Thesis
on
7

Farm, Shop, Landing

MARTIN BRUEGEL

Farm, Shop,

Landing

The Rise of a Market Society in the Hudson Valley, 1780–1860

DUKE UNIVERSITY PRESS   *Durham & London*   2002

© 2002 Duke University Press
All rights reserved
Printed in the United States of
America on acid-free paper ∞
Designed by Amy Ruth Buchanan
Typeset in Bembo by Tseng
Information Systems, Inc.
Library of Congress Cataloging-in-
Publication Data appear on the last
printed page of this book.

This project won the Dixon Ryan
Fox prize for best manuscript from
the New York State Historical
Association. The book has been
published with the support of a
grant from the Département
d'Économie et Sociologie, Institut
National de la Recherche
Agronomique in Paris.

To my mother HERTHA
and the memory of my father ALOIS,
and to my sisters, brothers, and
their families

Contents

Illustrations, Tables, Figures, and Maps

Figures

Maps

Acknowledgments

Many people have contributed to the completion of this project, and it is a pleasant task (and one I have looked forward to for a while) to acknowledge my debt to them. My deepest gratitude goes to the people who made Cornell such a nurturing, mind-opening experience for me. The very ability to express my appreciation owes a great deal to the patience of my teachers in the university's English as a Second Language Program, who introduced me to the dos and don'ts of their native tongue. Stuart Blumin, whom my family has come to call affectionately Doktorvater, supported this project as a mentor who influenced the questions I asked and the ways in which I went about answering them while finding time to introduce me to many things American, from baseball to fly fishing. Steven Kaplan's enthusiasm and critical acumen as well as his culinary and enological knowledge and most of all his willingness to combine all of them were crucial to my American experience, the writing of my dissertation, and the continuation of my career back home in Europe. Larry Moore's intellectual vigor and empathy made him an ideal reader and this a better book. Discussions with Glenn Altschuler and David Sabean solved questions pertaining to time consciousness and agricultural practices. Reference and manuscript librarians at the Olin and Mann Libraries proved to be as diligent and skillful as a researcher could wish them to be. Intellectual companionship and camaraderie with Bob Bussel, Clare Crowston, John Fousek, Chris Heindl, Connie Kindig, Cynthia Koepp, Liz Milliken, Jim Siekmeier, Sam Stoloff, Carlos Villamil, and Michael Wilson often grew in seminars but were mostly sustained and developed in college town bars and on hikes in upstate New York.

The republic of letters offered a great many benefits along the way, and many a scholar's generosity and broad-mindedness grew into the kinds of friendship that make life as an academic so exciting and altogether enriching. Richard Stott accompanied this project almost from its inception and greatly helped to sharpen my interpretation. Claude Grignon welcomed a freshly minted graduate to the Laboratoire de Recherche sur la Consommation (CORELA) and unfailingly supported this project through the highs and lows of the revising process. Discussions with Jean-Michel Chevet reinforced its comparative facets. David Galenson pointed out ways to strengthen parts of a narrative that sat oddly with his own explanatory inclinations. The members of CORELA generously and daily share their knowledge in economics, history, sociology, and statistics with me and so provide an excellent example of the benefits of interdisciplinary collaboration. My former colleagues at the University of Illinois at Urbana-Champaign were very patient in listening to parts of what became this book and suggested ways to improve it. I should also like to thank the reviewers and the editors of Duke University Press for their strictures and suggestions.

My research found help among the curators, archivists, and local historians in New York State. Margaret Heilbrun is a keen guide to the rich collections of the New-York Historical Society, a witty, ethnographically inclined observer of researchers and their habits, and a sharp commentator and lively conversationalist during breaks. Helen McLallen, Sharon Palmer, and Janette Johnson of the Columbia County Historical Society and Eileen O'Brien of the New York State Historical Association extended their schedules to accommodate my time constraints. (At this point I should also mention the Cooperstown night guard who commiserated with a foreign graduate student—and who not only pointed out a perfectly illegal spot in which to sleep under open skies but kept an eye on the fellow's nocturnal safety during his two-week sweep through the area). At the Greene County Historical Society, Raymond Beecher and Shelby Mattice liberally shared their erudition on local history and material culture. Across the Hudson in Kinderhook, Ruth Piwonka is a repository of knowledge on Columbia County's past. At the Institut National de la Recherche Agronomique (INRA), Catherine Cansot expertly produced maps, tables, and figures.

Money helped, too. Fellowships and other funding from the Swiss National Science Foundation, the Mellon Foundation, the INRA, the University of Illinois at Urbana-Champaign, and Cornell University made my research ventures possible.

Then there are other debts. The Yarme family did everything (and then some) to facilitate my life in the United States. They have a special place in these acknowledgments. Marie-Georges Compper accompanied the final stretch with humor and patience. Most importantly, I hope that my mother Hertha recognizes some of her own big-heartedness and brio in this reconstruction of past lives. My sisters and brothers have followed my itinerary abroad with affection, and it is to all of them, and their families, that I dedicate the following pages.

Introduction

Everyday Life and the Making of Rural Development in the Hudson Valley

Nothing denotes the profound transformation of society in the mid–Hudson Valley as plainly to an observer on the threshold of the third millennium as the introduction of the word *capital* into the vocabulary of its people around 1800. The notion never appears in records of the late eighteenth century. Neither does the substance, for "money, as yet, was a scarce commodity."[1] When the Hudson *Northern Whig* pondered the conditions of economic development by the second decade of the nineteenth century, its editor hoped that the city of Hudson on the east bank of the river would capture the commerce of "the almost boundless western country." The problem was geography because "the Merchants of Athens [on the Hudson's west bank] will stop that trade on their side of the river. Have they the Capital to do this?" the writer wondered, only to provide a short answer. "No. But Capitalists may move there." Still, his city held an advantage. "Merchants will rarely be induced to settle in Athens at all, as the city of Hudson must hold out greater inducements to capitalists."[2] As late as 1836, when "capitalists ha[d] purchased a new steamboat" to ply the river between Hudson and New York City, the concept of capital possessed a tangible quality. It was linked to merchants, and it stood for their assets.[3] Things were changing, however. George Holcomb, a farmer in Stephentown, rushed to a bank in Pittsfield, Massachusetts, on which the first check he ever received in his forty years had been drawn in 1838.[4] This elusive mode of payment in the wake of a severe banking crisis made Holcomb hurry to commute paper into hard currency. The dissociation of endorser and promissory note and the mediation of exchange by a financial institution were signs of the movement toward less transparent and propinquitous social relations in the mid–Hudson Valley. In the process, the use of the word *capital* grew to indicate impersonal attributes until in 1847 it assumed a life of its own when the president of the Greene County Agricultural Society declared that "capital is seeking investment through different channels. Manufactures are springing up on every hand, and amply rewarding investments that are made, and opening new markets for the proceeds of the farmer's labors."[5]

The ways in which people perceived the social universe and the activities they carried on in it betrayed its alteration between the 1780s and the 1850s. When Alexander Coventry met his cousin on the outskirts of Hudson in 1785, he described William Coventry as a man in homemade garb with "coat, vest and trousers of brown cloth—a check shirt, and boots on: in fact, dressed as a farmer at work." Three generations later young husbandman William Hoffman of Claverack demonstrated new ambitions when buying fine boots and broadcloth and trimmings that tailor Scutts sewed into a "tight Bodied coat" with which to appear in public.[6] Whereas Alexander Coventry lent his oxen to Caleb Lobdell to draw hay and borrowed Lobdell's plow in return during the 1780s, Theodore Cole of Catskill "paid Mr Dubois for use of his horse this spring $15.00 in full" and Wilbur Fisk Strong earned five shillings (62.5 cents) per day threshing buckwheat for his Uncle Joe in the 1850s.[7] Whereas the youth of the agricultural neighborhoods enjoyed dances after spinning and working bees at the end of the eighteenth century, Daniel and William Hoffman "concluded to get up a cotillion Party at our House as we thought we could make it profitable besides having a very social time."[8] The organization of trade at landings on the Hudson abided by new rules, too. At the turn of the nineteenth century, Joseph White drove his produce by wagon to Kinderhook and Schodack and Isaac Mills rode his load to the landing. These were real sites where farmers delivered their goods to merchants they knew personally. In the middle of the nineteenth century, Hannah Bushnell "sent off" her butter while Theodore Cole sent hay, squashes, and gooseberries. "The sleighing is magnificent," William Hoffman observed in March 1847. "Farmers are now busily carrying their produce to Market as it commands a good price."[9] The "market" had ceased to be a place only. Commercial transactions had moved from a physical setting to an abstract, intangible sphere where prices mattered more than people and relationships.

People's horizon of experience expanded. Hudson River landings—the tangent of their lives at the end of the eighteenth century—increasingly relayed information from New York City. The downstream metropolis evolved into a pole that staked out the compass of, and helped structure, daily activities in the countryside. The growing complexity of social interactions in the mid–Hudson Valley required new means of communication, organization, and coordination. Miller William Youngs had "heard" the election results and of Hanna Barker's marriage in 1811. Thirty years later, inhabitants of Chatham petitioned the Albany and Weststockbridge Railroad Company to build a depot near their village because the discontinuation of the mail route forced them to walk or ride four or five miles to get the "papers & letters . . . which fact must have the effect at last to shut out from those villages almost all the Journals of the day which they have been accustomed to receive." News of the world had begun to matter. Where the sun dial had answered the needs of the neighborhood in 1800, longer chains of interdependence spawned the systematization of relationships. "A town clock . . . which strikes the hours regularly" surprised a visitor to Catskill in 1824, a year after Kingston had acquired a public clock. The residents of Coxsackie Landing felt the need for a clock in 1837, while Kinderhook received its own in the late 1840s.[10] Clock faces, hour hands, and belfries began to determine the unfolding of quotidian activities, and standards of punctuality and timeliness that were disconnected from natural rhythms and occurrences entered everyday life in the course of the first half of the nineteenth century.

The reordering of rural society in the mid–Hudson Valley was so momentous that it affected conceptions of family relations. Jenny Vosburgh of Kinderhook left her home to find shelter with her father in 1792 because her husband had turned from a protector into a tyrant. The same image of patriarchal matrimony pervaded Mary Livingston's lament over the death of Henry W. Livingston: "A Twelvemonth has nearly elapsed since that dreadful event which deprived me of my friend, my Protector, my Guide—which left me for the first time in my life to my own direction, & which presented me to my own view as a Child unable from weakness to go alone, yet abandoned in a wide world, without one supporting hand, without one consoling voice." By 1846, very different premises could inform thoughts on domestic arrangements. A discussion of married women's property rights prompted the editor of the *Kinderhook Sentinel,* a paper opposed to a reconsideration of the inferior status of women in marriage, to exclaim that "in the contract of marriage, as well as in the contract of sale, there is no good reason why the maxim *caveat emptor* should not apply."[11] The social and economic processes that underlay the movement from an understanding of the world rooted in concrete and particular experiences to general abstractions form the subject of this book.

The emergence of the modern world from a rural past has long since preoccupied historians of Europe. Whatever approach scholars of European development between the sixteenth and eighteenth centuries espoused, they couched their models in macroeconomic terms that focused on international commerce or the organization of mercantile networks on a regional scale. The European vantage point illustrates the prominence of commerce in the settlement of North America. Indeed, their differences notwithstanding, all accounts agree that transatlantic trade fueled European growth and linked North America to an expanding intercontinental economy. The development of the rural Hudson Valley between the War of Independence and the 1850s was thus part of an ongoing process.[12] But long-distance trade alone, Karl Polanyi and Fernand Braudel showed, is not sufficient to define a market economy. Neither is private property or entrepreneurial activity. These factors, all with long histories of their own, may be conducive to economic efficiency. Yet their mere presence does not automatically add up to a market system whose core characteristic is, in Max Weber's ideal-typical description, unimpeded, competitive exchange between rational agents to satisfy material needs. Whether this intellectual construction ever fully materialized in reality (Weber assigned ideal types the virtue of guiding research, not of designating concrete configurations of circumstances), historical analysis investigates the context in which a utilitarian rationality and individual choice come to pervade, if not to dominate altogether, all aspects of life.[13] The rural population of the Hudson Valley exported goods to Europe and the West Indies before the American Revolution, yet it took the crucial step toward a market society and a market culture between the end of the War of Independence and the 1850s. These were the years during which it found, borrowed, and forged the practical and intellectual means to think of all exchange in market terms. In short, it was in these decades that it became possible to associate capital with investments rather than merchants, to conceive of marriage in free market terms, to devise a neighborhood dance as a moneymaking proposition, and to save time by checking a steamboat schedule rather than losing it by waiting for the next sloop to leave for New York.

To construe the social evolution of the Hudson Valley during the early American republic as the coming of age of a market society ought not ensnare historians in the teleological trap of taking the so-called market revolution for granted. The debate between "market" and "social" his-

torians may well oppose scholars who construe the market economy
an ideal against which to test all different forms of social organization,
and others who diagnose the burgeoning free play of supply and demand
between competitive individuals as a traumatic contamination of traditional community bonds. Methodological and interpretive disagreements
should not conceal that their often fine monographs follow the progress,
and corroborate the efficiency, of a market economy and culture. Histories of frontier settlement are likely to suffer from this fallacy. The con-
flation of geographic and chronological dimensions conveys the impression of a synchronous, linear development from wilderness to capitalist
society. Such a narrative validates the unquestioned reality of a timeless,
utilitarian individual making efficient economic choices. This assumption
permeates a vast range of older historiographies. From David M. Potter
to Jack P. Greene, many a historian construed the British North American colonies as the auspicious land of plenty where an acquisitive frame
of mind and enterpreneurial zeal blossomed naturally, removed impediments to commercial opportunities, and generated the modern world of
capitalism and democracy.[14] Studies that challenge such smooth "modernization" uncover customary notions and practices with which members of
rural societies resisted the advance of a capitalist order.[15] They point to the
social, spatial, and temporal discontinuities that mark every society.

It was Fernand Braudel's insight to construe economic activities within
a tripartite structure in which a local world of barter and an international
network of trade, each with its own rules and imperatives, surround a
market economy. The advantage of Braudel's construction lies with the
recognition of the segments' different logics, of their distinct definitions
of *interest* and *utility,* and of the moving boundaries between them. Labor,
land, capital, and agricultural and manufactured goods circulate within
these three planes, albeit in variable proportions and cadences and for different purposes. Institutional arrangements and technical limitations determine the apportionment of capitalist, market, and material economies.
These were the reasons why, in the early modern era, kin connections
inhibited rather than promoted the free exchange of land, even while
stimulating property transfers, or why transportation infrastructures facilitated international trade before the creation of a regional market.[16] Yet,
whereas Braudel conceived of a structural framework from which real,
individual women and men are largely absent, this study examines the different strategies that members of the rural population pursued to insure
their material lives. Instead of thinking of market and nonmarket sectors

as mutually exclusive aggregate economic entities in a necessarily chronological time line, their very coexistence characterized the social experiences of residents of the American countryside.

This brings us back to the mid–Hudson Valley, where twenty-one-year-old Vincent Morgan Townsend "thrashed oats as usual" on 3 January 1834. "Felt ill-natured, thought that he who thrashed the oats ought to have the fun of riding them to market. Memo," Townsend concluded, "don't mean to work very hard when Pap is gone to carry a load of my thrashing to market." Here, then, the marketplace was the scene of meetings and merriment where social interaction preceded, surrounded, and followed commercial exchange. The temptations at the landing in Fishkill, Dutchess County, doomed Townsend, who, upon returning home late from another grain delivery, was punished with "a blowing up . . . from Pap."[17] Beyond the singular case of Townsend's socialization—the inculcation of norms concerning work and time—and the young man's sense of injustice in the face of paternal authority, the events reveal the complexity of quotidian economics and its coordination in the rural North. Note how different networks shape economic processes. The family organized work. Neighborhood artisans produced and repaired equipment and tools, for which they received payment in kind as well as cash. The shipper warehoused and then freighted produce and other goods produced on the farm to New York City, trading it for imported merchandise, ready money, and credit. The sanctions incurred by transgressors show that different conventions ordered these relationships and hence constituted them into fields of experience with their own determinations and means of coordination: physical violence and perhaps disinheritance among kin, loss of honor and credibility and the concomitant marginalization in the community, and the denial of credit at the wharves on the Hudson. Farm, shop, neighborhood, and landing were so many social and economic contexts in which farmers, artisans, merchants, and their wives and daughters deployed vim and ingenuity to make ends meet. A family's success in achieving a decent livelihood required the articulation of the material, market, and commercial spheres (to return to Braudel's architectural conceptions of economic activities); it also depended on their capacity to mobilize resources such as power, prestige, relations, and wealth. The constitution and everyday operations of networks that organized the exploitation of natural resources and the circulation of goods form the focus of this analysis.

The local, microhistorical perspective offers a fecund approach to large-scale developments. Their aspect changes if it is construed from the view-

points of people whose routines helped them cope with the uncei
of the future and whose decisions aimed at improving it. Attent
the ways and means by which contemporaries interpreted what ha
to and around them makes it possible to explain their actions witnout
surreptitiously introducing the notion of historical necessity or its corol-
lary, the necessarily destabilizing, negative impact of large-scale change
on people's everyday lives. The discipline of context is at stake here. The
following chapters do not assume the existence of a timeless, unchanging
market in which anonymous agents purposefully calibrate their activities
on prices, come together fleetingly to exchange goods and services without creating lasting ties, and behave in ways that progressively remove
hindrances to the efficient allocation of their resources. This model derived from classical economics informed Winifred Rothenberg's macroeconomic study of growth in Massachusetts during the eighteenth century. "A self-equilibrating, self-regulating, hegemonic market-economy"
seemingly governed exchange in New England by 1750 and was firmly in
place before the construction of an efficient transport infrastructure because funds freely flowed toward optimal investments.[18] Rather than re-
lying on the market as a heuristic theory concerning abstract functions
and unchanging, indistinguishable individuals, [this history of rural development examines the emergence of a market society and culture as the
genesis of social rules and conventions that were themselves the result of
struggles, hesitations, and compromises among historical actors endowed
with unequally distributed resources to affect the world in which they
lived and whose constraints they faced.]

The mid–Hudson Valley presents the setting in which I shall study
the restraints farm families overcame, the incentives they perceived, and
the opportunities they grasped to participate in the transformation of the
countryside. The region elicited comments from foreign visitors startled
to discover manors on which tenants paid rent in cash, kind, and service
to landlords. These manors were, according to Francis Hall's account of
1818, "a considerable remnant of feudalism in a young democracy of North
America." Consensus historians who deflated the variety of conflicts in the
American past to reduce it to the liberal kind of entrepreneurial competition trifled with manorial conditions and the agitation they gave rise
to after the American Revolution. Such a perspective made these events
seem exceptional, different in kind from other social developments in
early republican North America.[19] The failure to acknowledge the historical relevance of manorial society inflicted serious limitations on the in-

terpretation's explanatory power. Its streamlined narrative screened out or misrepresented everyday concerns of many an inhabitant in the region. The lack of close attention to the manors and their population in the Hudson Valley deprived consensus historians of a corrective control for their ambitious, encompassing view of American society. It also closed off avenues of comparison and scrutiny of the social discontinuities that shaped daily experience among the area's residents. To posit a single set of motives behind the variety of economic practices foreclosed rather than furthered the study of exchange. It also allowed for the furtive intrusion of anachronistic notions into the historical analysis while denying people the capacity to hold different values and endow their lives with a sense of their own. For the coexistence of two regimes of landed property, with their mutually exclusive connotations of autonomy and subordination in an area where as late as 1850 two-thirds of the families engaged in agriculture and another 15 percent made a living from the land by providing services to farmers, stimulated contemporaries—and ought to prompt their historians—to investigate the meanings of the "market." Moreover, the legality of manorial conditions did not protect them from the perception that they combined economic and political dominion in contradiction with republican principles. The lengthy struggle to outlaw or, on the contrary, maintain the constitutionality of manorial leases, with their recognition of differential claims to property, allows the recovery of the competing social and political projects that animated different members of the regional population. It helps explain their propensity to come together in associations whose goal it was to load the issue on the political agenda of their day. This study, then, recognizes the particularity of manorial social relations yet it refrains from emphasizing their uniqueness to construe them as an extreme manifestation of a generally shared but increasingly contested value system and model of social behavior whose halcyon days predated the American Revolution.

Columbia and Greene Counties lie east and west of the Hudson River, roughly 130 miles north of New York City and 30 miles south of Albany (see map 1). Columbia's shoreline measures about 30 miles and its medium breadth 18 miles; its surface covers about 626 square miles (or 400,640 acres). Around 1800, 37 percent of the land situated in the southern part of the county belonged to the Livingston family, which rented it to tenants. Greene County abuts the Hudson for 28 miles and extends 42 miles westward. Its area is 586 square miles (or 375,040 acres), a large portion of which is mountainous. Columbia's topography is diversified, too, and

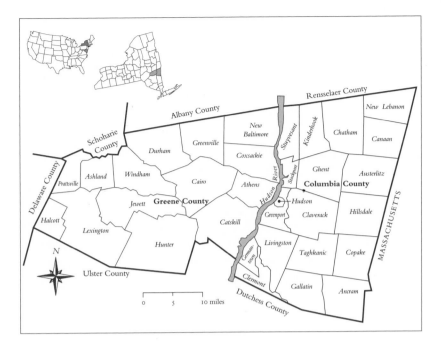

MAP I. The mid–Hudson Valley, circa 1850

when Alexander Coventry hiked up the Taconic Mountains on its eastern
border in 1791 he observed that "this place is rightly called Hillsdale . . . for
it is nothing but a congeries of hills and small vales." A generation later, a
German duke remarked upon the physical beauty, the wooded elevations,
and the pastures at the foot of the hills in the area. Rugged mountains,
broken but arable intervals, and extensive and fertile plains toward the
Hudson—the different altitudes imparted distinct climates to the region.
"The hills of the eastern towns of Columbia, though but 12 to 15 miles E.
of the Hudson, have a later harvest by 10, 12, and 15 days than the warmer
vallies on the margin of that river," Spafford's *Gazetteer* explained in 1813.
Plant life in the Catskill Mountains blossomed one month after the vege-
tation in the valley.[20]

The constellation of natural resources determined the choices of exploitation available to the area's population and influenced its social practices. The landscape of Columbia and Greene Counties bore witness to
the social transformation. Julian Niemcewicz described "the banks of the
Hudson on both sides ris[ing] up into the mountains covered with firs,
spruce, hemlock" in the 1790s. Tyrone Power had to travel into the hills to

find thick woods in the 1830s, and Washington Irving's "luxuriant wood-lands and picturesque streams" of the 1840s lay in the Shawangunk and Catskill Mountains. By the late 1840s, even the mountaintops exhibited signs of human activity. "The hills [had been] stripped of their timber so as to present their huge, rocky projections," the *Catskill Messenger* laconically reported.[21] Historians tend to tell the story of agricultural innovation in terms of demographic pressure, but the growth from 35,000 people in 1790 to 61,000 in 1820 and 76,000 in 1850 had less impact on the region's agricultural adaptation than the exhaustion of its soil and its suitability for new grass cultures.[22] The Hudson Valley's route to economic development relied on commercial agriculture whereas New England's hinged on the protoindustrial by-employment of its farming population. With the departure from mixed agriculture to an emphasis on cattle raising and fodder crops like hay and oats came the growth of a wage labor force and an expansion of commerce. Farmers began to produce for the extralocal market to a significantly greater extent than they had done before 1820, a development that constituted a critical moment in the extension of capitalist relations to the mid–Hudson Valley. At the same time, the resources of the environment, with its topography of creeks and waterpower, attracted manufacturers to the vicinity, which in turn created a new demand for agricultural produce.

An explanation of the mid–Hudson Valley's social and economic evolution between 1780 and 1860 hinges on an understanding of its society at the end of the eighteenth century. Historians of the area such as Alfred Young and Cynthia Kierner have asserted that farm life along the Hudson River revolved around the export market. The evidence suggests a different set of circumstances, for these were not people who fancied themselves in a land of plenty, all the less so as they were engaged in the reconstruction of their countryside after the devastations and deprivations of the war years. The fear of bad harvests and anxiety about material hardship gave rise to strategies of risk reduction and prudence in farm families and agricultural neighborhoods. In chapters 1 and 2, I examine this context along with its institutions, forms of sociability, and cultural models, all of which helped determine the categories through which neighbors assessed exchange equivalences among themselves and on the landings. The endeavors of farmers in the area revolved around the search for improvements in order to secure lives from which penury was absent; riches, as sometime valley resident J. Hector St. John de Crèvecoeur pointed out in the late 1700s, meant a decent maintenance, food, and shelter achieved through industry and assured primarily by neighborhood relations.[23] Farmers, only a minority of whom traded regularly at the landings around 1800, adopted new tools and stock and increased productivity and output. They reacted to growing competition from other areas with different comparative advantages and imaginatively adapted themselves to the soil's loss of fertility in order to maintain and enlarge their part in meeting the growing urban demand; these undertakings effected a new outlook on the most proficient organization of economic life in the Hudson Valley, where the institutional setup of markets changed under the influence of new ideas on economic efficiency (chapters 3 and 4). The income from exchange in the long-distance trade allowed families to acquire common goods of increasingly industrial origin with which to improve the material quality of their lives. The coming of industry altered the morphology of rural society in generating a new work force (chapters 3 and 5), and in chapter 6 I suggest that new revenues of the rural population—of factory hands no less than merchants, artisans, and farmers—translated into visibly different lifestyles indicative of the formation of classes in the countryside.[24] Lest we mistake the everyday strivings of the Hudson Valley population for an expression or simple reflection of economic conditions, chapter 7 takes up the changing conception of, and battle over access to, public space, where individuals joined formal and informal groups and engaged in collective actions to promote their social, economic, and political interests. Public strife occasionally produced the conditions under which ethnic labeling, with all its injurious connotations, marked out groups, but only the increased number of Irish immigrants in the 1840s expanded the purview of discrimination beyond the historical racism against African Americans. The struggle against manorial conditions during the first half of the nineteenth century offers a prism through which to review the different dimensions of social change in the Hudson Valley, and the conclusion brings together the strands of this analysis.

In 1871, Granby Spees delivered an address in Greenville, Greene County, to commemorate the town's first ninety years. He declared that

> a great mistake it would be to suppose that a secluded village like ours furnishes no names worthy of being preserved, no incidents worthy of being garnered into history, that blood and brains and exalted virtues and noteworthy events are to be found only in populous cities, in the camp of the capital; that the tillers of the soil, and the matrons and

the maidens of the farm-house were in a sphere too humble for public notice. For right here, on this mountain-skirted landscape, men have lived and events have occurred, worthy of the eloquence of the eulogist and the pen of the historian. And as for what we call blood and brains and exalted virtues, and whatever else is necessary to keep a nation going, they come, like the food and the implements that are necessary to keep life agoing, not from the palaces of the city, but from the farm and the shop.[25]

It is unlikely that Spees envisioned something like the transformation in the ways in which his villagers coordinated their economic activities on the farm, in the shop, and at the landings as the theme of a historical undertaking. Yet I offer these chapters as a contribution to the history of the region that saw farmer William Coventry struggle in the face of bad harvests, widow Mary Livingston fight her tenants, blacksmith Samuel Fowks help invent the cast iron plow, and Hannah Bushnell sell her butter in the market. I hope that both their descendents, who have a curiosity for details, and historians with an interest in generalizations will enjoy the retrieval of their story.

ONE

Exchange and the Creation of the Neighborhood

in the Late Eighteenth Century

Just about a year after he had left Scotland and immigrated to North America to settle near his kin in Hudson, New York, Alexander Coventry, a twenty-year-old physician in September 1786, decided to build a house. He hired two carpenters who spent eight days working on the building. At one point they threatened to walk out on him. He prevented their leaving by promising cloth in return for their work and offering a dinner that contained meat. Money being scarce and the doctor's practice intermittent, he turned to his cousin William Coventry to temporarily pick up the bill. The reckoning proved fairly complicated because it did not just involve the two cousins and the journeymen but also the neighborhood's tavern keeper, Caleb Lobdell. He had provided a part of the food and drink while the crew set up Alexander Coventry's future dwelling. Lobdell happened to be a character who enjoyed a reputation as one of the strongest men in the vicinity. His vigor came in handy, for Coventry needed another hand to finish his residence. So Alexander and his cousin William settled the debt with Lobdell with a pair of stockings and two pieces of homemade cloth; this remuneration, however, left the innkeeper in their debt for one day's work, which, they agreed, he was to perform by building the cellar foundation. The textile products that the parties in this deal swapped were the result of the toils of William's wife, yet none of the men paid attention to that fact. The whole transaction involved at least five people, rested on an intricate method of accounting, and revealed a good sense of self-interest. To the people concerned, however, the operation amounted to nothing more than everyday business. Alexander Coventry entered the amount of the carpenters' charges in his diary and then simply noted that his cousin "Wm Coventry gave them goods for it, and placed it to my account. Also gave Caleb Lobdell a pair of stockings at 10s. and a piece of cloth at 4s., and also another piece, for which he is to give a day's work, at stoning my cellar."[1]

The construction of Coventry's house had not begun with the employment of the carpenters, and it did not end with the completion of their work and the settlement of their wages. Alexander Coventry's main concern before the start of the project pertained to the mobilization of neighbors to help him raise the building. He drummed up nine men to cut and hew the timber to clear the construction site. In his diary he remarked that the three men who staked out the ground "drank two bottles of rum, and wrought pretty hard." On 28 September 1786, twenty people, including two male slaves, gathered to participate in the completion of the house frame, an exercise that required a sustained rhythm. "They wrought very briskly," Coventry chronicled with satisfaction, "and got it finished a little after sundown." Then things got out of hand. The house raising had, after all, occurred right after harvest, and after a period of intense exertion people called for an equally energetic time of merriment. Coventry recorded that

> a number of women, old and young, were present. They all went afrolicing to David Williams, and being hearty, having finished 2½ gallon of rum, their mirth ended in a quarrel between A[ndrew] M[artin] and G[hoes] who fought. I saw part of the battle. They were both naked, except their breech cloath, and lay on the floor, both their bodies besmered with blood. They had a poor manner of fighting. They did not box, but struck two or three strokes, then clinched and fell. G[hoes] had not fair play. Saw both A[llen] and W[?] strike him. Williams was quite merry, and struck W[?] who knocked him down with one blow. Andrew's face was much bruised.[2]

If nothing else, the events leading up to and accompanying the construction of Alexander Coventry's residence in the mid–Hudson Valley hint at the intensity of neighborhood relations. They also invite an analysis of the principles that organized exchange among neighbors. The minor role of an abstract and comprehensive medium of exchange—money—raises questions about the ways in which people measured the value of their respective contributions to transactions, about the nature and extent of spheres of circulation of goods and services, and about their units of equivalence. The house raising demonstrates how the object of a neighbor-

hood transaction receded behind social conventions. Plain material r\
sons underlay the pooling of assets to complete occasional, daily or se,\
sonal tasks. Families lacked the manpower and tools to perform the entir\
gamut of work on and around the farm. Cooperation proved necessary to
solve problems of scarce labor resources. Exchange of hands and communal efforts made survival possible. In other words, the apparent utility of
the traded good or service neither structured nor exhausted the meaning
of the exchange. Participation was what mattered. If the material results
of individual efforts surely counted in the eyes of the participants, their
involvement also expressed a sense of belonging and thus discloses, to us
as historians, the moral underpinning of collective undertakings. Because
tensions lurked beneath the organization of collective travails, rituals and
ceremonies like harvest home, weddings, and funerals, during which food
was shared, affirmed neighborhood reciprocities and helped contain jealousies in order to maintain a locality's social fabric. Indeed, the coherence
of the local economy did not hinge on single commodities or isolated acts
of exchange. When neighbors collaborated, when they swapped tools for
help and then partook in a meal, they worked at lasting relationships: these
constituted their moral community.

Personal alliances imprinted their mark on politics, too. Yet, while
long-term symmetry in the local give-and-take shaped the mobilization of practical support within neighborhoods, politics revealed that the
Coventry cousins lived in a society of ranks where chains of dependence
linked people in vertical arrangements. Personal acquaintance determined
a voter's political outlook. "Messrs. Lawrence and Thurston here from
Hudson, canvassing for the election," Alexander Coventry recorded in late
April 1788. At that very moment, members of the powerful Livingston
family were "out attending the election."[3] Manorial society most conspicuously operated on aristocratic values, and it is thus no wonder to observe the work of political deference most clearly in its realm. Influential
men grafted their ascendency on social networks that reached into neighborhoods. The acknowledged inequality of power came with a corrective
in the hands of those who conceded superiority to others. The counterpart of the submissive attitude found its fullest expression on the manor,
where tenants could withdraw their support of the landlord's candidates
if a proprietor refused favors or enforced lease agreements too harshly.
However, self-interest alone cannot explain the reasons why citizens of the
republic would acquiesce in elite leadership; they enjoyed, after all, more
than the paltry ability to switch allegiance from one notable to another

because they could promote candidates of their own. Electoral behavior exposed the persistence of the hierarchical principle, the view, increasingly questioned but still shaping conduct, that society functions as a whole in which assigned social stations apportion power and, with power, prestige, responsibility, and obligation. Politics was personal. It regularly stirred up the passion of some voters but most of the time left the majority of the population outside its purview. "Few people at the election," Coventry observed after the visit of Lawrence and Thurston. He himself was more excited at the sight of two camels than at the news of the adoption of a new federal Constitution on 26 July 1788.[4] The majority of the mid–Hudson Valley's inhabitants struggled to make ends meet, and, though polls and electioneering provided room for festivities, farm families that had cause to worry about their livelihood left the governing to members of the superior set in New York society. We begin, then, with a landscape in which neighbors are successively raising a house and a rumpus.

A World of Insecurity

The organization of material life in rural neighborhoods at the end of the eighteenth century owed as much to labor scarcity as to a worldview that Hudson Valley farmers shared with peasant populations in other parts of the world. In spite of the area's abundance, the seemingly endless expanse of land across the continent (which contrasted with Europe's difficulty in supporting its population), and their important contribution to the equivalent of a million bushels of wheat exported to Europe in 1788, the people of the Hudson Valley believed that nature would regularly fail them. This is not to say that its inhabitants were starving at the end of the eighteenth century. But the generation that came of age after the War of Independence knew hardship. Rather than adapting to the environment's average productivity, their experience taught them to prepare for bad years. The limited technical capacity to control natural events left people inured to nature's whims. St. John de Crèvecoeur, who owned a farm in the lower Hudson Valley's Orange County, described the burden of an agricultural existence through the perception of "the inconveniences and accidents which the grains of our fields, the trees of our orchards, as well as those of our woods, are exposed to." He concluded, "if bountiful Nature is kind to us on the one hand, on the other she wills that we shall purchase her kindness not only with sweats and labor but vigilance and care. These calamities remind us of our precarious situation," so much so that Crèvecoeur, a booster of settlement in Mid-Atlantic states, promised a "decent maintenance," not riches, to immigrants.[5] Poor harvests brought about by a variety of causes occurred one out of two years between 1780 and 1805, and the combination of memory and experience shaped the self-representation of rural society in the mid–Hudson Valley.

The war years with their requisitions, penury of goods, and inclement weather weighed down the area's farmers. "No provisions in Stores," a preoccupied John Beebe in the area of Chatham hastened to note in May 1780. "Continental Currancy almost Run out. Publick Spirit and Virtue gone. Religion losing ground." In June 1779, Beebe collected news on events nearby. Urban and rural consumers had retaliated against commercial practices that they perceived as patently unfair extortion. On Monday, 7 June 1779, Beebe reported "a Great Cry for Bread and talk of Gathering a Mobb to search for wheat." William Smith, who resided in Columbia County, had already noticed in 1778 that goods such as salt and linen were scarce in the Hudson Valley. Even wheat, a staple, had become rare.[6] In October 1779, Beebe complained that the wheat harvest tallied half the usual quantity. The following winter made things worse. "A great Cry for bread" resounded in his neighborhood. "The Corn mills Except on large Streams almost universally Stopt for want of water occasioned by want of Rain and frosty weather." People and cattle went hungry, and Beebe mentioned that this was the coldest season he had seen in his fifty-two years. So bitingly glacial was it, in fact, that farm animals froze in their sheds, a loss all the more unfortunate as their number had been reduced the previous summer when "the pastures yeald[ed] but small support for Cattle."[7]

After the war, farmers commented on good harvests, although many more of their statements betrayed the insecurity of their condition and the fear of loss that went with it. John Beebe chronicled "a fair prospect for a plentiful Harvest [of] wheat and hay" in the summer of 1785. In the fall he noted that "it has been a fine Season, a plentifull harvest and a kind providence." Five years later, William Coventry observed that "the people in general had good Crops of wheat & rye, & the Corn & other things looked very well." His cousin Alexander Coventry discerned in 1791 that "the people begin to have provision in abundance, and several have grain to sell, also hay is pretty plenty." The tenor of that latter comment, however, suggested an unusual circumstance rather than an expected regularity of bountiful harvests. In 1805 the *Hudson Bee* confirmed the precariousness of agricultural endeavors when it commented on a wheat crop that was going to be "more prolific than has been known for ten years."[8] Little had the editor's prudence foreseen the drought that was about to affect the city's food supply.

Hard years were the distinctive feature of and the standard against which farmers measured, their lives. In 1787, the *Hudson Weekly Gazette* alluded to the harm parasitic flies had inflicted on wheat. Insect plagues recurred several times. "The Grasshopers is so planty that they are eating every green thing up," William Coventry fumed in July 1799. "They were so planty on the rye that they eat the cheif of the Cornel. Thear would be from two to six on every head of rye. Thy would rise before one just like a swarm of bees." As if this scourge had not been enough, Coventry soon discovered "a striped bug thats far worse on the peotatoes & gardins then the Grasshopers. this bugg has wings and flyes from place to place. these bugs has killed all the peotatoes tops & every soft hearb thy come across." The striped bug returned in 1800, and Coventry's "peotatoes turned out but poor." Losses betided in 1807 when the "hushen [Hessian] fly or insect is cutting the wheat all off."[9] Wild animals attacked livestock. Alexander Coventry wrote in January 1791 that "wolves are very plenty." In April 1790 the legislature in the Catskill area passed an act that introduced a bounty for every killed wolf or panther, and tales about the adventures of hunters became folklore.[10]

Weather rendered harvests uncertain. In July 1787, Alexander Coventry's diary records that "all nature cries aloud for rain. The pastures are scorched up; the Indian Corn looks yellow; nay, even the foliage of the trees droops and seems deprived of moisture; the wheat ripens apace, the ear is dried before it received its proper quantity of nourishment." An early frost in September of that year left the corn hurt and the buckwheat ruined. And so the litany continued. Fall 1792 appeared to William Coventry as "the Dryest & hotest weather ever I saw. so dry that the mills could not Grind. the people was badly off on account that they could not get flour. the Grass looked as if it had been burnt. the cattle suffered for peasture." Coventry reiterated several times that this season was "the dryest time ever I saw," but on 24 August 1792 he groaned that "the mills was so scarce of water that people could not get grain ground for to eate. terrible dry."[11] The temperatures were high and the crops poor in 1795, but 1796 proved worse. *The Catskill Packet and Western Mail* had counted six weeks without rain in early September 1796 and purported that nobody could remember a similar drought. It dried up pastures and hurt cattle. Winter and spring crops were tenuous, and the water had disappeared from the wells. "The people is terrible bad off for Water," Coventry noted at the end of November, more than four months into the dearth. Similar climatic conditions prevailed in 1800 and 1801. Although the damage in the latter year appeared contained, summer and fall 1800 had left Coventry's well so dry that "we have to fetch the cheif of the water from the river." Two years later, the opposite quandary ravaged the area. The summer humidity led to mildew and rust on wheat fields and reduced yields.[12]

Agricultural pests and climatic hazards translated into serious predicaments. Silah Strong of Durham at the foot of the Catskills recorded that "provisions are very scarce here" in 1784. Alexander Coventry's in-laws bought thirty bushels of wheat in February 1791. When even neighbors had run out of produce, farmers became consumers of products that they had to purchase as customers at the very landings where they were used to selling their surplus. During fall 1798 and winter 1799, William Coventry went to Hudson to procure rye and corn. He had exhausted his reserve of seeds, which jeopardized the following harvest. The same cycle repeated itself in 1800 when Coventry secured first wheat and buckwheat flour and then another twenty bushels of rye to supply his family and stock and to put aside seeds. When wheat prices rose, hay seemed to follow closely. "People was terrible scearce of hay," Coventry remarked in April 1798. The consequence of this dearness lay in the opening of a price differential between foodstuffs and cattle. As Coventry put it, "wheat, rye and Spring grain Looked poor. the Maddows is poor, money scarce. . . . Cattle & horses cheap." In August 1805 the *Hudson Bee* observed that farmers were "foddering their cattle as in the depth of winter."[13] Crop failures drove the price of livestock down and depleted a farm family's assets. To offer animals for sale was supposed to reduce the consumption of fodder and raise cash so that the household could secure sustenance from the marketplace. Such tradeoffs imperiled the family's subsistence basis, for new beasts were needed to replace lost ones in order to ensure adequate production for home consumption. Coventry himself was at times able to benefit from the crises by purveying hay to Hudson, yet he never mentioned the acquisition of a cow or horse during hard times.

Changing Works, Finding Equivalence

The lingering memories of hardship experienced during the War of Independence heightened the customary awareness that a humid summer, an early frost, or a blight could destroy entire crops and turn an agricultural seller into a buyer of produce. The unpredictability of life in the countryside called for strategies with which families sought to increase their security or at least reduce the risks of scarcity. Farmers in the Hudson Valley practiced mixed agriculture. They allotted land to tillage, pastures and meadows, and woods. Although the cultivation of many crops and the raising of cattle helped attenuate the risks nature presented to the rural population and its livelihood, every commentator on farming in the area pinpointed, in Timothy Dwight's words, its "humble scale." The sequence of tasks allowed the farmer to spread the work more evenly over the year and reduced the strains that resulted from the short supply of agricultural labor. The situation persisted through the 1780s and 1790s when Alexander Coventry described the lack of hands as a drag during rich harvests and a cap on development.[14]

Contract labor was rare because the scarcity of farmhands maintained their remunerations at a level unaffordable to farmers. Alexander Coventry visited a neighbor who "has had the intermittent fever for about three weeks but has had no doctor, though he has been obliged to hire a supernumerary hand for the harvest, which has been very expensive for him." The price of this singular and unwanted outlay was much higher, Coventry concluded, because of "the insolence of what is called hired help, who must be humored like spoiled children, or they will leave you at their own will." The problem of discipline thus compounded the stiff cost and motivated farmers to avoid the employment of laborers. "I wish if any of My Children ever hapens to be farmers that thy never will hire a man or woman for more than one Month at a time," William Coventry expressed his thoughts on the condition of the independent yeoman. "And never hire done what they can doe themselves & never hire Except thy know that thy Can pay when the Labour is done. If they want to hire by the year they must make their bargain so that they can turn off the hireling when ever they pleas."[15]

The efforts of family members were often insufficient to accomplish the gamut of chores necessary to sustain a farm and feed its people, but fathers could at least exert control over them. Caleb Dill of New Windsor intended to prevent a situation of hired labor when he obliged his younger son Caleb to "stay with my [older] son David to help Carey on the labour of the farm. . . . If he should leave the fambly before [the age of twenty-one] then £10 per year to be deduced from his part more and applyd at the descretion of my son David for the benifit of the fambly."[16] Parental pressure, filial insubordination, family imperatives, and individual desires clashed around the exploitation of resources on the farm. If the demand for labor induced confrontations in which authority and autonomy were at stake, family labor—including the use of slaves, whose number varied from 0.5 percent of Canaan's population to 29 percent of Hurley's—proved to be the rule in the mid–Hudson Valley at the end of the eighteenth century. Farmers kept the labor market at a distance just as it kept farm families out of its reach.[17]

Some undertakings, however, required so much manpower that farmers had to recruit their neighbors. Alexander Coventry's house raising was such an event, and John Beebe participated in a construction project where "the Scaffold polls broke and 6 or seven men fell . . . but none killed." (Of course, not every house was erected by cooperative effort; still, the villagers of Marbletown and Hurley in Ulster County, where three in ten houses were "new" or "new, not finished" in 1798, must have been kept busy elevating dwellings.)[18] Mowing bees, too, mobilized whole neighborhoods. At one point Alexander Coventry marveled at twenty-five men engaged in cutting a meadow. William Coventry held, and collaborated in, a variety of such happenings, one of which was a "ploughing bee at Widow Uphams." These recurring episodes of prestation and counterprestation formed the elements of a strategy to overcome shortages of labor that impeded agricultural production. They also functioned as safety nets for neighbors in reduced circumstances, and, since misfortunes such as death or fire struck at random, precaution commanded that every family contribute a premium on their future security. These collaborations integrated the neighborhood and established it as more than a mere locality where farmers happened to live. They were one means by which to rise above exiguities and weather the turbulences in a precarious world. In a very precise sense, then, these relationships created a community.[19]

Material circumstances impelled farmers to rely on each other for many tasks and endeavors. Transactions between neighbors often appeared trifling, as when Alexander Coventry borrowed Thomas Van Alstine's boots to hike from Hudson to Claverack. These swappings proved vital because materially as well as symbolically they allowed families to walk in a world that still presented many risks and limitations. American historians have discussed the question of self-sufficiency of farm families and agricultural communities as if these were discrete units. But it is impossible to think about them separately because it was precisely the constant exchange of labor and tools that conditioned the family's subsistence and held the neighborhood together.[20] The paucity of utensils and draft animals in farm households lay at the root of these systems (table 1). To lend a hand and

TABLE I. Farm Animals and Utensils in Probate Inventories, 1787–93 ($N = 68$)

Animals and Utensils	Number	Percentage of N
Oxen	19	28
Horses	44	65
Ploughs	39	57
Cows	51	75
Sheep	35	51
Wagons	24	35
Sleds	26	38
Spinning wheels	42	62
Looms	22	32
Churns	34	50
Artisan's tools	15	22

Sources: Anjou, *Ulster County*, vol. 2; Probate Inventories, Columbia County Court House.

borrow a tool were necessary gestures to maintain production, sustain a family in the long run, and recognize the social boundaries of the neighborhood. To refuse certainly signaled an estrangement from, and often an enmity with, the community or one of its members.

Neighborhood exchange involved ordinary goods. Elisha Bashett and Zephaniah Chase of Lexington in the Catskills traded shoes finished in January 1787 for a pig delivered in April and a cradle remitted in May. Alexander Coventry bartered three pounds of butter and one bushel of potatoes for the sole leather of his wife's shoes. The balance of the give-and-take contained labor that one party performed in return for goods or previous services. Henry Lomfire asked Alexander Coventry to take a load of bark to Hudson; during Coventry's absence, Lomfire ploughed Coventry's field. George Holcomb of Stephentown, Rensselaer County, "threshed for Wm. Douglas" on 7 March 1814. He mentioned that "Wm. Dixon [was] with me for which Douglas indebted to me four days work and I am indebted to a days work to Dixon for his helping me today." Twelve days later Holcomb "chopped for Wm. Dixon in answer to his threshing for me at Wm. Douglasses a few days ago." John Palmer and Selah Strong in Durham swapped work and homemade cloth in the late 1780s. Stephen Skiff squared his account with Zephaniah Chase in 1799 with produce and work on Chase's farm.[21]

Transactions among neighbors took their meaning as a series of small acts that engendered "a prestatory sense of obligation" between them. The continuous threads of these dealings wove the social fabric together, for their result signified more than monetary debts. Indeed, Joseph Jenkins of Canaan omitted at times to jot down the prices of produce he and his fellow villagers exchanged over the years. William Coventry and his neighbors Whitlock, Lobdell, and Wright's wife, were unable to determine the size of their claims on each other.[22] These transactions connected people, and the settlements of accounts reveal the nodes of intricate webs of interdependence. The complexity of such entanglements emerged in George Holcomb's diary. "Today Wm. Dixon paid me eight dollars and I lent the same to Joseph Hill and I borrowed two dollars of Miriam and lent the same to Samuel Holcomb and today I wanted about two thirds of it for Wm. Dixon and he paid me in three trees of timber that I went and chopped and got home at night . . . this evening I went to Mr. Zach Chapman to a party, Mr. Foley came and dressed flax for half a cord of wood I drew him last winter to the school house."[23] The distribution of liabilities and debts among numerous fellow villagers increased their dependence on each other as well as their security. When George Holcomb jotted down in his diary that he "and Lyman Spring [worked] for us and Wm. for A. Harrison—we changed works," then he revealed how social arrangements prevailed over economic obstacles. Changing works offered a solution to problems caused by insufficient hands and tools. Labor was often the means of exchange. No comparative advantage determined the evaluation of different kinds of work, and in the absence of attention to specialization days—that is, time spent at a task—measured the equivalence of exchanged goods and services in the neighborhood. This mode of attending to the needs of people in the countryside revealed the inner workings of a world in which economic exertions served the social imperative of the reproduction of the neighborhood as a moral community with specific norms and sanctions. It unveiled a setting in which, according to Alexander Coventry, most people strove to have "a good farm and competency" as a means of achieving independence.[24]

Land, Family, Migration

Besides labor, the crucial factor of production was land. The link between the family and the turf they cultivated has intrigued many a historian who inquired about the compatibility of a lively land market and a familial orientation expressed in a strong attachment to a particular piece of real estate. The American context complicates an exploration of the degree of concern with family continuity on the land because westward migration, however arduous, offered a solution to problems of population pressure. Inspired by the European discussion on protoindustrialization and studies that depicted a colonial society as accelerating toward implosion as a consequence of demographic growth, Christopher Clark and James Henretta proposed to construe industrial by-employment in New England as an attempt to uphold the economic independence of the farm family as a unit attached to the land.[25] Yet how did acquisition and alienation of land relate to the family's imperative for long-term safeguarding of its offspring?

The answer to this question requires information on geographic stability and mobility and their influence on the social structure. Evidence on out-migration is hard to come by, although census and tax records from the early republic yield material with which to draw a sketch of population movement in the mid–Hudson Valley. The most straightforward measure gained from this documentation pertains to the persistence of heads of households, for we are unable to distinguish among the people whose track is lost from one decennial census to the next, between those who pulled up stakes and those who died. Further limitations concern the impossibility of ascertaining family strategies to place offspring and the distance of relocation. However, the benefits of these sources outstrip their shortcomings. They dispel conventional wisdom on geographic mobility and thus call our attention to the social dynamics in rural communities in the Hudson Valley. Kinderhook in Columbia County had an apparent persistence rate of 68.4 percent between 1800 and 1810: 307 household heads out of 449 stayed put.[26] Table 2 refines the categories in order to delineate the propensity to emigrate or, on the contrary, to stay in town. The objection of any reader of *Bleak House* notwithstanding, this analysis attempts to gauge the positive influence of families in people's choice of a residence because the nonalphabetical tax and census lists reflect clusters of homes. They show that ranking within three lines of a household head with the same last name on the tax or census lists halved one's predisposition to move away from Kinderhook. To share the family name with someone whose dwelling lay beyond this aggregation did not affect the decision on migration one way or the other. Being the single representative of a last name doubled one's chances of leaving. The likely emigrant was rather poorer and less connected than Kinderhook's average household head; he or she was probably young to boot. Newcomers, although

TABLE 2. Determinants of Migration, Kinderhook, 1800–1810

		APPARENT FAMILY			
Persons	Wealth	None	Distant	Close	N
Stayers	$1,403	53 (17.3%)	59 (19.2%)	195 (62.5%)	307
Movers	$750	77 (54.2%)	32 (22.3%)	33 (23.2%)	142
TOTAL	$1,196	130 (28.9%)	91 (20.3%)	228 (50.8%)	449

Sources: Manuscript Population Schedules of the Second U.S. Census, 1800 (microfilm edition); Manuscript Population Schedules of the Third U.S. Census, 1810 (microfilm edition); Tax Assessment of Kinderhook, 1800, NYSL; "Assessment Roll of the Real and Personal Estates in the Town of Kinderhood . . . in 1809," reprinted in Edward A. Collier, *A History of Old Kinderhook* (New York, 1914), 112–24.

four times more likely to settle with their families rather than as single-person households, owned property worth $402 in 1809, a mere 30 percent of the average wealth among Kinderhook's taxpayers. These findings support an interpretation that emphasizes continuity rather than change in the development of the countryside's social structure and, if we accept a certain degree of determinism, its conjugation with influence.[27] Since older, richer, and more influential families tended to stay, it solidified rather than enervated the community's structure.

The impact of migration on the land market is difficult to evaluate. Plenty of parcels and farms changed hands, and plenty stayed in families. In a random sample of land transfers in Columbia County between 1787 and 1793, 61 percent concerned people living in the same village. Motives driving this market certainly covered a wide spectrum, ranging from speculation to debt payments and emigration, but parental intentions to ease sons into adult life seem prominent, too. Patrick McClaghry had bought land over the years that would help his sons support families of their own. Isaac Belknap granted the "homestead farm" to his eldest son Isaac whereas the younger Jeremy got "all the Farm I lately purchased of Niel McArthur." In January 1800, William Coventry reasoned about conveying equal parts of his real and personal estate to his children, for he wanted "every one of them Doe for themselves, not for to Depand on any of the others for a living."[28] Land was not simply a commodity for these farmers. It represented the ground on which their way of life depended. It was a legacy. Not speculation but the desire to satisfy the needs of the family contributed to a lively market in land.

The nominal ownership of land was vested in individuals, but in practice it was encumbered with a great many moral and legal obligations. These checks frustrated the proprietor's freedom to dispose of real estate without considering the interests of kin. Lawrence Van Deusen Sr. enacted a bond with his three sons in which the transfer of the title to his grist mill coerced them to "jointly & severally, their Heirs and Executors to support & maintain the said Lawrence and his wife in meat, drink & Cloathing during their natural lives in a decent manner suitable to their rank and to bury them in the same decent manner after their death." In wills, testators summoned their sons to provide their widowed mothers with "a suitable and comfortable support" or to allow her "the Use of a Bed Room wherein is a small Fire place and convenient firewood, with sufficient meat and Drink during her natural life." Widowed women fulfilled the role of stewards until the heirs reached twenty-one years, but when Helmus Weller assigned his wife "the full power and management of my Estate personall and Real while she continues my Widow" he also added that "she is not to sell nor omercel anything to hurt my children." Sons who acceded to the title of family land saw their liberty of action curtailed by stipulations to care for their unmarried siblings.[29] Land was a link between generations. It established relationships and did not function as commercial property from which its life-sustaining aspect as well as its capacity as a store of wealth, a reserve, or an asset could be abstracted or isolated.

Property bound families together. Its possession sorted out relationships, and its distribution created a situation of inequality between fathers and children. Because married women could not own real estate, sons inherited the lion's share of land while daughters received household furniture and cash. The complementarity of the bequests was designed to endow a young family with the capacity to run a farm. Yet situations of inheritance could become convoluted. Tensions and jealousies could give rise to animosities and lawsuits between heirs. Alexander Coventry mentioned his enemies' "endeavors to deprive me of my inheritance." In 1792, three brothers appeared before Judge Bronk in Coxsackie to arbitrate the division of their family land. When Martin Van Bergen refused to take care of his sister Deborah Moore after their mother's death, the town of Coxsackie launched a lawsuit against him. William Coventry's brother and his two brothers-in-law contested the potential sale of the farm William had received and consulted with the lawyer Peter Van Schaack about how to recuperate their shares. William did not sell, but discord had replaced reciprocity. He commented bitterly that "my own Realations is my worst

Enimy in the world." Hostility marked Archibald McCurdy's last will, in which he forbade his executors to sell his farm to William Wilson, his brother-in-law.[30] Such interference affected the land market, and, although we do not know how prices were formed in the mid–Hudson Valley at the end of the eighteenth century, long-term family strategies influenced these transactions as much as purely mercantile considerations did.

Boundaries: Insiders and Outsiders

Questions of community self-definition were framed within a consciousness of unpredictable resource exploitation. The neighborhood offered the material and social wherewithal to its inhabitants to satisfy immediate needs and work at long-term security. While farmers could castigate deviants among themselves, they found threats to their existence from above and below their immediate environs. The boundaries of neighborhoods and villages were as much social as they were geographic, and their combination erected demarcations that distinguished between insiders and outsiders. These categories of perception, reminiscent of early modern European village affairs, originated in the daily experiences of exchange among neighbors.[31]

The river landings, where all the exchange with extralocal markets took place, had to combat the negative imagery associated with urban spaces and commercial deals. Merchants suffered a bad reputation, and they easily became the targets of distrust that stigmatized them as outsiders to the neighborhood. People from the country accused long-distance traders of preying on farmers. The words of an outraged dignitary at the end of the War of Independence set the tone. "Of late there has again been heard a Cry of War, but it proceeds from a few Merchants who would not Care if all the Inhabitants of America went into Perdition provided they could remain secure and enrich themselves, many of them I hope will suffer. In Fact they will deserve it as they have been sucking the Blood of their Fellow Citizens." Businessmen in Hudson were branded in 1786 as "a parcel of jockies . . . who want to take advantage of, and ruin country people." Twenty years later, the blame hit Catskill while Hudson appeared, curiously enough, to be a model of honesty in mercantile operations. "In Hudson, all low wretched arts to take in the countrymen are despised, but in Catskill such practices are openly avowed, that it is common to hear merchants boasting of some crafty piece of knavery by which they swindled a countryman out of the honest value of the product of his farm."[32] The public image of the middleman as a parasite who did nothing to contribute to the production of goods seemed to come with the job. Location and occupation situated him outside and beyond the farm community and its elaborate system of exchange and moral obligations.

"Outsiders" were held to be responsible for unexplained incidents in the neighborhood. Rumors of embezzlers who drew notes on imaginary ship captains and merchants to filch countrymen of their stock spread through rural areas in the 1780s and 1790s. Horses disappeared mysteriously. Such thefts and frauds undoubtedly happened. But in the search for an explanation the grapevine added a dimension to these events that revealed the fears of the farming population. A story Alexander Coventry heard while sitting in an inn illustrates how lively and fear driven the collective imagination was in the countryside. "The Gentleman and Moore," who shared Coventry's table, "said that the neighborhood of Kinderhook was infested by a gang of thieves who picked up every thing that was left-out and stole horses and cows, but were so cunning that they could not be found out. They said they inhabited the Pine Woods which are very extensive there: that they lived in little huts. There are supposed to be about 20 of them named Johnston, being of one family and a mixture of Negro, Indian and White. That they cohabited with one another sister and brother, etc." Farmers seemed concerned about real or fictitious threats of robberies that would deprive them of their share of worldly goods. Yet the description of the Kinderhook thieves revealed primitive and uncanny outsiders who bore more than a mere resemblance to European "brigands." They were outlaws, certainly, who almost allegorically embodied the insecurity of farmers in an uncertain world, and pariahs, too, onto whom a farming community projected its fears of impurity as if to cleanse itself of sin and temptation. Indeed, the outcasts not only stole valuable assets from cultivators and managed to do so without leaving traces, but they were also racially mixed and incestuous at the same time. And when people flocked to see hangings and trials it is possible to imagine this activity as a rite through which a community exorcised its demons.[33]

"Insiders" met at taverns to recruit their neighbors for collective undertakings, as Thomas Whitlock and Alexander Coventry did after deciding to erect dwellings for their families. They were the people who participated in common efforts and common feasts. They were the men and women who helped build houses and bring in the hay at harvest time. During such feats, men shared a large quantity of alcoholic beverages to relieve their thirst and fortify their bodies in the struggle against time and weather. William Coventry, "having finished his harvest, gave all hands a pretty good supper," his cousin Alexander noted in July 1786. Insiders also were women who visited each other or who, like Marietta Staats,

> went off with the young ladies to a frolic, or spinning bee. These are so-called, because each young lady that attends, has had a pound of wool sent to her that she must spin herself, by a certain day, and she must return the yarn to the owner; all the ladies meeting at the house, and having their dinner and supper there, helping the lady of the house in sewing perhaps, and after tea, have a dance. Generally the young men meet there, and draw wood or something to help the farmer, after which they go home, change their dress, and return and spend the evening dancing and drinking cider and spruce beer, and then see the girls home. Next day there is little or no work done.

The dance at the end of the day was tantamount to a theatrical reaffirmation of the bonds of community. It defined its boundaries and hinged on a moral code of behavior, and when Alexander Coventry described such an event, at which "the whole world was assembled, drinking tea with upwards of 20 people," his portrayal managed to catch neatly the horizon of country dwellers as well as the trust that bound them together.[34]

Fears rooted in a worldview shaped by an image of limited goods defined outsiders in the mid–Hudson Valley in the 1780s and 1790s. The same anxieties framed the structure of everyday life. The belief in a fixed fund of wealth that made one man's gain the loss of another informed the social dynamic of daily exchange, gave rise to tensions between neighbors. A sense of neighborliness prompted Simon Lathrop to inquire of John Beebe of Chatham whether the Wilbour family, which "does suffer for the Want of the Common supports of life," could get help in 1780. Empathy made William Coventry pay visits to Jeremiah Deans, whose daughter had swallowed a copper.[35] This world of farmers contained not only generosity and trust but circumspection and jealousy. When Thomas Whitlock's brother-in-law "was dressed very spruce, new boots, fine cloth, brown coat, ruffled shirt, the ruffles 2 inches broad," it was a singular logic that informed Alexander Coventry's judgment. "So great was the metamorphos," Coventry wrote," that I did not know him as he passed; a little good fortune tries a man more than considerable bad luck will. He has been a little fortunate of late, and means to show it to the world. . . . His land is not yet paid for, but his pride has had a surprising increase." The conspicuous display of success touched off immediate censure. In a universe of limited wealth, individual affluence could only be gained at the expense of one's neighbors. This outlook explained the limited scope of individual appetites. Brazillai Worth, a baker in Catskill, had no scheme to attain riches, but he hoped "that his friends and the community will consider him in his narrow walks and . . . assist him in his small earnings to a comfortable support of his family." Jacob's accomplishment, so suspicion went, resulted from cunning or a lucky streak to the detriment of his brother-in-law. Coventry observed that Jacob "now treats Thos. Whitlock, who was the making of him, with snears, and will not do anything to assist him now while building, though Thomas has wrought many a day for him, and never received recompance."[36] Jacob had not played by the rules, and Coventry's moral outrage and sense of treachery contained a sweeping endorsement of the communal yardsticks used to enforce social cohesion.

Reprimands of behavior that transgressed communal norms covered a wide repertory. Gossip ostracized scorned neighbors and was one of the means with which to settle accounts of contempt and insolence. In an argument about broken promises between Walter Tyler and Ruben Jeacocks, at least eleven neighbors appeared before the Justice of the Peace in Coxsackie to confirm or contest the litigants' honesty and reputation. Samuel Mott had "never heard any complaint" about Tyler but considered Jeacocks "a bad man." The testimonies drew the line between insiders and outsiders, and the escalation from bruits to damage to property seemed an easy step to take. After one of Alexander Coventry's pigs strayed from his barnyard into a neighbor's field, Coventry brought her home only to "find that the sow had half her nose cut off, and even the small pig had her nose cruelly cut by that savage Hubbel or his boys. On the 1st October found one of my best harrows shot on my own pasture near H[ubbel]'s and though he denies doing it himself seemed to have knowledge of his son doing so." Cruelty to animals served as a favored device for inflicting harm on a neighbor. A fellow villager of the Coventry cousins named Decker "lost his breading mare [because] some person tied a bush to her tail, and she ran until she dropped down and died." And William Coventry declared "Reuben Macey is a bad man" after the latter had set his dogs on three of Coventry's hogs, which, driven by fear, ran into a creek and died.[37]

Tension and violence marked neighborhood life as much as collaboration in the postrevolutionary mid-Hudson Valley. The exchange of work and the cooperation at large tasks that originated in a shortage of labor created a situation in which resentment between fellow villagers often arose. Solidarity had its cost: while joint efforts assured the maintenance of the neighborhood's economic underpinnings, symbolic work aimed at overriding divisions within the district. Heavy ritual expenditures thus formed a cornerstone of commutations, and like all occasions of commensality these get-togethers both celebrated the community and enforced its moral standards, for participating meant accepting the rules. Ceremonies at which people shared food fortified the sense of community and defined its insiders. Abraham Wells of Coxsackie related to Leonard Bronk that "Peter Van Bergen and Miss Witlock was married last Thursday & [the] wading continued till Saturday." When Widow Elias celebrated her second marriage, "a large company . . . danced all night" and the party lasted for three days. One regalement for thirty-three people in Coventry's environs featured eighteen pounds of beef, thirteen pounds of veal, one turkey, four gallons of hard liquor and two gallons of wine.[38] These feasts, whose purpose it was to strengthen the integrity of the neighborhood and the mutual bonds of nearby residents, also accompanied doleful events. A correspondent of the *Catskill Messenger* recollected in 1836 that funerals at the beginning of the nineteenth century "appeared more like some festival or convivial party than a house of mourning. A large concours of people, old, middle aged, and young, from far and near, were in attendance. Several rooms were occupied by tables, furnished with divers kinds of meats, pickles, pies, turts, &c., while an ample sideboard supplied with various sorts of drinkables . . . served both as a whetter of the appetite, and a libation to the memory of the deceased." When Doctor Graham's wife died after having given birth to her sixth surviving child, her burial was attended by "a considerable concourse of people. . . . The neighbors contributed and got 2 gallons of rum and one of wine."[39] In a world where subsistence depended on solidarity, such events confirmed and reproduced reciprocal relationships that entailed norms and sanctions. Insiders built networks of support whose very tightness elicited compassion and at times violence.

Masculine Microcosm: The Tavern

To a European beholder, villages in the Hudson Valley offered a curious sight. A captured Hessian soldier from the defeated Burgoyne army described Kinderhook in 1777 as "a type of market-town with widely separated houses." Nobletown consisted of "isolated houses." The farmsteads of Coxsackie and Kingston stood at a good distance from each other.[40] Hessian soldiers considered many of them "wretched huts." The Marquis de Chastellux saw log cabins in the environs of Kinderhook, and the English traveler William Strickland regarded their inhabitants as "miserable backwoodsmen." Houses, however uncomfortable (according to Alexander Coventry the home of his cousin William was "quite out of repair"), provided shelter to families, a function whose physical and symbolic importance was best demonstrated in the warmth of the hearth. In November 1786, Alexander Coventry wrote that it was "so extremely cold, that one does not dare to leave the fireplace."[41] The dispersion of the settlement and the constraints of family homes helped remove the setting of neighborhood sociability to the inn.

The village of Catskill sustained one tavern for every forty of its adult inhabitants in 1807, and a public house graced almost every mile of the Susquehanna Turnpike between Catskill Landing and Windham. Inns had multiple functions, yet with the exception of dances they remained exclusively male places. Juries deliberated and political meetings took place there; gambling, singing, drinking, and fighting were regular pastimes. William Coventry spent many an evening at the pub, although the binge of 25 April 1791 did appear rather extraordinary: "I was at Nicholas Vanderear's [tavern] to a Cockfite in the day; to David Williamson's the rest of the Night. Come home about day brack." He rolled dice at Delamater's while his cousin Alexander played cards. Innkeeper David Williams organized shooting matches with live targets. "They set up a turkey about 100 yards distant, and shoot at it with single bullets," Alexander Coventry described the amusement. "If blood is drawn, the turkey becomes the property of the shooter." George Holcomb's militia company ended its training at the tavern, a place where Holcomb also danced and sang at other times.[42] The inn, then, reinforced the proximity among neighbors. Because it brought men together in a public space and allowed them to engage in discussions in front of a crowd, the tavern provided a stage on which to parade and assert one's masculinity. It was a microcosm where the concerns, jealousies, and frustrations of the vicinity's men emerged, too, and whose heated atmosphere exacerbated the male code of behavior in the countryside.

Honor and masculinity, like all other resources, existed in finite quantity only. Human exertion could not increase them. This feature explains why tensions between men often led to fistfights in which insults gave way to blows. The ideal man united strength, toughness, agility, and mental sharpness—qualities that allowed him to establish ascendency over his environment. Alexander Coventry discussed one of the men in his neighborhood who corresponded to this profile. He called at a tavern, and "there was carpenter Frick, a brother of Caleb's [Lobdell], named John, Old Mr. Whitlock, and Thomas Whitlock. They were pretty merry. Caleb sang some nice songs, and even danced, using his feet with a dexterity I had never before seen. He is upwards of 40 years, and has been one of the completest men of his time. He has been, and still is, amazing strong; he is agile, and can do the work of any two ordinary people; he sings exceedingly well, and has withal, a very pleasant countenance, nor is he destitute of wit."[43] In short, he had a vocabulary and a punch.

This world teemed with tensions, but a series of rituals restrained the rampageous impulses. Trading insults could end with a shared board of bread and cheese. A shouting match could lead to a challenge and then to a fight. Alcohol played an ambiguous role in these events: it could serve as a peacemaker, but its consumption could also ignite the explosion of dormant aggressiveness. After a drawn-out brawl, John Van Buren proposed to "drink friends" with Sander Goes, who declined, fearing accusations of cowardice. The altercation continued until "the s^d Sanders call^d he had enough," soon after which surrender he expired. The outcome of a bout between James Jenison, Andrew Martin, and Thomas Mesick, all neighbors of William Coventry's, was less tragic, but the loss of control indicated the ease with which a man could inflict and suffer major harm. Mesick knocked Martin out, after which the whole tavern was up in arms to keep other fighters apart.[44]

The tavern operated as a forum where reputations were made or destroyed. In the fall of 1796, the Duke De LaRochefoucauld discovered that the arson of a bridge near Catskill had originated with an unsolved dispute at an inn. John Schuneman and Tunis Van Wagenen took their quarrel to the newspaper. Their standing in the community was at stake, and they worked hard to injure the other's name. "Notorious liar," "intruder to the rights of your fellow citizens," and "notorious drunkard" flew back and forth. The conflict had left the public house, but it returned to it when Van Wagenen published a statement that affirmed the tavern's central location in village sociability. It read, "and though I can, and will, enjoy myself with my friends, I never have been drunk; and if I was, not at your expense."[45] A place of solidarity and rupture within the frame of ritualized conviviality, the inn played a fundamental part in regulating the social equilibrium among neighbors. It functioned, in a way at least, as an alternative to the court of justice as a place of dispute settlement.

Honor and masculinity ordered life beyond the small world of the tavern. Home to a society where face-to-face relations made their existence as organizing principles possible, the Hudson Valley contained a people whose bonds were marked by social inequality. And a man was answerable for his honor exclusively to his social peers. "Honor, dignity [and] reputation" were at stake in an announcement published by merchant Benjamin Folger of Hudson and again in a lawsuit between two notable citizens of Columbia County, Israel Spencer and Peter Van Ness. Men had to respond to any slur on their reputation, and thus they went to great lengths to restore their good names. "Damn'd Rascals" was the epithet local patrician Killian Van Rensselaer threw at Peter Ten Broeck and two of his lawyer friends in Claverack, "upon which a short altercation ensued." Ten Broeck challenged the perpetrator per letter to a duel. To no avail, he explained in pretty formal language, because "Mr. Rensselaer has neglected my invitation — he has not answered it — he has never asserted that such an invitation is inconsistent with his principles of religion. But, to the contrary, has lately and publicly asserted, that he has frequently received and accepted such invitations, and add to all this he now sustains an office in the military department. Upon the whole, I now consider myself warranted in declaring Killian K. Van Rensselaer to be destitute of the principles of honour, and do publicly accuse him of cowardice and pusillanimity, and want of veracity." The same values informed the behavior of gentlemen and farmers, although the attributes of the honor code were less highly developed among the neighbors of the Coventry cousins than in the circle of lawyers and merchants.[46] It is to the interaction of men of different ranks that we turn in the final section.

Influence, Deference, Defiance

In March 1792, the *Hudson Gazette* announced the founding of the Society of Mechanics in the city of Hudson and the town of Claverack. Its purpose was to raise funds for its members because "in society, casualties are perpetually happening. He who flourishes to day, may be depressed tomorrow." Uncertainty was a fact of life, the article suggested, but it concluded that "one peculiar happiness attending mankind is that money may be handed down from heir to heir, but wisdom is the peculiar gift of heaven, and is found among the middle and lower orders of life as often as among the rich." It was a bold announcement, but one that still couched its defiance in terms of a society of orders. The divisions of society appeared to be vertical, and although the commentary contained remarks critical of the rich and superior rank it only implied that acceptance of the elite's wisdom was conditional. The discussion did not put forward an outline of a new mode of government and political authority. Indeed, it was indicative of deferential behavior in a world of factional politics where leaders from the upper stratum competed for influence among the rank and file.[47]

Influential families in the mid–Hudson Valley included the landed aristocrats of the Livingston and Van Rensselaer families in Columbia County, the Bronks in Coxsackie, and the dynasties of lawyers among the Van Schaacks, Silvesters and Van Nesses in Kinderhook. These notables owed their position to their wealth, which allowed them to hold political office without remuneration.[48] They sealed their alliances through marriages and fictive kinship, as when Stephen Haight asked Leonard Bronk to be the godfather of his newborn child. Members of the elite felt embattled after the revolution. Henry Livingston construed the county election of 1785 as "a Tryal between Demo and Aristo." But the assault on their dominion remained weak enough to confirm their continuing assurance that power properly belonged to them. Peter Livingston wrote to Peter Van Schaack in 1791 to inquire about places on the electoral lists. "As to my brother Walter," he declared in a tone that revealed his view of politics as a family affair, "if the Gentleman concludes upon a Senator to go from this Town, I do not think it belongs to him as a Non Resident, as I am the eldest and presume have as much Interest both here [on Livingston Manor] and in Hudson if not more than he. Thinks it my place to offer myself." Kin relations led Laurence Merkel to Leonard Bronk to lobby for support of the Van Vechten brothers Samuel and Abraham in a series of elections in 1800.[49]

The peddling of influence was indeed a private affair—yet everybody seemed to know about the constant violation of the republican ideal of common good that transcended factional concerns. Garrett Abeel, a consummate politician, stayed conspicuously aloof—or ostentatiously above—parties and denied any connection with a peculiar group of voters. So did Jacob Bogardus, whose claim it was to have reconciled opposing parties and accepted nominations only after vigorous and repeated solicitation by friends. Dorrance Kirtland cautioned Leonard Bronk that their adversaries "have been busy for some time having private meetings the result of which is that public meetings have been Frequent for the week past—they have had three in the latter part of the week past in the back parts of the Town." His own people had not idled either and managed to drum up a "respectable" crowd of thirty-two men to their meeting. When one interest controlled an area, however, others abstained from organizing there. The Livingstons commanded the manor towns in southern Columbia County, which persuaded their opponents to refrain from calling pre-electoral meetings.[50]

The polls, too, showed the effects of logrolling and arm twisting. The Livingstons guided their tenants through election days. They prodded their agent William Cockburn "to go around . . . to the tenants a few days previous to the elections and request them to come out and vote." Robert Livingston mused about the "good success" when members of his family led tenants to the election offices. Leonard Bronk kept a list of Federalists on whom to rely during balloting. Indeed, the description of an election in 1787 intimates that partisan voters arrived in droves in Coxsackie. "They came in by Eight or ten at the time to Vote & the Poll was Closed so that they was deprived of their votes. I expect about 40 or 50."[51]

The acquiescence in elite leadership found its sources on two grounds. Historically, the Livingstons, Bronks, Van Schaacks, and Van Nesses had assumed stations of consequence in the mid–Hudson Valley. Their self-confidence grew out of the prestige associated with their traditional roles in a society whose social structure prescribed leaders and led.[52] Economically, these great families distributed patronage and protection—resources, that is, that mattered in a world of insecurity. "I am very much rejoiced that you will be pleased to extend your Charity to me and advance me with a charitable Gift of some cloathing," a man named Backer wrote to Chancellor Robert R. Livingston upon deciding to return to Germany in 1801, "for nothing as hardship perhaps famine would undoubtedly be my fortune here in my old days." Charity implied Backer's inability to return the gift in kind, and that guaranteed his subjection to the landlord's power. More importantly, the owner of Clermont Manor could release his tenants from the payment of rent during a bad harvest. Or he could lend them money to buy livestock. Leonard Bronk, too, irrigated the local economy with credit extended to dozens of men in Coxsackie until 1815.[53] These ties established vertical lines of dependence and protection. Influential men stood at the center of networks of clientage. Patronage created reciprocal bonds. It fostered and sustained attitudes of obligation and loyalty. Such connections made life more predictable for farmers in need, and they paid part of their debt on election day.

Other mechanisms braced deferential conduct. Augustin Prevost was "a gentleman of distinguished character and fortune," a description that captured his patrician lifestyle, which was supported by an income from his landed estate. Categories of a hierarchical nature classified the men who sold and bought land in the mid–Hudson Valley from the genteel esquire and gentleman through the merchant and lawyer to the ordinary farmer and cordwainer. A rigorous etiquette regulated social interaction between persons of different ranks. William Coventry referred to "Squier Delamatter," and Backer, the beneficiary of a gift offered by Robert R. Livingston, was awed by the prospect of calling at the manor house. "My Cloathing is in such a situation that it would be the greatest impudency to appear in such apparel before you and your illustrious Family," he wrote. "If it is your will to see me down I must obey and appear before the Gentlemen and Ladies in my ragged cloths but I pray you, Sir, to spare me this shame." The hierarchy of pews at the church in Coxsackie offered an accurate replication of the distribution of prominence (and social capital and leverage) in town: Leonard Bronk occupied "Num^r 1"; then followed other dignitaries from Jonas Bronk to Philip Conine and Mathias Van Den Berck.[54] Official records did not simply codify economic transactions but marked social positions. Reenactments of social roles and ranks on Sundays projected the image of a hierarchical society and conveyed the message of a social landscape in which plain people looked up to elevated men and women. Hierarchy, as a value, explained the competition for honors that recognized and confirmed a man's standing in the community with a "place in view" at public events.

Suffrage requirements under the New York State Constitution supported the three-tiered scaffolding of society. Forty percent of all adult white males could not cast a ballot in state elections in 1790. In Catskill, Coxsackie, and Freehold, 40 percent of the adult white male population could vote for the Assembly, while 25 percent could do so in Columbia County. The governors and senators were elected by 20 percent of adult men in the towns on the Hudson River's west bank and 35 percent on its eastern shore. In spite of such limitations, elections were, Alan Taylor writes, "festive, competitive, masculine assertions of dominance," and it is true that "the duch & English got afighting" in Coxsackie in 1787. "Some times thirty or Forty together at once. I certanly exspected that some whood have been killed. The duch upon that whole made out well, for the Number of the Yankes had but one Eye to look out of."[55] But what needs emphasis, too, is the modest voter turnout even at unrestricted federal polls in the late 1780s and early 1790s. The disfranchisement surely accounted for electoral participation that ranged from 28 to 47 percent of the white male population between 1789 and 1793; so did a government that was distant and a material existence that required close attention.[56]

The interweaving of influence and deference, condescension, and disaffection created an atmosphere in which "a plebeian" complained about the "usurpation of rights . . . by a few individuals" who ran political affairs at their "private conveniendum." If the elite drew legitimacy from its traditional preeminence in politics, then the unfulfilled promise of the Amercian Revolution inspired a defiant attitude in the 1780s and 1790s. As early as 1780 John Beebe marveled at the sweeping transformation. He "reflected back on the State of Affairs in the Government ten years ago when Publick affairs were conducted by Sutch who look:d Down with Desdain on those that now are set at the Helm." A correspondent of the *Hudson Weekly Gazette* wondered in 1787 what had happened to "all the advantages which you have been promised from the late happy revolution." The electors of Freehold were thought to oppose James Barker, "the candidate of the oppressors, [and] even pride themselves in doing him an injury."[57] These were attempts to stretch the bonds of authority, however, and not to promote a new plan of government.

The rhetoric advocating "the views of the majority" and outraged by "the infringement on the rights of the people" was fierce, but it hit a wall of obstruction. A paternalistic and contemptuous reception greeted the plebeian as "a little fantastical, up-start, malevolent boy" who had stepped beyond his rightfully ascribed position in society. Even the rather more active voters in Coxsackie discovered the limits of their exertions. They expressed their resentment of elite rule by holding up candidates "out of the Woods . . . for Publick Officers." Leonard Bronk himself "was greatly in dispute for supervisor, that is to say among the bog inhabitants." In the end, however, "when it came to a vote there was no Imposition." In the early nineteenth century oppositional candidates ran against "the all-grasping family of the Livingstons [who] seduced by their intrigues or corrupted by their enormous wealth." Yet the impotence of these activities and verbal assaults—"Crazy Bob Livingston" was deemed "from a moral point of view . . . too abandoned almost for public animadversion"—came to light in the extent of the electorate almost a generation after the initial skirmishes had occurred. In 1814, only 70 percent of all adult white males in Greene County and 78 percent in Columbia County could participate as voters in the political life of the region. Forty-six and 48 percent could consider themselves full citizens who exercised their rights without any property restrictions.[58] Civil equality remained twice removed, and in spite of the hustle at the polls power continued as the privilege of the traditional elite.

THE WORLD in which Alexander Coventry, Thomas Whitlock, and their neighbors built new houses was a thoroughly local place. Haunted by the lean years of the War of Independence and inspired by the ideals of the American Revolution, the mid–Hudson Valley remained an uncertain universe. Its people invented strategies to reduce the insecurities that nature thrust upon them. But rural culture exacerbated these fears through its construction of natural resources as finite and, more importantly, of the creation of wealth as impossible by means of gains in the productivity of human labor. Inheritance practices linked generations to sustain a family's ability to make ends meet and to help increase comfort in children's lives, not to engage in real estate speculation, as would be the case on the western frontier. A network of exchange constructed the neighborhood. Labor operated as the currency in the majority of the transactions between adjoining families. Production time rather than market value established the exchange standard. The constant give-and-take to insure the reproduction of families, and fellow villagers created reciprocal ties whose importance lay perhaps as much in emotional security as in economic shelter from shortages. These interdependencies spawned zones of friction. Teamwork gave rise to conflict, sympathy to jealousy. Violence formed an accepted part of everyday life. A culture of masculinity imposed tough conduct, because honor called for vindication whenever it was cast in doubt. Because anxiety about material conditions shaped lives and the social equilibrium in the neighborhood hinged on foundations that required constant maintenance, rituals of commensality defused tensions and reasserted the bonds of community.[59]

The conjunction between hierarchy and limited goods, the two values along which rural society in the mid–Hudson Valley organized itself, appeared in a dispute opposing one Isaac Rosa of Coxsackie and Leonard Bronk, the most eminent man in the area in 1801. Rosa accused Bronk of executing a plan to "have my Labour for Naught." The reason and origin of the conflict remained unclear, but Rosa continued: "*Sir* there is a golden Ballance wich oat to be in the Breast of Every Man wich is conchens." The powerful Bronk had defaulted on the expectation that a high rank came with obligations toward those in lower stations. He had forsaken probity when taking advantage of, rather than showing respect to, a weaker member of the town's community. Rosa went on to depict the consequences of such disregard of fair play. In a world where material improvement of one family appeared to be possible only because of the decline of another, Bronk's conduct endangered the basis of Rosa's existence. "The hand of god is Iracisabel," he exclaimed. "It is so that som men build upon the Ruens of others and why we no not."[60] The purpose of the golden balance was to assure an equitable, not an equal, distribution of the area's resources. Bronk had, in Rosa's view, violated the social norms that promised a decent livelihood to even the humblest family in the neighborhood.

Distinct mechanisms that centered around the reduction of risks ordered life in rural society. But it was not a world apart. Beyond the confines of the neighborhood lay towns whose population needed foodstuffs, whose houses required lumber, whose stoves burned wood. There was a state whose agents began to arbitrate disputes that farmers had hitherto solved by asking neighbors to adjudicate right or wrong.[61] These services led to taxes, which the inhabitants of the countryside had to pay in cash. The minimal import of currency to neighborhood transactions must not seduce us into believing in the absence of self-interest or rationality in neighborhood economies. Nor should we conclude, by negative inference, that cash was the sole limiting element whose lack thwarted the blossoming of market behavior until financiers and banks poured fiduciary or coin into the economy and thus set off a round of development that allowed the market to come into its own in the Hudson Valley countryside. Payment, however, required farmers to produce crops that could be shipped to other areas. Comparative advantages gave rise to long-distance trade. The modalities of this commerce, and its extent and importance in the lives of farm families, now require inquiry.

TWO

To Market, to Mill, to the Woods

The uncertainty of agricultural production pervaded the attitudes of farmers toward life. "I cant buy for I have nothing to sell," Abraham Wells informed Leonard Bronk in 1798. "I can tell you so farr as this we dont suffer for nothing but money. Our little crops are promising and if they dont fail we are in hope to do better."[1] Wells's first priority was to produce enough to reach the threshold of home consumption, although the account betrayed his appreciation of the amenities that income from sales would afford his family. Comfort required the exchange of farm produce for articles of merchandise like molasses or rum that only importation from remote regions afforded the people in the Hudson Valley. However much the main preoccupation of farm families was producing enough provisions to cover their own needs, long-distance trade was necessary to the regional economy at the end of the eighteenth century because it lacked certain goods. These commodities—from tropical products to English crockery—proved useful and attractive to farm families, which obtained them at the neighborhood store or in shops located at Hudson River landings.

Farmers dealt with merchants and storekeepers who perforce operated as importers and exporters, too. As intermediaries, they linked farmer and neighborhood to the wider economic world. They conveyed country produce to the city and passed on signals from the distant metropolitan market to the local population. If the merchant was the pivot of long-distance trade, the farmer's situation shaped its organization. Long-distance trade bore the imprints of both the imperfection of information from the city and the concern of farm families for subsistence security in the face of the precarious conditions of agricultural production. Hudson Valley resident and gentleman farmer J. Hector St. John de Crèvecoeur (who supplied the title for this chapter) explained that "the limits of our trade do not permit us to send our produce where we might find a ready vent for it." His observation suggests a social geography that determined the mechanisms of price setting. Beyond the neighborhood in which labor time defined exchange equivalents, farmers who commercialized produce chose between taking a "chance for the market of the world" and a course in which "that chance is fixed by a certain price then received." When it came to exchange for extralocal goods, Crèvecoeur thus distinguished between a market where impersonal forces of supply and demand ordered the value of local merchandise and an exchange relation in which the risk factor declined as a consequence of a customary determination of a good's value. In practice, farmers straddled two worlds that historians and ethnologists have often tended to construe as incompatible. In the fall of 1798, Daniel Sahler and Henry Graham earned credit for flax seed at six shillings per bushel when it remained in the local exchange system and nine and one-half shillings when Kingston merchant Abraham J. Hasbrouck shipped it to New York City.[2] Two different social circuits—not a single competitive market—determined the prices of produce. Farmers and merchants decided how to distribute the expendable produce between the local realm in which relations and repute were built and maintained and the world of alluring commodities beyond the neighborhood to which merchants provided access.

The organization of business at Hudson River landings hinged as much on credibility as credit. In this currency-poor economy, credit capitalized trade and made it possible in the first place. It bound farmers to merchants and merchants to farmers. These were ties of fidelity that lasted for years. They reduced suspicion between producer and shipper, whose relation tended to be construed as antagonistic. They ordered exchange and brought stability to the long-distance trade. Trust lowered transaction costs and reduced the insecurity inherent in trade by providing guarantees for the quality of the merchandise. Both parties benefited from its accrual in this long-term arrangement. Yet the balance of power may well have tipped in favor of the debtor, whose defaulting the creditor prevented by keeping produce prices stable even though they varied in the metropolitan market.

Commercial exchange, part of the farm families' strategy to achieve a competence, as Daniel Vickers argued, did not occur in a market free of personal relations: these bonds actually predicated trade on the Hudson. Abstraction from the social context in which these transactions took place dilutes Winifred B. Rothenberg's cliometric insights into the economy of rural New England between 1750 and 1850. In her analysis, sellers and buyers, whom she construed without regard to social ties and the organization of commerce, met in frictionless markets where their decisions to produce, sell, and buy were based on rational calculations aimed at maximizing profits.[3] In the Hudson Valley at the end of the eighteenth century, social imperatives shaped economic choices, and that field of force also influenced the goings-on beyond the neighborhood. Not anonymity but relational considerations that reduced uncertainties through the introduction of personal obligations characterized commercial interactions in Catskill, Hudson, and Kingston. This physical quality of the association between merchant and producer disappears when the market, disguised as an analytical tool to measure efficiency of commodity and utility allocation, becomes a metaphor for the encounters of what were, after all, people who struggled to secure a decent livelihood.

The farm family's efforts to produce and acquire the necessaries of life form the subject of the following pages. Seasonal rhythms and the willingness to dispose of several assets led country people to pursue multiple occupations under one roof in order to procure their living. Some of these activities connected them to their neighbors while others attached them to long-distance traders and urban consumers. Just how many farm families carried produce to merchants at landings—and what part of their production these goods represented—is the treacherously simple question raised here to help us understand how farmers responded to marketing incentives and opportunities for growth. The goal of this analysis is to understand the extent of, and the social rules that governed, commercial exchange.

Farm Work and Farm Production

"Great parts of the profits of summer are expanded in carrying a family through this wintry career," Crèvecoeur summed up the rhythms of production and consumption on the farm. Agricultural labor followed, of course, a seasonal pattern. Celerity marked work during the summer, when neighbors helped each other to reap crops and bring in the harvest. Scottish immigrant Alexander Coventry found the pace of harvesting "rather hurried in this country." Winter's chores required much less haste and, according to the author of *American Husbandry,* often came to a halt altogether. Crèvecoeur labeled the cold months the "season of festivity," and William Strickland called them the "season of amusement and recreation" for farm families. While these comments pertained to the cadence of labor and the length of the working day, they did not imply the advent of leisured inactivity after fall. Housework continued for women, while the farmers in the Catskills chopped trees to heat their houses and fabricate shingles and barrel staves. Barns allowed women and men to thresh corn and clean flax, necessary steps in the transformation of farm products for final use.[4]

Observation of farm families in his native neighborhood led Chancellor Robert R. Livingston to assert that they made virtue out of necessity and strove to supply all their wants. The quest for economic security indeed impelled farmers to pursue a variety of activities. William Coventry wove baskets. He made rope. "I was making indian shoes the cheif of the day," he recorded on 24 January 1796, and in November 1798 he stitched and sewed leather mittens. He made and mended shoes during rainy or wintry weather, an activity that occupied him for an average of ten days per year between 1790 and 1802. Alexander Coventry happened onto a farm whose owner also ran a small tannery and a shoe shop.[5]

The diversification of economic activities increased the number of sources of nourishment for rural families. The creation and maintenance of a wide register of social connections informed the strategies of farmers as well as artisans. Zephaniah Chase's experience in the Catskills illustrates this logic. A carpenter who had migrated from Martha's Vineyard to Lexington Heights, Chase immediately found work. His neighbors, also pioneer settlers, needed his skills to mend their tools while they were clearing land. He furnished their houses with beds and chairs. In 1786, Chase's entire income of £35 9s 1d (or about $90) flowed from his trade. Eleven years later, Chase had carved out a farm from the woods, and agricultural produce brought 20 percent of his revenue of £30 and 8s (or $76). His craft earned him a little over two-fifths of his income while services like writing deeds for his fellow villagers generated 38 percent of his proceeds.[6] Chase had, within a few years, minimized risks to his family's livelihood by multiplying connections in the community and by increasing his assets. Instead of following one occupation, he pursued three, all of which integrated the Chase family into the neighborhood. Multiple activities rather than specialization ordered economic pursuits among Hudson Valley residents in the late eighteenth century.

Artisans like Chase owed their economic welfare to the state of agriculture around them. A good year could mean more orders from farmers while their own produce supplied their families. A bad year could shrink demand and contract their provisions. A good harvest offered craftsmen the opportunity to hire themselves out or to participate in work bees. Zephaniah Chase did not record any income in July 1797 when he was probably busy working his own soil. David Cullen, a shoemaker in northern Dutchess County, hired Mills Garrit in July 1793 to help harvest his land.[7] The extent to which seasonality determined the monthly income of artisans appeared in the accounts of Kingston shoemaker John Masten. His shop brought £51 and 9d (about $129) in 1798. Summer and fall saw him least at the cobbler's bench, and indeed the distribution of his revenues inversely followed the pattern of John Wedges's workdays as a farm laborer in Canaan in the late eighteenth century (figs. 1 and 2). Masten, it is safe to assume, spent much of the harvest season in the fields. The combination of agricultural and artisanal occupations and their alternation throughout the year were devices of the search for security in a world where the anticipation of mediocre harvests shaped behavior.

Work was the pivotal factor in production on farms at the end of the eighteenth century. Its availability marked the limits of the land a family could cultivate. The size of a farm mattered insofar as agricultural practices exhausted the soil. Predatory agriculture required husbandmen to shift cultivation from plot to plot to allow depleted lots to recover some of their fertility as overgrown fallows. The larger a farm, the easier it was to maintain its output. Smaller farmsteads curbed a family's ability to support itself without finding another source of income because they thwarted the necessary rotation of tilled fields. So, while the total acreage of a farm denoted its long-term viability, if not its productivity (research on seventeenth- and eighteenth-century European farms demonstrated the absence of a significant correlation between farm size and productivity), it was a family's capacity to work the land that determined the volume of crops. Only a parcel of less than forty acres rendered the sustenance of a farm family precarious.[8] About one-quarter of the farm households in the environs of the city of Hudson encompassed fewer acres (table 3). These were the people who principally relied on artisanal skills to earn a living. Remember that 22 percent of the probate inventories listed artisanal tools in the 1790s, and 108 (or 27.4 percent) of 394 identifiable accounts kept by Catskill merchant Teunis Van Vechten between 1753 and 1782 belonged to men with an interest in crafts.[9]

Farmers divided their land into tillage, pasture, hay meadows, woods,

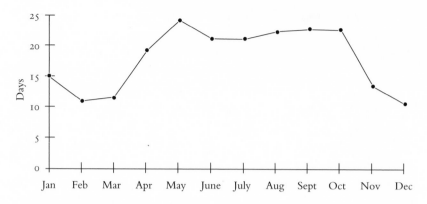

FIG. 1. Average number of workdays of a farm laborer, April 1789 through March 1791. (Data from Elijah Hudson Farm Account Book, Canaan, Special Collections, NYSHA.)

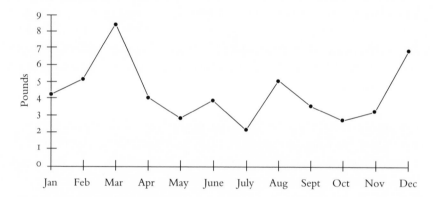

FIG. 2. Shoemaker's monthly income, 1798. (Data from John E. Masten Account Book, Kingston, N-YHS.)

TABLE 3. Size of Farms in Columbia County around 1800 ($N = 130$)

Size	All farms	Top decile	Bottom 30%
Mean size (acres)	98.1	210.8	35.1
Median size (acres)	97.0	197.0	35.0

Source: Daniel Penfield Deed, 15 Oct. 1806, Deeds TT, 354–366, Columbia County Court House.

and fallow. Robert R. Livingston of Clermont described common farms in the Hudson Valley as divided "into lots, of from fifteen to twenty acres, and ploughed in succession every third year." English gentleman farmer William Strickland visited a tenant farm on Clermont Manor in Columbia County where fifteen acres carried wheat and forty acres were grasslands. Data from nearby Ulster County corroborate the observation: its farmers cultivated between ten and fourteen acres of grains around the turn of the century.[10] A farmer whom Alexander Coventry considered "a sober, steady, clever man" had kept "an account of the expenses he was at in getting in a crop of wheat and rye" in 1790. It was a lot of work: fifty-two days from breaking the soil to bringing the crops into the barn. The harvest, moreover, proved modest. It consisted of 56 bushels of wheat and 17 bushels of rye. In 1791, William Coventry expected a harvest of 50 bushels of wheat and about the same in rye; nine years later, he expressed his satisfaction after harvesting 140 bushels of corn, but often weather and pests foiled even average outputs. "Buckwheat is poor," he noted in 1801. "I sowed one bushel and got eight from it."[11] The volume belied Crève-coeur's upbeat assessment of an industrious family's capacity to sell, not just grow, 100 bushels of wheat. Good yields in the Hudson Valley stood at 12 bushels of wheat per acre, 25 bushels of corn, and 15 bushels of buckwheat. In peacetime under Napoleon I, yields in the Paris region averaged 22 bushels of wheat and 16 bushels of buckwheat per acre (no maize was grown), and even poor areas like the Aveyronnais near the Pyrenees could expect 10 bushels of wheat, 9 bushels of buckwheat, and 11 bushels of maize on average.[12] Hudson Valley soil productivity did not measure up to the best cereal regions in France at the end of the eighteenth century.

Mowing meadows occupied the farm family from June to the end of September, although it permitted a great deal of flexibility. According to Chancellor Livingston, one acre of grass usually produced one ton of hay. William Coventry swung the scythe on fifty-one days in 1802 and brought

TABLE 4. Mean Number of Animals per Farm around 1790 ($N = 68$)

Animals	Average number	Number of farms and %
Cows	3.8	51 farms, or 75.0%
Oxen	0.7	19 farms, or 27.9%
Horses	2.2	44 farms, or 64.7%
Sheep	7.3	35 farms, or 51.5%

Sources: Gustave Anjou, comp., *Ulster County: Probate Records* (New York, 1906), vol. 2; Probate Inventories, Columbia County Surrogates' Court.

fifty-three loads of hay into the barn. A year earlier, he had gathered forty-nine loads. He never mentioned the sale of grains, but residents of Hudson purchased seven wagon loads of hay, which made Coventry £21 5s 6d in 1801. The rest, probably fifteen tons of hay, provided fodder for his cattle.[13]

Between Robert R. Livingston, who described farm animals of the eastern states as generally large and comparable to those of France, and Alexander Coventry, who found them insufficiently fed and meager in Columbia County, their number rather than their appearance surprises. Stock, of course, required constant attention, and women supplied the work necessary to run the dairy, from milking to buttering and cheese making.[14] The shortage of labor and the neglect of fences affected the size of herds, however much cows were necessary for a balanced diet, oxen and horses were needed as draft animals and slaughter beasts, and sheep were used as providers of wool. Hillsdale's 635 households kept 2,270 head of cattle aged two years and older in 1799, an average of 3.57 bovines in an area well suited for stock. A comparative perspective again confirms the unexceptional situation of Hudson Valley agriculture: an average farmstead (table 4) was roughly on a par with its counterpart in Central Europe, where Tamás Faragó found three draft animals (oxen and horses).[15]

What exactly did it mean for a family to live and work on a farm in the mid–Hudson Valley? I have avoided speculating about the total volume of farm production because the bases of evidence are narrow. Moreover, contemporaries' own assessment of their world as a place of limited goods and the comparison with conditions among European peasants ought to warn us away from precipitous conclusions about the security of their material lives. Even Crèvecoeur sounded a levelheaded note when he cautioned, "I do not mean that every one who comes will grow rich in a little time; no, but he may procure an easy, decent maintenance by his industry. Instead of starving, he will be fed; instead of being idle, he will have employment." There was more than enough land to till, but the structure and composition of farms in the Hudson Valley environment limited the output a family could expect from its toil. Traveling through an area at the foot of the Catskills in 1788, Alexander Coventry observed that "the inhabitants are very poor, but seem industrious," a description with which his cousin William agreed six years later.[16] As an assessment of the rural condition, the statement summed up the lives of the majority among the inhabitants in the Hudson Valley countryside: they engaged in multiple activities to secure a decent competence.

Food Consumption

Farmers evaluated their circumstances by means of the degree of satisfaction of their families' needs, that is, by the relation of output and consumption rather than the amount of monetary profit. An analysis of allotments conferred to widows in men's wills allows us to catch a glimpse of expectations about sufficiency at the end of the eighteenth century. Testators set aside goods and stock to maintain their surviving wives. Wills imposed legal as well as moral obligations on heirs. The widow's position in the world was precarious, and Abraham Donaldson of New Paltz acknowledged it when he provided "unto my beloved wife Catherine a suitable and comfortable support from the farm I now live on . . . to be given her by my two sons John and Samuel."[17] Not everybody made a will and not every will contained instructions on the share allotted to the surviving spouse, but some husbands expressed their concern for their wives in more precise, quantifiable terms. Some only specified the amount of food with a heavy emphasis on bread cereals and one type of meat. Others provided cash. Still others bestowed sheep to assure that a widow could spin and weave cloth in order to dress herself and trade at the neighborhood store. Cows supplied milk for daily meals and the possibility of churning butter. Table 5 collects a medley of data, and yet the evidence out of which it is built offers the closest approximation of the individual maintenance that people deemed necessary to live competently. The multiplication of the allotments for single widows provides an estimate of family requirements, even though differentiated needs were likely to reduce the calculated averages.

The widows' parts were generous, for only rich farmers owned the

Commodity	Widows' part	Family needs (widows × 5)
Wheat	6.5 bu	32.5 bu
Corn	4.0 bu	20.0 bu
Beef	62.5 lbs	312.5 lbs
Pork	100.0 lbs	500.0 lbs
Cows	1.5	7.5
Sheep	4.5	
Wool	10.0 lbs	
Yearly allowance	14£	70£

Sources: Wills A, 1787–1798, Columbia County Court House; Anjou, *Ulster County,* vol. 2.

number of cattle extrapolated from the widows' parts, and average family incomes were hardly large enough to spare £14 to support a widowed mother. In all likelihood, the wills represented the vision of the wealthier inhabitants of the rural Hudson Valley. Weekly meat consumption attained a level of 3 pounds per person, a truly aristocratic volume compared to that of Europe and an intake that would have condemned two-thirds of Columbia County's neat cattle to the butcher block in 1800.[18] Wheat portions came to 7.5 pounds per week. In a precious diary entry recorded in December 1787, Alexander Coventry stated, "have used, since housekeeping, which began in June [to] the 10 present month, 15 bu. wheat, besides some corn." Four adults lived in the household, and so the calculation allowed each to consume 7.5 bushels of wheat per year. Coventry's piece of information, originating from a professional head of family, reasonably corroborates the wheat allocation in the widows' parts. It also indicates a somewhat lesser dependence of the Hudson Valley diet on cereals compared to the intake of French peasants. They consumed on average 11 bushels of wheat and saw much less meat in their soups than did Hudson Valley farmers.[19]

Less wheat but more maize and meat on a more regular basis distinguished the Hudson Valley's from a European peasant diet. Beyond those staples, diversification of their food repertoire ranked high among the efforts of the Coventry cousins. The cultivation of gardens suffered from the shortage of labor, yet the combined exertion of wives, husbands, and other household members increased the variety of vegetables in kettles and pots. They raised beans, cabbage, celery, cucumbers, and turnips and dug up potatoes, all of which required few means and manipulations for preservation because they could be stored naturally, dried, or salted. In October 1787, Alexander Coventry set aside five bushels of apples for winter. In New England, where similar circumstances prevailed, diversified production on the farm and improved skills in food preservation afforded, according to Sarah McMahon, "many rural households an ample, diversified fare" toward the end of the eighteenth century. McMahon concluded that a "deseasonalization" of food supplies reduced the disparity between winter and summer provisions, all but eliminated the "six-weeks want" in spring, and put an end to the specter of scarcity in rural households.[20] These achievements were impressive, but in the Hudson Valley their foundations were more precarious. Spring, for one, still appears to have been a season of austerity. Then legumes and vegetables seldom graced the bowls of the valley's rural inhabitants. Their seasonal eclipse occurred at a time when even staples could, and did, run short. In May 1789, Alexander Coventry "went to the Mill in the morning, but got only ½ bushel of Rye, grain being so scarce that there does not come enough to miln for the family." Six days later he returned "and got one bushel of Rye from the Miller, there being only two bushels in the miln." William Coventry, too, sought agricultural produce when the year had been lean. In spring 1795, he expressed a consumer's exasperation because "grain is terrible dear." In February 1799, he purchased corn, in January 1800 he procured wheat and buckwheat flour, and in May of the same year he was forced to buy rye because he had exhausted his seeds during the winter. Early 1801 saw him again ride to Hudson to acquire grain for his family. Circumstances compelled farm families to practice prudence and habits of frugality. Edward McGraw of New Windsor remembered his family's kitchen table mostly for its routine. Breakfast consisted of tea, bread, and butter; dinner was boiled pork and vegetables; and supper comprised soup and milk. If anything guided the McGraws' disposition toward daily nourishment around 1800, it was the "economy of expenditures" that patterned their behavior.[21]

There was, then, a factual basis to the conception of the world as an uncertain place where a farm family's existence was one of vulnerability and exposure to hardship. That reality is difficult to fathom if we simply compare a farm's probable output with the family's subsistence expectations because average figures do not capture the contingencies of rural life. Those numbers indicate that most families produced enough supplies to feed themselves and engage in exchange. But cases of misery and deprivation occurred often enough to keep town authorities vigilant and warn paupers, as in early republican Coeymans, "to Leave this town or give secourety to the Overseer of the poor [to] not becom Chargeable to said town."[22] The mere comparison between one series of data, a reasonable assumption that farms brought forth between sixty and one hundred bushels of grain (plus milk for dairy, vegetables, and hay), and another, that the needs of a family stood at approximately thirty to forty bushels, obfuscates the struggle to balance different kinds of work and hides the fear of events—a death, a frost, a pest—that endangered sufficient harvests. Their precariousness fostered the logic of neighborhood exchange. It incited women to make and barter goods at the neighborhood store. And it influenced the forms of trade in Hudson River towns.

Female Economies

At her death in January 1805, Catherine Overbagh, the widow of Godfrey Brandow, left two shillings in cash, two sheep, a spinning wheel, two pounds of wool, and eight pairs of knitting needles. *Stoddard's Diary* for 1801 summed up women's toil and, in a somewhat unintended manner (note the use of pronouns), contrasted its length to the presumably shorter days of men: "The thrifty housewife cards and spins, / Whose talk with rising *sol* begins, / Nor till he long has sunk from sight, / Does she to labour bid good night."[23] Beyond household chores like cooking, washing, sewing, and cleaning, women pursued tasks whose products were also objects of exchange among neighbors or in the neighborhood store. Younger women did stints with families and earned monies as spinners and weavers. John Teller of Clinton, Dutchess County, paid Sarah Husted 2£ 4s "in ful for weaving" in 1798. Betsy Martin, Linda Patterson, and Lucy Hubbel spun and wove for their neighbors, the Coventry family, in 1791 and 1792. Wives could run farms. "Found everything in good order," Alexander Coventry recorded in his diary after returning from an extended journey to western New York. "The business of the farm as forward as though I had been at home. . . . My good wife had superintended the business and has done as well as I could." On another occasion the young physician noted that widow Elias "has no hired men, but with her daughters, who are but children, takes care of a large stock of cattle."[24] These activities, like Catherine

Overbagh's knitting, formed part of the family's strategy to square needs and the supply of labor and to balance expenses and income.

The majority of women's trading occurred within narrow local confines. Between 1785 and 1787, Zephaniah Chase, the Lexington Heights carpenter, built furniture for ten women, a signal indication that they ran the domestic side of family life, where they assumed the control of the exchange equivalents, whether in goods or cash. Nine of them paid at least part of their bills with textile goods: Peggi Doggett knitted stockings, Abigail Doggett made woolen gloves, Sarah Norton sewed trousers and a linen shirt, and others spun and wove. James Mason settled his account at a Claverack store with yarn, thread, cloth, and carpets. Since he was the only man in the household, the articles, whose value added up to 22£ in eighteen months, were the products of the women who lived under the same roof. Although dairy products appeared rarely in store ledgers, Mason's account listed butter and Alexander Coventry once noted that a household help "took three skim milk cheeses and two pounds of butter for my wife [to Hudson] and got a black silk handkerchief." Betsy Coventry enjoyed the independence of a household that most of the time was above the subsistence threshold. She was free to spend at least part of the income she had generated without her husband's interference (although he knew about her expenditures). Yet when the Coventrys' household helper Sally gleaned wheat after harvest it was her husband Cuff who disposed of it.[25]

Men recognized women's economic contribution to the household's material well-being. Wives enjoyed a degree of autonomy in their activities on and beyond the farmstead, and in their productive and reproductive aspects these endeavors followed the family imperative of achieving a competency. Yet gendered definitions of responsibilities circumscribed women's sphere of independence in this patriarchal order: just like Hannah Brockway, who traded in the name of her husband Gideon at Selah Strong's country store in the early 1790s, wives could represent the household in economic matters. But authority lay with their spouses. What further distinguished women's part in the strategy of multiplying the household's relations to increase its security was both the geography of their connections and the nature of the products they exchanged. While men established and entertained contacts at the Hudson River landings where they delivered produce, women traveled shorter distances and confined their deals to the neighborhood. However, the goods they brought to shops resulted from their transformative work on raw materials from the farm, whether flax, wool, or milk. Most of these articles left their area of origin as merchandise, although country stores happened to serve occasionally as clearinghouses for local production. The absence of collection circuits for dairy products in the mid–Hudson Valley suggests the limited extent of such traffic, especially in comparison with the Philadelphia hinterland, where butter and cheese engendered a lively long-distance trade. It also hints at the way in which commerce could graft itself on neighborhood transactions and, as in the case of dairy, appeal to women less as a strategy of empowerment than as a means of access to greater familial well-being and individual gratification. The effect of such a development consisted of the confluence of two logics of exchange at the country store, where neighborhood give-and-take, with its variable value equivalents, could coexist with marketing.[26]

"Riding 1 Load to Landing"

While women and men participated in local exchange, men alone organized the transport of produce to merchants in river towns. Joseph White of Canaan borrowed Elijah Hudson's wagon eight times in 1788, yet only once in September did he "carry flower" to Hudson. William Goodrich used Joseph Jenkins's cart to drive to Hudson in 1803, while Abraham Van Dyck earned credit at a Kinderhook store "by riding 1 load to landing" in January 1804. Timothy Persons of Windham had one Reynolds's "waggon to get a load to the Road and go to the River" in June 1809. Samuel Crocker, too, borrowed Reynolds's wagon, once in 1808, once in 1810, and twice in 1811. These journeys to landings were few. Among the fifty-seven customers who shipped goods to the metropolitan market in New York City on the sloops of Kingston merchant Abraham J. Hasbrouck in 1798, forty-seven delivered their freight in a single trip. A wagon, according to Crèvecoeur, could carry two-thirds of a cord of wood, five barrels of flour, or "thirty bushels of wheat, and at sixty pounds to the bushel, this makes a weight of eighteen hundred pounds."[27] A rough measure of farmers' involvement in long-distance trade, this first piece of information suggests the limited amount of products that left the neighborhood for the outside world.

Not all farmers who came to the landings shipped goods to New York. Some exchanged a portion of their produce for merchandise that they could not obtain through the area's networks. Their business responded to a need for indispensable things for which they traded a part of their

TABLE 6. Long-Distance Trade among Freighters' Customers, Late Eighteenth
Century

		ACCOUNTS	
Freighters	Number	Long-distance	Percentage
Snyder, 1774–77	120	39	32.5
Hasbrouck, 1798	159	57	35.8

Sources: Benjamin Snyder Account Book, 1774–1777, N-YHS; Abraham J. Hasbrouck Journal,
1797–1799, N-YHS.

farm's output. Others delivered products that they forwarded to the metropolis with the help of a shipper's services. Surplus production made this
extralocal orientation possible, and it established a distinction between
farmers in the mid–Hudson Valley. The ledgers of Benjamin Snyder of
Saugerties and Abraham J. Hasbrouck of Kingston, both merchants who
owned sloops in the 1770s and the 1790s, respectively, discriminated between long-distance and local customers. Although we know little about
the competition that Snyder and Hasbrouck faced from other freighters,
the ties of fidelity between merchants and customers help delineate as
accurate a chart as we can hope to get of the degree to which farmers from
Ulster County were involved in extralocal trade (table 6).

Only one-third of the farmers doing business at the landing participated
directly in the world of long-distance trade. The shipping accounts at Hasbrouck's belonged without exception to farmers selected among the top
third of property owners in Kingston, Hurley, and Marbletown. Wealth
not only determined involvement with the world beyond the neighborhood; it also correlated closely with the worth of the goods that a farmer
sent to New York. The richer a client, the wider the variety and the higher
the value of the products he consigned to the merchant (table 7).

Agricultural households traded at the merchant's, storekeeper's, and
miller's, but only a minority among them sent produce to the metropolitan market. The transactions between long-distance traders and these
intermediaries complicate an evaluation of the extent and importance of
long-distance trade among the rural population. Hasbrouck's five most
important sloop patrons ran businesses of their own in Kingston and
Marbletown. Lemuel Winchel, for example, operated a gristmill and a
forge in Marbletown. He and four other local service providers contributed 1,195 (54.2 percent) of the 2,204 bushels of wheat shipped to New

TABLE 7. Long-Distance Trade and Wealth in 1798, Kingston Area (*N* = 57)

Value of goods sent to New York City (£)	Number of customers	Property per customer (£)	Wealth (percentile)
100–200	5	2,924	2
50–99.9	5	2,450	2
15–49.9	14	1,472	5
5–14.9	12	1,370	6
0–4.9	21	504	33

Sources: Abraham J. Hasbrouck Journals, 1797–1799, N-YHS; Tax Assessment for Ulster County, 1799, Garrett Lansing Papers, NYSL.

York. The accounts of John and Tobias Teller of Clinton, Dutchess County, shed some light on the scope of a country store that sent produce to the landing. These data allow us to reckon with the volume of business among Hasbrouck's mercantile partners, even though the Tellers delivered their goods to Poughkeepsie. Of their 131 customers in 1798, 28 (21.4 percent) earned credit with wheat, only 2 brought corn, and 3 transported rye. The average quantity of wheat exchanged was 9.9 bushels. This was a small amount, and incidental evidence confirms the prevalence of slim pickings. Alexander Coventry's father-in-law sent 8 bushels of wheat to New York in 1787, an event seemingly so extraordinary that the diarist considered it worth noting.[28] Local storekeepers and artisans (like millers and tanners, for example) skimmed off the surplus of a farm family's output in exchange for groceries and services to their fellow neighbors and then relied on shippers like Hasbrouck to dispatch these local goods in exchange for extralocal merchandise.

Wheat was the most important of the fourteen articles that Hasbrouck's sloops carried downstream. The twenty-seven farmers who dealt with it brought 35.6 bushels on average to the dock on the Hudson. But the average volume masked differences. The nineteen farmers in the top half of Hasbrouck's list sold 50.1 bushels, and the eight accounts in the bottom half forwarded 5.5 bushels. The former group earned 27£ 11s 1d ($68.89) from wheat sales, the latter 3£ 4d ($7.56). Remember that these farmers stood among the wealthiest third of the area's inhabitants; note that buckwheat, butter, corn, and rye played a minor part in their transactions; and recall that apples, nuts, and soap—products that Alexander Coventry assigned to an economy of expediency in which the region's poorer families were steeped[29]—appeared rather prominently in the barrels of the lower half of Hasbrouck's lineup. The contours of exchange in the long-distance circuit now acquire more definition: it was a confined province in the lives of most Hudson Valley farmers.

Robert R. Livingston calculated at the end of the eighteenth century that a hundred-acre farm produced a profit of £11 to £14 ($28 to $35). It was an informed computation. The average long-distance customer at Hasbrouck's Kingston store earned £14 2s 4d ($35.30), but that figure covered great disparities. The twenty-three farmers in the top half of the roster made £26 6s 5d (or $66.05) while the twenty-nine in the lower half secured 3£ 12s 10d (or $9.01) in 1798. The monies that Hasbrouck's customers took in represented returns of less than 2.5 percent on the real estate value of their farms. Even if we grant that they likely, but rarely, engaged in smaller transactions with the few other merchants at the landing, these terms emphasize the limited importance of trade among mid–Hudson Valley farmers. Such circumstances of parsimony explain why Alexander Coventry "lent William Coventry a dollar to pay taxes with."[30] They also reveal the economic foundations of the neighborhood's distinct social identity.

Personal Relations and the Marketplace

Visitors and villagers noted the increasingly busy trade that the landings on the Hudson maintained with their hinterlands. New England emigrants had founded Hudson "for the purpose of establishing a commercial settlement" in 1785. When Elkanah Watson traveled through the area in late 1788, he reckoned that the new city exhibited "a progress at that period almost without parallel in American history. It had emerged from a Dutch farm into a position of a commercial city, with a considerable population, warehouses, wharves and docks, rope-walks, shipping and the din of industry." William Strickland considered Hudson the "natural mart" for the backcountry, and John Lambert "conceived that a considerable trade was carried on between this town and the interior." Catskill Landing stirred up similar comments and sustained comparable growth. It consisted of 5 dwelling houses and 1 store in 1787. By 1792, 10 buildings lodged inhabitants and merchandise. Another ten years later, 180 houses and wharves composed the village. Two sloops had plied between Catskill and New York in 1787. At the turn of the century, twelve vessels commuted between the two locations, for good reason, indeed, because the quantities of wheat brought to the pier continued to increase as a consequence of, as the *New York Magazine* observed in 1797, "a considerable extent of back-country, which is rapidly settling by an industrious people."[31]

Contemporary evaluations of the volume and value of this long-distance trade are exceedingly rare, and prudence should temper boastful claims with more levelheaded assessments. According to the *Catskill Western Constellation* of 1801, the late 1780s and early 1790s saw the incremental burgeoning of wheat deliveries to Catskill Landing. Totaling 257 bushels in 1787, they amounted to 4,002 bushels in 1794. By the turn of the century, the newspaper's estimate put the volume somewhere between 35,000 and 45,000 bushels of wheat per year, whereas the Rev. Clark Brown reported the shipment of roughly 10,000 bushels. Computations based on demographic data from Catskill's hinterland and Hasbrouck's account yield an upper limit volume of 18,000 bushels for 1800.[32]

These were developments to dazzle anybody, and it is tempting to conflate this growth of long-distance trade volume with the amplification of the impersonal market and the solidification of market behavior among farmers. An observation by the curmudgeonly shrewd Rev. Timothy Dwight in 1804 invites a more careful analysis of the goings-on at Hudson River wharves. This Connecticut Yankee described how in Catskill "much of [the] business is done in the way of barter and is attended with all the evils incident to those modes of exchanging property, in which there is no settled standard of dealing." Dwight stumbled on, and then dismissed, the principle that regulated trade at the landing. Barter did not simply mean the substitution of one article of merchandise for another without the mediation of money. It first and foremost displayed the primacy of personal relations. In a world of insecurity, where risk reduction guided the behavior of farm families, the establishment of dependable and durable credit and debt connections lay in the interest of both merchant and farmer. Personal relations helped counteract the potential harm of natural events. The accretion of debts bound farmers to particular merchants but accorded their families the acquisition of extra-local goods in return of future deliveries of produce. The extension of credit to farmers assured merchants of agricultural supplies to sell at a profit in the metropolitan market but obliged them to ponder the probability of failures among farm families. Trust between merchant and farmer sealed this relationship. The marketplace turned out to be a site where people entered long-term relationships so as to introduce a measure of stability in a precarious and volatile environment.[33]

To ride a load to the landing and deliver it to the warehouse of a freighter did not culminate in the spontaneous, impersonal encounter of seller and buyer. Abraham J. Hasbrouck, the shipper of cargo and dry goods dealer in Kingston, agreed to deal with Jesse W. Baker only after having received a recommendation from one of his familiar patrons. A farmer's reputation with his neighbors constituted the ante of commercial relations with merchants on the landings. Credibility preceded credit, but once two men engaged in such an association it lasted for many years. Unsettled and running accounts, and at times even loans in cash from the merchant to the farmer, fortified these ties.[34] The link was built to last: it assured that the merchant would receive produce on a regular basis and the farmer would obtain the necessaries of life unavailable in the neighborhood. The privileged bond not only furthered reliability in a commercial setting, but it also helped diminish the farmer's prejudice against the conniving merchant that so delineated the margins of the rural community.

The personal—or *pratik*—relationships that characterized transactions at the market sites in the mid–Hudson Valley shielded farmers and merchants from the "invisible hand" and the uncertainties of supply and demand as they ruled the New York City market. In Kingston, Hasbrouck gave two kinds of credit to his customers, and while this custom seemed to have puzzled Reverend Dwight in Catskill his contemporary Crèvecoeur took the existence of parallel circuits in stride. The Kingston merchant took cherry boards "at the New York price" from Solomon De Graff. He noted that Jacob Hunt's "barrel poles we have not counted; we are to allow him 8s p[r] Hundred if they sell for more than 10s p[r] Hundred in New York. If not, then we are to allow him 7s p[r] Hundred." Price differentials marked nuts and butter, which earned 1s 10d per pound when sent to New York and 1s 6d when used as truck in local exchange.[35] The shipper acted as the conduit of Hudson Valley farmers to the wider world, but the local price did not simply correspond to the New York equivalent, from which he subtracted transport costs. Over long periods of time, prices of locally produced goods in the neighborhood trading center remained constant and unresponsive to metropolitan fluctuations. Pressure from the neighborhood—or what we might call its economic culture—kept long-distance traders inserted in networks that gauged exchange values on the basis of the effort it took to produce a good rather than on its reaction to New York City market forces. The system guaranteed farmers a secure level of income for their goods and the prospect of garnering additional monies in New York while merchants could count on recurring entrustment of farm produce. Indeed, this mutual interest generated trust which, in turn, sustained long-distance commerce within the conventions of personal relationships.

The sense of security found another support outside the link between shipper and husbandman in the towns' ordinances on the quality of flour and the price of bread. Since urban markets immediately felt the effects of agricultural shortages, town authorities in Catskill and Hudson followed an impulse toward sociopolitical regulation and nominated inspectors to enforce the assize on bread. Governmental regulation of the marketplace through licenses and control of merchandise responded to popular concerns about supplies. It also helped to create a climate that reinforced notions of social responsibility and fair price. To transgress these rules was to risk the opprobrium of the neighborhood and the action of the law. James Sackett, a witness at a trial that opposed two inhabitants of Coxsackie in 1798, testified that "Mr. Pomroy in Genl is called a Fair dealer." In Hudson, Ephraim Whittaker complained of Peter Ten Broeck's breaking of the mutual obligations of friendship, even though their dispute had originated with an unpaid cobbler's bill in 1787.[36] Exchange did not amount to an individual act but took place in enduring partnerships whose particular honor codes bore a great deal of likeness to those between friends. Fair business principles sanctioned some profit but prohibited caveat emptor practices. They respected an implicit notion of a "just price."

Merchants had, of course, an interest in knowing the evolution of New York City prices, and in the long run the metropolis's higher quotations would attract farmers and determine local trade, too. But in the 1790s there was a distinctness to the local marketplace that made New York figures of commerce irrelevant to rural people. In March 1793, the *Catskill Packet* announced a regular column of produce prices dispatched by Manhattan wholesalers. "To gratify many of our country customers, who have expressed a wish to know the price current in New York for some articles of their produce, we have selected those of the most important from a New York paper of the 9th inst.," the initial statement read. Then it toned down the expectations for a new departure because "the prices of produce, however, are so fluctuating, that they may have suffered considerable variation since that date; we cannot therefore pretend to vouch for their accuracy." The column faded from the newspaper. The reason of its eclipse pertained as much to the editor's inability to secure up to date intelligence than to the indifference with which it was met in the countryside. Only once in the more than thirty years during which he kept a diary did William Coventry take note of developments in New York City. When prices were high in spring 1801, he wrote that "wheat sold in New York at 19s 6d pr bushel." Then, in another unique gesture, he crossed the sentence out, as if this piece of information had no pertinence to his family's existence.[37]

The struggle to eke out the family's subsistence explains the farmers' aloofness from the opportunities of the long-distance trade. Winifred Rothenberg argued that Massachusetts farmers responded to the incentives of urban demand and began to specialize their production and increase the number of their trips to sell goods in market towns in the middle of the eighteenth century.[38] The Hudson Valley suggests another experience, one in which farm families lived by a social rather than an economic imperative. In response to an insecure environment and resources whose exploitation proved to be a formidable task, circumspection and diversification mapped out the behavior of rural people. Relationships, not the abstract forces of the free market, channeled the allocation of labor and the flow of goods first in, then beyond, the neighborhood. This is not to propose a Malthusian model of a contradiction between population and carrying capacity to explain the conduct of farm families in the mid–Hudson Valley. Population limited production rather than the other way around. The goal of farm families did not consist in making large profits. It was to protect themselves from the vagaries of an unpredictable and unmasterable world.

The strategy encouraged flexibility. In the extremely cold winter of 1791 William Coventry spent his days alternately chopping wood and conveying it to Hudson. Many other farmers in the area, including Coventry's neighbor Ghoes, engaged in similar efforts. They found encouragement in a note published in the *Catskill Packet* of 1793 that illustrated some of the hardships of life in the Hudson Valley. "The printers wish, as their woodpile is already reduced to *freezing point,* and will shortly be down to 0, if not replenished, that such of their customers as have promised wood for papers, may not neglect to improve the present good sleighing in fulfilment of their engagement."[39] Yet even lumbering was an activity mediated by the seasons and second to the production of family supplies. The demand for wood helped farmers earn supplementary revenues in winter. It did so without pushing them into an exclusive dependence on the income that resulted from such sales, just as the credits of women's domestic textile production constituted another source from which to sponsor the family's well-being rather than to accommodate an individual's pursuit of gain. Theirs was an understanding of the marketplace as a concrete, physical setting in which people knew each other. The elusive market of supply and demand neither governed their outlook nor directed their economic behavior.

ONLY A MINORITY of Hudson Valley farmers directly engaged in long-distance trade at the turn of the nineteenth century. This did not mean that two-thirds of the farm families abstained from trading at the storekeeper's. On the contrary, they, too, obtained goods produced elsewhere, and women's role in assuring family supplies by exchanging produce of their own at the local retailer's illustrated the importance the rural population attached to extraregional commodities like molasses, tea, or rum. But long-distance commerce conformed to rules that differed from the conventions of neighborhood swapping. Price making and price levels hinted at the difference and the coexistence of nonmarket and market rationality in the rural economy. Among neighbors, labor was the standard in the establishment of exchange equivalence. When it came to exporting goods, however, the freight forwarder and the vicinity's wealthier farmers combined to neutralize the volatility of the New York City market in establishing relationships that lasted for years, sometimes decades. As a consequence, prices fluctuated much less in the Hudson Valley than in the metropolitan market. It was credit that tied farm families to merchants, who thus increased the likelihood of siphoning agricultural products out of the neighborhood into New York City and beyond. Yet credit was a personal arrangement before it was an economic deal. While it sustained and perpetuated commerce, it depended on the neighborhood's value system, for its attribution hinged on a farmer's standing and reputation in local society. Once established, the balance in the relationship tipped toward the debtor, whose very obligation to the creditor provided the leverage to maintain access to merchandise from beyond the Hudson Valley.

The relational strategy operated in a field of force that offered room for innovation. The circumstances of life in the countryside explain why farmers were eager to improve their condition. We can locate this desire and the willingness to introduce changes in the transformation of agricultural practices. As long as examples taught innovative practices, farmers were willing to appropriate methods that increased yields. Alexander Coventry conversed with a husbandman in Ancram in April 1790 about the cultivation of corn, which, according to Crèvecoeur, was the grain attended "with the greatest labour . . . but the most subject to accidents from seasons, insects, birds and animals." Coventry's interlocutor raised "a great deal of corn and finds ashes exceed all other manures for the corn," the physician noted with curiosity. "He puts a single handful around each hill when the corn is about three inches high . . . and harrows the first time." Six weeks later Coventry distributed ashes in his cornfield. Within ten years, his cousin William Coventry had adopted the same procedures. Another case concerned the discovery of a new kind of grain, which John Whitlock related to Coventry. It "grows larger, and has whiter flour: They call it 'White Wheat.' He says a man found a set of wheat in his field, which was larger than the other wheat, he sowed it by itself, and sowed it by itself, and from it—the rest is propagated."[40] These were, quite literally, seeds of change. Such ameliorations helped farm families improve their standard of living and made the countryside more attractive to people who intended to exploit its resources. It was this combination that induced the transformation of the rural Hudson Valley. However, improvements in soil or labor productivity often occurred without market incentives, and their multiplication did not ineluctably lead to the rise of a market society. Such a development required alterations in the mental, institutional, and infrastructural makeup of rural society.

THREE

Natural Resources and Economic Development

The Hudson Valley scenery changed considerably in the first half of the nineteenth century. Forests receded in the face of economic appetites that claimed land, wood, and waterpower. Metropolitan demand for food-stuffs, fodder, apparel, and building materials promoted the expansion of agricultural and industrial activities in the counties of Greene and Columbia. This process of economic prospection and development happened elsewhere, too. During the ensuing constitution of a wider trading zone, the Hudson Valley area began to specialize in the production of goods for which it possessed natural advantages. Long-distance trade grew with the exploitation of local resources. The "meagre utilitarianism" that seemed to animate his contemporaries as they exploited natural sources of wealth and built a more complex web of interregional dependencies deeply disturbed the painter Thomas Cole (1801–48) who had moved to the village of Catskill in the mid-1830s. "The ravages of the axe" became an underlying motive of Cole's artistic project, and it is by no means accidental that he should have found his subject matter in the vanishing natural landscape of the Hudson River valley.[1]

The emergence of nature as an aesthetic category in American art around 1820 coincided with that moment in time when human diligence transformed it from an encompassing and mysterious world of insecurity into a repository of factors of production. Of course, wildly beautiful nature could offer solace from civilization and to Cole it represented "a sovereign remedy" to city life. The artist's vision perhaps idealized a pristine state of nature, but in his valorization of the sublime he meant to maintain the integrity of people as social beings. In a lecture to the Catskill Lyceum, Cole enjoined his audience to leave behind "the low pursuit of avarice" and behold the cultivated scenery so "important to man in his social capacity."[2] That distinctive quality diminished with the extension of market relations, the replacement of cooperation with competition, the separation of products from producers, and the increasing importance of prices that originated beyond the confines of the neighborhood in the volatile play of supply and demand. Cole's was a pessimistic view of the evolution of American society. While we hear echoes of his unease among the utterances of the Hudson Valley's population, we also encounter entrepreneurs and farmers who eagerly contributed, as one of them put it in 1832, "to develop the resources" of the area.[3] With this register of voices in mind, the following pages explore the large processes to which the artists of the Hudson River School alluded. The aim is to illuminate the conditions that made the creation of their works possible. But whereas Cole's canvasses were both composite and detailed (they realistically represented imagined landscapes), our panoramic view takes its clue from their statement about the concrete traces and transforming effects that women and men inscribed on the mid–Hudson Valley landscape and how, in turn, these actions reshaped their conceptions of space and time.

Economic developments in the rural Hudson Valley hinged on the exploitation of natural resources. Soil-depleting methods forced farm families to modify their agricultural practices in the face of competition arising from newly settled lands to the west. At the crossroads of ecological and economic pressures, farm families capitalized on topographical diversity. They began to emphasize grass cultures and livestock rather than field crops to carve out a niche in an increasingly commercial and competitive world. Waterpower and abundant hemlock formed other comparative advantages and attracted textile entrepreneurs and tanners to the area after the embargo of 1807 had sharpened their awareness of growing domestic demand. Merchants acted as intermediaries between metropolitan demand and rural society. They promoted the construction of roadways to facilitate the hauling of produce and merchandise. Roads that one observer characterized in 1824 as "rather too numerous to be good" opened up the countryside.[4] Agricultural specialization, industrial beginnings, and improved transportation combined to accelerate the rhythms of life in the Hudson Valley. Its population increased production, and often productivity, and in the process discovered that time was a resource, too.

Keener attention to schedules formed but part of a social project whose aim it was to systematize human behavior in order to improve productivity or, as Cole felt, to toil "in order to produce more toil." In 1816, the *Hudson Bee* ran an advertisement that captured the tenor of these efforts under the headline "Book-keeping," a notion that appeared for the first time in a public statement in the mid–Hudson Valley. It read, "James Bennett, Accountant, most respectfully announces to those gentlemen of Hudson, who may wish to acquire a complete knowledge of Book-keeping by double-entry, that he intends to deliver a course of [twenty] Lectures on that art." The announcement exposed the trend toward a formalization of business methods and commercial practices.[5] And, though its success was still limited among farmers in the 1850s, even they talked about conforming their ways to a rational design.

The rise of a society in which the pursuit of profit rather than the mere satisfaction of material needs (to follow Max Weber's distinction) defined economic behavior required a transformation of habits in the countryside. Lawyers and merchants advanced an ideology of laissez-faire, which they carried into the local marketplace where face-to-face relationships still predominated at the beginning of the nineteenth century. Participation in governments helped them use the state's institutional power to promote laws that aimed at reorganizing the business sphere and encouraging economic growth by chartering private, profit-oriented corporations. Local councils adopted ordinances to enforce liberal tenets of economic theory, to enhance the public nature of market transactions at the expense of traditional personal relations, and to link prices to the metropolitan market. Political interventions in favor of deregulated internal commerce show that there was nothing natural about the rise of a market society. Unease about the displacement of traditional exchange practices demonstrates that there was nothing predetermined about the outcome of, to use George Taylor's expression, "the great turnabout" of 1820 in the history of the Hudson Valley.[6]

The Rise of the Market Principle

In America, Alexis de Tocqueville found in the 1830s that "an immense field for competition is thrown open to all." Restless, mobile people were vying for material advantages. Laissez-faire economics provided the framework for this frenzied behavior, and if Tocqueville's own historical studies taught him about the political origins of the free market in France he considered the American experience to be a natural consequence of abundance and social equality. But the market principle, like any social project, had a history. Political authorities played a crucial role in the promotion of a free market society. One of the government's most important state-making interventions in the economic sphere stemmed from the belief that economic growth and welfare were best achieved when state laws framed an order from which moral concerns were largely absent. The process toward the liberty to dispose freely of one's property encompassed the departure from a substantive theory of contracts that held that community customs and habitual values of goods and services validated agreements. In its place there emerged a doctrine that rested entirely, in the words of legal historian Morton Horwitz, on "the convergence of the wills of the contracting parties."[7] The law, then, sanctioned the primacy of supply and demand at the expense of the notion of a good's just, intrinsic price. Face-to-face relationships yielded to business dealings between anonymous sellers and buyers. In the place of moral obligations, the maxim caveat emptor began to hold sway.

State intervention and the rising tenets of laissez-faire, however awkward their coexistence appeared in the early nineteenth century, did not exclude one another. Yet on the local level social practices that made up networks of privileged association between merchants, farmers, and consumers acted as obstacles to the development of a free market. Ideas of economic liberalism needed assertion in public discourse and action. The *Hudson Balance* declared in 1803 that "every man in a free country, whether he be gentle or simple, has an undoubted right to offer his wares at public market; and even though they should appear unfashionable and bungling, if they had been wrought according to his best skill, it would be cruelly hard to hiss him out of the market-place." The achievement of the free flow of goods in an open rather than a private space not only invited the abolition of governmental licensing but it entailed the removal of special relationships. The legal curtailment of the personalized—or pratik—system that undergirded much of the exchange in the city of Hudson began in 1810. A city ordinance regulating the public market stipulated that "the first person applying for meat publicly exposed in the market shall be first attended to and served, any pretence of prior engagement or sale notwithstanding." It was the law's aim to do away with the favored client status that liberal theory construed as collusion. Its prescription for anonymous, transient relations in the market required inspectors to enforce behavior that did not come naturally to the participants in the marketplace. Success seemed tenuous at first, for six years later another ordinance increased the penalties for infractions and expanded the statute's purview to include vegetable vendors, too.[8]

Legislative activism by local authorities, whom mercantile interests increasingly dominated in Hudson and Catskill as the reconstruction of the mid–Hudson Valley progressed, also advanced the geographic integration of the Hudson Valley into a single market space during the second decade of the nineteenth century. Of course, New York City had held an important place in the merchants' mental map ever since the Hudson Valley was settled. The occasional publication of metropolitan prices in Hudson Valley newspapers during the first half of the nineteenth century notwithstanding, it was only in 1849 that the editor of the *Catskill Messenger* confidently stated that "the prices of produce in this vicinity will be guided altogether by the prices of produce in the City."[9] In the meantime, the promulgation of new laws attempted the alignment of Hudson Valley towns with New York City, an endeavor of cultural and economic importance. "By virtue of an Ordinance of the Trustees of the village of Catskill," a proclamation read in 1819, "the assize of Bread is directed to correspond with that of the city of New York." In the metropolis, however, supply and demand acted as the arbiter of grain and flour prices. The assize functioned as a cap on bakers' profits rather than a guarantor of affordable breadstuffs, and by December 1821 a new constellation of economic assumptions steeped in Adam Smith's theory of the free market as the most efficient purveyor of goods and services led to the abolition of regulations altogether.[10] That measure and its repercussions marked a fundamental step in the formal inauguration of the free market era in the Hudson Valley. And, indeed, the parallel fluctuations of produce prices at mid–Hudson Valley locations and in New York confirm that the valley region was on its way to forming a single market one year before the Erie Canal opened (fig. 3).

The introduction of liberal precepts into the countryside did not advance in smooth progression. When a committee on petitions in the state legislature recommended that Thomas Frothingham be granted the right to "Lands covered with water for the purpose of Erecting a Wharf" on the Hudson at the end of the eighteenth century, it made sure to respond to a petition signed by inhabitants of Claverack. While authorizing individual enterprise, it supported the maintenance of "common uses . . . for General Advantage and convenience" in order to secure their customary rights to fishing grounds "without Molestation and Controversy."[11] Certain re-

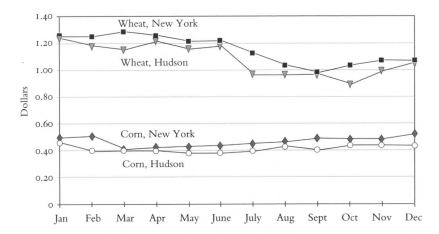

FIG. 3. Prices of produce in New York and the Hudson Valley, 1824 (in dollars per bushel). (Data from Henry Dubois Account Book, NYSL; John and Tobias Teller Ledger, NYSHA; Abraham J. Hasbrouck Journal, N-YHS; John Masten Account Book, N-YHS; *New York American,* Jan. 1824; *New York Spectator,* Feb.–Dec. 1824.)

sources, water for one, still passed as common, public goods on which society could lay claims that obliged the government to exert its police function in order to guarantee access to their utilization.

Concerns about how to strike a balance between the common good and the pursuit of individual gain based on the unimpeded, free use of private property accompanied the rise of the market principle. In a unique reflection about market development in 1818, the *Catskill Recorder* expressed its worries about the possible consequences of the new economic configuration in which liberty, rather than leading society to well-ordered prosperity, could plunge it into chaos: "The spirit of enterprise has produced an excessive competition among Merchants, which, if not checked, will ultimately terminate in the serious embarrassment, if not ruin of many—witness the sacrifices made last winter in the purchases of grain, 17, 18 s[hillings], and sometimes as much as a man's conscience would permit him to ask, was paid per bushel of wheat, and that at a time when the quantity in this country was well known to be greater than it had been for many years past." Profiteering was morally reprehensible and socially corrosive, the article continued. The only way to avoid permanent harm in the Catskill market was that "the Merchant or purchaser always inform the *seller* what his commodity is fairly worth in New York. If he wishes to sell, purchase it so as to make a reasonable saving, and always observe uniformity in the offer, and price, according to the existing state of the market."[12] It was a curious piece of advice to people who made a living from long-distance trade and were likely to appreciate the risks of their business. In principle, market forces seemed to regulate the divergent utilities of sellers and buyers harmoniously, but when it came to describing desirable business practices, notions of "fair worth" and "actual value" pervaded the article in the *Recorder*. And yet if the "ground" of the market, a physical designation that the author used to capture the place of economic transactions, remained a site where morality—"a man's conscience"—needed to restrain the impulses let loose by the increasing prevalence of the market principle, the author did not call for a reinvigoration of the state's role in the marketplace. The market principle threatened to bring about disorder and hasten reversals of fortunes among the agents of commercial exchange and in the communities they served. However, regulatory intervention by local or state authorities did not appear to the author as a valid alternative to moral exhortation.

Reflections on the community's health and integrity in the face of rising competition among its members remained a regular feature and a constant measure of the advance of free market forces in the first half of the nineteenth century. "There is no trait in the character of the inhabitants of a country town much less forbidding than a disinclination to sustain their own mechanics, artists or artizans, tradesmen, &c.," the *Coxsackie Standard* stated in 1838, just to fume that "this, we regret to say, is a prominent trait in the character of a considerable portion of the citizens of this place." Within a dozen years, another report pertained to residents who "patronize foreign or city labor, if it be a tithe the cheaper. Such men are of no benefit to a community; they are the reverse—a drudge." In an echo of the optimistic adoption of the free enterprise creed at the beginning of the century, the *Catskill Messenger* editorialized in 1849 "that every man has a perfect right to engage in whatever business he may fancy. . . , but we doubt the utility of the system of 'cutting in' upon each other's trade, business, or profession." The entitlement to a competence, rather than the reliance on competition in the market, made a lot of sense. "A poor man, an earnest laborer, by the toil of whose hands comes the support of his family, sees before him many obstacles in the path of life. Imagine that man's feelings when he sees a prosperous neighbor ready to snatch the means of existence from him. . . . Is it right and just to deprive a man of his only means of subsistence?" The question was rhetorical, but the author had yet another point to drive home in the face of "the present generation of gain-lovers." The unrestrained pursuit of profit destroyed the local community.

> Were it properly considered that each and every member of a community is, more or less, dependent upon the others, there would be no interference in their respective callings; but as long as it is thought the more they injure their neighbors, the more benefit it is to themselves, so long will they continue to walk in this path of folly. Even in this village there is much talk in relation to this matter; there is much of anger generated continually; and in a small place like this, where the business of many men is limited to the immediate vicinity, the result must be injurious not only to the aggressed, but equally to the aggressor.

The moral vision conjured up a state of anomic disarray, but as an injunction it did not call for any other remedy but self-restraint. By 1850, governmental powers did not appear as valid instruments with which to regulate the market.[13]

Legislative actions endeavored to impose the free play of supply and demand. If the enforcement of the market principle aimed at the transformation of exchange practices in the marketplace, manorial relations, with their recognition of differential claims to property, created altogether different obstacles to the mobility of goods. Unlike sharecropping contracts, which required the landowner to supply all capital inputs in exchange for labor, manorial leases bound landlord and tenant together as proprietor and possessor of the same piece of land. Manorial conditions not only compelled the lessee to raise money to acquire a farm and to invest in stock and implements. They empowered the landlord to exert extraeconomic pressure to make the tenant comply with lease terms that assured him the right to first purchase of the farm's annual production and the collection of levies at the farm's sale. "All the catalog of incidents, fines, tolls, quit-rents, reservations, proprietorships of mills, &c. &c. common to old European tenures," as the English visitor Francis Hall labeled manorial conditions in 1818, remained in place until 1846, when New York's new Constitution eliminated "feudal incidents" in the state. The highest state officials subscribed to the view, now enshrined in a constitutional precept, that "leasehold estates are peculiarly unfavorable to the development of the country and the progress of the people in improvement and enterprise." The political decision formally lifted the stain of restraint from the Hudson Valley real estate market. Its adoption owed much to tenant activism, but it also marked the halcyon days of the market principle. Now manorial land, too, could change hands as an unencumbered commercial commodity.[14]

Roads and Hinterland Development

New York City's population grew from 60,000 inhabitants in 1800 to 202,000 in 1830 and 813,000 in 1860 and created an extensive demand for foodstuffs and natural resources. Merchants tapped into the potential wealth of the countryside to satisfy urban wants. Horatio Gates Spafford sensed the possibilities of development in 1813 when he predicted Catskill's or Athens' "rapid growth as the market-town for an extensive hinterland." Businessmen at the landings recognized the countryside's value as a repository of agricultural produce. Economics of scale induced them to promote the construction of turnpikes. Between 1799 and 1806, five toll roads sprouted from Hudson, two linked Coxsackie with its catchment area, and one highway ran between Catskill and Freehold.[15] The projectors of these roads hoped that they would not only lower transportation costs but "increase the products of agriculture." In this respect, they considered farmers handicapped in their productive efforts by the absence of an adequate, efficient transportation network rather than steeped in subsistence agriculture because of an antidevelopmental, anticapitalist mentality. Polish traveler Julian Niemcewicz discerned both the idea behind, and the physical effect of, this project when he discovered with some astonishment that "instead of following the mail routes, as they so obviously do in Europe, they [roads] cut right into the interior of the provinces, toward the lands whence come the produce and the principal commodities."[16]

The extension of roads looked like the forward march of civilization to Benjamin DeWitt. Searching for a metaphor to describe the emerging transportation system, he anticipated some of the insights, if not the vocabulary, of central place theory in 1807. A hierarchy of locations that fulfilled distributive functions in the service sector reminded DeWitt of the body's circulation of the blood (map 2). He urged his readers to "consider the city of New York as the centre of commerce, or the heart of the state, Hudson's river as the main artery, the turnpike roads leading from it as so many great branches extending to the extremities, from which diverge the innumerable small ramifications or common roads into the whole body and substance; these again send off capillary branches, or private roads, to

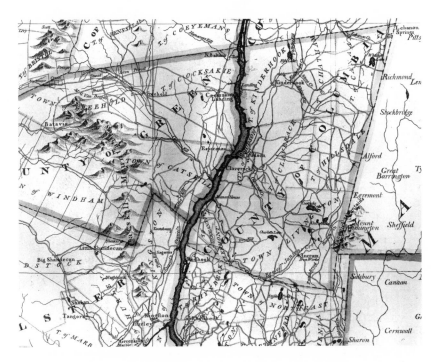

MAP 2. Roadways and turnpikes in Columbia and Greene Counties, circa 1800. (Detail from Simeon De Witt, *A Map of the State of New York* [Albany, 1804]. Courtesy of the Division of Rare and Manuscript Collections, Carl A. Kroch Library, Cornell University.)

all the individual farms, which may be considered as the secretory organs, generating the produce and wealth of the state." The turnpikes connected production sites to the metropolitan market. They helped feed extraregional demand and in turn facilitated the flow of goods into the mid–Hudson Valley.[17]

The cost of this transportation system was high. Because the state of New York could not raise the monies to finance it, private companies mobilized $195,000 to build 150 miles of roads in Greene and Columbia Counties. A share in these ventures sold for $20 to $50, a price that limited the number of investors. When a proposal circulated in Columbia County to enlarge the Union Turnpike between Hudson and Chatham to thirty feet, the editors of the *Hudson Bee* surmised that "gentlemen living on the route will undoubtedly be induced to exert themselves, as they have no convenient way of getting to market." Mercantile and professional involvement in the capitalization of commercial infrastructure was crucial. Four of the five warehouse owners at Kinderhook Landing bought stock in the Chatham Turnpike. Thomas Jenkins, a merchant in Hudson, served on three turnpike committees. Merchants and shippers like the Reed brothers, Dorrance Kirtland, Tallmadge Fairchild, and Archibald McVickar from Coxsackie Landing financed the Coxsackie Turnpike in 1805. Merchant George Crawford of Hudson had a stake in the Farmer's Turnpike, and sloop captain Jehoakim Bergh of Rhinebeck acquired $350 worth of shares in a turnpike with a terminus in his home port. Away from the river, country storekeepers like Aaron Kellogg and Abraham Holdridge invested in these roads. But so did lawyers like Elisha Williams, Francis Silvester, and Peter Van Schaack, all of whom entertained a wide network of friends and business partners beyond their neighborhoods.[18]

While turnpikes contributed to the opening of the countryside and helped induce the likely appreciation of land values, their maintenance was expensive. A few toll roads proved lucrative and long-lived. The Columbia Turnpike, connecting the city of Hudson to Claverack and Hillsdale, opened in 1802 and yielded an average yearly dividend of 8 percent between 1811 and 1845. In general, however, investors with no direct interest in transportation who had expected a return on their capital saw many corporations abandon the business and convert their private highways into public freeways by the 1820s. As early as 1811, Mary Livingston, a scion of the powerful landed aristocracy in Columbia County, evaluated "218 Turnpike shares worth nominally $5450 Being $25 each—worth in reality $1090." The Highland Turnpike, which ran from New York to Troy, never paid any dividends. Its president expressed his discontent to William Wilson of Clermont as he searched for ways to make a profit: "The toll collected at the gate on the Columbia section is so small as to induce a belief that something is wrong about it, which ought to be corrected. Can it be that the present situation of the gate is the most eligible one, or that the gate keeper is dishonest, or that the stages pass over the gate?"[19] Whatever other reasons kept traffic low, slow rural development put a low ceiling on the revenues of mid–Hudson Valley toll roads.

The development of the hinterland was an ongoing project, and the construction of ever more roads seemed necessary to its success. Business leaders built thoroughfares to places like the Catskill Mountains, which were difficult to reach and where the exploitation of resources had promoted the tanning industry and, somewhat incidentally, agriculture. "Who can doubt," the *Catskill Recorder* asked in 1827, "that the completion of the road by the Catskill and Mountain Turnpike Company . . . intending to intersect the Clove turnpike at the foot of the mountains, would secure to ourselves the valuable trade and freight of a large extent of country, fast increasing in population and wealth, while now on account of the almost impassable state of our roads to that section of our country, it is bending its course to various landings below us, and thereby enable us under favorable auspices to reap greater benefits from our situation." The benefits appeared uncontestable to the president of the New York State Agricultural Society, whose address extolled the virtues of plank roads in 1849. The farmer's productions, he declared, "which are bulky, have to be moved, before they are placed at the disposal of the merchant, an average of twelve miles. . . . Upon roads as they now are, 1200 lbs is a good load; upon plank roads, three or four times that weight can be safely carried: making a saving of twenty-five per cent in the cost of taking a crop to market, besides a saving in time, and wear and tear of wagon, teams and harness, etc."[20] The purpose of roads remained the opening of the countryside, but the argument in their favor had taken on new elements: it alluded to increased agricultural productivity and the importance of husbanding time.

Agricultural Adaptations

In 1833, the *Albany Argus* published an article entitled "Hints to Farmers." Its author promoted the selection of crops and stock "which promise the best reward" and emphasized, as if to make the point unmistakable, "that the farmer should apply his labor to such objects as will ensure him the best profit." Production and exchange went hand in hand, and so the summary read that "the farmer who undertakes to raise all kinds of crops upon one kind of soil misapplies his labor. He had better confine himself to those which make the best return — sell the surplus, and buy with a part of the proceeds that for which his neighbor's soil is better adapted than his own." In however many words the *Argus* couched its admonition, it urged farmers to abandon mixed for specialized agriculture. It asked rural people to place their faith in the distant market and leave behind their traditional motives, which were centered around the preservation of the household and the continuity of the family. That strategy had led to the exhaustion of the soil in the Hudson Valley, where the development of western New York was aggravating pressures on farmers. "Genesee flour" not only competed in the New York City market with North-River produce but stores in Catskill began offering it for sale shortly after the opening of the Erie Canal.[21]

These circumstances compelled Hudson Valley farmers to explore the comparative advantages of their region. They introduced clover and spread the use of timothy grass. Clover, a green crop with nitrogen-fixing properties, altered the traditional long-fallow rotation, and with timothy it provided a boost to terrain that had been exhausted by, or was ill-adapted to, grain cultivation. Jesse Buel observed in 1839 that "forty years ago [clover] culture may be said to have commenced in the United States; but its progress was slow till within the last few years." Indeed, evidence of fertility-maintaining agriculture appeared in the second decade of the nineteenth century. Storekeepers like G. W. Merrick in Durham began to sell clover seeds. By the mid-1820s, Abraham J. Hasbrouck was selling them to a majority of his customers while some purchased timothy. Within a few years, John Fowler commented on the cultivation of hay. Another traveler, Patrick Shirreff, observed "sloops, carrying well-formed hay and straw stacks, glide towards New York." Land use reflected the change. While the area devoted to grain cultivation increased by less than 1 percent in Greene County and decreased by 4 percent in Columbia County between 1845 to 1855, hay production grew by more than 24 percent in Greene and almost 16 percent in Columbia between 1840 and 1855. By 1860, French's *Gazetteer* noted that "the whole region [Greene County] is best adapted to grazing; and the principal exports are butter, cheese and pressed hay." The entry for Columbia simply read that "an immense quantity of hay, annually sent to the New York market, forms the principal export of the county." [22]

New grasses supported more animals. The *Rural Repository* reveled in its description of Hillsdale, where "a domesticated flock now quietly graze o'er fields of blossoming clover" in 1842. As a consequence the use of manure increased. *The Cultivator* placed the turning point in the 1820s when it sketched the change from wheat to cattle and sheep raising that farmers had combined with "coarse grains." Eyewitness accounts help refine the timing of agricultural adaptation. John P. Beekman, a lifelong resident of Kinderhook, recalled in 1843 that "forty years ago, farming in the river counties was of the worst possible description. The virgin fertility of the soil had been exhausted by frequent croppings." Spafford's *Gazetteer* commented on soil exhaustion in Kinderhook in 1813. By 1823, Isaac Holmes mentioned that farmers applied manure to their land, though he considered the quantities too small. Another ten years later, James Stuart mentioned the richness of Kinderhook and noted that the application of manure had allowed the cultivation of a tract of pine woods formerly believed to be sterile. The progress of fertilizer usage caused Freeman Hunt to write in 1837 that "the old town of Kinderhook, for richness of soil, fertility, and adaptation to every branch of agriculture, is not surpassed by any land in the state." Daniel Curtiss of Canaan asserted in 1841 that "the profits arising from stock, as far as a farm will sustain it properly, are obtained with less labor and expense than from grain. By this I mean to be understood to say that I think it far better to feed and mow our clover fields, and have the returns from our flocks and yards than to plough under the clover and enrich them." And, though it still scolded farmers for underestimating the value of manure in 1844, the *Kinderhook Sentinel* also rejoiced, "the more sheep, the more wheat," and hence the higher the profits for farmers.[23]

While areas near the river specialized in large cattle and hay, the hill region expanded pastures to support smaller, less demanding stock. The introduction of the strong breed of Merino sheep, whose wool was finer, more easily processed, and thus more marketable, sustained that transformation after 1810. This combination of circumstances—economic pressures, new and permanent grasses, and a novel breed—drew the highlands into the circumference of the long-distance market. As one husbandman recollected, "every farmer had a certain number of what are usually called *common sheep,* sufficient to furnish him with wool for domestic uses. It was not in his interest to have more, for as manufactures had not arisen, and it would not bear exportation, wool was an article scarcely marketable in large quantities." In 1820, the New York State Board of Agriculture speculated that "wool will be grown largely in counties too distant from markets for grain or meat, and there the pastures ought to be permanent." By the mid-1820s, sheep had become Columbia County's most valuable stock according to Spafford's *Gazetteer,* and Erastus Pratt of Austerlitz advised his "Dear Cousin" to populate his farm "with fine wool sheep, & you soon will be free of debt & in the way of making money as fast as reasonable." At the height of the sheep boom between 1821 and 1835 the ratio of sheep to cattle increased from two to five sheep per cow.[24] This development constituted a critical moment in the extension of capitalist relations to hill areas because farmers were not merely making up, or simply substituting a new product, for a small market crop lost to lower prices. Sheep raising brought them into the extralocal market to a significantly greater extent than they had been before, so much so that the Pameacha Manufacturing Company of Middletown, Connecticut, advertised in Hudson Valley newspapers that it would pay the highest price for wool in cash.[25]

Permanent grasslands induced a rearrangement of the environment. William Cobbett found Americans to be rather clumsy and awkward farmers compared to English peasants, but he easily discovered their talents. "An *ax* is their tool," he observed in 1819, "and with that tool, at *cutting down* trees or *cutting them up,* they will do *ten times* as much in a day as any other man that I ever saw. Set one of these men upon a wood of timber trees, and his slaughter will astonish you." The receding forests in the Hudson Valley corroborated Cobbett's observation. Where Hessian soldiers had savored the sylvan beauty and bounty during the Revolutionary War, where Julian Niemcewicz beheld lush woods that rose from the banks of the Hudson to the mountains in the 1790s, where an article entitled "Notes on the Natural History of Kinderhook" described attractive falls in a nearby creek that could, however, "only be seen by those who are willing to endure the fatigue of scrambling through thick woods" in 1802, the following generation saw, like Scottish traveler James Stuart, tracts of pine woods transformed into arable fields. In the mid-1820s, a German duke found the district between the Taconic Mountains and the Hudson "extremely charming," with "rather well cultivated fields and rich pastures." On the other bank of the river, the *Greene County Republican* brought up the scarcity of lumber in the Catskill market. Alexander Coventry, traveling through Durham in 1822, stumbled on the cause of that situation. He noticed the expansion of fields and noted that "wood is quite scarce, although this was all forest 30 years ago." And by 1850 architect Andrew Jackson Downing attributed the high cost of construction in the Hudson Valley to the shortage of suitable timber.[26] No wonder Thomas Cole discovered the Catskills and his vocation as a landscape painter during these years of change.

The opening of the landscape was one of the consequences of the expansion of pastures and meadows. They covered more than 60 percent of the improvable surface in certain areas of the mid–Hudson Valley region in 1855. Their expansion also gave rise to novel divisions in the rural scene. Cattle and sheep, which used to live in barnyards or roam and forage in the woods, now found themselves enclosed within solid stone fences. The link between pasture and enclosure appeared in Isaac Bromyhan's labor performed on Henry Dubois's farm in Schodack in May 1823: he was consecutively "sowing plaster, making fences."[27] The farms in Durham were surrounded by fences in 1822. Peter Roggen's homestead in Oak Hill, a neighborhood of Durham, was divided by stone walls into nineteen lots of five to nine acres. In Greenville, Lewis Sherrel's stone fences were three to five feet thick and at least five feet high. A farmer in Albany County combined stone and wood rails so "as no sheep or cattle get over it." John

Burroughs took a more romantic view of the ten miles of stone fences around his family's farm on the western slope of the Catskills. They were

> the only lines of poetry and prose that Father ever wrote. They are still very legible on the face of the landscape and cannot be easily erased from it. Gathered out of the confusion of nature, built up of fragments of the old Devonian rock and shale, laid with due regard to wear and tear of time, well-bottomed and well-capped, establishing boundaries and defining possessions, etc., these lines of stone wall afford a good lesson in many things besides wall building. They are good literature and good philosophy. They smack of the soil, they have local colour, they are a bit of chaos brought into order.[28]

Human diligence was transforming the face of the mid–Hudson Valley.

Specialization locked the mid–Hudson Valley area into an increasingly intensive interregional trade. Greene County exports of butter, one of the most important articles of merchandise shipped from Catskill, rose from 11,864 firkins worth $164,096 in 1832 to 19,901 firkins worth $199,010 in 1843 to 31,128 firkins worth $435,792 in 1847. The district's dependence on imported foodstuffs became noticeable in the 1830s and was unmistakable by 1860 when French's *Gazetteer* explained that the people in counties upon the Hudson "are almost exclusively engaged in stock and sheep raising and in dairying. Little more grain is raised than is strictly necessary for a proper rotation of crops; and the greater part of the grain for home consumption is imported from other sections of the country." Its entry on Greene County laconically stated that "the grain grown is insufficient for the consumption of the population."[29] The state census of 1855 showed the extent of interdependence when it revealed the vast wheat deficit of the mid–Hudson Valley region. It indicated marketable surpluses for hay and oats, both of which articles the horses of New York City consumed (table 8).

The opening of the Hudson Valley landscape conditioned the expansion of its inhabitants' mental horizon and social experience as well. Not only were the Dubois, Hoffman, and Bushnell families constrained to purchase flour because soil conditions and heightened interregional competition propelled the specialization of their farms in hay and other produce for the long-distance market, where they enjoyed a comparative edge, but they and their neighbors began to follow news from distant regions. In July 1832, a customer inquired of Oliver Jones in Hudson whether the New York hay market "affords a decent proffit." James Reynolds recorded in 1847

TABLE 8. Marketable Portions of Agricultural Production, 1855 (percentages)

Commodity	Columbia County	Greene County
Corn	25.1	−92.2
Hay	29.5	35.8
Oats	77.6	57.2
Wheat	−95.2	−94.2

Sources: Census of the State of New York for 1855; Jared Van Wagenen, Golden Age of Homespun (Ithaca, 1953), 68. Calculation parameters were adjusted from information gleaned in Winifred B. Rothenberg, "A Price Index for Rural Massachusetts, 1750–1855," Journal of Economic History 39 (1979): 988–1001.

that "news from Europe advanced flour to $7.00 per bbl" in the Pough-keepsie area. "Starving Ireland," William Hoffman pointed out in his diary, was crying out for American foodstuffs.[30] This extralocal orientation stood in clear contrast to the neighborhood's encompassing universe at the turn of the nineteenth century.

Natural Resources and Industrialization

In 1811, the *Hudson Bee* carried an advertisement for a "Valuable Property for Sale." The seventy-acre plot was "situated on a good stream of water well calculated for a factory of any kind." A prospector traveling in Greene County a few years later jotted into his diary that "there are several mills below the falls—their situation is advantageous, the Kauterskill having its origin in the mountains is a never failing mill stream." The observer specu-lated that "there would be water enough with proper dams for twenty overshot mills, but in this present state weaping abundantly from a miser-able old age, the river is scarcely sufficient to carry the four mills situated by the falls." When William Darby crossed Kinderhook Creek in 1818, he discovered "a fine merchant mill and," he continued, "directly opposite the mill stands a large cotton factory. During the last war a little village rose around this factory, inhabited by weavers, spinners and other workmen." Indeed, the embargo of 1807 had pushed mid–Hudson Valley merchants, who had hitherto invested their capital in maritime trade, to turn toward manufacturing. Because water was the most efficient source of power, they explored creeks whose banks were high and narrow. The shape maximized the amount of energy channeled into the operation of the wheel while minimizing the width and construction cost of the dam. And, although waterpower relied on a felicitous climate—William Youngs had to close his mill because it was "obstructed much with ice" in January 1814 while Abner Austin noted in his diary on 14 July 1818 that "water failed so as to stop mill"—as late as 1850 only 16 out of 236 industrial mills (or 6.8 percent) in Columbia and Greene Counties used steam as an energy source.[31]

Whatever industrial enterprise sprang up between 1807 and the 1840s in the mid-Hudson Valley, considerations bearing on natural resources played a primary role. The introduction of steam changed that pattern and began to disconnect mills from creeks. When the *Kinderhook Sentinel* announced the building of a steam factory in the village of Kinderhook in 1846, the editors exclaimed that after a generation of manufacturers had taken advantage of the streams in the neighboring village of Valatie, "the business prospects of our village are beginning to brighten. . . . The noise of the loom and shuttle will soon be heard in our midst" and would provide "employment for a large number of persons." Until the advent of steam, however, a close correspondence between the sites of resources and manufacturing exploitation characterized the mode of industrial development. Describing Claverack and Kinderhook Creeks, whose last stretch had been renamed Factory Creek, Gordon's 1836 *Gazetteer* stated that its "water power has given rise to several manufacturing villages." The link between enterprise and geography occurred to Sterling Goodenow as early as 1811. He concluded in his *Brief Topographical and Statistical Manual of the State of New York* that "some spot favorable for manufactures, or for the transaction of mercantile or other business, suddenly becomes populous, and, if remote from an earlier settled or more noted part of the same town, requires a separate name."[32]

The exploitation of natural resources altered the landscape. The industrial village of Stockport on Factory Creek five miles north of Hudson emerged in an area of "wilderness" according to a Columbia County native in the second decade of the nineteenth century. Hudson River clay and sand in combination with wood from the Catskills allowed the emergence of brickyards that altered the riverbanks. The tanning industry was one of the main springs of industrial development and environmental change. It blossomed in the Catskill Mountains between 1817 and the 1850s after William Edwards discovered a process using hemlock bark as a tanning agent. Bark was difficult to transport because of rapid loss of the chemical properties so crucial to tanners. As a consequence, skins from South America were carried into the hemlock-covered Catskills. Greene County produced more leather than the rest of the state of New York in the 1830s and early 1840s. "Where three years ago was the wilderness, is now one of the most extensive manufactories of leather in the state," the *Catskill Recorder* noted in 1820. "We allude to the settlement of Messrs. Edwards at Hunter, which is already assuming an air of neatness and comfort; and, what in these times is not the least to be regarded, of profit, importance and utility." The Catskills proved a territory of opportunity, and tanning entrepreneurs followed its woods to pursue their activities. In 1832, the *Recorder* breathed excitement: "From having been formerly acquainted with this section of the country, we were struck with astonishment at the change in its condition. But seven years ago, the section which bears the name of Schohariekill, was an extended plain, owned and occupied by some half dozen farmers, for agricultural purposes only. Now it is almost one extended village, and is not surpassed, in appearance, industry, enterprise or situation, by any village in the county. On the noble stream that meanders through its valley are three large leather manufactories."[33]

The rise and fall of the tanneries in the Catskills depended exclusively on the availability of hemlock. In its very brevity, the existence of the Catskill tanning industry represented a poignant prototype of economic development with its individual benefits and ecological costs in the countryside. Hemlock and riches went hand in hand. Yet with the exhaustion of hemlock supplies the tanners left behind an entirely transformed area dispossessed of a large portion of its woods. Either with foreboding or self-delusion, on 4 July 1832 Zadock Pratt toasted "the tanneries of the county of Greene. . . . May they never want hemlock bark to keep them in operation." But the forests were receding. Pratt had cleared 3,666 acres of woods in twenty years, while all the tanning establishments had consumed an average of 1,500 acres per year. Where "heavy hemlock" in the mountains had formed a "dense wilderness" in the 1820s, the *Catskill Messenger* commented in 1848 that the hills were being "stripped of their timber so as to present their huge rocky projections." Erosion was one of the consequences of the extensive exploitation of timber.[34] The scarcity of bark ended the short existence of the tanning business in Greene County by the late 1840s. It is not without irony that William Henry Edwards, a grandson of one of the first tanners and businessmen in the Catskills, should have lamented the predatory mode of getting bark. "From the time I first knew the region [around 1828]," he recalled in an addendum to his grandfather's

Memoirs, "it was but a few years before the border of the living forest re-treated up the mountain sides, and there was a large extent of land that gradually was cleared up, and occupied by farmers. But the beauty of the mountains had departed forever." Eventually people withdrew from the area to search for other opportunities and trees began to grow again in neighborhoods that had been requited to nature.[35]

Time: A Cash Article

Enhanced agricultural productivity, the more complex division of manu-facturing labor, and a growing long-distance trade altered the relationship of the Hudson Valley population with time. Watches and public clocks came to play an increasingly important role in their lives during the first half of the nineteenth century. General explanations of the development of time consciousness attribute changes to such phenomena as urbaniza-tion and industrialization. Both Lewis Mumford and David Landes assert that temporal compulsiveness remained confined to cities until railroads penetrated the countryside and subjected its population to urban fetters. The urban experience suggests that the social utility of timepieces in the organization of work appeared upon their introduction. The Hudson Val-ley, on the contrary, underwent a two-stage process: only when the dif-fusion of clocks and watches had reached a majority of its households in the 1820s did they begin to attract people's attention to their capacity as timekeepers. Comments on the importance of timeliness and punctuality after that moment alert us to an alteration of the categories by which the inhabitants of the Hudson Valley perceived and measured time. An abun-dant resource that suffered squandering at the beginning of the nineteenth century, time became a scarce one that required husbanding.[36]

At the turn of the nineteenth century, people in the Hudson Val-ley lived with notions of time that dated back to the waning Middle Ages. Noon divided the days, and Lexington Heights carpenter Zepha-niah Chase charged Edmon Cottle for "2½ days work on your stoop." Joseph Wedges received credit for labor performed during half days on Elijah Hudson's farm in Canaan around 1790, while James Mason's wife sewed for ten and one-half days on behalf of Henry Van Schaack in spring 1795.[37] The Reverend Prout of Jewett in the Catskills remembered the early 1800s, when "seldom a clock was to be seen among the inhabitants. Laban Andrews brought a brass clock and a sun dial from Connecticut. The dial governed the time. From that the neighbors made noon-marks in their windows, by the shadow of some object as seen at the sun's meridien." A Shaker clock maker confided in his diary that clocks were scarce in the Hudson Valley area in 1803. When state tax assessors counted clocks and watches in 1800, their survey confirmed the observation. They listed 937 timepieces among the 48,000 inhabitants of Columbia and Greene Counties, numbers that meant that one in eight households at most owned an instrument to measure time.[38]

Seasons rather than years, harvests rather than profits, and reproduction rather than accumulation loomed in people's consciousness. John Beebe of Chatham noted on 4 August 1785 that the inhabitants in his vicinity "had finished Harvesting." He continued that "it has been a fine season, a plentiful harvest and a kind providence." Sojourner Truth, who lived and worked as a slave in Ulster County, recollected the years before her escape to freedom in 1827 in seasonal terms. Her master had sold two of her siblings "when there was snow on the ground" and she took flight after the "fall's work" was done.[39] Time received its meaning from its immediate relations to people's experience and the organization of agricultural work.

The development of long-distance trade increased the complexity of scheduling. A sample of twenty-four farmers who employed Abraham J. Hasbrouck's services in 1824 to send wares to New York came to the store between five and six times in 1824. In Catskill, M'Kinstry, Penfield and Porter began to systematize the purveyance of cargo in 1818. They introduced regular shipments, removing themselves from the traditional modus operandi that had hitherto entirely depended on the length of time it took to fill a sloop. "The advantage to the Western Merchant by the appointment of stated days on which to sail from Catskill and New York are apparent," their explanation read. "It will enable them to calculate with accuracy on what day to be at Catskill with produce &c. which they wish supplied to New York and on what day to order teams to meet them here, to transport their goods to the west."[40] Timetables represented a step toward increasing predictability and order. Their introduction marked a momentous change because they forced a new type of regularity onto people living in the rural Hudson Valley.

It was only when a sufficiently dense network of timepieces existed in the rural Hudson Valley that they began to function as dependable timekeepers and organizers of social interaction. Connecticut entrepreneur Chauncy Jerome had learned early in his life that the countryside represented a vast market for clocks when he saw a neighboring mechanic "on horseback with a clock on each side of his saddle-bags, and a third lashed

TABLE 9. Clocks and Watches in Greene County Inventories, 1800–1850

Years	Inventories	With timers	Percentage	Price per clock	Price per watch
1801–10	27	7	25.7	$26.64	$22.74
1811–20	49	20	40.8	$19.91	$16.25
1821–30	46	29	63.0	$9.13	$10.47
1831–40	35	23	65.7	$5.48	$7.67
1841–50	41	30	73.2	$5.14	$7.82

Sources: Probate Inventories, Greene County Surrogates' Court, Catskill.

behind the saddle with the dials in plain sight" in the second decade of the century. Harriet Martineau commented with ironic keenness on the mode of distribution and the effect of timepieces in rural areas in the 1830s. "The Yankee pedlars, with their wooden clocks, are renowned. . . . These men are great benefactors to society: for, be their clocks what they may, they make the country people as well off as the inhabitants of towns, in the matter of knowing time. . . . It appeared as if the clocks themselves had something of the Yankee spirit in them; for, while they were usually too fast, I rarely knew one too slow."[41] The dissemination of clocks and watches progressed rapidly between 1810 and 1830 when a majority of inventoried estates in Greene County listed a timepiece (table 9).

Increasing awareness of time revealed how much clock faces and hour hands began to determine the unfolding of daily activities in the 1820s. Not surprisingly it was William Bessac, a repairer of timepieces and distributor of fare tickets for Hudson Valley steamboats, who in a single account in 1826 recorded the precise time spent at work. The occasion concerned the credit Thomas Johnson had earned "by 3 hours writing." The urge to log time appeared in somewhat contradictory form in the ledger of Kingston tailor and farmer J. D. LaMontanye. Titus Jansen cradled oats on LaMontanye's farm "about ¾ of a day" in August 1835, the first reckoning of accounts that applied quarter-day units. LaMontanye also borrowed James Dubois's "horses & waggon to draw 1 load hay & one horse & waggon to draw 4 loads all home & horse and waggon about 1 hour to draw 15 cocks in the barn." The degree of precision reverted to older, more approximative norms the following spring. Eli Cristiana plowed "with oxen between 5 & 6 days [and] did about 3 or 3½ days work." The trend, however, continued. A dozen years later William Hoffman of Claverack hinted at the ubiquity of horologes in the countryside. After having read a book on scientists in the winter of 1848 when farm labor was light, he wrote that "Galileo another great character first invented the Pendulum & formed the present time piece we have at present, the clock which measures time for us & of which we could not very well dispense with." Hoffman's own experience proved that time discipline pervaded his life. On 23 August 1847, he noted that he had spent the hours from 8 A.M. to noon and from 1:30 P.M. to sunset plowing. Earlier in the month his diary chronicled that it had taken him about three hours to transport ten bushels of rye and seven bushels of potatoes over a distance of about five miles from his family's farm to the market in Hudson.[42]

Hoffman's observations summed up an evolution whose achievement consisted of introducing the notion of productivity into the countryside. If William Cobbett could still assert in 1817 that "an American labourer is not regulated, as to time, by *clocks* and *watches*[,] the sun . . . tells him when to begin in the morning and when to leave off at night," by the 1840s agricultural reformer Jesse Buel was admonishing farmers to "work it right . . . by redeeming time." Husbandmen heard a novel discourse that not only suggested the introduction of new crops and the adoption of improved methods but constructed time as a resource that required judicious treatment. The connection between market rationality and time consciousness appeared unequivocally when the president of the New York State Agricultural Society proclaimed in 1852 that "time and labor have become cash articles, and he [the farmer] neither lends nor barters them."[43] Among the farmer's resources, time had come to assume an important place.

Longer chains of social interdependence spawned the systematization of social relationships. Rural dwellers recognized pressures emanating from vaster business connections, but they still contrasted their social rhythms to the cadence of urban life. The bylaws of the Lexington Temperance Society stipulated in the 1820s that "this Soc. shall meet on the tuesday evening of each month preceding the full moon." Paper manufacturer Abner Austin apologized in 1828 for "the impossibility of my coming up to City punctuality, where it is no inconsiderable part of business to receive and answer letters promptly."[44] The transformation did not disconnect rural inhabitants from the seasonal modulation of their lives. In 1786, William Coventry reveled in the blossoms on the cherry and apple trees, and the spring of 1855 kindled poetic feelings in Hannah Bushnell, who wrote that "the Plum and pear trees are in bloom. currant and goose berry are in blossom. pleasant season. the little birds singing so sweetly." But the seasons had acquired additional significance. James Hopkins informed Charles Hopkins that "things go swimmingly at Catskill," alluding to the imminent opening of the Hudson River, which marked the commencement of the commercial season in 1843. When the *Catskill Messenger* reported six years later that the village had the "same dull appearance that is prevalent in winter," it too perceived the situation in terms of markets and trade. "One can scarcely notice any change in the business of the Village," it lamented, "what is the reason—is Catskill behind its neighbors in enterprise?"[45]

Economic rationality imparted to work a new content in the mid-nineteenth century. While William Coventry and William Youngs went fishing in the middle of the harvest during the century's first dozen years, the *Kinderhook Sentinel* related the persistent efforts of farmers in the fall of 1845 to drive "a brisk business in transporting to market all they have to spare (and a little more, too) of these staple articles [hay and potatoes], before the close of navigation." The language of artisans tells the same story. In 1811, shoemaker Nathaniel Reeve adhered to the traditional principles of spoken goods. He promised his customers that "all orders from distant and adjacent towns will be strictly attended to," a notion that defined accuracy and skill before it implied promptness. Cabinetmaker George Doak still made furniture "to order" thirty-three years later, but now the pledge included delivery "with punctuality." The new imperatives affected women's domestic labor. While prescriptive literature emphasized efficiency and warned against the dangers of idleness, it also stressed the importance of women's adherence to regular and precise mealtimes to avoid slowing the work performed outside the home. Time had become a resource whose management mattered increasingly as the nineteenth century advanced, and we understand the reason why the inhabitants of Coxsackie desired "a town time that can be relied upon" when they discussed the virtues of a "town clock" in 1837.[46]

On 31 July 1836, Thomas Cole "took a walk . . . up the valley of the Catskill, where they are now constructing the railroad. This was once my favorite walk," he wrote, "but now the charm of solitude and quietness is gone." Eight years before, Hawthorne had depicted the locomotive as the embodiment of industrial power and a source of human alienation from communion with nature. Cole sensed the dislocation engendered by economic development.[47] Industrialization, however, did not provide the lone cause for his anxiety. Brooks and creeks in Greene and Columbia Counties offered sites for manufacturing. The setting in the countryside could, as was Thomas Jefferson and Tench Coxe's view after they had assessed the European experience, change the character of the cotton mill and promote economic and moral benefits rather than degeneration in North America. Cole easily accommodated the pastoral idea in which farmers cultivated land and strove for a competence. But he could not reconcile himself to, in Max Weber's terms, "the boiling heat of modern capitalistic culture [that] is connected with the heedless consumption of natural resources, for which there are no substitutes." And, to pursue the comparison, Cole appreciated days that were, like Thoreau's in Concord, "not minced into hours and fretted by the ticking clock."[48] In brief, he dreaded the rise of a culture of economic rationalism.

With the Catskill artist, we have delineated the physical transformation of the mid–Hudson Valley in the first half of the nineteenth century. The expansion of the market had altered the meanings of space and time for the rural population. Even the market principle that had caused such misgivings had found wide, if not general, acceptance by the middle of the century. In 1810, the *Hudson Bee* carried a long article in which it still had to refute claims about the detrimental effects of manufacturing on agriculture, emphasizing its contribution to the general prosperity. The argument became a staple used to drum up support for industrial establishments in the wake of the embargo of 1807 and the promotion of domestic development. "Public opinion has long been divided, and even distracted, on subjects connected with *Domestic Manufactures*," Horatio Spafford remarked in 1824 when he described the Matteawan Cotton Factory in Dutchess County. He continued: "A market is here made, to a certain extent, for the surplus productions of the surrounding country, profitable alike to those who make that market, and those who supply it, and . . . in its influence exactly proportioned to that establishment itself. It is making a market at home, at the very door of those who have a surplus of products for such a market, where raw materials, manual labor, water-power, and the labor of ingenious machinery, are all converted into money." Increased social differentiation fueled agricultural development in the region. In the case of the tanning industry, it is tempting to speak of capitalist islands that spurred economic growth in the woods. "The solitude of the deep mountain glens was made vocal by the hum of industry, the buzz of the waterwheel, and the rattling of machinery," John Homer French wrote in 1860. The *Catskill Messenger* revealed just as much when it reported in 1834 that "several of the extensive tanning establishments in the country have been obliged to suspend their operations and discharge their hands. The effects of this suspension will be sensibly felt by the farming interest in the county, who have found a ready market for their produce at these factories."[49]

The critique formulated at the beginning of the century had given way to a new outlook. Economic development and growth within a market framework now appeared as a desirable process. The new appreciation shaped Theodore A. Cole's conception of his farming activities. He noted in 1857 that "the first hay that I sent to New York only brought 40^c per 100, the straw 55^c. I think perhaps we would make more money if we let the hay go and pasture more cows if there should be a prospect of its being so low next year. Hard times tend to lower the price of all kinds of produce."[50] There could be no better illustration of the way market rationality now informed people's cast of mind: Cole's father would not have understood his son's calculations.

FOUR

Farms Woven into the Landscape:

Agricultural Developments, 1810–1850s

Paper manufacturer Abner Austin was a keen observer of the social and economic goings-on in the Catskill area. In the mid-1830s he noted in a letter that "farmers near the River are turning their attention to cultivating grass. . . . Every considerable farmer has his hay press, & sends all his surplus hay on to market. They are raising less grain & keep less stock to make the amount the larger for sale. This change of management has given quite a spring to farming operations." The transformation of arable land into pasture and the extension of the cultivated surface opened up the Hudson Valley scenery. The serene prospect allowed Thomas Cole to remark on a journey through the Taconic Mountains into the Massachusetts Berkshires that farms and dwellings "wove themselves into a vast and varied landscape." The two contemporaries focused on different scales of the process that engaged the Hudson Valley population during the first half of the nineteenth century. While Cole saw the big picture, so to speak, Austin zeroed in on one of its constitutive elements. The artist reminds us that even as late as 1845 four-fifths of the mid–Hudson Valley's inhabitants—artisans and shopkeepers no less than farmers—worked and lived in neighborhoods where agriculture provided the large majority of people with a livelihood. The manufacturer alerts us to the participation of farm families in the developments that altered their lives and their environment and in turn conditioned their existence.[1] The burgeoning market orientation of farmers who began to specialize in grass culture forms this chapter's subject of investigation. After all, if political authorities and increasingly stronger commercial middlemen implemented laws and launched ventures to foster economic development, and indeed growth, in the countryside, the success of their schemes depended on the willingness of farmers to go along with, and contribute to, their projects.

The stakes were high for Hudson Valley farmers. The expanding national market, with its sharper competition, pressured the region's agriculturalists into reinventing themselves after the second decade of the nineteenth century. Grain yields, for one, remained very low compared to those in newly settled areas to the west.[2] The conversion to meadows and animal husbandry bespoke more efficient land use in the region, a shift that helped increase the agricultural output that farm families sold in the market. Specialization induced the reorganization of labor processes on the farm. Although improved equipment and livestock sustained rising production, technological enhancements of traditional tools and the adoption of new breeds did not impose the acquisition of unfamiliar skills. Productivity growth relied on the intensification of well-known work practices. But the continuity in agricultural methods did not entail stability of the labor force. On the contrary, families increasingly turned to hired, paid men and women to work on farms. The proliferation of agricultural wage labor was one of the salient features in the Hudson Valley of Cole and Austin's generation.

More voluminous trade and a larger pool of salaried hands led to the decline of neighborhood swapping and the eventual predominance of cash transactions in the Hudson Valley. Direct, personal obligation gave way to mediated, financial dealings. Account books offer clues to this reordering of social relations. Timothy Persons used Reynolds's wagon to deliver produce at the landing in Catskill in June 1809; he also received foodstuffs between 1808 and 1810, for which he returned "smith work." Their transactions amounted to 25£ 15s 10d during this period, but Reynolds cleared his debt of 1£ 5s 2d with a bushel of wheat and 12 shillings. The pattern held for four of the ten accounts in Reynolds's ledger. Six men, however, never used cash and performed work to maintain the balance. A few years later, Green Blevin of Upper Catskill paid one-third of his debt of 19£ 14s to blacksmith Samuel Fowks in cash. The rest was covered intermittently between 1817 and 1822 with work, cabbage, potatoes, buckwheat flour, linen, and pork. Fowks's income of £413 over these five years from twenty customer accounts was made up of 60 percent goods and services and 40 percent cash. At Butler's general store in Greenville, where accounts were squared regularly in the 1850s, only seven out of thirty-one customers carried produce to the counter to pay for their purchases and only John Garruson worked off his debt. Financial institutions began to transact payments, too, and in September 1857 farmer Theodore Cole settled his butcher's bill with "a note for sixty days payable at the Tanners Bank."[3]

The adoption of new payment methods had to overcome the suspicions farmers entertained vis-à-vis banks as much as the uninterest bankers showed in the farming population. In 1815, the inhabitants of Canaan launched a petition to the state government to warn against the dangers "monied institutions" posed to society. Throughout the first half of the nineteenth century, farmers remained reluctant to deposit whatever savings they had in local banks while bankers revealed their distrust of agricultural equity by awarding very few mortgages to farm families.[4] Yet, if behavior changed haltingly, pressure to alter economic and social practices rose with the century. When in 1803 one Mr. Stebbins of Hillsdale lost house and store to fire, the *Hudson Bee* reported that "with an alacrity deserving the highest praise, the neighbors of Mr. Stebbins have raised a new store, and it is said, intend to volunteer their services, until it is completely finished." Twenty-five years later, this kind of generosity elicited some commendation and a great deal of criticism. "Fire!" a headline in the *Catskill Recorder* read in 1828 after the tannery of May and Gillum had burned down. What followed was a poignant editorial indictment of neighborly compassion in the name of economic efficiency.

> Although in the present instance it gives us pleasure to announce that a very considerable portion of the loss sustained by Messrs. May & Gillum has been made up to them by the liberality of their fellow citizens, yet as a general thing, we are opposed to the practice of assisting by public subscription those who sustain losses by fire. At the present day, when the competition between the numerous companies has reduced the rate of insurance to a moderate premium, every man who is not able to be his own underwriter, or who in other words has not the ability to sustain the losses fire may occasion him, without embarrassing himself or his friends, should be at all times insured. The practice of correct businessmen is in conformity with this principle. The plan, therefore, of dividing upon community the losses of those who from negligence or parsimony are without insurance, is in theory wrong, and in effect, prejudicial to the interests of society.[5]

In this emerging order of new contingencies and opportunities, farm families sought openings to maintain and improve their comfort and style of life. In this quest, many succeeded but some failed. In the neighborhood, expansion of production and growing participation in the long-distance market induced the redistribution of land and a rearrangement in the orchestration of farm labor. The conjunction of agricultural specialization, the appeal of western lands, and a more competitive demand for workers to enter industrial employment led to the rise of extrafamilial wage labor on Hudson Valley farms.[6] In families, the new economic constellation tipped the balance toward women's greater involvement in market-oriented activities. This more visible participation in the family's economy fostered women's self-confidence, and we must wonder whether this economic shift—rather than the waning supply of land or enhanced literacy in an area where farm size tended to grow and schools were ubiquitous—did not lead to a renegotiation of power relations between the sexes and a reduction in birth rates.[7]

Marketing Agricultural Produce

In the first half of the nineteenth century, ever more farmers produced more goods for the long-distance market. In 1801, 108 (or 39.7 percent) of Abraham J. Hasbrouck's customers in Kingston shipped produce to New York City. Twenty-three years later, 55.8 percent—that is, 213 out of 382 accounts on the merchant's ledgers in 1824—forwarded cargo to the metropolis. Not only did a larger number of agriculturalists participate in trade, but the average value of the produce conveyed to the city rose from roughly 70 to 170 dollars between 1798 and 1824. The combined effect of growing numbers and larger volumes induced a change upon which the *Greene County Republican* commented in 1828 with the observation that the Hudson's "waters which but a few years since were occasionally disturbed by a tri-weekly steamboat, and here and there a solitary sail, now scarcely find a rest from an uninterrupted agitation by the craft floating upon its bosom."[8]

The paucity and heterogeneity of extant data permit only an approximate reconstruction of the development beyond the insights provided by Hasbrouck's journals. Occasional farm accounts published in newspapers and agricultural magazines depicted the mercantile acumen of substantial farmers. They indeed enlarged the crop repertory destined for trade; potatoes, for example, seemed to have been barely cultivated for home consumption at the beginning of the century but began to penetrate the market in the 1830s when new, more productive, and better appreciated varieties appeared in the Hudson Valley.[9] The general purpose of published

TABLE 10. Value of Farmers' Marketed Goods, 1798–1853

Year	Clients	Amount ($)
1798	Hasbrouck clients, Kingston area	70
1813	Adam Shaver, Livingston Manor	250
1815	Unidentified Farmer, Catskill	389
1824	Hasbrouck clients, Kingston area	169
1828	150 acre farm, Dutchess County	1,000
1835	Samuel T. Vary, Kinderhook	2,284
1847	Peter Crispell Jr., Hurley, Ulster County	2,154
1850	Ephraim P. Best, Kinderhook	2,287
1853	G. W. Coffin, Amenia	1,192

Sources: Abraham J. Hasbrouck Journals, 1798 and 1824 (sample), N-YHS; *Northern Whig,* 12 Oct. 1813; Great Imbaught (Catskill) Farm Account Book 1815–16, N-YHS; *Niles' Weekly Register,* 29 March 1829, 77; *Catskill Messenger,* 3 March 1836, 1; *Transactions of the New York State Agricultural Society* 7 (1847): 217–19; *Transactions of the New York State Agricultural Society* 14 (1854), 120; Ephraim P. Best Account Book 1846–1855, COLCHS.

accounts was, however, to incite emulation among the less striving husbandmen. Such information is valuable because it is rare, but its bias will require us to balance its contents with other evidence (Table 10).

Prosperous farmers like Samuel T. Vary of Kinderhook could, according to the *Catskill Messenger* of 1836, expect a return of 13 percent on their farm's real estate value, a middling figure compared to the 17 and 8 percent that David Harris of Dutchess County and Ephraim Best of Kinderhook, both of whom cultivated extensive farms in fertile areas, reaped in 1835 and 1850, respectively.[10] Between Harris's optimistic assertion and a pessimistic estimate in the *Catskill Democrat* that put a poor farmer's yearly return at a level of 2 or 3 percent of the land's value in November 1844, Ephraim Best's gross profits averaged roughly 10 percent of his property value between 1844 and 1854, with the exceptional peak of 21 percent ($4,156) in 1853 driving up the mean revenues the commercialized goods brought him during this decade. At the same moment in time during the mid-1850s George W. Coffin's balance "in favor of the farm" stood at about 5 percent of the value of his real estate located in Amenia, Dutchess County.[11] These numbers, used with circumspection, permit us to estimate the value of produce that farmers marketed in the 1850s on the basis of real estate values assessed in the agricultural census. If we assume that farms yielded yearly produce worth one-tenth of the real estate value and all other things remained equal (admittedly a strong but not arbitrary hypothesis by mid-century), then the average farm in the prosperous vicinity of Kinderhook carried goods worth $900 to the landing, a figure in line with Ephraim Best's results on a farm more than twice the size and value of Kinderhook's mean unit. In Greenville, the load amounted to $400, while farmers from Lexington in the Catskills brought products valued at about $200 to the river.[12] All these amounts surpassed the value of goods that Hasbrouck's customers shipped to New York in 1824.

The price of land, with respect to which these figures acquire their significance and which we take to encompass information on its relative economic productivity, soared in the first half of the nineteenth century. On a visit to the Kinderhook area in 1828, Alexander Coventry noticed that "the pitch pine woods which 40 years ago shaded the road had disappeared. These formerly extended from Kinderhook 15 miles North, with only 2 houses and clearings, but now are entirely gone, the country cleared, not 10 rods of shade in the distance. . . . About 1790 this land was sold for $1 an acre; now it brings $75 or $80." The *Kinderhook Sentinel* reported the sale of a 216 acre farm at $95 an acre in 1839. This kind of information mattered to its readers, who began to take an interest in the active land market. Russell Cady wrote a letter to his brother Elias in which he detailed the prices of farms in Kinderhook. They fetched between $52 and $70 an acre in 1835. He concluded, "Allen Cady has sold his farm for 1700 dollars and has bought out Thomas Lyon in Chatham for 27 dollars per acre. A good round price for stony land." The average value of an acre in Columbia County increased, according to state assessments, from $10.10 in 1799 to $21.20 in 1835 and to $28.50 in 1847.[13] Land appreciated in value because capital improvements led to a larger volume of marketable produce, regardless of whether the merchandise was butter and cattle from the hill country or hay, oats, and swine from areas closer to the Hudson.

The marketing of the increased agricultural production—Hasbrouck's customers sextupled their trips to the Kingston merchant between 1798 and 1824 to deliver their goods for the New York market—changed social relations at the landings. Competition among traders increased, and whereas Horatio Gates Spafford had anticipated economic development in 1813 in the 1830s Thomas Hamilton recorded that "from the large number of warehouses which these [villages on the Hudson] generally contained, they were evidently places of considerable deposit for the agricultural produce of the neighboring country."[14] It was not only that more long-distance traders offered their services to farmers. They began to specialize. Clearly, routine and credit assured general shippers of Hasbrouck's ilk (if not longevity) a loyal clientele. But farmers began to avail themselves of a wider array of intermediaries to market their goods. They turned to drovers to have their stock routed to the landing and shipped to the metropolitan market. Village storekeepers like Reuben Rundle of East Greenville collected hay from farmers in the neighborhood and then had it transported on Hudson River sloops specially equipped to carry bales. Butter, salted and stored in firkins, became the object of brokers who contracted with families in the spring for fall delivery of the farm's production.[15]

The exposure to a larger number of mercantile middlemen loosened the long-term, personal ties at the landings. Farmers consigned their various goods to different shippers. The Burroughs family, which ran a large farm in the Catskills, dealt with a butter factor and delivered the rest of its production to a freighter in Catskill. George Holcomb of Stephentown peddled his apples and potatoes at militia trainings, noted when his wife used butter and eggs to get store credit and generate cash income, and traded other goods in Troy. Kinderhook's Ephraim Best shipped hay and potatoes to New York with trader Alexander Davis while local merchants Blanchard, Miller, and Brown organized the sale of wool and buckwheat. By midcentury, when steamboat travel had achieved commonplace status among the enterprising part of the rural population, Ambrose Austin of Hillsdale sought to do without commercial intermediaries altogether by speculating in poultry at the metropolitan markets, which he attended in person.[16]

With the loosening of ties of confidence at the landing came the possibility of larger monetary profits for farmers. Brokers now regularly visited farm families to secure produce for the metropolitan market. In a letter to his brother-in-law, Frederick Kirtland, Cooper Sayre of Rensselaerwick rejoiced in 1836 that "you are probably aware of the high prices of produce in all parts of the county. Everything is raised to its highest pitch. Wheat is worth 16/9–rye 9/6–corn 8/1–oats is worth 4/ at the barn and emptying in proportion so that we have no reason to complain of the price we get for our produce." It became possible to play one wholesaler against the other. However, a wider playing field involved higher risks. In a saturated market and in the absence of privileged relations with long-distance traders, the disposal of goods proved uncertain. The sale of rye and potatoes in August 1847 caused sorrows for William Hoffman, who found "the market very dull" on the pier in Hudson and encountered "a great deal of trouble" in interesting customers, so much so that he had to lower his asking price.[17]

The intensification of long-distance trade in the first decades of the nineteenth century affected transactions between neighbors and helped carry the market principle into neighborhood exchange. Of course, mutual visiting and philanthropic events like quilting bees remained, formally unchanged, on the social agenda where drinking in taverns subsisted despite assaults from the temperance movement. The traffic in goods, however, now happened in competitive proximity to extralocal commerce. It was as if the two circuits through which produce (or labor and tools for that matter) used to move had collapsed into one. Now immediate and utilitarian rather than long-term considerations began to govern material dealings between neighbors, and the values of exchanged goods and services found monetary equivalents whereas earlier they had involved social obligations and rewards. Ephraim Best saw no difference between his neighbors and long-distance merchants: all sensibly paid the same price for his produce. Hannah Bushnell was keenly aware of produce prices at Coxsackie in the 1850s, and, contrary to Nancy Grey Osterud's contention that women recoiled from engaging in market relationships and maintained an attitude of social reciprocity when dealing among themselves, had no compunction about charging female neighbors at the current rates when the opportunity presented itself. In July 1855, Bushnell noted that she "did not send off any butter. I sold 7 pounds to the neighbors today." A year later, Adaline Plank "came here. She wanted 5 or 6 pounds of butter to fill up their pail to send to market. I let them have 5 pounds 18 cents a pound."[18]

Do these novel practices prove the claim that farmers in the Empire State had evolved into rational profit maximizers? This was certainly the opinion of the New York State Agricultural Society's president, who in 1852 trumpeted that "farming is no longer that uncertain, profitless work, which it once was. It is now reduced to a system, securing returns far more certain in their character, and at the same time as remunerating as any investment in any other pursuit." His vision surely exaggerated the methodological behavior of farmers, the deficiency of which continued to trouble census takers. "Owing to the Consequences of Farmers not keeping diaries of the Productions of the farms which come under the head of this Schedule," the marshall for Kinderhook noted in 1855, "I was under the necessity of taking it at their Own Estimation, but no doubt it is as correct as it possibly could be under the Circumstances." The exactitude of accounting on the farm remained approximate according to James Callanan of Albany County. He acknowledged that his "farming operations are not guided to a very great extent by actually weighing and measuring, nor are they registered very minutely by daily accounts. The annual expense of improving my farm has never been kept with a precision that would enable me to strike an accurate balance of debt and credit. I generally know, however, the amount of net gain every year."[19] In spite of its merely rough accuracy by the 1850s, the measurement of cost against return to determine either income or profit mattered in the routine of farm families' everyday lives. In this respect the president of the Agricultural Society was right to stress the emergence of a more calculating outlook as a consequence of farmers' growing involvement with the produce market.

Land and Livestock

The squeezing scissors of extralocal competition and the regression of grain yields pressured farmers in the Hudson Valley to train their eyes more closely on the long-distance trade. They enhanced production in ways that would assure them a safe position in the vaster sphere of exchange. Land reclamation was one way of increasing production, and it proved to be an important factor in the expansion of agricultural output in the mid–Hudson Valley. Between 1821 and 1855, census data show a 24 percent increase in improved land in long-settled Columbia County and a 70 percent expansion in Greene County. Growth of the cultivated surface exceeded the region's demographic course until the mid-1830s when Columbia's count of inhabitants rose faster than its improved acreage. The general movement after 1820 resulted in a smaller number of people per improved acre by midcentury while the total population density in both counties increased, a first hint that during this period the mid–Hudson Valley area succeeded in releasing additional marketable goods per inhabitant because constant individual consumption levels did not use up produce supplied by the larger surface in production (even if we grant lower average productivity per acre on more marginal land). However, waves of different magnitudes extended the cultivated surface of the area, whose geography brought about distinct rhythms in development (Table 11).[20]

The opening of the countryside altered the proportions of the uses to which the land was put. Fields carrying grains, pastures supporting animals (cattle, horses, and sheep), and meadows devoted to the production of hay continued to grace the landscape. But incentives to develop the land encountered soil and climatic conditions that limited the degree of transformation. Hudson Valley farmers clung to a minimum of grain cul-

TABLE II. Change in Cultivated Surface, 1821–55

Terrain	Total acres	IMPROVED ACRES					ANNUAL CHANGE (%)			
		1821	1825	1835	1845	1855	1821 1825	1825 1835	1835 1845	1845 1855
Columbia County										
Hill	223,953	144,175	149,244	173,485	174,778	177,495	0.7	1.6	0.1	0.2
Midlands	99,276	67,302	75,270	82,963	83,008	84,074	2.4	1.0	0.0	0.1
River	50,303	33,323	39,646	50,907	54,012	42,708	3.8	2.8	0.6	−2.1
TOTAL	373,532	244,800	264,160	307,355	311,798	304,277	1.6	1.6	0.1	−0.2
Greene County										
Hill	264,597	79,879	90,296	117,261	132,323	146,748	1.7	1.9	0.9	0.7
River	98,233	45,040	51,710	57,580	66,776	65,476	3.0	1.1	1.6	−0.2
TOTAL	362,830	124,919	142,006	174,841	199,099	212,224	2.7	2.3	1.4	0.7

Sources: Data from "Census of the State of New York for 1821," in New York State. Assembly, *Journal,* 45th Session (Albany, 1822), appendix; "Census of the State of New York for 1825," in New York State. Assembly, *Journal,* 49th Session (Albany, 1826), appendix; *Census of the State of New York for 1835* (Albany, 1836); New York State Secretary, *Census of the State of New York for 1845* (Albany, 1846); and *id., Census of the State of New York for 1855* (Albany, 1857). For regional subdivisions, see map 3.

ture below the threshold of which they did not want to fall because it was necessary for crop rotation and supplied winter fodder for horses partially fed on oats, but the hill country in the Catskills and the Taconic Mountains confined the extent of tillage. Geography influenced the arbitrage between meadow and pasture. River towns favored the production of hay while inversely, but not surprisingly to a Swiss historian, hill towns emphasized grazing, a distribution delineated by the 1850s (when the New York census introduced these categories): pastures occupied almost two-fifths of the improved surface in the hills of both counties while meadows covered roughly 20 percent in Columbia County and 30 percent in Greene. Towns on the Hudson kept more than one-third of their improved land in hay-producing meadows (map 3). Turnpikes of dubious quality made it easier to transport compact dairy products or walk cattle to the landings than to carry bulk hay on wagons to the Hudson.

Crop rotation, to which Hudson Valley farmers increasingly turned in the second decade of the nineteenth century, and the repeated exploitation of plots during the agricultural year render an extrapolation of land use difficult. This was true for grasslands, too. After June and July, when mead-

MAP 3. Land use in Columbia and Greene Counties, 1855

ows were cut for hay, they served as pastures for cattle. Ruminating cows fertilized the soil and helped prolong the life span of temporary grasses, which needed reseeding every eight to ten years. To complicate retrospective assessments of land use patterns, farmers intercalated tillage, too, so that it was not uncommon to plant potatoes on a one- or two-acre patch before it reverted to grass. Or, as Chancellor Livingston detailed around 1810, some farmers "plough between the corn and sow wheat or rye while the corn still stands." Important mid–Hudson Valley crops like rye (which accounted for approximately 10 percent of Columbia County's improved land and 5 percent in Greene's between 1845 and 1855), oats (13 percent in Columbia, 8 percent in Greene), and buckwheat (between 3 and 5 percent in both counties) complemented each other's growing cycle almost seamlessly, for a farmer could sow rye at the end of September and harvest it toward June, use part of the same surface to plant the fast-growing buckwheat as a catch-up crop in July and cut it in October, and plow and manure the field for winter oats to be reaped the following July, which added up to triple use of at least some of the soil over two seasons.[21]

Figures on cattle and sheep, whose numbers were regular features in New York State census after 1821, help bring some light to the puzzle of land use. Columbia County contained about 18,800 head of cattle (bulls, oxen, and cows) at the end of the eighteenth century. This number meant that the size of the herd almost doubled over the following twenty years to peak and then decline quite regularly afterward. The most extensive demands by animals on local agricultural output fell into the decade 1835–45. In these years farm animals were most numerous, and hence their consumption needs were largest in absolute terms. General estimates put the need of 1 cow at three to four acres of pasture and meadow (for hay during stabling in winter) per year while the same allotment could feed 8 sheep. The expansion of improved land mitigated the impact of animal requirements on other farm production, and although measurement is approximate the late 1820s and 1830s in Greene County and the 1820s in Columbia emerge as the most intense periods of animal farming in the mid–Hudson Valley in that they saw the largest number of animals per improved acre of land. In Columbia County this density owed both its increase and its contraction to the rise and decline of sheep raising (Fig. 4). With the acceleration of the demand for wool, four-fifths of the newly cleared land between 1821 and 1825 were laid down in grass to feed sheep. In Greene County, where neat cattle proved to be an important factor in the conquest

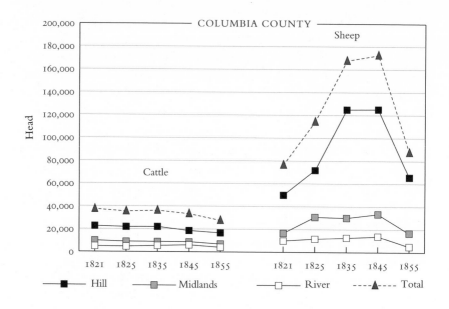

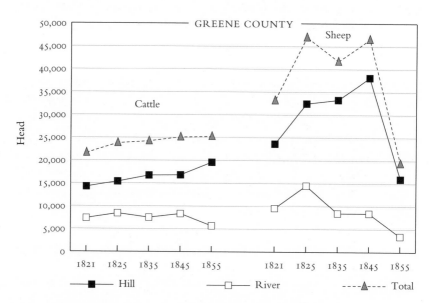

FIG. 4. Cattle and sheep in the mid–Hudson Valley, 1821–55. (Data from New York State Censuses, 1821–55.)

of the hill country, sheep were less momentous, accounting for roughly 30 percent of the newly improved land.[22]

The 1830s brought about a stronger emphasis in the different subregional strategies of agricultural adaptation. River towns in both counties, while abandoning improved land, maintained and even enlarged the tilled surface. Coxsackie, for example, almost doubled its fields of rye while slightly increasing the allotments for corn and oats between 1845 and 1855. At the same time, farmers in river towns drastically reduced their stock, an indication of the increased importance of meadows to produce hay for the export trade on which Abner Austin had commented. Columbia midland towns maintained the extent of their improved surface (although with variations that make any robust statistical analysis impossible) but engaged more pronouncedly in the cultivation of grains in the 1840s. In the hills, where sheep had dominated the landscape for twenty years, the driving force behind the development of land was the creation of meadows. Austerlitz gave up 1,152 acres (19 percent) of its fields to add 3,204 acres (30 percent) of new grasslands between 1845 and 1855, even though the land requirements of its animal stock fell by 5,900 acres. A similar if less striking reallocation occurred in the Catskills, where Cairo surrendered 777 acres of fields (about 10 percent) to 1,054 acres of grassland (about 9 percent) in the decade following 1845 while the minor decline in animal requirements freed more hay for trade.

These developments did not alter the general pattern of animal farming. Milk cows and other stock were more numerous on hill farms than along the river by 1850. In the Catskills, an average farmer milked 6.2 cows and pastured 9.5 other bovines, while the numbers in river towns were 4.2 and 2.5, respectively. Midland farms in Columbia County kept 5.4 milk cows and 3.8 head of neat cattle, roughly one fewer of each than the average farm in the area of the Taconic Mountains. Competition from the rising dairy belt in central New York diminished the market share of dairy products from the mid–Hudson Valley after 1820. Dairy farms in Oneida County sustained more than 15 milk cows and about 5 nonmilking animals in 1850. The comparative advantage of Columbia and Greene sections lay with grass in the form of hay and, secondarily it seems, with animals fit for slaughter. Both George W. Coffin of Amenia in northeastern Dutchess County, where he cultivated a 108 acre farm, and George W. Best of Kinderhook sold "beef cattle on foot," but whereas Best sold hay, too, Coffin seems to have used his mowing to feed 22 bovines through winter in 1855.[23]

The possibility of expanding the amount of improved land to extend production in conjunction with slower paced demographic growth eliminated the danger of agricultural involution in the mid–Hudson Valley. This was a process that Christopher Clark uncovered to explain the increasing involvement of land-poor and underemployed Connecticut River farm families in networks of market-oriented industrial outwork such as weaving, straw hat making, or even shoe production in order to stay on the land during the first half of the nineteenth century.[24] Hudson Valley families like the Duboises of Catskill, whose sons left homestead and agriculture in the 1830s and 1840s while their sister and her husband remained, combined the out-migration of some of their offspring with the development of unbroken land on their farms and the acquisition of new lots to increase the overall farm size. Manor tenants on the Livingston family's estate in Clermont enlarged their farms from 79 to 104 acres between 1799 and 1826, a surface that amounted almost to the 107 acres of an average freehold property. These were still the dimensions of Clermont farms in 1850. In the Catskills, the average farm size in Lexington increased from 105.4 acres in 1813 to 117.3 in 1850. The other method of avoiding a progressively inadequate relation between the land and the people who worked it was to extend the cultivated portion of the land. In New Baltimore, where the average farm size actually diminished from 127 to 110 acres between 1813 and 1850, the contraction was set off by a 36 percent increase in improved land. Farmers in Austerlitz opted for the conjunction of the two palliatives between the mid-1820s and 1850, when their average real estate holdings grew from 120 to 127 acres while they extended the improved portion from 90 to 101 acres on average. Commercial agriculture rather than proto-industrial by-employment helped farm families to survive, and prosper, in the increasingly mercantile environment.[25]

The process of land accretion induced a redistribution of real estate that flattened its dispersion. The portion of farms of less than 40 acres swelled to about 15 percent in Austerlitz and Baltimore toward 1850, while the share of the largest exploitations, at 250 plus acres, diminished to roughly 5 percent. In the middle ranges, size shifted toward units of 100 to 130 acres (fig. 5). By midcentury, the mid–Hudson Valley farm population was part of a development that produced more equality as well as a noteworthy, if slight, increase in the precariousness of livelihood on the lower rungs of the social ladder. Midland communities in Columbia County were home to more affluent farmers at the top of the social pyramid in 1850; at the same time, with a less than 10 percent portion of small farms, the district was living up to its reputation as "proverbially rich" or becoming "rich by improved management."[26] In general, then, the accentuation of animal farming after the War of 1812 through the late 1830s, the conversion to more intensive exploitation of grasslands, and, partially, tillage afterward profited the majority of the farmers who stuck it out in the area.

Labor

Mixed agriculture, with its combination of tillage, stock raising, dairy, and hay making, offered the advantages of a certain degree of flexibility in the organization of work on the farm. There were the everyday operations of householding and stock keeping that could not suffer any inattention. Seasonal operations like preparing fields, sowing, and hoeing, but also mowing and harvesting, added changing cadences to agricultural toil even while leaving some latitude in their execution; farmers could gather ripe corn at any time in the fall since it does not spoil (illus. 1). Countercyclical activities filled in time left unoccupied by the farm's major seasonal imperatives; all types of repair work on tools, fences, ditches, barns, and houses, but also the fabrication of boots for family members, barrel staves for trade, and spinning for domestic use and commercial exchange, could be accomplished in winter or in September precisely before corn stalks might be cut and stacked.[27]

The increased emphasis on grass culture during the first half of the nineteenth century altered the proportions within, but not the principles of, mixed agriculture. The basic rhythms of farm work changed little. But the introduction of red clover and the use of gypsum in the early 1800s inaugurated the departure from long-fallow agriculture and intensified labor demands. As the landscape opened up and farmers improved the soil, fences to prevent animals from breaking into tilled fields became one of the area's permanent features. They signaled the continuous use of the land, which farmers stopped from reverting to weed and brush. The extension and intensification of land use induced a more pronounced pattern of labor demands over the year, a heightening of peaks and valleys already apparent in the number of man days necessary for the cultivation of Isaac DeWitt's Kingston, Ulster County, farm in 1823 (fig. 6).[28]

More improved land called for increased plowing. Among farm implements, the plow occupied the position of the "most useful instrument to the farmer," and it was the subject of the most notable technical improvements in the first quarter of the nineteenth century. The beginning of the

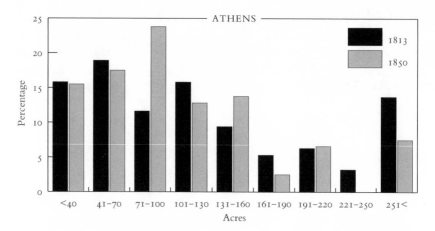

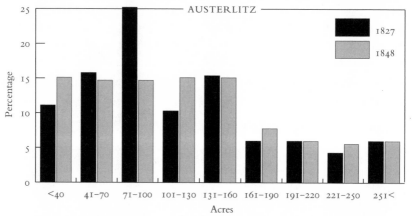

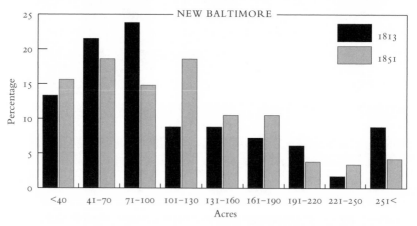

Opposite: FIG. 5. Changes in land distribution, Athens, Austerlitz, and New Baltimore, 1813–51, percentage of total number of farms. (Data from Greene County Property Assessment Roll for 1813, MV 109, GrCHS; Manuscript Agricultural Schedules, Federal Census for 1850; New York State Census for 1825, Austerlitz, Austerlitz Town Clerk; 1827 Tax Assessment for Austerlitz, ColCHS; Assessment of the Town of Austerlitz for 1848, ColCHS; Assessment of the Real and Personal Property and Tax Book of the Town of New Baltimore, County of Greene, in the Year 1851, New Baltimore ms. file, GrCHS.

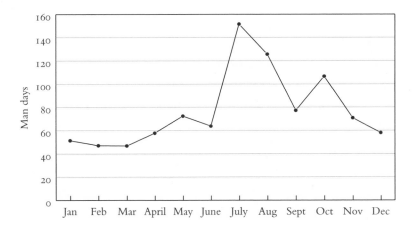

FIG. 6. Man days of labor on Isaac DeWitt's farm, Kingston, 1823–26. (Data from Isaac DeWitt Farm Account Book, Albany Institute of History and Art.)

Last Q 7th, 3h 58m morn | First Q 23d, 6h 49m morn.
New ● 15th, 9h 0m morn. | Full ● 39th, 10h 13m after.

ILLUS. I. Picking corn. (From *Stoddard's Diary; or, the Columbia Almanack* [Hudson, 1830]. Courtesy of the Division of Rare and Manuscript Collections, Carl A. Kroch Library, Cornell University.)

century saw wheel plows in interval lands and foot plows with mostly one, but sometimes two, handles on heavier or stonier ground. By 1826, the New York State Board of Agriculture rejoiced in reporting on a major advance in agricultural technology. The gain was not due to the efforts of gentlemen farmers. The invention of the cast iron plow owed everything to blacksmiths, who talked to farmers and observed them at work. Samuel Fowks of Catskill played a crucial role in the inventive adaptation and subsequent dissemination of the cast iron plow in the mid–Hudson Valley. An advertisement in 1821 explained the advantages of the castings, "which are so constructed as not to require any smith's work to finish them, and by which strength and durability are added to the plough, by the art lately discovered of hardening the metal in the three places most likely to wear, namely point, share and landside." Fowks's business prospered, for farmers quickly recognized an improvement that did not alter agricultural methods. His shop sold twenty-four plows at $8.75 in 1822 and eleven in April 1823 alone, and by 1824 a New York City newspaper reported that he had transformed his blacksmith shop into an air furnace that produced mostly plowshares.[29] The Board of Agriculture chronicled the proliferation of the new implement in the Hudson Valley and communicated that "the substitution of fallow crops [i.e., clover] for naked crops, a practice which is rapidly gaining ground and which greatly economizes labor is principally to be ascribed to the perfection with which we are now enabled to perform the operation of ploughing." According to agricultural reformer Jesse Buel, the cast iron plow doubled productivity between 1820 and 1840: it allowed a farmer to turn one to two acres of land whereas the wooden plow permitted only one-half to one acre in a day.[30]

Better plowing and new fodder sustained healthier livestock. They produced more manure with which to fertilize the soil once farmers collected it in stables, a practice that began after Robert Livingston described Hudson Valley agriculture in 1809 but seemed quite general by the 1840s when Barney McGuiniss spread manure for four days in April 1848 on Asa Beach's farm in Cairo. Labor organization proved to be the key to these improvements. To John Burroughs, cows represented the world in the 1840s, and "to keep her in good condition, well pastured in summer and well housed and fed in winter, and the whole dairy up to its highest point of efficiency," he recalled, "to this end the farmer directed his efforts." Constant attention to the needs of farm animals, not technology, increased output. No innovation eased the toil of milking and butter making between 1801, when J. B. Bordley detailed these activities in a handbook, and the 1840s, when every family member over ten years old lent a hand in milking and young Burroughs tied a big dog or a wether to the wheel of the churner. The intensity of labor increased, too, when sheep supplied fleece to the wool industry rather than satisfying domestic needs. If by 1810 "everybody [knew] that sheep live upon next to nothing," the concern for the quality of the raw material spurred better care of the animals after the 1820s.[31]

The apparent formal simplicity of farm tools, it is worth recalling here, should not hide their functional specificity from our retrospective gaze. The use of harvesting implements changed with the relative importance of the crops. A grain's place on the scale of appreciation determined by and large the way in which it was cut. At the beginning of the nineteenth century, when economic conditions and the attendant strategies compelled farmers to cling to tillage as much as stock keeping, they used sickles to reap grain. Edward McGraw "had seen many a harvest cut with sickles" in the Ulster County of his youth during the 1820s and 1830s. He recalled that "cradles were used as long ago as I can remember, but few [were] owned in the old neighborhood, and very few knew how to use them or cared to learn. They were not generally liked; cradling was called a wasteful and slovenly way of gathering grain." The shift from the labor-intensive sickle to the labor-saving cradle scythe to cut sheaves resulted from the reapportionment of tillage, pasture, and meadow on farms and the larger part that coarse and less nutrient demanding varieties took among grains. Lucius

Moll of Schodack recorded the cradling of oats and rye in 1821, but the treatment of the more delicate wheat was gentler: it was still cut with sickles, then bound (illus. 2 and 3).[32]

The changing mix of agricultural pursuits, their expansion, and the intensification of work in stables and fields altered the organization of work on the farm. Eventually it also affected the labor force. Recall that Chancellor Livingston took it for granted that farm families executed all the accruing tasks on their homesteads at the turn of the nineteenth century, while observers from William Cobbett to James Stuart considered family labor the rule in the northeastern United States. Its cause seemed self-evident to Thomas Hamilton, who wrote in 1831 that "the price of labour is high, and besides, it cannot always be commanded at any price. . . . What a man produces by his own labour, and that of his family, he produces cheaply. What he is compelled to hire others to perform, is done expensively." A great deal of ideology informed this view, for the Hudson Valley population had always pooled neighborhood resources to accomplish large-scale work efforts; harvests and house raisings imposed concerted efforts and collaboration and kept the postrevolutionary generation busily engaged in neighborly, nonmonetary intercourse. That situation, with its very specific organizing principles, no longer obtained in the mid–Hudson Valley after the 1830s. The market now limited problems of moral hazard with

1830. VIII Month, August, begins on Sunday, hath 31 days.

Full ● 4th, 8h 2m morn. New ◑ 18th, 6h 58m morn

Last Q 11th, 5h 13m morn. First Q 26th, 9h 8m morn.

ILLUS. 3. Representing the harvest of wheat. (From *Stoddard's Diary; or, the Columbia Almanack* [Hudson, 1830]. Courtesy of the Division of Rare and Manuscript Collections, Carl A. Kroch Library, Cornell University.)

rare, unruly, insubordinate, and expensive farmhands whom the Coventry cousins and their neighbors had refrained from hiring in the 1790s and 1800s. William Thomson noted their ready availability in northern Dutchess County, where, he discovered in the early 1840s, "farmers . . . have no difficulty in getting laborers." This was an important change: the reluctance with which farmers had occasionally engaged people to perform work had given way to hiring as a matter of course.[33]

Two features dramatize the coming of wage labor. For one, the combination of catch-up and fodder crops stretched the need for labor at a time when the rising number of animals, too, induced more steady work because cows required constant attention. As a consequence, the length of seasonal work agreements for male laborers grew from 4.2 months in the first decade of the nineteenth century to 6.6 in the 1820s and 7.1 in the 1840s. These men, by the 1820s, depended for the preponderant part of their living on the earnings they received as hired hands in agriculture. Remunerated labor was becoming a fact of life in the agricultural sector of the Hudson Valley. Although we cannot ascertain the extent of their seasonal employment, between one-fifth and one-third of farm families used the services of a live-in but unrelated laborer or female domestic over sixteen years of age in 1850 (the census was taken in June when, as labor needs on DeWitt's farm in Kingston suggested for the 1820s, jobs were numerous and work arrangements common in the area). A significant segment of the region's agricultural labor force subsisted on wages from April through October.[34]

Farmers employed more paid labor for longer periods as the century advanced, but its relative cost declined. The larger pool of women and men willing to hire themselves out seemed to keep their real cost to farmers down while the larger volume of produce increased farm income. Monthly remunerations for male laborers throughout the first half of the nineteenth century varied between $9.30 at its beginning and $10.50 in the 1840s, with the 1830s representing something of a peak when a male farm hand earned slightly more than $11.00 on average per month. In farm accounting, however, the proportion of these expenses diminished in spite of the rising tendency toward individual remuneration. Wages for yearly contracts with men, the first of which I located in December 1827 when Isaac Reed of Chatham hired Henry Van Hosen for "12 months for 100 dollars and do his own washing and mending with an allowance for 3 day and a half gratis," also showed a trend toward augmentation since they averaged around $106.00 in the 1840s. Overall, the proportion of labor cost to income on the farm at Great Imbaught was 57 percent in 1815–16. By midcentury, it had decreased to about 20 percent for Ephraim P. Best in Kinderhook; George W. Coffin in Amenia, Dutchess County; and Peter Crispell in Hurley, Ulster County, all of whom hired laborers for the year and the season.[35]

The extension of employment length distinguished a new labor force from the neighbors who still helped each other during the crest of harvest work, as when John Webster lent a hand to farmer Lowry in Hillsdale for ten days in August 1849 toward the end of the haying season. The neighbors stayed, but the seasonal laborers would eventually move on. They were young, more than half of them under age twenty, and on their way to acquiring both the skills and savings to settle elsewhere. Their part in the overall effort in Hudson Valley agriculture had become more important while the form of their remuneration was more particular. Seasonal contracts combined cash payments with board. The Hoffmans of Claverack paid their hand George $10.75 per month for seven months' work in 1847, the use of a house and a garden included. Ephraim P. Best "hired Dick Ebo for 7 months at a rate of $11 per month including old wood for 7 months which he is to get himself in his own time. The house he is to have for $20 per year for the sole benefit of himself and family. The house wrent to be paid out of his 7 months salary." Ebo received $5.00 for labor in December and continued to work at varying rates for Best through 1848. Of course, everybody engaged in a collective effort received rewards in kind. Asa Webster provided liquor to the people who helped him bring in hay in 1849. Itinerant William Thomson, who worked for a prosperous Dutchess County farmer in the summer of 1840 during his North American tour, delighted in an enumeration of "a piece of boiled pork, a piece of cold beef, cold mush (very good), flour bread, green Indian corn (smoking hot), cucumbers, pumpkin pie, silver spoons, clean knives and forks, water in clean tumblers, and a cup of tea after" that he was served during harvest meals. But if the purpose of shared meals and drinks was to foster a congenial work ambiance for neighbors and strangers alike, food and lodging were part of the wages for seasonal labor and hence remained subject to calculation and negotiation. The employer's authority showed in the deductions he made from the agreed-upon wage for days lost to sickness, military training, or public celebrations.[36]

Such stark asymmetry did not prevail between neighbors. Their interactions continued to encompass the swapping of goods and services as well as other gestures of attention. While the Olmsteds worked occasionally for other residents of Austerlitz in the 1830s, they received food and wood from them to make ends meet during the difficult winter of 1837. Lucretia Warner Hall "experienced much kindness from friends and neighbors." Births and deaths called for affective gestures that reproduced the social bonds in the neighborhood: Neighboring women assisted George Holcomb's wife in delivery, and Sara Mynderse Campbell sewed a shroud at the death of a neighbor's child.[37]

The nature of economic relations between neighbors changed nevertheless. The regular pooling of collective resources diminished. Common events like mowing bees that had astonished Alexander Coventry and kept his cousin William busy in the 1790s faded from the fabric of the district's social life. Extraordinary occasions such as accidents or house raisings still mobilized neighbors. But the cycle of agricultural labor with its everreturning harvest progressively appeared to be income-generating input in production. The new context lessened the significance of the exchange of hands as a link in the chain of prestations and counterprestations between neighbors and emphasized the market orientation of farm output. In the second decade of the century, Daniel Hatch of Canaan could still ascribe a one-for-all daily rate for the jobs that neighbor David Horton accomplished on his farm while Lucius Moll of Schodack participated for several days in Daniel Van Beuren's harvest without calculating a daily wage. These examples notwithstanding, the classification of work on farms grew more precise and insistent. The same Moll identified assignments on his homestead and allotted them different per day compensations in 1821: hoeing potatoes and corn in June was worth 4 shillings (50 cents), mowing grass in July came to 5 shillings 6 pence (about 69 cents), and cradling rye in July paid 1 dollar. What increasingly mattered was not the relation work created and sustained but its result. The transformation eventually affected families, too. Teenager William Hoffman drew a salary on his family's farm in the 1840s, and Wilbur Strong "threshed Rye for Uncle Joe in the afternoon for six pence a bushel" in 1858 at a time when Ephraim P. Best was charging his kin for the use of labor and implements.[38]

Authority and the Sexual Division of Labor on the Farm

The rise of a social order in the countryside in which wage labor became an everyday fact for the rural population must not, of course, obfuscate the continuity in the entire farm family's involvement with agriculture. "The family upon a farm in the United States must all labour," Isaac Holmes reported in the early 1820s. "The father, mother, sons, and daughters, must all work." Neither a task's inherent quality nor the difficulty of learning the skills it required implied the choice of a taxonomy based on anything other than the strength necessary to execute different jobs on the farm. And yet historical and anthropological research shows that gender played a considerable part in, even if it may not have presided over, the organization of agricultural labor. It most certainly informed the classification of tasks, often assigning inferior value to women's work. To raise the question of whether and how the increasing prevalence of the market principle in the mid–Hudson Valley countryside altered the patriarchal frame within which women and men still interacted at the end of the eighteenth century invites an analysis of social norms and an examination of the variance at which everyday behavior evolved from such ideal standards. This close look at quotidian practices in a circumscribed setting proves all the more necessary as historical writing tends to rely on discursive evidence or technological inference to broach very general assertions about the status of women during this epoch.[39]

A resident of the city of Hudson, Hannah Barnard charted prescriptions of conduct in rural households in 1820. Her awareness of women's vital contribution to the family's material existence clearly set her codification apart from the emerging urban middle class ideology of domesticity, with

ILLUS. 4. Women's work, men's work. (From *Stoddard's Diary; or, the Columbia Almanack* [Hudson, 1830]. Courtesy of the Division of Rare and Manuscript Collections, Carl A. Kroch Library, Cornell University.)

its stress on female superintendence of homes as sites of consumption and dispensers of health and education. Whereas people lived by working the land (and it is good to remember that this was the case for a large majority of the Hudson Valley population), acknowledgment of women's productive input in the reproduction of the farm household prevailed over the exposition of urbane ideals of republican motherhood and gentility. Barnard's tract reads like praise of manual labor and a diatribe against those genteel folks who did not "by any manual labour, increase the quantum of the real articles for human sustenance, or useful clothing, yet . . . were fed and clothed."[40]

The agricultural family, in Barnard's depiction, was a collective in which men and women joined their forces and talents to turn out a great many of life's necessities and certainly enough to engage in trade for the needed and desired goods they could not produce on the farm. Albeit distinct, the responsibilities of women and men were not exclusive and discrete (illus. 4). Barnard studiously rejected the division between a female world of reproduction and a male world of production—or the alignment of female with nature and male with culture. If anything determined the sexual division of labor, it was geography. Women tended to stay in proximity to the family's residence whereas men attended to activities located away from the home. Her domain extended to "the garden, cow-yard, kitchen and dairy room." She controlled the fire that heated the house and the soup pot; she cultivated vegetables and preserved and prepared foods; she fabricated, sewed, and mended textiles; she kept the house clean; and she also milked cows and churned butter. His main duties began in the barn and extended to fields, pastures, and woods. He was "hoeing corn, potatoes, mending fence, spreading manure." He cared for the horses and oxen that drew plow and wagon. This blueprint did not induce Barnard to intimate a ranking of male and female labor in which the former was both more arduous and more valuable than the latter.[41]

These norms provided no directions to guide rural women into domesticity. Even the boundaries between ascribed responsibilities were not hermetic enough to institute clearly gendered definitions of economic roles on the farm. If the marketing of agricultural produce in general accrued to the husband, the management of the dairy devolved to the wife's "mind, two hands, and bodily strength." It endowed her with the capacity to deal in the commerce of the goods she produced: butter and cheese. In the absence of the husband, his spouse walked "the rounds now and then, to see whether all is going right out doors." Conversely, men helped in transformative or preservative labor processes like "cutting and salting down meat." Barnard's recognition of the dignity and importance of labor performed by men and women in the maintenance of the farm and the procurement of its income did not, however, result in the acknowledgment of status equality between the sexes. Normal circumstances, so she postulated, put the male at the head of the household. Barnard tempered this patriarchal understanding of the family bond with a wife's almost organic and certainly indispensable consulting advice on matters domestic. She nevertheless endowed the pater familias with the power to direct the household and represent the family's interest in the world of politics, where he and his homologues deliberated "on the laws necessary to be enacted for the good of the community at large."[42] The family's sole breadwinner the father was not, but he surely occupied the position of an enlightened and well-meaning ruler of the farming realm.

Much evidence supports this prescriptive view of the sexual division of labor in the rural Hudson Valley. We have seen the Coventry cousins in the 1780s as well as the men of the Best family in the 1840s work in the fields. Women like Jane Claw of Coxsackie (who assaulted Samuel Burns in 1808 with "pails of Buttermilk and other Vessells of offensive liquid matter . . . which she held in her hands") and John Burroughs's mother, Amy Kelly Burroughs (whom he "never tired of seeing lift the great masses of golden butter from the churn" in the 1840s), ran or worked in family dairies, although all members of the Burroughs family "took a hand [in milking] when we had reached the age of about ten years, Mother and my sisters doing their share." A typical entry in Ann-Janette Dubois's diary read, "wash; hard work; then churn."[43] Historians of nineteenth-century northern rural development by and large accepted this conventional classification, discussing less its factual bases than the importance of women's indoor activities to total farm revenues. Had not the illustrious commentator Harriet Martineau portrayed the strict separation of indoor and outdoor labor along gender lines as the principal feature distinguishing the northern American from the European countryside? The less renowned but usually well-informed traveler James Stuart put a rather downhearted spin on American circumstances when he noted that "the harvest work being altogether performed by males. . . . , the cheerful appearance of the harvest field all over Britain, filled with male and female reapers and gleaners, is nowhere to be seen in this country."[44]

And yet economic reason would mandate that a labor-scarce environment like the Hudson Valley countryside at the beginning of the nineteenth century must mobilize all available resources to assure the most efficient production. How, then, do we explain the fading of the European tradition of female fieldwork in the face of the numerous and constant claims on the labor potential in the area? Historians concede that extraordinary pressures confounded the normative division of male and female labor; threatening rain, for example, brought women into the fields to gather crops alongside men almost everywhere. Besides, exacting conditions in the pioneering Midwest spurred the collaboration of women and men in sowing and reaping corn in the second quarter of the nineteenth century, a fact that invites a reconsideration of the received wisdom for longer settled and labor-scarce regions.[45]

It was actually routine for farm women to cooperate with men in fieldwork. When Robert R. Livingston, owner of Clermont Manor, composed his portrayal of American agriculture for the *Edinburgh Encyclopedia* around 1810, his immediate surroundings in Columbia County and its people's agricultural practices entered the picture. "Most of our farmers cultivate their farms with their own hands, aided by their sons when of proper age to be serviceable," Livingston wrote. Then he described the role of wives and daughters: "Women labour in harvest, and in haying, and in planting corn, before they are mothers, but very seldom afterwards; the care of their children, and their domestic concerns, occupy their time after this period." Livingston went beyond Hannah Barnard's normative discourse because he confirmed women's outdoor activities. But because he restricted these contributions to the period when women remained childless, he also seemed to corroborate her gendered geography of work while justifying it like the spokespeople of the urban middle class with women's nurturing responsibilities. Killian Scott, a farmhand born in Columbia County in 1785, entertained no such prejudices. He who had actually cultivated the land rather than merely observing people at work remembered on the eve of his life that "women worked out of doors in the field during harvest and haying."[46]

Agricultural development in the first half of the nineteenth century affected women's outdoor activities nevertheless. Its consequences on women's visibility had, however, less to do with ideological considerations than the reapportionment of the farming mix. Haying time remained one of the most strenuous periods of family work, and the expansion of meadow land in the mid–Hudson Valley may well have intensified women's collaboration. Ann-Janette Dubois helped her husband Peter Withaker "to finish the hay stack in the back field" or "raked after two loads of hay in Square lot," after which she felt "very tired." According to Burroughs, who recalled haying seasons lasting thirty or forty days in the Catskills during the 1840s, "the scythe, the handrake, the pitchfork in the calloused hands of men and boys did the work, occasionally the women even taking a turn with the rake or mowing away." On 14 August 1844, Thomas Cole observed that "Mr McDaniels & his sons & wife were making hay in the meadow." The Hudson *Rural Repository,* a genteel publication, depicted a woman with a rake in 1839 (illus. 5).[47]

Until the late 1820s, more grasslands had meant more animals. The shift in emphasis compelled women to spend more time close to the farmstead. Sheep required little supervision while grazing, although their fleece suffered from their freedom to forage near underbrush, but, as the New York State Board of Agriculture lamented in 1820, "as to the scab, the burrs, and the briars in the wool, that is the women's concern."[48] Cattle, as we have seen, induced a steady working rhythm. In Europe, areas specializing in dairy production showed a greater incidence of domestics per farm than those whose population cultivated grain.[49] In New York, this circumstance took a peculiar twist because the rise of the dairy state was predicated on female labor. It surely is no coincidence that dairymaids signed the first year-long labor contracts in the mid–Hudson Valley in the second decade of the nineteenth century (ten years before the first men in

ILLUS. 5. A break from haying. (From *Rural Repository,* 17 Aug. 1839, 33. Courtesy of the Cornell University Libraries.)

my documentation began to work for wages year-round), when butter and cheese production had not yet begun to suffer from western competition. Women earned paltry wages. Ruth Taylor and Phebe Spencer, who had yearlong contracts with Reynolds of Windham in 1811–12 and 1816–17, respectively, were paid thirty dollars. When hired on a weekly basis, they received seventy-five cents in the 1820s and not quite a dollar in the 1830s and 1840s. George Holcomb paid Fanny Roberts one dollar a week in 1832, but because she had shown some hesitation to leave home and join the Holcomb family he promised her "a set of silver tea spoons to cost nearly five dollars" at the end of her five-month stint. Despite this initial bargaining, the New York State Agricultural Society considered the low rates particularly propitious to the maintenance and even the expansion of dairy farms. "Another advantage of the butter dairy over wheat crops consists in the cost of the labor of production and transportation to market. The labor of females and boys is used mainly in the milking of cows and the making of the butter, which is cheaper than the labor required in plowing, sowing, and threshing the wheat and carrying it to market."[50] Within the patriarchal system, it was comparative economic advantages that kept women toiling in the stable and the dairy rather than the field.

The third change in Hudson Valley agriculture concerned the increased cultivation of coarse grains at the expense of wheat. While the former were harvested with scythes and eventually cradle scythes, the latter, more delicate and more valuable, was cut with sickles. The English experience suggests a male monopoly on the manipulation of this heavy tool, which doubled productivity. Sickles, however, were handled by women and men. And that was the case in the Hudson Valley as long as wheat remained important and the competition for female labor in dairy and wool preparation was low. Killian Scott of Hillsdale remembered that all family members worked outdoors with sickles to cut wheat sheaves at the beginning of the nineteenth century, an observation corroborated by Edward McGraw of New Windsor in Orange County, who had observed "men and women engaged in using them [sickles]."[51] The connection of crops with harvest technology thus diminished the place of women in the fields.

At this point, a synopsis of agricultural development and labor demand between 1800 and 1850 would state that a coalescence of factors led to the all but complete disappearance of women from outdoor activities except at harvest time: new technology engendered productivity gains, which reduced the number of hands needed in fieldwork, while the rise of dairy production, in which few inventions alleviated the execution of the diverse chores, created a stronger demand for female labor; and the emergence of wage labor facilitated the recruitment of both female dairymaids and male hands. This summary, however, proves insufficient. The transformation of the rural economy from tillage to a heavier emphasis on animals induced a modification in the region's crop mix. Agricultural reformers from Robert R. Livingston to Jesse Buel recommended potatoes and turnips as winter fodder for sheep and cattle. These vegetables required weeding and hoeing so that the effort of their cultivation was at least three times the input needed to grow the same unit of wheat or rye. Of course, turnips played a very marginal role in Hudson Valley agriculture and farms seldom contained more than two acres of potatoes (producing more than one hundred bushels). On these small and hence easily overlooked but labor-intensive parcels, women manipulated hoes and reap hooks. Ann-Janette Dubois planted potatoes (and occasionally corn) and pulled weeds. Lucretia Warner Hall in the 1840s and Hannah Bushnell in the 1850s toiled in the potato patches of their families' farms. Men, too, participated in these strenuous efforts, and on one memorable occasion Ann-Janette Dubois caught a glimpse of her "Father dig[ging] potatoes alone," which caused him to be "mad."[52]

In 1835 the Scottish traveler Patrick Shirreff "observed several women engaged in the fields weeding, cutting, and planting potatoes, and none of them seemed in poverty, or tinged with black blood. Mr. Stuart, in his *Three Years' Residence in America,* says, that women are not allowed to work in the fields, without saying whether the prohibition arises from custom or by law. Women are actively employed in different occupations when their services are wanted, which does not, however, often occur."[53] Shirreff caught a long-term trend. There certainly was a decline in the size of the female agricultural labor force in outdoor work. Harvests, however, still mobilized women and men and girls and boys in the 1850s, and this general mobilization suggests the suppleness of the sexual division of farm labor. No rigorous taboo prevented women from working outdoors. No transgression of a strictly enforced customary rule was necessary year after year to bring in crops and hay. Women's working sphere spanned the dairy and the plot of roots and legumes, which all continued to demand a great deal of regular manual labor. If the rise in importance of the cattle that tradition largely but not exclusively assigned to their care accounted for the increasingly larger chunk of time women spent with cows and in dairy production in the first decades of the nineteenth century, it may well be that this new demand resulted in a shortage of labor in grainfields, which sustained the adoption of the labor-saving cradle scythe to reap oats, rye, and barley. These properly agricultural developments, rather than law or social norm, explain the altogether relative absence of women from the fields, an absence that became the rule only when mechanical improvements enhanced agricultural and dairying productivity and forced women out of fields and butter and cheese making.

Before this momentous change at midcentury, agricultural development carried paradoxical consequences for women in the Hudson Valley. It brought about more repetitiousness in their tasks and maybe increased their burden in the productive process, but it also provided room for more independence from male control. Women were acutely aware that their endless toil contributed to the family's well-being and men were not the only breadwinners. Silvina Bramhell spun, dried fruit, and accomplished a heap of "other business," which included the making and commercializing of butter and cheese. Sarah Mynderse Campbell was "busy" during harvest time and often ran her husband's general store during his absence. The refrain of Ann-Janette Dubois's diary echoed her entry of 2 September 1837: "We bake pies; churn; I worked hard." Summing up her winter days in 1835, Lucinda Davenport wrote that "various occupations employ my time. Sometimes *sewing, knitting, spinning,* making scrap books when I can get wherewith to make them—performing the numerous offices of *cook,* seamstress, spinster, housekeeper etc. all in one day . . . I am continually hurried, and if interrupted at all, it is by another greater hurry."[54] Just as Hannah Barnard had outlined, women did not withdraw from gainful pursuits to achieve predominance in a domestic and restrained sphere. These income-producing activities enhanced the social position of rural women, and it inspirited them to sustain domestic conflicts, which Barnard quite naturally omitted from her manual.

Unlike their English counterparts, commentators on agricultural matters in the northern United States had no doubt about the importance of women in the successful home dairy as late as the 1840s. The measure of a farm wife's worth, Gaylord and Tucker asserted in their *American Husbandry* (1844), without frowning, consisted of her skills in producing marketable goods. "Every dealer in butter knows," they wrote, "that the most decisive test which can be offered of the skill and neatness of the housewife or the dairywoman, is furnished by the quality of the article offered by her in the market."[55] The implied autonomy of women in the marketing of dairy and farmyard products held true in practice. James Callanan paid "but little attention to the amount of butter and cheese manufactured, as my wife generally has the avails of them." George Holcomb knew what his wife was doing but did not interfere when she "carried butter and eggs and traded" them at the store for cotton yarn and other wares. Hannah Bushnell, whose family owned three milk cows in 1855, enjoyed the same freedom and was in charge of butter sales. On one occasion, she noted, "this morning Euralia and I went down to the store. Carried 5 lbs of butter got 2 yards satinett for Elijah, a pair of pantaloons, 5 shillings, yarn and some other notions." At another time, while "our folks picked a bushel of peaches and sold [them] to J. Drake," she stressed that "I sold 20 lbs of butter to day at 20 cents a pound."[56]

Butter money emboldened women on the farm and exacerbated latent conflicts. This income remained in the hands of the Dubois women in Catskill, but over time control of the purse shifted from mother to daughter. Soon after her marriage to Peter Whitaker, Ann-Janette Dubois scribbled in her diary in July 1838 that "Mother divide butter money with me." Two months later the entry read "mother divide money; give me 5 dollars." Ann-Janette "talked to mother about taking turns to do housework." Their relationship changed slowly, and in July 1842 Ann-Janette recorded, "I wash; Mother churn—I looked over my account with Mother;

she has worked 17 days more for me than herself." The daughter kept a careful tally: "Mother worked three days for me and milked 5 times." The balance of authority had tilted, and the management of the dairy proved a good indicator of a woman's weight in the household. This assertiveness transpired in Ann-Janette's marital relations. Although we will never know what happened between them when she wrote on 20 January 1840 that "Peter & I had much to say to each other," we may take this diary entry as an indication that she imparted her view of things and circumstances in order to modify her husband's.[57]

There was another development that fortified women's position. Nothing had changed in married women's legal subjection to their husbands between 1790 and 1840. Yet the proportion of property transfers in which women appeared on the deed increased from one-fifth to three-quarters between 1790 and 1827 in Columbia County.[58] Equally important, although not as pervasive a transformation, fathers now bestowed more real estate on their daughters. Joseph Peckham devised "to my eldest son Nathan Peckham and to my two daughters Sarah the wife of Henry Becker and Abigail Peckham . . . all my freehold estate in the town of Chatham aforesaid and elsewhere, share and share alike." Fifteen (39.5 percent) out of 38 wills codified in Columbia County in 1827 and 1828 bequeathed land to women, while 7 (18.4 percent) arranged for the sale of real estate in order to confer cash to both daughters and sons.[59] Geographic and occupational mobility transformed land into a commodity with which to raise money. The Dubois brothers left Catskill to pursue artisanal and mercantile careers. Members of the Pratt and Cady families moved from Austerlitz to western New York where they established farms. William Hoffman became a store clerk in New York and Calvin Bushnell learned the trade of a wagon maker.[60] This is not to say that women began to inherit the same amount of goods and monies, a problem difficult to address because of inter vivos devolutions. Yet less discrimination between real estate and mobile property in wills, the growing importance of monetary inheritance, and the waning imperative of the lineal family's attachment to the land improved the status of daughters in the configuration of heirs and in marriage.

In practical terms, if not in principle, this evolution strengthened women's position within marriage. Married women's property rights — the right to secure her property for her own use by means of a premarital settlement — entered the law books only with New York's constitutional convention of 1846, and, if we listen to the editor of the *Kinderhook Sen-*

tinel, the passage of such a provision meant that "the whole law of domestic relations is overthrown."[61] Unquestionably other societal processes, not least the ideologically inspired reform movements that often antagonized as many newspaper editors and residents as they mobilized, helped promote an improvement in women's status. Just as undeniably, rural development and the rise of a market society increased opportunities for farm women to generate revenues, which they then converted into a measure of authority. They used the conquered sense of strength to command new respect within conjugal as well as intergenerational relations.

HUDSON VALLEY farm families engaged in agricultural development to remain competitive in an increasingly commercial environment. They took advantage of the region's suitability for grass culture, plowed up the soil, and sowed it down in permanent, nitrogen-fixing grasses after timothy and red clover had become more readily available in the early nineteenth century. This resolution helped sustain the region's comparative advantage in the expanding market without, however, pushing it toward a degree of specialization that would have meant the end of mixed agriculture. The extension of grasslands, varying according to an area's distance from the Hudson, made the increase in stock raising possible and shifted the apportionment of farm labor toward the regular needs of milk cows while augmenting the land's requirement of plowing on farmsteads, whose improved acreage had, on average, grown in size. Soil exhaustion, easier importation of breadstuffs, and the growing demand for animal feed, but probably also the relative lack of hands, led to the substitution of less prestigious grains for the more delicate wheat, a modification that promoted the use of cradle scythes in the place of sickles. Because both the cow and the scythe connoted integration into a gendered division of labor, the rise of dairy production and the wider cultivation of lesser, larger grains heightened the appearance of discrete labor spheres for women and men whereas they simply intensified (and probably enhanced efficiency in) traditionally assigned tasks. The erroneous representation seemed to authorize the equation of women with nature and men with culture when in fact women continued to work outdoors in production on smaller, labor-intensive plots of land and during harvest.

The overall development created a greater demand for work, the most expensive factor in agricultural production at the beginning of the nineteenth century. It furthered the introduction of permanent wage labor. Three factors explain the ease with which farm families entered into the new kinds of social relations. First, better transportation and increased involvement in the market removed the fear of scarcity that had characterized farmers' worldview at the end of the eighteenth century, and increased material well-being benefited the majority of the agricultural population. Second, wage labor advanced slowly, although the second decade of the nineteenth century formed a crucial pivot in the transformation of the countryside and farmhands and dairymaids participated in family life and events. And, finally, if the rise of wage labor meant that "competitive small capitalist farms" dotted the landscape by 1850, as Allan Kulikoff has surmised, then we must also say that these qualitatively different social relations had not engulfed all aspects of life before the Civil War. Networks that tied the neigborhood together still mitigated the effects of development on farm families. Abner Austin's neighbors, artisans and farmers, had joined forces to rebuild his mill after a freshet destroyed it in 1822. Such collective efforts occurred less often and included fewer people as the nineteenth century advanced. Hannah Bushnell's in-laws "had a small bee to raise their house up about one foot" in 1856, an event whose rarity and narrow scope suggest the transformation of the countryside.[62] That such community efforts still occurred also proves the attachment of farmers to a meaning of work that remained social even as they moved toward an experience in which cash would function as the medium of exchange. But the shift in the forms of economic interaction denoted the advent of a new society.

FIVE

Country Shops and Factory Creeks, 1807–1850s

The coming of industrial enterprises to the mid–Hudson Valley owed a great deal to national events. "The late interceptions of our commerce have redoubled the attention of our citizens to the culture of raw material and the establishment of manufactures," the *Hudson Bee* observed in 1810. Six years later, the *Northern Whig* assessed the consequences of "the Embargo [that] swept our ships from the ocean—our trade withered—our sources of wealth dried up." Yet the article concluded on a somewhat more positive note: "It is true that a little relief was afforded a considerable portion of our citizens, during the latter part of the war, and particularly the laboring class, by the extensive manufacturing companies in our vicinity."[1] Failing importations from the British Isles incited merchants who had suffered losses at sea to invest in textile factories. They harnessed the waterpower of local creeks to supply the American market with cloth. Seth G. Macy, a former sea captain, built a woolen mill "being a permanent stone building, contemplated to manufacture 100 yards daily" in 1810. Merchants Thomas Lawrence and John F. and Seth Jenkins incorporated the Columbia Manufacturing Society in 1809 and hired Englishman James Wild to construct cotton machinery that eventually propelled fifteen hundred spindles. Wild left the partnership in 1811 to found the Kinderhook Manufacturing Society with his brother Nathan and local merchant Benjamin Baldwin. In the course of its thirty miles, Kinderhook Creek gave "motion to many mills," a gazetteer reported in 1836. It was "extensively employed for manufacturing purposes" and had "given rise to several manufacturing villages."[2] Other large-scale ventures took off in the second decade of the century to satisfy increasing domestic demand. By middecade, Joseph Foster and Nathan Clark of Athens were advertising large quantities of bricks for sale. William Edwards of Hunter and Foster Morss of Windham announced the introduction of tanning in the Catskills with their search for eighteen journeymen in 1817.[3]

Industrial development in the United States took a variety of paths. Historical accounts no longer depict the centralized factory as the embodiment of the industrial revolution. Lowell, that blend of entrepreneurial pluck and mechanical ingenuity, thrived alongside an elaborate putting-out system in rural New England and the single-trade town of Lynn, Massachusetts. The sweatshops of New York City and the foundries of Newark, New Jersey, formed part of a regional economic space. While machines replaced the human hand in spinning and weaving, other labor processes in the shoemaking and clothing trades achieved higher productivity through increased division of manual labor.[4] A rippled pattern emerged from the reverberations of industrialization on the economic structure of the countryside during the first half of the nineteenth century. Still, after tracing the multiplicity of change in rural Massachusetts, Jonathan Prude and Christopher Clark concluded that the rise of a poorly skilled wage labor force distinguished the transformation. Richard Stott surmised that "the victim of the expansion of semiskilled work was not the highly trained urban craftsman but the rural artisan and the farm wife—it was their work New Yorkers were taking."[5]

The growth of the manufacturing sector in the mid–Hudson Valley does not warrant such a saturnine assessment. Quite apart from the fact that overburdened wives welcomed factory cloth as a relief from one of their many chores, artisanal shops persisted while textile mills imprinted their character on some neighborhoods. The village of Valatie harbored the only tenements in the 1840s to house mill workers in Columbia County while George Doak went on manufacturing "cabinet furniture, such as Book Cases, Sofas, Bureaus, Dining and Breakfast Tables, of Mahogany and Cherry, likewise all kinds of Work Stands, Bedsteads, &c., made of different qualities of wood." Mosher's Mills on Lebanon Creek, which had given rise to "a small village with considerable mechanical and other business" by 1824, demonstrated the agricultural impulse behind local economies. When floods destroyed dam and buildings, the hamlet of Rayville, where artisans and shopkeepers occupied a cluster of thirty houses, began to function as the service center for the surrounding area in the 1850s.[6] Economic development expanded not only the number of jobs for workers but also those for artisans, and for a short period textile mills created opportunities for supplementary income from putting-out work for farm families.

In England, Raphael Samuels has argued, "capitalist growth was rooted in a subsoil of small-scale enterprise." A similar metaphor of organicity helped Jeremy Atack explain the survival of small industrial firms in the United States by pointing out their symbiotic relationship with large units. The Hudson Valley experience provides a richer and more nuanced view, for a look at its industrial structure reveals a segmented world. Its manufacturing sector contained two distinct components. The "extent of the market" accounted not only for the division of labor and the pace of growth and expansion, but it divided factories on creeks from shops in the country according to their location, origin, and level of investment, rhythm of employment, tools, and to a large degree recruitment of the work force. Change came with factories springing up on brooks around 1810 while continuity characterized many craft shops, although large-scale production of capital and consumer goods altered the skills required in some artisanal occupations. Whereas construction jobs or fine furniture making remained unchanged, the crafts of blacksmith and shoemaker did not encompass the same range of skills in 1850 as in 1815.[7]

Deskilling, many historians contend, was one of the causes of artisan radicalism in European and American cities, and among the rare occurrences of labor unrest in the mid–Hudson Valley the shoemakers assumed a preeminent role in the 1830s, for which they received a fair share of attention from an older, union-centered historiography. Conflicts erupted over the organization and control of the labor market. Masters strove to impose the market principle and more flexibility in hiring while mechanics fought to keep shops free of wage-reducing "green hands."[8] Such confrontations remained exceptional and occurred more often than not during widespread economic downturns. Crises revealed the vulnerability of workers and artisans, whose numbers had increased with industrial development and population growth between the Embargo of 1807 and the 1850s. The *Catskill Messenger* disclosed the ordeal of "those in the more humble walks of life" during the predicament of 1837 when it noted that "our village abounds with families of slender means who depend exclusively upon their daily labor for sustenance; who, while they can find employment, support themselves well," but who suffered hardship while out of work.[9] Artisans and workers got by in good times and thus saw few

ILLUS. 6. The mill village of Columbiaville, circa 1830. (Courtesy of the Columbia County Historical Society, Gift of the Estate of Sue G. Rowe.)

reasons to pursue aggressive conflictual strategies to improve their conditions in workplaces where they were few, but they rightly feared economic recessions, which threatened to push them into poverty.

Continuity and Change in Industrial Development

The agricultural economy of the mid–Hudson Valley forced artisans to live on the crest of local demand while textile mills, tanners, and brickyards largely depended on the state of the national market. Two- to six-story factory buildings on creeks where several dozen hands labored were the most spectacular structures created during the period of early industrialization (see illus. 6). But Stephen Whittlesey's 1805 advertisement for a 14 × 20 foot shop located near Adijah Dewey's tavern on the Susquehanna Turnpike and "calculated for a mechanic or merchant" remained the rule among nonagricultural work sites throughout the first half of the nineteenth century.[10] By 1850, almost three-quarters of the 641 manufacturing enterprises with capital above $500 counted in the federal census of Greene and Columbia Counties employed four or fewer workers and, to emphasize their differences, the largest 15 plants provided work for more hands than the smallest 500 shops taken together (table 12). The experience in

TABLE 12. Employees per Workplace in Columbia and Greene Counties, 1850
($N = 643$)

Employees	Shops	Total workers	Percentage of total	CUMULATIVE TOTAL	
				Number	%
1–4	478	982	23.5	982	23.5
5–9	73	459	11.0	1,441	34.5
10–14	29	341	8.2	1,782	42.6
15–19	18	296	7.1	2,078	49.7
20–29	12	276	6.6	2,354	56.3
30–49	16	532	12.7	2,886	69.0
50–99	9	525	12.6	3,411	81.6
Over 100	6	769	18.4	4,180	100.0

Source: Manuscript Schedules of Manufactures, Federal Census for 1850, Columbia and Greene Counties (microfilm).

the small shop was thus just as important, real, and typical as the encounter with the mill site.

Although the geographic distribution between mill villages and country shops hinged upon the availability of power sources, it also indicated the nature and extent of a shop or mill's market. Carpenters, blacksmiths, harness makers, wagon makers, and so forth served the needs of neighborhoods. Textile factories, brickyards, and Catskill tanneries supplied the national market, and with the exception of brickyards on the Hudson River they gave rise to compact factory villages where the families of their employees lived.[11] Distinct physical settings illustrated the dichotomy in the Hudson Valley's industrial makeup. The Kinderhook Manufacturing Society sold its cloth at auctions in Albany and New York and added Philadelphia in the 1820s, and Reed and Watson sent their textile goods to New York, from whence they were shipped "all over the country" in the late 1820s and 1830s. The construction boom in New York City after the recession of 1816–17 created a vast demand for Hudson Valley bricks; New York "is our only Market," three brick makers of Athens declared in 1820 when they employed "10 sloops . . . in transporting bricks to New York from all the establishments in this Village." And the immense quantities of leather tanned in the Catskills entered the market through the New York "Swamp," the metropolitan leather district.[12]

The integration of these industries into the extraregional market re-

TABLE 13. Capital and Employees per Workplace, 1820 and 1850

Workplace	Year	Capital	Employees	Capital per employee	N [a]
Textile mills	1820	$8,800	13.8	$638	5
	1850	$22,066	30.6	$721	32
Brickyards	1820	$950	10.5	$90	11
	1850	$2,991	19.0	$157	25
Tanneries	1820	$6,244	4.3	$1,452	22
	1850	$12,294	10.5	$1,171	24
Blacksmith shops	1850	$609	2.1	$290	62
Flour mills	1850	$4,595	2.0	$2,298	69
Shoemakers' shops	1850	$552	3.2	$173	53

Sources: Federal Census for 1820; Manuscript Schedules of Manufactures for 1850 (microfilm).
[a] Given the caprices of the 1820 census, this column does not represent any measure of industrial development.

quired much more capital than the establishment of country shops. At the outset of the sheep boom in the second decade of the century, it cost between $100 and $200 to acquire a carding machine to disentangle wool fibers before spinning yarn in farm homes; when prices for machines declined, so many people made the relatively small investment to start a carding business that the bottom fell out of the market. The ante was much higher for businesses that wished to compete in the national market. "Respecting a Slitting & Rolling Mill," Samuel Adams of Canaan wrote to John A. Thomson in 1817, "I would observe that, exclusive of the Mill Privilege & any uncommon expensive site for the foundation & Blooms of a Mill, & regarding use more than appearance, I should suppose $7000 would build works of that description in your neighborhood [of Catskill]."[13] As table 13 shows, this amount of money far exceeded the low-level investment necessary to set up a blacksmith's shop in 1850.

Where did incipient entrepreneurs raise capital? Financial institutions in the mid–Hudson Valley seem to have been unable to back industrial ventures. Freeman Hunt assessed the situation in 1837 in severe terms: "Columbia County ranks among the five wealthiest in the state, and yet it has but one bank located at Hudson, with a capital of but $150,000, a sum altogether inadequate to furnish accommodations to the business community of a county whose manufacturing, and other business operations, will compare with almost any section of the state." The limited availability of credit on a local basis left two other possibilities, both of which paper manufacturer Abner Austin explored in the early 1830s. "I constantly see the various amounts of money advertised in N. York to loan—but understand it must be on property in the City of N. York, and therefore have never tried to obtain it from there," he wrote to his local lender, attorney Elisha Williams. "It would suit me to owe the debt in N. York, there is the place of my greatest operations, & I would there best make myself known to the satisfaction of a creditor." The transfer did not work out, and Austin then considered putting himself "in the hands of Mr. O[rin] Day," a Catskill businessman.[14] Significantly, Austin did not mention a local bank as a source of capital.

Local support for industrial businesses was limited. Contrary to Jeanne Chase's suggestion that industries remained in the hands of Hudson Valley residents because metropolitan New Yorkers showed little interest in investing beyond the city's hinterland, New York funds increasingly matched monies put up by local merchants unable to pursue their maritime calling after the Embargo of 1807. The pattern appeared most clearly in the tanning industry. The erection of William Edwards's New York Tannery in Hunter was backed by Gideon Lee, Richard Cunningham, William Boyard, Herman LeRoy of New York City, and Joseph Xifie of Cuba, each investing $10,000 in 1817. Five years later, Jacob Lorillard of New York helped Edwards to buy a large share in the business. The New York Equitable Insurance Company and Charles McEvers injected more money into the enterprise, but Lorillard dominated the supply of hides and the sale of leather. Zadock Pratt also depended on New York merchants for finance capital and the purchase of hides in South America.[15] The development of the textile industry proceeded in various ways and did not progressively limit the sphere of action among its entrepreneurs, who reinvested their profits in improved machinery. After the initial combination of capital on a local basis and with help from state authorities in the form of loans, tax exemptions, and other prerogatives, metropolitan investors acquired stock. The Marshall brothers financed their print works on Claverack Creek with profits accumulated as operators and agents of a similar factory in Huddersfield, England. John J. Van Alen sold the Beaver Company to Abraham Godwin, Thomas Rogers, and John Clark of New Jersey in 1829. Benjamin Baldwin disposed of his share in the Kinderhook Manufacturing Society to Richard Lawrence of New York in 1837. Nathan Wild, considered an "ingenious mechanist" by the agent of Dun and Company in Columbia County, mortgaged part of his property to Seth Grosvenor, another New Yorker, in 1847.[16]

Local shops or stores mobilized family rather than metropolitan capitalists for financial support. Virtually all entries on small businesses in the credit report ledgers of R. G. Dun and Company contained information about kin relations. F. S. Lynes, a tailor with few assets, had "no wealthy relations," which presumably indicated the precariousness of his enterprise. The father of the Miller brothers, who ran a gristmill and general store, was a "rich farmer." Nelson Hyde sold dry goods and crockery in Catskill, and the "aid from Dr. Ford, his brother-in-law" averted doubts arising from his lack of sufficient funds. A network of indigenous and often related backers could launch an artisanal shop or a country grocery, but the passage from artisan to manufacturer or storekeeper to merchant was fraught with obstacles. Accumulation alone did not meet the requirements of expansion. For every Samuel Fowks, who successfully moved from blacksmithing into the casting of plows in an iron foundry in the early 1820s, there were fifteen Daniel Clarks in 1850 who still hammered iron into horseshoes on an anvil. For every Edward Brousseau, who came from Canada to Coxsackie in 1839 at age twenty to work in the brickyards and ended up employing thirty-five men in Stuyvesant in the 1870s, there were many hundreds of "Kanaks" who returned home. The opportunities and limitations of manufacturing careers appeared in the woolen industry, too. The boldest artisan–entrepreneurs successively amalgamated the different processes of wool preparation until they achieved a vertical integration that proceeded from carding, spinning, and fulling to weaving and dressing. In the most elaborate course of events, farmers consigned the entire fabrication to "a mill or manufactory, where it is put through a regular process, and one half of the cloth made from it returned to the owner of the raw material, without any expence save one-third of the cost of dressing." Most artisans, however, specialized in one or two steps of wool preparation, and like Moses Barber devoted their "whole time to carding country work," leaving other tasks to the family or different artisans.[17]

Artisanal shops providing ancillary services to farmers not only evolved with agricultural development; they also lived by seasonal rhythms. Henry Booth's carding shop began work in March 1808 when farmers were shearing their sheep. Busy throughout summer and fall, its machines stood still during the winter months. The conjunction of agricultural and artisanal labor more often occurred contrapuntally. Craftsmen left their shops during harvest to earn supplementary wages. John Burroughs described how coopers and blacksmiths hayed in the 1840s. Scotsman William Thomson, who traveled as an itinerant wool carder in 1841, hired himself out to cut and bind oats when the stream alongside his country shop in Dutchess County dried up. Shoemaker Lucas Moll of Schodack spent several days every year in the fields. His income from fabricating and mending footware from April through August 1818 hardly added up to 20 percent of his yearly revenue, a pattern that held true for farmer, sawmiller, and cobbler Daniel Hatch of Canaan in 1808. Similar seasonal cycles characterized the work of sawmiller Lester R. Skidmore at Union Vale in Dutchess County in 1822–23 and of Kingston tailor J. D. LaMontanye in 1835, both of whom divided their energies between major artisanal occupations and minor farming pursuits (Figs. 7–10).[18]

Factory work proved much more constant throughout the year. At the Kinderhook Manufacturing Society, Joseph Lathrop received wages for 326 days of labor in 1814, which meant that he occasionally toiled on Sundays, too. James Hawkins, who was part of his father's crew in 1815, was paid for 301 days. Across the Hudson River at Abner Austin's Paper Mill, George Gibbs's work days added up to 307.5 in 1825 and 306.5 in 1826. The same pattern appeared a generation later in a textile mill in Dutchess County, where J. Knapp spent 312.5 days in the factory in 1848 and 308.25 in 1849. Tanners in the Catskills also hired their workers on a yearly basis, and the advantage of a regular income rendered such employment rather more attractive. Indeed, master artisans promised "constant employ" and "steady support" in their job announcements so as to attract journeymen.[19]

Larger scale and regular, year-round business fortified factories against hard times. The agent of the Farmers' Manufactory of Cotton in Schaghticoke may well have described the fits of the market between 1828 and 1832 in terms of overstocking, relief, commotion, and loss, but the plant's nominal profits nonetheless oscillated between 7.5 and 15 percent, which provided it with enough robustness to weather contrary economic cycles. Others did not cope so well with the market's mercurial movements, and the mid–Hudson Valley had its share of tragic events. In 1816, Nathan Wild wrote to his brother James in England that "business continues as dull as ever. Cash is scarce and Failures taking place continually, the most prominent of which you will be the least prepared to hear is Ruben Folger & Son, 'tis said for seventy thousand dollars." Their own company, the Kinderhook Manufacturing Society, fared slightly better. "We have done nothing there since you left," Nathan admitted, but the plant survived tem-

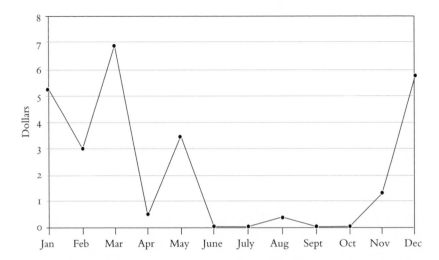

FIG. 7. Daniel Hatch's income from shoemaking, 1811 (in dollars). (Data from Daniel Hatch Account Book, NYSHA.)

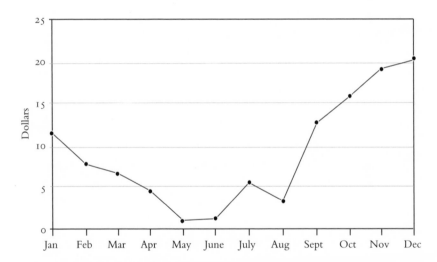

FIG. 8. Lucas Moll's income from shoemaking, 1818 (in dollars). (Data from Lucas Moll Account Book, COLCHS.)

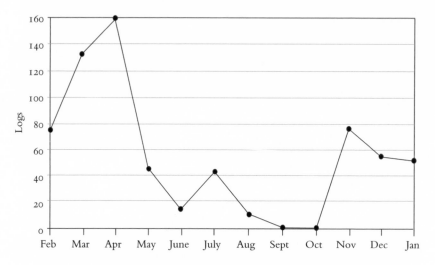

FIG. 9. Sawmill activities, February 1822 through January 1823 (in logs). (Data from Farm and Saw Mill Account Book, Dutchess County Historical Society.)

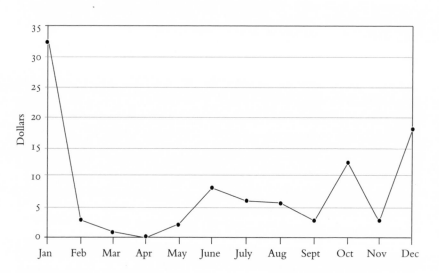

FIG. 10. J. D. LaMontanye's income from tailoring, 1835 (in dollars). (Data from J. D. LaMontanye Account Book, Ulster County Community College.)

porary adversities for the next generation. In October 1818, Abner Austin recorded that "to the surprise of many the failure of Ira Day became publick." Events took a sad turn six weeks later when "Ira Day hung himself in his garret—supposed to be occasioned by his failure in business—a most [illegible] & awful manner of avoiding trouble—said to be insane." Austin himself suffered losses of nearly $3,000 through failures between 1817 and 1821. The cause of a "bad year for business," crockery dealer Thomas Thomson laconically stated, was "markets completely glutted with European goods of almost every description."[20]

The mainspring of periodic hardship changed, but instability remained. In the mid-1830s, newspapers complained about "the slumber" into which the mid–Hudson Valley had fallen. Peter Ousterhout surmised that "in regard to our population 3/4 are bankrupt and 9/10 of them are in debt more or less." Francis Hopkins of Catskill informed Charles Hopkins in March 1842 that "all who come from Catskill lately speak of it as about used up & talk of emigrating." The same expression imbued a letter written by James Hopkins a year later when railroad speculation had ended in a burst bubble and brought ruin to Greene County. "The failures have decreased lately so that there's not more than one a week. This I suppose is partly owing to their being nearly all used up. But it is a sorrowful sight to see a whole village insolvent. To see men who were once in easy circumstances now reduced to want and poverty." Across the river in Columbia County, the agents of Dun and Company counted 332 "out of Business Traders" between March 1843 and September 1849. The tally, which included people who left as well as bankruptcies, revealed a turnover rate of 5 businesses per month. One-half of all enterprises in Columbia County, the large majority of which were one- or two-men ventures, had either changed owners or disappeared altogether during these five and one-half years.[21]

Individualism did not always preside over the ways in which entrepreneurs and master artisans grappled with economic difficulties. Corporatist actions aimed to counter the market's vicissitudes. When the number of wool carders pullulated in the 1810s and competition made that line of business a losing proposition in Greene County, they combined to keep prices high enough to guarantee the profitability of their cottage industry. The members of the Master Tanners Friendly Association agreed in August 1825 to control the price of hemlock bark, the raw material that had attracted their business to the Catskills, so that competition between them might remain on an equitable basis. During hard times in the mid-1830s, blacksmiths and carpenters organized meetings to establish common price rates among the members of their trades in Greene County in an attempt to rein in the volatility of the market and to enforce customary notions of fair remuneration. These guildlike economic organizations disappeared with the end of the crisis, and the market principle again ruled supreme.[22]

Artisans and Workers in the Countryside

Advertisements for jobs alert us to the composition of the labor force in the manufacturing sector. On the threshold of industrialization around 1810, the Columbia Manufacturing Society offered "Employment for Women and Children" while shoemaker John Starr sought to hire "two or three steady journeymen capable of performing men's work in the best manner." The demand for lesser-skilled hands in industrial occupations opened up employment opportunities for women and children, who remained largely excluded from the trades, where men enforced a monopoly on jobs through, among other measures, credentialing by means of apprenticeship. It comes as no surprise, then, when we find women in textile factories and larger shoemaker's and tailor's shops as custom work gave way to a series of single, routinized tasks. But job announcements not only exposed the normative view of the sexual division of labor in the industrial sector; they also hinted at the scope of artisanal and industrial employment. The proportion of locally oriented craftsmen remained stable at 15 to 20 percent of the total work force between 1820 and 1850, while the number of factory hands increased dramatically. Towns in Greene County listed between 15 and 26 local occupations (exclusive of trade and services) in which 1 in 7 people earned a living in 1850, about the same ratio as in 1820. But where factories existed in the mid–Hudson Valley this stable set of local producers was joined, and even in some places outnumbered, by workers in larger shops producing for extralocal markets. Of Kinderhook's total labor force of 1,253 men, 311 (24.8 percent) were employed in factories and shops in 1820. Thirty years later, however, there were 250 artisans and 421 factory operatives, 19 and 32 percent of the gainfully employed population, respectively.[23]

Wages that were high compared to the monetary (not the total) remunerations of agriculture accompanied the expansion of the industrial sector. In the textile industry, men's monthly payments were about twice as high as those of farm laborers while women earned three to four times as much as dairymaids. Such figures did not seem to impress observers, who had no apparent reason to share in an anti-industrial bias. A paternalis-

TABLE 14. Monthly Wages in Various Occupations, 1850 (in dollars)

Occupation	Wages	Shops	Percentage compared to textiles
Textiles, men	19.18	33	100
Textiles, women	12.43	33	100
Tailoring, men	26.59	15	139
Tailoring, women	9.51	15	77
Blacksmithing	23.64	65	123
Brick making	20.91	25	109
Carriage making	20.15	32	105
Furniture making	20.94	27	109
Foundry worker	23.84	12	124
Shipbuilder	38.89	2	203
Shoemaker	22.99	53	120
Tanner	16.29	25	85
All Men	22.43	243	117

Source: Manuscript Schedules of Manufactures, Federal Census for 1850, Columbia and Greene Counties (microfilm).

tic paper manufacturer with twenty employees in the 1820s, Abner Austin once remarked in a moment of unselfconsciousness that "our workmen are all poor, and must be paid as they earn, frequently before." And when Alexander Coventry visited the mill village of Columbiaville in 1828, he arrived at the same conclusion. "The operatives," he wrote, "get a bare subsistence: no instance having yet occurred of a single individual's having gained an independence."[24] The seasonal rhythm in agricultural and artisanal occupations, however, as well as rewards in kind and housing, make it difficult to assess intersectorial differences. It is quite plausible that regularity of employment was a major factor in attracting women and men to work in factories while high monthly wages promoted artisanal jobs. Indeed, monthly artisanal wages exceeded those of mill operatives by more than 20 percent in 1850. Relatively steady activities such as coach, carriage, sleigh, and furniture making offered payments exceeding those of mill operatives by 5 to 10 percent (table 14). Lower earnings were the tradeoff for steadier incomes.

These wage data concerned a mobile labor force. James Montgomery mentioned the rapid turnover of workers in his *Practical Detail of the Cotton Manufacture in the United States* (1840), an observation confirmed by recent studies.[25] No factory records survive from the mid–Hudson Valley that precisely measured the length of mill careers. Other evidence, however, is suggestive. Mary and Malica Segue stayed one and four months, respectively, at the American Manufactory Company in 1815. While the extent of the work force and the age of the youngest and oldest factory hands in Kinderhook and Stockport remained stable between 1855 and 1860, the average age of female workers rose from 22.6 to 22.8 years and that of male operatives fell from 30.1 to 26.9 years. These numbers hint at the temporary status of mill occupations in people's lives. The patterns of journeymen's existence in the countryside are difficult to trace, for no trade associations in the image of European *compagnonnages* provided institutional support and rituals for artisans on the road. Craftsmen did, nevertheless, travel from shop to shop. The Total Abstinence Society of Jewett in the Catskill tanning area lost almost 20 percent of its members to "removals out of town" in 1834, 1835, and 1836, a period of depression for tanneries. As early as the 1820s, the Master Tanners Friendly Association attempted to quell their journeymen's wanderlust by offering financial incentives to those who stayed for 3 years at the same workplace. During a strike of cordwainers and cobblers in Catskill, an article defending their cause in 1839 stated that "it is true, journeymen shoemakers have had a rather hard name; fifteen years ago, they were perhaps more given to roving about than other mechanics, tramping from place to place." Thomas Logan, a shoemaker, left Catskill to find work in Hudson in early 1836. Unsuccessful and unwilling to break a shop boycott organized by his fellow shoemakers, he moved on to find a position in Claverack.[26]

Most manufacturers were unambiguous about the reasons why female hands arrived at their mills: the prospect of significantly higher monthly wages than women could earn in agricultural jobs was the principal motivation. The owner of the Phoenix Cotton Manufactory in Middlefield, Otsego County, declared in the early 1830s that "the confinement of females so many hours in the day [twelve, that is], renders them unwilling to engage in this business without more wages than they could make otherwise." Thomas Dublin's research on the women at work in Lowell, Massachusetts, confirms this reasoning, and he also documented the sense of pride and independence these female operatives found in spite of unremitting and grating conditions on shop floors.[27]

No evidence allows for a similar portrait of mid–Hudson Valley mill sites, but at least two male witnesses noticed a sprightly quality among women in the factories. Their impressions cannot substitute for female voices, but they do open a window on the world of the mill village. Chandler Holbrook, an inspector for the Manhattan Fire Company who examined factory buildings in 1828, noted that mid–Hudson Valley mills provided constant employment to their workers. Then he observed that women's "wages being more than could be obtained by the hitherto ordinary occupation of housework—they [the female operatives] are enabled to dress with more neatness and taste." In Columbiaville, Alexander Coventry recorded the long hours of factory work. Yet he also saw "many good looking girls," which prodded him to speculate that "they submit to this constraint to acquire fine clothes and dress gay on Sunday: their hands can be kept whiter, their clothes more clean, than at Housework." However skewed this perspective on women's possibilities and goals in the job market and their position on the pay scale—after all, women's responsibilities in agriculture were consequential and went far beyond work in the house stricto sensu, between 1830 and 1850 the difference separating male and female remuneration narrowed. The relative improvement of women's position from roughly one-third to two-thirds of a male wage in the textile branch between 1830 and 1850 amounted, however, to a mixed blessing. While monthly salaries for female operatives rose from $9.50 to $12.43, men's fell from $24.36 to $19.18, an indication of the growing labor pool among the male population and of the effects of competition from women.[28]

Seasonality and gender-differentiated developments make it difficult to analyze long-term trends in manufacturing remuneration. According to Kenneth Sokoloff and Georgia Villaflor, artisans in labor-intensive sectors improved their real wages during early industrialization while workers in capital-intensive enterprises trailed behind. The decline of the wages of male operatives in textile factories corroborates the second part of the observation in the Hudson Valley. The lack of data and craftmen's irregular incomes combine to resist generalizations about the artisanal condition. Tanners, whose industry Sokoloff and Villaflor singled out for consequential growth in a capital-intensive business, did not realize any significant enhancement in Greene and Columbia Counties between 1820 and 1850, when their average yearly revenue rose from $189 to $196. In labor-intensive brickmaking, wages for the usual six-month employment period increased from $86 to $125.[29]

A most surprising picture emerges from a comparison with wages in

New York City. The average journeyman's yearly pay (except in tanning and brickmaking) was $184.00 in the mid–Hudson Valley in 1820, whereas a city craftsman earned $312.00. By 1850, the average monthly wage for a rural artisan was $22.43 (243 firms), whereas the average monthly wage in the city amounted to $20.70; women received $9.46 in the mid–Hudson Valley (based on 65 firms that employed women), while city jobs paid $7.70.[30] An appraisal based on the data of the 1820 census must acknowledge their shortcomings and a comparison of the rural and urban labor markets cannot overlook the seasonal impact that is likely to be bigger in the countryside than in the city. And yet in a period of thirty years the manufacturing sector in the countryside had done well and probably substantially caught up with that of the metropolitan area. It is clear that artisanal families in the mid–Hudson Valley did earn comparatively good incomes, especially in the presence of garden plots and lower rents. Indeed, puzzled census marshals in Greenville did not know how to classify "about 75 families" who lived on 150 improved acres, owned 75 cows and 100 swine, dug up 500 bushels of Irish potatoes, cultivated 500 bushels of Indian corn and 500 bushels of oats and produced $1,000 worth of orchard and garden produce in 1850 but were not full-time farmers. These were, in all likelihood, artisanal households. In 1825, fourteen out of the sixteen clearly identifiable families in Austerlitz whose gainfully employed men all ran or worked in craft shops owned cattle. William Thomson, the perspicacious Scotsman who journeyed through the Hudson Valley in 1841, easily picked up on the advantages a rural existence offered to artisans. He detected several weavers who lived in comfortable houses on a few acres of land and "owned a cow or two, a pig, some chickens, lots of Indian corn, and potatoes." He concluded with the observation that "emigrants of the handicraft class come crowding to manufacturing towns and well-known districts, where they frequently cannot get work until their means are expended: besides, they glut the labour market, when other places are in want of them: instead of which, if they would just shut their eyes, and walk twenty miles straight into any ordinary well-settled district, they would find profitable employment in this and many other ways."[31]

Thomson had a point: compared to New York City's 51 percent foreign-born residents in 1855, Columbia and Greene counties, with 44,400 and 31,100 inhabitants, respectively, counted 11.8 and 7.3 percent immigrants among their populations. Some newcomers had of course discovered Thomson's commonsensical notion before he had wandered through rural regions. And if we believe contemporary comments then these Euro-

TABLE 15. Employment of Foreign-Born Men, Columbia County, 1850

| Ethnicity | AGRICULTURE | | FACTORY | | CRAFTS | | OTHER | | |
	N	%	N	%	N	%	N	%	N
Irish	622	76.1	52	6.4	98	12.0	45	5.5	817
English	67	31.8	60	28.4	64	30.3	20	9.5	211
Other	188	70.4	12	4.5	67	25.1	9	3.4	276
TOTAL	877	67.3	124	9.5	229	17.6	74	5.7	1,304

Source: Manuscript Population Schedules, Federal Census for 1850, Columbia County (microfilm).

peans did have a tendency to flock to the factory creeks. In 1810, the *Hudson Balance* defended the contribution of manufactures to the area's prosperity with the indication that they were not detrimental to agriculture in that they siphoned off farm laborers, for "the principal workmen [in factories] are generally foreigners." The Marlborough Woolen Factory hired mostly Englishmen in the 1820s, and Alexander Coventry found that the calico printers at the Marshall establishment in Columbiaville were "mostly Englishmen, good sized, healthy looking men."[32] Census figures for the 1850s do not quite bear out these perceptions. Although three-fifths of the English immigrants found jobs in crafts and manufacturing, agriculture absorbed the majority of foreign-born residents in Columbia County, with three-quarters of Irishmen ending up working on farms (table 15). Among factory operatives in Stockport and Kinderhook, the two towns with the largest industrial populations, immigrants appear to have been overrepresented. Yet it was in the brickyards of Greene County, where work was seasonal, that native-born men were a minority and Canadians made up almost half of the work force (table 16). This, then, was a work force the recruitment of which assured it of an important new component. Immigrants helped industries in the Hudson Valley to grow.

The desire to escape poverty motivated Europeans to leave their continent and enter what one guidebook designated as "the paradise of the working classes."[33] By and large, immigrants to the Hudson Valley found an open labor market in which to make a living. The patterns of employment further indicate that skill rather than ethnicity determined a job applicant's chances of success, for the predominance of native-born men in the crafts did not prevent immigrants from entering these lines of work. While the Irish, who had come from the countryside in their largely rural country, ended up in agricultural jobs, they also found employment in the

TABLE 16. National Origins of Operatives in Some Occupations, 1850

Occupation	AMERICAN		IRISH		ENGLISH		CANADIAN		OTHER	
	N	%	N	%	N	%	N	%	N	%
Factory worker[a]	193	61.5	41	13.1	61	19.4	—	—	19	6.1
Brick maker[b]	121	31.3	74	19.1	3	0.8	189	48.8	—	—
Blacksmith[c]	89	75.4	18	15.3	5	4.2	—	—	6	5.1
Carpenter[c]	49	77.8	6	9.5	6	9.5	—	—	2	3.2
Shoemaker[c]	241	86.3	12	5.0	6	2.5	—	—	15	6.2

Source: Manuscript Population Schedules, Federal Census for 1850, Columbia and Greene Counties (microfilm).
[a] Stockport, Kinderhook
[b] Athens, Coxsackie
[c] Columbia County

region's crafts and factories. The English, the next largest foreign-born group in 1850, when their mother country was the most industrialized nation in the world, were divided almost equally among agricultural, artisanal, and industrial occupations, and we may infer from eyewitness accounts by Alexander Coventry and others that factory owners seemed to have prized their qualifications. Nationals of both countries were actually overrepresented in artisanal and industrial jobs, although the shoemakers, as the largest craft contingent, appeared to be the least open to foreign-born colleagues. The concentration of Canadians in brickyards, however, attests to the importance of social conditions in access to employment; word of mouth at home helped publicize job opportunities down south along the Hudson and bring about seasonal movements of migrant workers.

African Americans, who made up less than 3 percent of the population in the mid–Hudson Valley in 1855, confronted a very different reality. They faced a narrow spectrum of occupations. A traveler to the Catskill Mountains remarked upon the presence of black laborers in agriculture prior to 1820, and Edward Abdy observed "coloured servants" in the 1830s. The census of 1850 confirmed these views. Eighty-two percent of black men toiled in agriculture in Columbia County; seventeen (6.5 percent) of them worked on boats plying on the Hudson, three swung the hammer as blacksmiths, and a handful of others were employed as porters, cooks, whitewashers, waiters, or musicians. Martin Cross of Catskill and B. H. Greene of Hudson ran barbershops. Greene owned $2,200 worth of real estate;

Cross, whom the agents of Dun and Company described as the "King of negroes in this part of the country," had accumulated $1,200 by 1852. These amounts were substantial and spoke to the resourcefulness of the two black entrepreneurs in a severely confined environment. The boundaries imposed by white society on their existence appeared in reform efforts that proposed an African School in 1830 to groom black domestics and in the credit ledgers of Dun and Company, where one of Cross's entries states that he was "good in his way."[34] If immigrants could hope to do well in the mid–Hudson Valley as long as its economy was flourishing, discrimination was a sorry, ordinary fact of life for African Americans who had resided in the area for almost two hundred years.

Industrialization was changing both the circumstances and the profile of artisanal pursuits. Itinerant weavers and shoemakers had disappeared from the mid–Hudson Valley by the 1850s because cloth and shoes were cheaper to buy than to produce on the farm. The reconfiguration of society, which now included property-poor factory operatives and propertyless migrant workers, enhanced the status of artisans, whose inferior prestige had conferred on them a low rank in colonial America. There is, indeed, no evidence that they felt déclassé as a result of the effects of industrial development on their trades.[35] Technological innovations and increased division of labor, however, had altered the social relations of production in the workshop. The dimensions of the transformation come into view when we compare the fabrication of furniture at the beginning and in the middle of the nineteenth century. In July 1808, Martin Lane boarded for two weeks on the Reynolds farm in Windham and built 1 bureau, 1 painted bedstead, 1 wagon chair, and one candle stand; by 1848, a "cabinetware manufacture" supplied the local market, and in nearby Hunter the twenty men and thirty women employed in B. J. Wheeler's waterpowered plant turned out 16,000 chairs while P. Howard's factory produced 4,000 bedsteads with a staff of ten men in 1850. Specialization had brought shops into existence that produced only one article: horse rakes in Windham, steel forks in Ashland, plow castings in Taghkanic and Catskill, rocking chairs in New Lebanon, and 22,000 hat bodies manufactured exclusively at S. G. Bidwell's Hat Manufactory in Ashland.[36]

Shop and factory redefined the boundaries of their markets. The production of iron implements had moved from the blacksmith's to the better equipped furnace shop. Samuel Fowks cast plows; repaired wagons, shovels, chains, and candlesticks; sharpened drills; and ironed wheels and sleighs in the 1820s. Joseph McMurdy accomplished the same variety of tasks for the Bristol Glass Factory in 1816 and 1817. By midcentury, Carl Ludwig Fleischmann described the village blacksmith as a jack of all trades who could perform all kinds of labor on iron but did not use it as a raw material to mold implements. Durham blacksmith D. E. Rugg still bolted wagons, set shoes, ironed whippletrees, plows, and crowbars, and fixed and sharpened forks in 1846, but he no longer fabricated plows, hooks, hinges, shovels, spades, and tongues. Shoemaking saw an increasing subdivision of labor. Lucas Moll of Schodack had cut and stitched 82 pairs of shoes and boots in 1818; Daniel Ives fashioned "Morocco shoes" for Herman Miers's wife in 1824. A generation later, ten shoe shops with fifty-eight men and nine women in Hudson produced 36,265 pairs of footgear in 1850, roughly 550 per employee. Tailors seemed to have escaped the sweep of mass production at least until 1840 when ready-made clothes diminished their market share and relegated them to occasional sartorial luxury assignments on the one hand and continual repair jobs on the other. Henry Cherrytree had sewn shirts and a coat for Samuel Fowks in 1822, and in the 1830s Kingston tailor J. D. LaMontanye still created vests, pantaloons, coats, and shirts.[37] The development of a market for mass-produced goods had, it is worth repeating, two contradictory effects on artisans: more confined to repair assignments and tasks that required fewer skills and represented just one step in the productive process, the owners of small shops, if not their journeymen, had improved their social and economic condition.

The probability of prospering as a blacksmith, carpenter, harness maker, shoemaker or tailor in the mid–Hudson Valley was small. Millers, at least those who stayed in business in a period of concentration, did rather well: their numbers in Columbia and Greene Counties steadily declined, from 108 in 1820 to 69 in 1850, with the conversion of the area to more grass-based husbandry. The capital requirements for a mill (a dam, a building, a run) and real estate rose from about $2,200 in 1813 to roughly $4,600 in 1850 (illus. 7). Part of these more important investments stemmed from the rise in land prices, for no substantial improvements in grinding technology seem to have found their way into the mid–Hudson Valley. In 1803, the Rev. Clark Brown described Ira Day's flour mill in Catskill as "the most curious and complicated piece of machinery, which perhaps is of the kind in the United States." Its two waterwheels propelled four stones that allowed it to grind between 500 and 600 bushels of wheat into 125 to 150 barrels of flour per day, about 70 (or maybe somewhat fewer) per run. This output was impressive even by later standards. Within ten years miller William Youngs of Coeymans, just beyond the border of Greene County,

ILLUS. 7. Marks Barker's flour mill on Stockport Creek, early nineteenth century. (Courtesy of the Columbia County Historical Society.)

jotted in his diary, "grinding night and day—Make 50 barrels per day." Another forty years later, William Carter Hughes estimated that 50 barrels was a "good amount of business" for a typical country mill operated by two men. Although varying grain supplies and lack of wood barrels translated into uneven production, on an average, unhurried day in the second decade of the century Youngs seemed to have ground about 30 barrels of flour from 120 bushels of wheat or oats, which he then sold in the neighborhood or in Albany and New York.[38] In any case, millers distinguished themselves from other local artisans. As a group they fell into the more prosperous ranks of the area's inhabitants in the beginning and middle of the nineteenth century.

Outwork

If harvests pushed artisans into the fields when agricultural work became pressing, the difficult mechanics of weaving forced manufacturers to move this part of cloth production from the factory to farms and country shops. When putting out the yarn spun on water-driven jennies, textile entrepreneurs took advantage of the widespread competence of farm women to operate manual looms. While one advertisement claimed that looms and other mechanical devices permitted every farmer to have "a manufacturing establishment in his own family, under his own management," it was quite patent to see "female dexterity" in manipulating these instruments, and women used their cloth to settle accounts at the neighborhood store.[39] Indeed, domestic production of woolen or flannel clothing actually limited the market for imported textiles. Abner Austin, then still a storekeeper in Hudson, informed a supplier in 1809 that a few cotton goods usually sold in spring but "shirtings cannot be disposed of in this market to any considerable extent." Reuben Moore, also of Hudson, offered "his normal quantity of Home Manufactured Goods" for sale in 1815. This competition relied on the widespread diffusion of hand looms in the mid–Hudson Valley, where Horatio Spafford's *Gazetteer of the State of New York* publicized figures from Tench Coxe's industrial census of 1810 to indicate that one in four families owned a weaving device, a figure confirmed by an analysis of fifty-six probate inventories from the Austerlitz area in which fifteen households (26.8 percent) preserved a loom. As late as 1837, Kinderhook grocers J. and P. Bain still carried "Home-made Woolen Cloths, also low priced Broad Cloths" despite the stiff commercial rivalry of factory-made goods.[40]

Technical obstacles in the mechanization of weaving, not the rigid and insufficient urban labor supply and seasonal agricultural underemployment as in early modern Europe, obliged Hudson Valley industrialists to mobilize households to weave for their factories. The putting-out system saved them money because families owned the means of production. Between 1810 and 1830, textile plants spawned networks of rural industry on the east bank of the Hudson River. Spafford's *Gazetteer* described their setup in the article on Greenwich, Washington County, in 1813. "In these cotton factories, one of which is in Greenwich, and one in Easton, about 50,000 pounds of cotton wool are annually wrought into yarn, and a considerable portion of it into clothes of various kinds. They employ about 70 hands at the works; and from 100 to 150 families are constantly employed in weaving for these establishments." But the mobilization of family labor did not suffice to satisfy the needs of woolen and cotton mills. Manufacturers encouraged weavers to set up shop near their mill sites. The Leeds Woolen Factory in Amenia, a town in northern Dutchess County, offered employment "on liberal terms" to local weavers in 1810. J. N. Knight and George Cunningham announced in 1816 that they had "commenced the weaving of Cotton, Linen and Woollen, in its various branches, at the Shop of the Columbia Manufacturing Society" in Hudson. The result was the emergence of a belt of artisanal satellites that revolved around the central factory. The Matteawan Cotton Factory of Fishkill, Dutchess County, contained the insufficient number of fifty waterpowered looms in 1824 and hired out work to "about 60 handlooms . . . in shops and in the neighborhood." In 1828, *Niles' Weekly Register* reported, the Glenham Woollen Factory in Dutchess County, with 122 hands working "within the establishment," also enlisted about 30 weavers outside its mill. There was something quite symbiotic about these relationships between the central factory site and the scattered artisanal shops.[41]

The Kinderhook Manufacturing Society, besides employing about thirty hands in its factory on Kinderhook Creek, put out yarn to sixty-nine weavers between April 1814 and 1816. The factory faced at least one competitor in the Columbia Manufacturing Society, which had already begun to recruit outweavers, and so its agents followed the roads northeast toward East Nassau, Stephentown, even New Lebanon and Canaan and easterly toward Chatham and Ghent to find weavers. It is possible to trace thirty-four of the sixty-nine outworkers in the federal census of 1820: eighteen resided more than twelve miles (or about half a day's journey) from the mill; twelve made their homes in Claverack and Chatham, at a distance of four to seven miles; and four lived in Kinderhook. These locations covered a large district, and the length of the journey to the factory determined the number of deliveries per weaver over the two-year period. People from the periphery of the catchment area came to the Kinderhook Manufacturing Society 3.1 times on average, those living in the central plant's adjacent towns 3.9 times, and residents of Kinderhook 7.0 times. The manufacturers received 4.75 deliveries per month during the first year of the existence of this *Verlagsystem*. In the second year their number had more than tripled to 16.00 while the average conveyance rose from 77.2 to 114.6 yards. The amplification resulted from the increased involvement of families with a full-time artisan among their members. Robert Williams and Hassel Brewer, both engaged in industrial pursuits in 1820, wove 125.2 yards per month between October 1814 and April 1815 when they were the most active outworkers. A year later, John Nelson and James Nichols, both with manufacturing families in 1820, supplied 366 yards per month throughout the same period. Overall, then, families with a full-time craftsman played a more consequential role in the labor force because they produced more cloth and did so in a more predictable way than their farming neighbors (table 17).[42]

Manufacturers had two reasons to prefer artisanal to farmer's fabric. They could count on the regularity of deliveries, which helped reduce

TABLE 17. Outweavers' Production and Income, April 1814 through March 1816

| | TOTAL | | PER FAMILY | | |
Outweavers	Yards	%	Yards	Trips	Income
All 69 outweavers	26,399	100.0	382.6	3.6	$43.96
17 farm families	4,395	16.6	258.5	2.6	$26.21
11 artisans	10,008	37.9	909.8	5.9	$117.18

Sources: Kinderhook Manufacturing Society Journal, 1814–1816; Manuscript Schedules, Federal Census for 1820 (microfilm).

the amount of their frozen capital, for yarn in farmhouses restrained the sale of cloth. Because artisans depended on their income from outwork much more than farmers, whose earnings from weaving formed a supplementary, not the main, source of their livelihood, they were not only more regular but, if price serves as an indicator, delivered articles of better quality: they earned 25 percent more per yard than farmers, and no instance occurred in which the owners of the Kinderhook Manufacturing Society penalized an artisan for "damage of cloth" or "bad weaving." Nor did artisans neglect to return their goods to the factory, as happened with farmer William Chace of Chatham, whose default provoked a loss for the society.[43]

The decline of putting-out systems began with the introduction of power looms, first in cotton and then in wool weaving. The inability of mechanical devices to produce finer goods perpetuated the heterogeneous nature of rural industrialization. It allowed hand loom weavers to supply articles whose higher quality fared well in urban markets. But mechanization pushed prices down and squeezed handicraft shops out of business. The market value of cotton sheeting dropped from an average of 27.25 cents between 1812 and 1819 to an average of 11.30 cents from 1820 to 1827. If outworkers received approximately 40 percent of the selling price of a yard of cotton prior to 1820, a constant cost of their labor would have doubled the price of sheeting in the 1820s. "It has become more fashionable and cheaper," Sterling Goodenow explained not surprisingly, in 1822, "to dress in the fabricks of our rapidly increasing manufactories."[44] Rolla M. Tryon has argued that the growth of a transport system consisting of canals and railroads undermined domestic manufacturing because it made the products of distant, mechanical factories accessible to rural people. But mills on creeks dotted the landscape in the countryside, and the agent of the Glenham Company's factory in Fishkill dated the decrease in manufacturing costs to 1822 and the installation of power looms. William Crippen knew better, too. Long before steam engines pushed barges through artificial waterways and pulled wagons on tracks, Crippen stated in November 1820 that his shop, with one billy, one jenny, and three looms, "has not done anything for years." Competition from factory fabrics had wiped out his cottage business.[45]

Outwork had proved beneficial to manufacturers because it required little fixed capital at the onset of rural industrialization. Artisans and farm families used their own hand looms to weave cloth. The market for textiles was expanding, and demand outran the supply of fabrics produced in a labor-intensive process. The power loom reduced the cost of manufacturing by 50 percent according to the Glenham Company's calculation and by 80 percent if we believe the agent of the Utica Cotton Factory. Outwork had in a sense contributed to its own demise. It had helped to generate the profits that provided the basis for investments in labor-saving machinery. Eventually, farm families found it advantageous to acquire factory goods rather than spin yarn and weave cloth in their homes. Ann-Janette Dubois purchased muslin and calico in the 1830s, Ephraim P. Best bought "cloth for coat," and Hannah Bushnell picked up "20 yds factory cloth for 8 pence a yard, 5 yds cotton flannel—1 shilling a yd," prices that defied home manufacturing in the 1850s.[46]

Intimacy and Tension in the Manufacturing World

Industrial development in the countryside created two rather distinct work forces. While factory operatives toiled in a novel work setting that often imposed a degree of geographic mobility, artisans had traditionally passed through some form of apprenticeship and then pursued their trade as journeymen in ways that valued, and at times imposed, nurturing in mechanics' organizations.[47] Their dissimilarities notwithstanding, an attachment to the family as a model of labor relations suffused the social practices and the rhetoric of the industrial world in the first half of the nineteenth century. The uses of the family were multiple: whereas employers perceived it as a disciplinary agency, employees evoked it to emphasize their responsibilities for the well-being of their wives and children. As a social entity, an economic preoccupation, and a rhetorical image, the pervasiveness of the family furnishes part of the explanation for the smooth process of social change in the mid–Hudson Valley. Its real and symbolic presence in the factory and the workshop allayed unrest into which, elsewhere, dissatisfaction caused by industrialization occasionally spilled. Conversely, the absence of family ties allowed workers to quit their jobs when tensions arose with employers, an individual act that succeeded under favorable economic conditions. When times were hard, however, the fear for the family's subsistence heightened the sense of antagonistic interests and led to strife that took on a public character and caught the attention of the press and political as well as judicial authorities.

Families, of course, existed elsewhere, and ambitions to re-create close bonds with their workers motivated mill proprietors in rural Massachusetts and Philadelphia as well as the Hudson Valley. Paternalistic concerns about the proper conduct of women and men employed in factories motivated the organization of boardinghouses in Lowell and Waltham, Massachusetts, however much they served as instruments of social control. Similar considerations influenced Hudson Valley proprietors. In Matteawan, Spafford's *Gazetteer* reported, "a busy little village has grown up here, which now comprises 21 dwelling-houses, occupied by the proprietors of the works, the managers, workmen &c., and several more are about to be erected, all owned by the company." The owners enforced their moral vision through the prohibition of liquor and establishment of a school for children. Abner Austin of Catskill viewed his paper mill work force as a family. In 1826, he "cultivate[d] with my own hands . . . a very large garden, daily to provide for a family averaging over 20 souls."[48] Its members were none else but his male and female workers.

Note that families were in fact important in factories. They reduced transaction costs in hiring. Most of the wives of Abner Austin's workmen sorted and cut rags for the paper mill. Five of the 15 accounts for workmen in Austin's ledger concerned families in which both husband and wife had incomes from the factory in 1816. Austin also paid William Shortman's expenses in "moving your family from Kinderhook to Catskill." At the Kinderhook Manufacturing Company, the Hawkinses, Van Valkenburghs, and Vosburghs, all in all 17 hands, provided two-thirds of the original crew inside the factory walls between 1814 and 1816. The recruitment of family members did not just represent an early strategy to staff mills. In 1847, the owner of a textile plant in Dutchess County scribbled in the employee time book that "David Brown has a famely of 5 hands 4 Girls and 1 Boy — 3 of the Girls weavers — address Leads Green County N York — to be written to on or before the 1st Nov. [1847]." The utility of female spinners and weavers, whose earnings were low, propelled manufacturers to scour the countryside—and competing factories—for families willing to work in their plants. Paternal authority facilitated the initiation of novices into the factory regimen while family wages reduced labor costs. The employment scenario remained in place until the outbreak of the Civil War. Almost two-thirds of the 441 factory operatives in Kinderhook and Stockport had at least 1 other family member working in the same mill.[49]

Just as in families (or other moral communities), the collective partaking in comestibles and libations figured prominently among the gestures of employers to institute a sociable atmosphere on the shop floor. These happenings were intended to endow the workplace with stability. Abner Austin supplied homegrown vegetables and occasional meals at his paper mill. William Edwards, a tanner in Hunter, often shared breakfast with his journeymen from the 1820s through the late 1840s. Scottish wool carder and spinner William Thomson described his experience at a small mill in Washington Hollow, Dutchess County, in terms evoking the intimacy between master and journeymen in the 1840s. He "boarded with the Boss (at two dollars per week, including washing)," while his weekly wages varied between five and seven dollars. Journeymen and the boss's family shared breakfast, dinner, and supper, where "the workmen sat at table without their coats, with their shirt sleeves rolled up." Thomson recalled the "good feeling" that prevailed in the family and how, on his first Sunday, "the *Boss,* thinking, I suppose, I felt lonesome, asked me to go into the room, where his daughters were chattering, laughing, and amusing themselves. When they understood that I liked music, they sung me the 'Braes of Birniebousle,' and 'Jessie of Dunblane,' as pleased and as innocent-like as young lambs." The sheer number of workers in larger enterprises engendered difficulties for the construction of an image of shared interests, if not intimacy, between owners and operatives. Still, Nathan Wild purchased "20 lbs coffe[e]" for the hands at the Kinderhook Manufacturing Company in 1816. The owners of Wadsworth Woolen Factory in Poughkeepsie bought "food for support of laborers" at the beginning of the 1830s; in Livingston, the cotton manufactory of Reed and Watson spent a thousand dollars a year for "agricultural productions of the county" to feed its two dozen workers.[50]

And, just like in families, the fabrication of harmony in shops always contained the germs of dissonance and conflict. Close relations do not necessarily mean warm relations, and intimacy can also further friction and unveil concord as a fiction. Apprentices ran away. The situation at James Clark's store in Kinderhook seemed already tense when he and John Olmsted, his clerk, "had some talk." Olmsted reported that Clark "wanted to devil me and I would smile and turn up my face at him." The strain grew worse, and after a blowup, Olmsted left to take a clerkship in New York City. When tensions arose, manufacturers resorted to coercion. Abner Austin's employee Jabesh Crandal was "turned away because he would get drunk & abuse his family — and also neglect his business." Charles Wilson was "a pretty good Vat man — is a drunken man & much given to quarrelling & abuse — turned away for the above faults." The owner of the Bristol Glass Factory fined "Patrick Swift $5 for neglect of duty as a masterstoker on night of 11th inst. & 12th [November 1816]." From the opposite angle, however, the mobility of artisans and the turnover among factory laborers suggest that they rarely invested much energy in translating individual dissatisfaction into collective movements. Economic self-interest led them to negotiate their wages in good times. When things turned sour and departure did not seem to be an option, as in the case of a few local brick makers, they resorted to the courts to settle disputes over remuneration.[51]

The defense of a lifestyle with its autonomy, habits, and necessary income, aroused artisans, who organized journeymen's associations. After the master tanners had created their association in 1825, the journeymen did the same, "fearing an encroachment of our just rights from the meeting of Master Tanners, lately called, . . . [we] immediately form ourselves into a society for supporting our own poor, and defending these our rights to the last extremity." They did not explain their conception of traditional rights but resolved to "regulate the number of working hours in each day" and "to acknowledge no person as a journeyman tanner who has not previously served a regular apprenticeship to the trade." The issue of the regulation of the labor market to prevent the depression of wages as a consequence of the hiring of unskilled laborers resurfaced during the economic downturn in the mid-1830s, at the same time as the "United Society of the Journeymen Cordwainers of the City of Hudson" adopted a closed shop strategy to defend their livelihood. Seeing their wages reduced and perpetuated at a lower level because of an abundance of hands, thirty-five or forty shoemakers agreed that "no member should work for a boss who employed men who were not members. If the boss refused to give the price, the journeymen belonging to the society would not work for him." The same principle of having a say in who got hired prompted a shoemakers' walkout in Catskill in 1839 after a master had taken on a non–society member who worked for lower pay. The control of supply aimed at the maintenance of wages, which the masters were able to reduce because, so the journeymen protested, they could take advantage of their artisans' numbers and dependence on income from labor.[52] In both cases the masters had shattered the atmosphere of intimacy and paternalistic concern, and that breach of trust signified a new kind of relationship in the shop. Economic development had undermined the fiction of the atelier as family and transformed master and journeyman into employer and employee by the 1830s.

The organization of economic life stood at the center of the public and legal discussion of artisan activism. The dispute pitted models like the family against the atomistic, liberal conception of the most efficient allocation of labor. The district attorney who prosecuted the Hudson journeymen shoemakers in *People v. Cooper* did not contest an individual's prerogative to ask for higher wages. But, he argued, "they had no right to meet together and fix those prices by combination," an objection newspapers made in 1834 to the organization of master tanners intent on fixing the prices of leather and in 1839 to the striking shoemakers in Catskill. The prosecution's opening statement in the trial of the Hudson shoemakers explained the dangers trade associations represented to the social order: "The tendency of these societies was to restrain the free circulation of wealth through the country." The point here is less that the artisans had to stand trial even though the masters, too, circulated their own list of wages, which they sought to enforce citywide. Rather, the debate shifted from the primacy of moral relations to the active construction of a market economy in which individuals earned wages according to the laws of supply and demand.[53]

The journeymen contested the efficiency of the new principle because it did not guarantee them a decent living. The Catskill shoemakers developed their opposition into a practical initiative; they opened their own shop to bring home sufficient incomes. In Hudson, the cordwainers' attorney delivered an impassioned speech about the poverty that had impelled his clients to fight for "adequate compensation for their labor." The declamation freed them of the charge of combination and conspiracy, "rescuing the rights of the Mechanics from the grasp of Tyranny and Oppression." The real danger to the social order and its economic foundation came from masters, whose cupidity and greed deprived journeymen of the indispensable and deserved means of a decent existence. Organized artisans, their spokesmen insisted, were neither hotheaded nor misguided. They were men who assumed responsibility for their families. Elisha Babcock, one of the leaders of the Hudson cordwainers, was "a man of family," and the Catskill shoemakers emphasized that ten out of eleven strikers were heads of families. If, under other circumstances, family ties reduced the willingness to resort to strikes as means of defending one's livelihood, here the very anxiety about their families' well-being sustained the artisans' resolution to resist their bosses. While we do not know what became of the Catskill shoemakers and their cooperative workshop, in Hudson the family argument won them the sympathy of, and acquittal by, the jury.[54]

The motivation of the shoemakers in the mid–Hudson Valley did not proceed from consternation over deskilling or the opposition of a corporate, civic-republican ideal of mutuality and independence to the rapacious individualism of entrepreneurs, two causes adduced by historians to construe nineteenth-century artisan radicalism in a period of sustained economic development. The twin fears over the loss of skilled, well-paid jobs, which provoked alarm over the descent into economic dependency, on the one hand, and the concomitant assault on artisans' self-perception as stalwarts of the republican political order on the other, did not seem to inspire the cordwainers or the foundry workers who withstood the application of new rules on the Catskill shop floor of Griggs and Bullock in 1835. Indeed, both groups recognized the advantages of dividing the productive process into small tasks. There was no hostility to the "systematized arrangements of the respective operations" in the machine shop at Griggs and Bullock. The shoemakers of Catskill even stated that "it is true that Journeymen have refused to work at different branches of the business as they could not do it without great loss to themselves; in fact, most of them can work at one branch only." If artisans fought against the imposition of systematic surveillance on the job, it was wage consciousness and its relationship with family subsistence that drove their actions in the 1830s. Journeymen were willing to work hard, and they expected fair remuneration in return.[55]

INDUSTRIAL DEVELOPMENT created a segmented nonagricultural labor force after the Embargo of 1807. Although seasonality still shaped artisanal activity at midcentury, the occasional farmer-shoemaker, like fifty-nine-year-old Stephen Hedges in the mid–Hudson Valley countryside, was an archaic survivor of an older era. Large-scale production of consumer goods had favored farmers' specialization because the opportunity costs of home manufacturing grew too important to warrant its persistence on the farm. The largely native-born artisans, whose part in the working population remained stable but whose numbers increased with demographic growth, served the local economy, and within predominantly agricultural neighborhoods their revenues depended on the farming population. Factory operatives, among whom there was a sizable, almost 40 percent, segment of foreign-born individuals in 1850, worked on goods destined for mostly extralocal markets. Both artisans and factory hands seemed to have improved their financial circumstances between the 1820s and the 1850s. As long as economic conditions were auspicious, their living standards in a rural environment where they were able to cultivate a garden were certainly on a par with those of urban areas. But tough luck or an economic contraction revealed the precariousness of their existence. "I have heard no other news since you left except the death of young Smith of the upper village, a son of Mr. Smith the brickmaker," the wife of the Rev. Thomas Mallaby wrote from Athens to her absent husband in 1843. "He died of the bilious fever. They say he will be a great loss as he was the main support of the family." Bad times like those of the mid-1830s also bred artisan discontent, and, if "of all journeymen indicted during this period the Hudson shoemakers were the most audacious in enforcing the closed shop," it was an extraordinary event that differed in kind, not merely intensity, from artisans' usual conduct. As a matter of fact, stricter discipline increasingly characterized the workplace. The journeymen of the Bristol Glass Factory near Woodstock, Ulster County, celebrated Blue Monday in spite of sanctions meted out by their masters in the 1810s; the operatives at the Marshall Print Works north of Hudson did, according to Alexander Coventry, "sometimes keep blue Monday, and even Tuesday" as late as 1828, after which date the ritualistic habit of voluntary idling seemed to have vanished, for no later mention of it appeared in local newspapers or diaries.[56]

Economic and social change not only removed long-standing habits, but it injected new meaning into established institutions. Just as spatial and occupational mobility stirred up society in the mid–Hudson Valley as mill owners recruited foreign-born hands and farmers' offspring moved west or into artisanal jobs, the family became more important as a real and symbolic device of social integration and assimilation. It served as an instrument of labor recruitment, an organizational ideal type, and a voucher for morality. Its importance appeared clearly, although in negative form, during a cholera crisis in the early 1830s. It was the absence of kin that designated the suspected vectors of the disease. In the words of physician E. Pierce, the *Catskill Messenger* reported in 1832 that "as early as May last, it was evident that a disordered and relaxed state of the bowels was a general complaint in the village [of Athens], and particularly among those who had come in from the country around for the purpose of labouring on the brick yards, docks, shops, &c. — and nearly one third of our population is of this transient, floating character." The deficiency in personal, familial attachments in the vicinity distinguished this most modern work force. As long as the family presided in actuality or in spirit over economic development, growth delivered widespread benefits. But when it did not, it was only a small mental leap to transform working classes into dangerous classes.[57]

SIX

"Things, Not Thought": Wealth, Income, and
Patterns of Consumption, 1800–1850s

Economic development and increased market participation in the Hudson Valley countryside raised disposable incomes among its population in the first half of the nineteenth century. The effects were not lost on contemporaries. In 1828, the *Catskill Recorder* emphatically exclaimed, "ten years ago we had *nothing*—now we have *everything.*" Then the article listed sites and symbols of improvement. "Ten years ago we had indeed a highway through our streets—now we have side-walks and flagging which are not surpassed in this region of country. Ten years ago we had a sort of smoke-house upon the roof of our church—now a beautiful steeple, its spire pointing the way which we all wish to go—to heaven. Ten years ago we had watches, if we were able to pay the tax upon them—now we have a clock untaxable." Here was a revolution. However much we must inquire about the speed and comprehensiveness of the change in living standards to correct for journalistic hyperbole, the selection of timekeepers as tokens of material well-being suggests the rise of a new understanding of the world. Manmade schedules rather than the sun's natural periodicity took over the rhythm of daily lives. Timetables became, as we have seen, both an object of strife over norms in the workplace and a means of co-ordination of shipments on the river. Time turned into a scarce resource, the *Recorder* alerts us, precisely when industrial commodities whose prices declined with respect to those of agricultural produce entered the reach of the area's residents and acquired a more commonplace presence in their lives. The epochal shift concerned the gains in comfort: the mid–Hudson Valley population stepped over the threshold of scarcity into the experience of sufficiency.[1]

The countryside, where people were amplifying their involvement in extralocal commerce as producers of agricultural and industrial products, represented a large market for consumer goods. While American historians agree about the vast expansion of the number and volume of commodities available to consumers in the course of the nineteenth century, they disagree about the social effects of commercialization in the early republic. Taking their cue from Adam Smith's trickle-down theory on the diffusion of material goods by means of emulation of gentlepeople by the poorer sorts, Gordon Wood and Richard Bushman elaborate the economist's hypothesis into a confirmation of the American promise of equality. "In the nineteenth century gentility spread downward through the social structure to large segments of the middle class and, in small doses, into the lives of working-class people," Bushman observed. Wood offered the same assessment, asserting that "the blurring of distinction between gentlemen and plain people in America corresponded to a steady vulgarization of eighteenth-century gentility." The dissemination of articles of taste and the adoption of polished comportment led to the rise of a "middle-class order" according to Wood. Bushman surmised that "the spread of gentility confused rather than clarified the issue of class. For one thing, what did gentility mean when common clerks and small-town farmers lived in houses with parlors, read books, and tried to be mannerly?" Vernacular gentility, so these historians tell us, promoted a classless or, better, a one-class society in the United States of America.[2]

Scholars more sensitive to social discontinuities find much to amend—or complicate—the narrative of the peaceful and encompassing conquest of American society by vernacular gentility. Stuart Blumin has demonstrated that income levels and well-being, as expressed in material possessions, clearly differentiated the middle and working classes in American cities. David Jaffee showed that portraits delighted only people "who sought symbols of middle-class identity," not every inhabitant of the rural North. And Sally McMurry detailed the critique leveled by the agricultural press in the antebellum period against conspicuous consumption and its negative view of parlor culture as a wasteful outgrowth of ostentatious behavior.[3]

Yet we know little about patterns of consumption in rural areas. Probate inventories indicate the extent to which carpets, curtains, and pictures embellished homes—and, lo and behold, it was not as sweeping as the observations of the *Catskill Recorder* intimated (table 18).

The tabulation to measure the proliferation of paraphernalia of respect-

TABLE 18. Consumer Items in Probate Inventories, Greene County, 1801–50

Items	1801–10 (N = 27)	1821–30 (N = 46)	1841–50 (N = 41)
Carpets	2 (7.4%)	14 (30.4%)	17 (41.5%)
Curtains	3 (11.1%)	10 (21.7%)	14 (34.1%)
Mirrors	15 (55.6%)	28 (60.9%)	27 (65.9%)
Silverware	6 (22.2%)	15 (32.6%)	18 (43.9%)
Framed pictures	3 (11.1%)	4 (9.8%)	10 (24.4%)

Source: Probate Inventories, Greene County Surrogates' Court.

ability shows that their strewing remained limited even by midcentury. The circumscribed diffusion of consumer items ought to inflect any interpretation. It should also encourage historians to heed the precautionary advice of sociologists about the different uses of things. Technical qualities of goods never exhaust their social meanings and do not direct the modes in which people adapted them to different contexts and needs: family silver may have sentimental value or constitute economies for emergency expenses, carpets vary in quality, and watches lost social prestige as their price fell during the first half of the nineteenth century. This is not to deny the interest of an analysis in terms of luxuries and necessities. But critical prudence steers our attention toward the material conditions of life, and it invites an examination of housing and foodways before we conduct an inquiry into the dissemination and meaning of consumer goods.[4]

John Burroughs's recollections illuminate the process by which agricultural income helped buy mass-produced articles of merchandise that substituted for discarded homemade gear in the 1840s. And they illustrate the uses to which these goods were put. "When the produce of the farm was taken a long distance to market [in Catskill]—that was an event, too," he recalled. "Then the family marketing was done in a few groceries. Some cloth, new caps and boots for the boys, and a dress, or a shawl, or a cloak for the girls were brought back, besides news and adventure, and strange tidings of the distant world." These purchases served immediate, practical purposes. The Burroughs family, like many other residents of the Hudson Valley region, could not afford the luxury of refined possessions. Their acquisitions did not represent "the psychological competition for status." If, with Daniel Bell, "one can say that bourgeois society is the institutionalization of envy," then their example suggests that rural consumerism had not reached that stage by the 1840s.[5] Rather, the dissemination of everyday articles projects the image of a world whose demands remained moderate. Shelter, clothing, and food dominated everyday material concerns, but the residents of the mid–Hudson Valley countryside naturally found satisfaction and even pleasure when comfort was available. In other words, the quest for necessities, not luxuries, propelled the consumer behavior of the majority of rural dwellers. There was relief in escaping a world marked by the fear of scarcity that had informed the practices of everyday life among the valley's population at the end of the eighteenth century. Two generations later, a more confident outlook informed their conduct and anticipations.

Expanding opportunities and enhanced living standards did not prevent the exacerbation of social stratification in the mid–Hudson Valley. For instance, the proportion of residents who rented rather than owned their dwellings increased steadily between 1801 and 1821, a development that illustrates the uneven distribution of economic gains in a society that prized private property above all. Social discontinuities in consumer choices do not surprise. But these rifts replicated themselves along the same fault lines in a series of consumptions. The tie between getting and spending comprised a large dose of occupational determination because the differences in consumer behavior originated in the circumstances of people's work. Houses, gardens, and foods expressed the alignment of work and well-being. The great economic disparities among farmers obviously complicate this portrait, and yet the acquisition and possession of consumer goods helped congeal rather than confuse social identities.[6]

The distribution of consumer goods depended on merchants, retailers, and peddlers. They cultivated contacts in New York City. They knew local demand and evaluated what their catchment area could bear in commodities and prices and thus opened markets for goods on a larger scale. They also mediated between metropolitan and rural culture. Their role as mercantile and cultural middlemen has inspired many a historian to describe them as the central agents in the transformation of the countryside.[7] In the following pages, traders and storekeepers figure as promoters of rural consumerism as they offered an increasing range of things to their clientele. To be sure, it was the customer who, based on his or her family's financial ability, made the choice of what to purchase, and much of the following discussion will focus on consumers. But I will begin by examining merchants, and modes of merchandising, for these provided the specific means by which Hudson Valley residents were able to translate rural surpluses and village incomes into material possessions.

Merchants and Storekeepers

The cadence of the seasons inflected the flow of goods in the Hudson Valley because the river regulated the rhythm with which merchandise arrived in the countryside. Advertisements for "New Goods" appeared in spring and fall. New York City was where the area's storekeepers acquired their wares and perforce maintained accounts with wholesalers, which they usually settled with sixty- or ninety-day IOU's. During the first decade of the nineteenth century, Reuben Swift of Canaan journeyed to New York City where he did regular business with the firms of Lawrence, Van Sinderen & Co. and John I. Glover soon after the ice had disappeared in the spring and again just before the closing of the river in the winter. Catskill merchant Alexander Thomson imported crockery from Liverpool in England with the help of his brother Thomas, who resided in New York City. John Olmsted of Spencertown recalled his father's small country store in the second decade of the century from which "twice a year he went to New York to bring goods. It usually took him three weeks to make the trip and get his goods home, which allowed one week each way on the River and one week in New York City." The passage became shorter with the introduction of steamboats, but spring and fall still marked the busiest times for merchants and storekeepers. "Winter set in on Monday of last week in good earnest," the *Kinderhook Sentinel* reported in December 1844 under the headline "The Weather—the River." It continued, "there was a great stir among the merchants and others who had to go to New York to make purchases to complete their winter supply, and off they hurried to the 'Great Metropolis.' They were all fortunate enough to get up their 'goods, wares and merchandise.'" And during the summer slack in 1850, when he worked as a store clerk in New York, William Hoffman observed that "trade this last spring has been somewhat lighter than formerly. We anticipate a heavy fall trade."[8]

In 1821, William Dalton described the rural storekeeper as "a general merchant. He is a grocer, draper, mercer, haberdasher, spirit-merchant, corn-factor, &c.—his stock being formed of a multifarious selection of every article which he can sell." The depiction applied to the store of John and Tobias Teller of Clinton Town in Dutchess County; they kept an inventory of about 100 articles between 1797 and 1815. John Toffey of Pawling, Dutchess County, increased the number of commodities in his shop from 90 in 1824 to 119 in 1833. Both establishments offered textiles from calico to twist, foods and medicines from allspice to whiskey, tools and materials from axes to vitriol, and household goods from baking dishes to stone pots. As late as 1852, Carl Ludwig Fleischmann employed the same terms as William Dalton to portray the wide array of products presented in rural emporiums.[9]

Lack of specialization characterized a majority of distributors in the rural hinterland. But villages at landings and those fulfilling central place functions in the countryside became more specialized as the century advanced. Dun and Company agents delivered credit reports on forty-nine stores in Columbia and Greene Counties in the 1840s that suggest the decreasing homogeneity of economic space. Thirty-three among them were country or general stores. Sixteen establishments, located in Catskill, Coxsackie, Hudson, and Kinderhook, dealt in one line of products; Charles Whiting of Kinderhook ran a hardware store, and Solomon Cornwall sold leather goods like coats and shoes. Kingston, Stuart Blumin found, developed a specialized commercial sector between 1840 and 1860, and the first signs of the trend in Kinderhook appeared in the mid-1830s when a bookseller, a jewelry and watch shop, a stove and hardware store, and a hat establishment evolved alongside twelve dry goods and grocery dealers. In contrast, the fifteen entries in the Dun and Company ledger originating in Catskill Mountain towns carried the label of "country store" without exception.[10]

Little data survive with which to trace the evolution of store inventories in the first half of the nineteenth century, and wide differences marked the stocks-in-trade of individual firms from year to year and from landing to rural crossroads. George Crawford of Hudson, for example, imported a great variety of commodities worth $2,004 from New York in 1824–25, and $6,956 in 1826; he put the value of his inventory at $4,009 in 1826, whereas the probate inventory of Simon Sayre's general store in Cairo revealed $1,150 of merchandise three years later.[11] Table 19, though based on a small number of observations, suggests that retail inventories of general stores grew between 1790 and 1830, especially when we account for commodity price reductions as a consequence of the productivity gains in manufacturing.

Such capital requirements made partnerships in mercantile enterprises

TABLE 19. Average General Store Inventories, 1790–1830

Decade	Value	Observations
1790s	$1,771	4
1800s	$2,172	4
1810s	$2,831	7
1820s	$4,396	8

Sources: Moore and Burrel Ledger 1793–1794, GrCHS; Titus Bedell Papers, Business Group I, 1795–1796, NYSL; *Andrew H. Heermance v. Richard R. Lawrence,* Greene County Court of Common Pleas 1801, GrCHS; Reuben Swift Receipt Book 1802–1809; George Crawford Inventory 1816–1834; Jehoiakim Berg Ledger 1801–1818, 130, Rare Book and Manuscript Division, NYPL; John and Tobias Teller Day Book, 7 June 1815; *Rural Repository,* 3 Feb. 1827, 143; Probate Inventories of Richard Stone (1813) and Simon Sayre (1829), Greene County Surrogates' Court.

indispensable. Grocer J. B. Concklin "saved some $500 from wages [as a mason] & commenced a small grocery & afterwards took in his brother who had about the same," the Catskill agent of Dun and Co. reported in 1843. Solomon Cornwall began his store with $1,500 in 1838, the same sum Joshua Fiero initially invested in his dry goods shop with the help of an uncle in 1844. These amounts represented at least twice the monies needed to conduct an artisanal shop at midcentury. The launching of a store in the countryside required the coordination of resources because the purchase of goods was expensive and metropolitan wholesalers required at least some collateral to open a short-term credit line. The insufficiency of financial institutions to help capitalize country stores compelled aspiring entrepreneurs to look for associates, and kin relations figured prominently in sixteen of the forty-nine mercantile firms listed in the Dun and Company ledgers during the 1840s. James G. Foster was "perfectly safe with the endorsement of Edward Green, his son in law, who sustains him." Obadiah Lampman of Coxsackie received advice and help from his father, who owned a farm of more than four hundred acres. Milton Martin's father, a wealthy farmer in Claverack, supported his son's general store. "I think I will run the risk of making one bold attempt towards gaining a living by Merchandize," Solomon Crandell informed his parents after his term as a store clerk in Kinderhook had expired in March 1829. Relatives would support his business, and he did not consider a partnership with a stranger. Crandell concluded his letter, "Franklin says you must light a candle in

Mid-days sun to find an honest man."[12] Crandell's untainted (and maybe yet untested) faith in the integrity of family members provides another example of the ways in which commercial development depended on trust and strengthened rather than weakened family ties.

An increasing number of stores with growing inventories affected public perception of the difference that separated metropolitan possibilities of provisioning from the country market. If in 1815 the publisher of the *Catskill Recorder* acknowledged a certain backwardness, and consequently a more limited offer of goods among Catskill merchants, the selection of commodities available to the provincial consumer appears to have matched New York's abundance in the 1840s. By the latter decade, newspapers in the Hudson Valley were boldly comparing local merchants to those in the metropolis. The *Catskill Democrat* meant to boost hometown business in the spring of 1845 when its editor had "tried the experiment of buying goods in New York, and truth compels us to say that in both instances we have been *shaved* a trifle, and we do have in the stores of this Village, as full and as good an assortment of necessaries and luxuries either for external show or internal use, as will be found in the State, at prices which must suit, and that they will meet with as gentlemanly and upright merchants as ever measured muslin or molasses."[13]

Merchants as gentlemen and commodities as objects of conspicuous consumption and articles of common use—did the author of this account allude to the consequences of an economic development that not only brought a larger number of consumer items into the countryside but induced a realignment of social taxonomy in the course of which nonmanual businessmen climbed up the hierarchy and maybe even marked their ascent with the acquisition of luxuries? Expanding retail assortments certainly enabled consumption as a practice to be invested with new meaning. Let us turn, then, to the incomes generated by the new retail stores, and by farm and other sources of family revenues, to begin our investigation of the conversion of growing inventories to new ways of life.

Wealth, Income, and Well-being

When Solomon Crandell decided to enter a business career in the late 1820s, his experience as a store clerk helped him gauge his chances for success. Although the failure rate of any kind of enterprise in the countryside was high, merchants and retailers did well in the 1840s, when R. G.

Dun and Co. began to collect credit reports. A particularly conscientious agent related in March 1844 that the three country stores in Durham sold about $3,500 worth of goods per year: the Pierce brothers and Alfred Tripp transacted $4,000, while Reuben Pierce "sells 2 to 3^m $ a year." The seventeen dealers in Columbia and Greene Counties for whom the Dun and Co. ledgers yield the same information recorded average sales of $3,733 per year. Markups of 100 percent and overhead costs of 25 percent brought yearly profits to approximately $1,400.[14] This sum remained substantially below the revenues of nonmanual businessmen in Boston and New York, who cleared between $2,000 and $6,000 yearly. Nevertheless, general traders made good livings in the mid–Hudson Valley. An artisanal shop with capital of $500 or less realized an average gross profit of $702 in 1850, just about half the return a retailer could expect from a country store. Only those manual enterprises with capital of $1,500 made a similar gross profit at $1,528, although their average staff of four reduced the net earnings to a level still considerably lower than the income of a dealer in general goods.[15]

The difference that marked the incomes of artisans and merchants translated into different volumes of wealth. Eighteen men who ran freighting establishments at the landings owned $12,586 worth of real estate in 1850. Agents of Dun and Co. reported that Barker, Kirtland & Co. in Coxsackie was "called the richest firm here" in April 1850. Joseph Sherman was "one of the richest men in the town" of New Baltimore in August 1848, and Penfield, Day & Co. was a "very wealthy house" in April 1848.[16] Merchants were not as successful, but they managed to accumulate more property than their artisan neighbors. In a comparison of 1,231 artisans (40.9 percent of whom indicated real estate ownership in 1850) and 393 merchants (56.7 percent with real estate), the businessmen possessed 2.5 times more land than the craftsmen (table 20).

Farmers, who made up the majority of the work force, mix up the picture. Calculations indicate that a farm family's revenues varied from 5 to 15 percent of the homestead's real estate value. Such a proportion resulted in gross incomes that lay between two hundred and two thousand dollars and consequently covered the spectrum of gross profits among artisans and storekeepers.[17] This wide variety is not surprising—in all regions there are larger and smaller farms—nor should we be astonished to see in table 20 that in some towns the average real estate wealth of farmers exceeded that of merchants. Farmers made their livings from the land, while

TABLE 20. Real Estate Wealth in 1850 (in dollars)

Town	Artisans	Merchants	Farmers
Athens	1,150	4,138	3,815
Cairo	734	2,454	2,367
Catskill	1,288	3,468	4,722
Coxsackie	1,574	4,571	3,891
Durham	1,374	2,275	2,830
Windham	835	2,503	1,790
Austerlitz	1,141	1,333	4,288
Chatham	1,261	2,458	5,970
Hillsdale	1,499	1,900	4,951
Hudson	1,609	5,517	—
Kinderhook	1,304	3,329	8,970

Sources: Manuscript Population and Agricultural Schedules, Federal Census for 1850 (microfilm).

to merchants (and artisans) real estate was a supplement, an investment or in some instances a commodity. If we could add the value of inventories and personal goods to table 20 we would no doubt discover a clearer hierarchy of total wealth, one dominated by merchants not only in central place locations like Coxsackie, Cairo, and Windham but in peripheral towns like Austerlitz and the rich agricultural districts around Chatham and Kinderhook.

Among these occupational groups artisans were most vulnerable to economic adversities. In 1811, shoemaker Nathaniel Hinman detailed losses of $505 over a twelve-year period and claimed not to have reached any "better circumstances, as to property, than when I commenced business." Cabinetmaker John Morrison saw himself "after several years industry and tolerably successful labor . . . under the necessity of selling his situation in the village of Catskill." While in 1813 the average assessment of property holders in that village amounted to $2,297, twenty-four identifiable artisans owned $937 on average. A generation later, when shoemaker George Larned moved to Catskill, the agent of Dun and Company still commented, "there are so many shoeshops here he cannot well succeed." Michael Canover, a blacksmith and one of the few craftsmen who appear in the credit ledgers, was considered "good for small amounts."[18] The agency definitely preferred shipping establishments.

Although business cycles brought difficult times to the mid–Hudson

Valley, as elsewhere, permanent poverty among white people occurred rarely in the area. A list of nineteen indigent individuals of Coxsackie and Athens shows that they were either young children or elderly in 1815. The town of Austerlitz approved a yearly amount of $400 on average between 1818 and 1828 to support its destitute inhabitants, again either infants or seniors. Harriet Olmsted, whose household lacked a regular income, informed her brother John in 1834 of a coincidence of dire circumstances through which the family was "learning to live without eating, have been one week without flour." Theirs was a temporary deprivation. But conditions were changing. The construction of a poor house in Greene County in 1825 unveiled the contours of a rising problem. The *Catskill Recorder* observed an "alarming increase of expence" in poor relief, which had almost doubled from $575 in 1824 to $1,085 in 1825. In 1832 and 1833, the town meeting of Austerlitz "voted that no Cattle Run in the Highway" but immediately amended the regulation by registering "that if a man have but two cows they may run in the highway." The criterion included every artisan in town. It also evinced the town's concern for the working poor.[19]

Workers' lives were hanging by a thread because economic unpredictability could precipitate a fall into indigence, an invariant in the life of working people. An economic crisis or a string of bad luck could easily disrupt the existence of working families and erase the distinction between working and poor people. Public reactions to the calamitous years of 1817 and 1836 testify to the change in the perception of the most likely social categories to fall into poverty. Indeed, the growth of an industrial work force aggravated the problem of penury and added an unprecedented social dimension to the threat of hardship. "Soup for the Poor," a headline in the *Hudson Bee* announced in February 1817. "At no period since the incorporation of this city has there been so great a number of suffering Poor as at the present time. . . . Little do people in general know the extent of suffering and wretchedness at this moment, even in this small city. Many are for whole days without a mouthful of food in their cold and cheerless habitations; not only are they destitute of food, but they have neither clothing nor fuel." This generic and undifferentiated description of the poor gave way to a more circumscribed delineation over the following twenty years. In 1837, an appeal for charity stated that "the existing severity of an almost Greenland winter bears with particular rigor upon those in the more humble walks of life, and should stimulate the affluent and those blessed with an abundance of this world's goods, to seek out and relieve the necessities and sufferings of the poor. Our village abounds with families of slender means who depend exclusively upon their daily labor for sustenance; who, while they can find employment, support themselves well;—and who not having been accustomed to ask charity, prefer living upon scanty stores." In the process of economic development, the perception of poverty gained in specificity: work now figured at the center of social construction. Economic differentiation had brought forth a sizable class of people whose only resource was their labor, but their eagerness to work did not insure them against exposure to hardships. Able-bodied adults now found themselves, at least temporarily, on poor relief rolls.[20]

Thus, there was no mistaking the fact that the descent into poverty represented a real fear for working-class families, even if good times provided them with adequate means for living. Frugality presided over expenditures in workers' households. Balancing income and expenses proved difficult for the workmen at Abner Austin's paper mill in Catskill. Sally and Joseph Oliver were on Austin's payroll in 1818, and their account illustrates the thriftiness with which they spent their monies. When their garden supplied vegetables, the Olivers' store statement was in their favor. Through the winter, however, they accumulated debts. Although they showed savings of about 6 percent of their annual income in July, their deficit on the ledger at the end of 1818 amounted to 2.4 percent of their combined salaries (table 21), a small sum, perhaps, but large enough to demonstrate that their material lives were still precarious, for they had acquired only food and a few clothes during that year. The Olivers just managed to provide for their basic needs without running into excessive debt. And yet the accounts reveal that an emergency could easily shift the scales and wreak havoc on their existence.

Thomas Cole exclaimed in 1834 that "in this world, where to be poor is to be considered criminal, there is much to be suffered by those whose purses are usually empty."[21] His struggle as a young artist in Catskill differed from his neighbors' endeavors. Their wealth and income assured them a decent, if not always solid, measure of well-being. But dire straits threatened those with no other means but labor to support their families. Cole's reference to the purse was certainly idiomatic, and although he exaggerated fears when equating poverty and criminality his utterance pointed to a new social phenomenon in the Hudson Valley: industrial development had generated a group of people in manual occupations and under economic conditions that did not always protect them against want. In the next section we will take Cole's reference to the purse liter-

TABLE 21. Sally and Joseph Oliver's Income and Expenses in 1818 (in dollars)

Month	Income	Expenses	End of month balance
January	43.71	46.14	−2.43
February	35.56	33.74	−0.61
March	43.03	44.36	−1.94
April	43.01	36.54	4.53
May	45.79	49.53	0.79
June	42.67	29.35	14.11
July	39.46	23.82	29.75
August	31.21	41.77	19.19
September	34.32	35.41	18.10
October	38.62	44.13	12.59
November	39.63	52.49	−0.27
December	34.36	45.48	−11.39
TOTAL	471.37	482.76	−11.39

Sources: Workmen's Ledgers 1816–1820, Austin Collection, MV 1052, MV 1058, GฅCHS.

ally and analyze the ways in which people spent their money in order to learn whether consumption deepened or narrowed the fault lines between classes.

Neighborhoods and Houses

Housing manifested the hierarchy of wealth and the differing circumstances of merchants, artisans, factory operatives, and farmers in the Hudson Valley. Neighborhoods (just as central place theory suggests) mirrored the economic functions to which they served as habitats, and so they often attracted a quite homogeneous population whose concentration tended to express something akin to distinct local identities. Farmers (as noted in chapter 4) lived in dispersed settlements. The average size of a farm household in 1850 was between 5.0 and 5.5 people. In villages that provided services to the agricultural population, households were larger. The thirty-eight hamlets for which it was possible to collect information typically contained 23 houses in 1836 with an average occupancy from 6.25 individuals in West Coxsackie to 7.00 in Kinderhook. The landings at Athens, Coxsackie, New Baltimore, and Stockport, where commercial transactions made their mark on the goings-on in the business district, incorporated from 50 to 150 dwellings with the same number of residents as those in smaller villages. Catskill and Hudson, with 285 and 500 buildings, counted 7 individuals per home. In Columbiaville and Stockport industrial workers lived near their factories in tenements that averaged almost 10 people per flat. The dimensions of these buildings varied widely—the Olmsteds in Spencertown lived in 744 square feet in 1826 while hatter William Chapman in Durham occupied 1,512 square feet with his family in 1818 and Peter Crispell's farm home measured 1,056 square feet in 1847—and so we ought to be cautious in interpreting these numbers.[22] Nevertheless, the distribution indicates that residential clustering separated rather than united farmers, artisans, industrial hands, and merchants.

Economic functions and opportunities sorted out the places where the Hudson Valley's white population lived. Its black inhabitants suffered from the pervasive racial prejudices that imbued mid-nineteenth-century society, and housing segregation was yet another element in the discrimination. Sojourner Truth remembered the slaves' accommodations as being in cellars whose "only lights consist[ed] of a few panes of glass" and whose depths were "often filled with mud and water." She also recalled "a rude cabin, far from any neighbors" that the freed slaves of her family received in the environs of Kingston and Hurley. Hudson's black population was clustered on the edge of the city. In Kinderhook, Matilda Metcalf described "Guinea Hill, a settlement of negroes at a little distance from the village." Because their economic opportunities were restricted to a few low-paying occupations, the incomes of black families limited efforts to improve the quality of their dwellings. Metcalf described "huts [that] are of very rude construction, some of them partly underground."[23] Marginalized and underpaid, blacks in the countryside strove to escape deprivation and were fortunate to cover the basic costs of living.

Adjusting the focus to the smaller scale of homes, the connection between wealth and shelter appeared obvious to architectural writer and Hudson Valley resident Andrew Jackson Downing. He envisioned three types of country residence. "An industrious man, who earns his bread by daily exertions, and lives in a snug and economical little home in the suburbs of a town, has very different wants from the farmer, whose accommodations must be plain but more spacious, or the man of easy income, who builds a villa as much to gratify his taste, as to serve the useful purposes of a dwelling." Downing graded refinement according to income. He expected [good] taste to find its pinnacle and least inhibited expression at the [wealthy] top of the social pyramid. While his scheme had necessity-driven consumption at its base, Downing did not insinuate an imitation effect driving consumer behavior among those of the lower classes who meant to catch up with the trend-setting upper crust. In spite of this concession to the cultural autonomy of social groups, Downing was spontaneously carried toward the luxurious residences of the rich and spent little time on the dwellings of the majority of the population. "Many of our readers will be farmers of small means," he nevertheless speculated at one point, and they would "not expend more than $500 or $600 on a farm-house." In the mid–Hudson Valley, between 92 and 94 percent of all homes conformed to this description in 1855: frame houses whose common value stood at $491 in Greene and $615 in Columbia Counties. These were probably the buildings James Stuart, the Scottish traveler with an optimistic inclination toward all things American, had in mind when he judged "the permanent dwelling-houses [in the Hudson Valley] fully equal to the average farm-houses in Britain" in the early 1830s. In Downing's hierarchy these "average buildings" corresponded to the cottage, "a dwelling of small size, intended for the occupation of a family, either wholly managing the household cares itself, or, at the most, with the assistance of one or two servants." Such abodes were characterized by modest simplicity rather than costly refinement, comfort rather than ostentation. When their attributes expressed a search for notability, John Fowler priced them at a whopping $1,500 to $2,000. They were built of stone rather than the much more common wood, and only then were they comparable to English homesteads. This appraisal applied to fewer than one in twelve buildings in the valley.[24]

Building materials offered marks of social distinction. Although brick making was an important business on the banks of the Hudson River—both Alexander Coventry and the Rev. Thomas Mallaby commented on the "many brick kilns around the village" of Athens in 1822 and "Athens brick" in 1843, only one in nine houses in Athens was constructed with bricks by the 1850s. Brick houses, worth $2,618 on average, formed less than 5 percent of dwellings in Columbia and Greene Counties, and only the city of Hudson, where conflagrations had ravaged entire blocks of wood-framed structures early in the century, contained these more fire resistant houses, which accounted for one-quarter of its residences. Austerlitz in the Taconic Mountains and Windham in the Catskills contained no brick buildings at all. The cost of such constructions put them beyond the reach of the vast majority of Hudson Valley inhabitants. Among those who could afford tasteful dwellings (to come back to Downing's categories), nonmanual businessmen and professionals occupied a disproportionate place: they owned roughly 44 percent of all brick structures in Columbia and Greene, while the much more numerous farmers held 41 percent. Conveying their sense of social status and material success, former president Martin Van Buren of Kinderhook, cotton entrepreneur James Wild of Stockport, merchant James G. Foster of Athens all lived in expensive brick houses.[25] In one way or another, they were all persons of consequence in their neighborhoods, and though I do not want to overstate their presence, for they were few in number, it is this kernel of families that most resembled the emerging urban middle class. The breadwinners in these families pursued nonmanual gainful activities. If physical distance left them mingling with popular classes in the mid–Hudson Valley, their residences erected social barriers that clearly set them apart from those of their neighbors who made their livings in manual work. Type of dwelling was one of the clearest indicators of middle-class status.

The intrinsic advantages of brick over wood in the construction of fire-resistant houses certainly justified the extra expense and may have blurred their contribution to outward signs of distinction in neighborhoods. But the pecuniary standard of taste, as Thorsten Veblen labeled it, was unmistakable in the uses to which Hudson Valley residents put gardens. To agricultural reformers, who surely knew about the work-intensive efforts required to keep up kitchen plots, and foreign observers, who often seemed to forget these input requirements, most of the immediate surroundings of dwellings offered a rather sorry picture. In 1833, the *Albany Argus* urged farmers to pay closer attention to gardens because their produce enriched the kitchen table and added to the household's reputation and respectability. Farm families, and especially the women in a household, cultivated their gardens, albeit in ways that impressed neither James Stuart nor John Fowler, who considered them neglected and disorderly. But beauty lies in the eye of the beholder, and these judgments reflected gauges of order and financial investment that mattered little to farmers and artisans. People in the Hudson Valley understood the practical merits of greens and tubers: during the 1830s shoemaker Amos Chapman rented a house and garden from George Holcomb in Stephentown; factory operative John Bower cultivated cabbage, lettuce, onions, potatoes, and spinach in Pine Grove, Dutchess County, in the 1840s. Farm wives Ann-Janette Dubois and Hannah Bushnell worked and pulled weeds in their gardens in the 1830s and 1850s. They obviously appreciated the contribution of vegetables to their food basket, infused their efforts with pride, and found joy in their accomplishments, as when Caroline Morss of Durham considered it note-worthy to inform Frederick Kirtland that "Ma has peas in her garden."[26] If these people, all in manual occupations, relished the results of their garden work, they would not waste labor and money for ornamental purposes. Theirs was an aesthetics of prowess and utilitarian achievement.

Pleasure gardens, on the contrary, displayed their owners' ability to invest in nonproductive aesthetics. The aristocratic landlord Chancellor Robert R. Livingston and his family lived in "one of the most extensive and elegant county-seats in the state," the *Gazetteer of the State of New York* announced in 1813, continuing that "its gardens are extensive, in a high state of cultivation, and laid out with much taste." The emergence of a rural middle-class after the turn of the nineteenth century added, and can be perceived in, an intermediary mode between the courtly, ostentatious enjoyment of gardens and the popular, efficient cultivation of vegetable plots. Sarah Mynderse Campbell, the wife of a storekeeper in Schodack, noted in April 1825 that "we have been much engaged in laying out our garden. I worked very hard for me and [have] sown all my seed and set out all my flowers and herbs. We have laid out our garden very handsome, more so than ever, in diamond squares." Four days later she recorded that the garden was "handsomely laid out in order and beauty." Decoration and utility combined to create an original form that was labor intensive and required additional outlays for an obvious pleasure effect. The purpose of enchanting the eye complemented the garden's function as a supplier of foodstuffs in this mercantile family, a combination of the five senses and material rewards that sustained "rural felicity" according to a 1834 install-ment of the *Rural Repository*.[27] The faculty of allocating time and means to maintain the exterior appearance of houses and their close surround-ings (and then to write about it or, better yet, to have others rave about it in print) divided merchants from farmers and artisans as well as genteel families.

Interiors

In 1817, Henry Fearon journeyed north on the Hudson and stopped to visit Judge Verplanck in Dutchess County. Fearon explored the area and con-cluded that despite its reputation for rising prosperity "the general style of living consists of a plentiful supply of the necessaries of life, but few of what in England we should call its comforts." China crockery from Liverpool clearly fell into the category of luxuries, for which there was, according to merchant Thomas Thomson, only a small market in Catskill. Twenty years later, Richard Weston noted when traveling in the Tappan area of the Hudson Valley that "it is needless to mention the furniture of a farmer's house, for it is very simple; yet I have seen chests of drawers with crystal handles, and lamps made of glass in place of tin, which is very convenient, as they have no shadow. The farmers rarely study the luxuries of life; indeed, they cannot afford or easily procure these, and seldom even the necessaries." Weston then speculated that the ingenuity of rural dwellers sprang from the lack of a market in which to purchase tools and goods. In contrast to this somewhat glum view of country life, William Thomson described an affluent farm family's "comfortable little parlour, with a painted floor, a Yankee clock, and cane-bottomed chairs" in Dutchess County at the beginning of the 1840s. And when members of the Hoffman family in Claverack whitewashed their "little room," which may have served as a substitute for a parlor, in spring 1848 they removed a carpet, chairs, tables, a standing clock, and window curtains.[28]

These descriptions confirm other evidence suggesting the decent, if by no means lavish, way of life that was the rule in the countryside. Most interiors contained furniture that assured the degree of comfort to farm families that Adam Smith defined as "not only the commodities which are indispensably necessary for the support of life, but whatever the custom of the country renders it indecent for creditable people, even of the lowest order, to be without." But while the material living standard of people as well as expectations about it were rising in the first half of the nineteenth century, the acquisition of consumer goods did not respond to a frenzy for luxuries or items for ostentatious display. Cooking stoves, for example, became widely available in the mid–Hudson Valley in the 1830s and seemed to have entered the category of necessary household equipment by the early 1840s, when the Dubois family of Catskill acquired their model, because it facilitated women's activities in the kitchen. At the same time, however, the *Coxsackie Standard* detected in 1838 "a petty aristocratic narrowness of mind" among a number of the town's inhabitants, who seemed to prefer imported merchandise to what the journal facetiously called "vulgar" country products. The comment, uttered in a period of economic difficulty, aimed at defending local artisanal and industrial activity, but it also offers a clue to a development concomitant to the widespread improvement of material well-being. It hinted at the differentiation of consumption patterns in the second quarter of the nineteenth century. It was by no means accidental that the first issue of the *Rural Repository*, a magazine that emphasized genteel activities and aspirations (including the leisure to spend time reading a bimonthly publication), appeared in 1824. It targeted members of an incipient rural middle class in quest of self-representation, which they found, of course, in family portraits. Thomas Cole deplored the intentions (and maybe the parvenu awkwardness) of these people: "Those who purchase pictures," the artist complained in a moment of exasperation, "many of them [are] like those who purchase merchandise: they want *quantity*, material—something to show, something palpable—*things* not *thought*."[29] In short, they were engaged in conspicuous consumption so as to build and uphold their reputations.

Paintings and pictures in households indeed indicated social differences. Seven of the ten probated inventories that listed pictures in the 1840s belonged to men with mercantile interests: Joseph Seely of Athens owned a likeness of himself and one of his wife; in Prattsville, Joseph Sturtevent's estate contained one family picture and four other paintings; and Abraham Salisbury may have pushed vanity furthest with four family pictures, two of himself and two of his wife, worth altogether $25. But two humbler inhabitants of Cairo, Silas Scribner and Shubalt Lockwood, both assessed at less than $200 in terms of personal property, owned family portraits, too. The third, a farmer named William Stewart of Greenville, had a sizable library, lots of silverware, and person goods worth $450 besides his family portrait. While the propensity to decorate rooms with paintings was most pronounced in the households of businesspeople, it existed among wealthier farmers as well. Furniture shows a similar pattern. Shipper David C. Porter of Catskill owned two bedroom carpets and two parlor carpets worth $90; paper maker Abner Austin's front room was carpeted, and a "gilt-framed" looking glass decorated the wall. A few miles distant from Porter and Austin, members of the Dubois family embellished their farm home, too. Yet they produced rather than shopped for "window curtains with fringe on" and wove more than thirty-three ells of fabric, which grandmother, mother, and daughter cut into "rag carpet[s] for kitchen and bedroom."[30]

The configuration of ownership was less pronounced in the 1820s, when fewer of these goods and no family portraits appeared in probate records. The accoutrements in the household headed by storekeeper Simon Sayre of Cairo comprehended two carpets, one mirror, window curtains, and a wooden clock. They were not commonplace even a generation later. Master tanner Henry Ashley of Catskill accommodated his dwelling with Venetian blinds and carpets, while farmers Hiram Clarke and Benjamin

Decker of Greenville owned, respectively, a carpet and curtains. The most evident distinction in the first quarter of the century thus separated those who could afford uncommon commodities from those who could not, and within the first group the businessmen who owned several rare items from the farmers who possessed just one. The dividing line still held for such luxury goods as curtains and paintings in the 1840s.[31] Farmers and artisans invested in necessaries and income-producing assets such as livestock and tools before they acquired more sumptuous items for living, and so the axis that by then divided the haves from the have-nots when it came to the combination of luxuries such as paintings, carpets, and curtains tended to align itself with the division between manual and nonmanual occupations.

Household Budgets

Farm families spent an increasing amount of money at stores as the nineteenth century advanced. Ephraim Depuy was an average client of Abraham J. Hasbrouck in Kingston at the end of the eighteenth century. He disbursed $34.57 in 1798, yet only the spectacles he acquired on 16 February for 2 shillings 6 pence (about 31 cents) fell outside the categories of cloth, tools, utensils, and groceries. Half a century later, in 1848, Asa Beach of Cairo expended a total of $105.17 on goods and services at the shoemaker's and the general store. About half of these monies went into cloth and shoes, $14.88 (14.1 percent of the total amount) bought crockery, a few dollars purchased brooms and candles, and about one-third paid for such exotic foods as coffee, tea, and sugar. While Asa Beach brought his footware to cobbler James Rogers in the late 1840s, Ephraim Depuy and William Coventry had mended their shoes at home a generation earlier.[32] This development, a consequence of agricultural specialization and intensification as well as large-scale production in the shoe industry, helped substitute one indispensable commodity for its homemade equivalent.

No average or standard summary of expenditures survives from the mid–Hudson Valley to indicate how families spent their household money and operated arbitrages among competing budget groups. However, ledgers and account books contain clues to the careers of consumer items during the first half of the nineteenth century. Table 22 presents a synopsis of outlays incurred by three farm families in 1815–16 and around 1850. None of the three families paid rent, all had access to firewood on their farms, and they settled at least a portion of their debts in kind. The owner or operator of the farm at Great Imbaught in Catskill remains unknown,

TABLE 22. Mid–Hudson Valley Budgets, 1815–54

Purchases	1815–16		1846–47		1853–54	
	$	%	$	%	$	%
Merchandise/groceries	34.95	7.8	172.29	19.0	119.17	10.0
Miscellaneous						
Shoemaker	—	—	26.65	—	—	—
Clothing	8.80	—	17.85	—	—	—
Total	16.56	3.7	44.50	4.9	286.35	24.0
Newspapers/books	—	—	14.00	1.5	23.80	2.0
Minister's salary	—	—	25.00	2.8	—	—
Medicine/physician	—	—	—	—	26.00	2.2
Taxes	47.82	10.6	50.00	5.5	37.77	3.2
Total consumption	51.51	—	255.79	—	455.32	—
Total farm expenses	449.59	—	905.96	—	1191.56	—
Consumption/total expenses	—	11.5	—	28.2	—	38.2

Sources: Unidentified Farm Account Book, Great Imbaught, 1815–1816, N-YHS; *Transactions of the New York Agricultural Society* 7 (1847): 217–19; *Transactions of the New York Agricultural Society* 14 (1854): 120.

but his expenses concerned the household, in which there were "the boys." The accounts by Peter Crispell of Hurley, Ulster County, and G. W. Coffin of Amenia, Dutchess County, both concern small families that farmed about one hundred acres in 1847 and 1853, respectively, which assured them a place among the top 20 percent in the wealth distribution of their towns. Budgets, like snapshots, allow us to look at one moment in time and extract a rough estimate of household disbursements. However sketchy and uneven, the data at least trace the increase in expenditures. Their absolute as well as relative part with respect to total farm expenses (including wage payments) grew from one-tenth to about one-third of overall expenditures. Within the different budget lines, expenditures for books and newspapers by midcentury surely indicate the widening of the mental horizon of the valley's inhabitants while taxes in 1815 seem high compared to those at midcentury. Merchandise and groceries may not have grown in relative terms, but their consumption in dollars expanded greatly, a sign of the area's integration in wider marketing systems.

Groceries played a significant part in farm budgets throughout the first half of the nineteenth century. The farmer at Great Imbaught in Catskill bought exotic products such as sugar, molasses, tea, rice, pepper, and rum in 1815–16, and so did Ephraim Best in the 1840s, but in constant prices the quantities increased quite substantially. The Bests and the Coffins purchased not only groceries but also beef, indicating the growth of the cash economy and perhaps a proclivity to prefer finer cuts on the farm. Indeed, meat appeared regularly on the tables of the mid–Hudson Valley, so much so that owner-sponsored meals for workers at the Glenham Woolen Factory in Dutchess County contained meat and breadstuffs as staples. Widow Harriet Van Orden, née Schuyler, whose food budget for a family of five children accounted for almost 60 percent of her expenses despite a garden, bought fish and meat every week in 1834.[33]

Meat consumption serves as a good index of people's well-being. It also expresses something about the consumer's standing in society because, in the nineteenth century as today, beef, pork, veal, and chicken do not easily substitute for each other. Carl Ludwig Fleischmann described the "common doings" of farmers as meals of pork and cornbread accompanied by tea or coffee. "Chicken fixings" were rather more extraordinary, an observation confirmed in 1828 by Marks Barker, who, upon visiting an old friend on a farm in Ancram, received "an acceptable refreshment of a good dish of tea and stewed chickens." Turkey and fowls marked special occasions in the families of miller William Youngs in 1811 and farmer Vincent Morgan Townsend in 1834. At celebrations, geese and chicken graced the Dubois's table. Sarah Mynderse Campbell commemorated birthdays with "fine fat turkeys." On 24 February 1827, she noted in her diary that "yesterday it was eleven years since we moved to Schodack. We had a fine large turkey for dinner to cellebrate the day of joy that we have landed at Schodack, this happy place." Against common sense, the vast numbers of sheep in the area did not make mutton and lamb into items of general consumption. Two Scotsmen (who must have known) reported that mutton and lamb were of inferior quality and farm families disliked their cuts. So they sold the carcasses to the growing number of workmen. That market was expanding, and by 1849 the New York State Agricultural Society stated that mutton was on its way to become a staple food.[34]

Bread, by the way, was not wheaten for everybody. Having lost his way in the Catskills in October 1826, Thomas Cole happened on a log cabin whose residents shared a "plain supper of cheese, rye-bread and butter" with him. Sojourner Truth's *Narrative* implies that rye bread was something of a gratification for slaves, whereas John Burroughs considered it a normal part of his farm family's diet in the 1840s. Merchant widow Harriet Van Orden of Catskill got crackers and white bread from the baker. All in all, and not surprisingly, the choice of comestibles was more varied for Hudson Valley residents than European farmers. But the hierarchy of food-stuffs nevertheless reflected the pecking order among social groups: just as with meat, the whiter the bread the more becoming it seemed to the upper classes; only on special occasions would subaltern groups indulge in such treats.[35]

Miscellaneous expenditures included the purchase of cloth and cloth-ing, and dressing was enough of a matter of respectability to justify extra expenses. This was a limpid proposition at the beginning of the nineteenth century, when Horatio Gates Spafford reported, "in the country, among those immediately employed in husbandry, a large part of the clothing is *home-made,* while sabbaths and holidays are set apart for boughten clothes." Sundays, when the neighborhood congregated at church and tavern, im-posed different canons of decency. They had their monetary price. On weekdays, however, a "coarse, homely appearance in dress" distinguished the residents of Hudson as well as the farmers in the countryside. Martha Hoag of Coxsackie begged her relative James Van der Poel of Kinderhook to send her money in order to acquire winter garments around 1815. Noth-ing plush was required; she simply longed for a warm coat and boots to protect her against the vagaries of the weather. Baker John Ashley of Cats-kill suspected the seduction of fashionable clothing when he implored his clients in 1811 to settle their accounts with him before thinking about new apparel.[36]

The advent of large-scale textile production facilitated the acquisition of a more extensive wardrobe. Between the 1790s and the early 1820s, the average assessment of accoutrements in the probate inventories of Columbia County grew from $14.46 to $21.78, an increase that masked the presence of more numerous pieces of clothing.[37] Some observers be-lieved that one of the main incentives of factory labor lay in the cash with which to buy fashionable outfits. A generational effect appeared to drive the purchase of clothing. Like the industrial work force (which was, as noted above, quite youthful), young people seemed capable of satisfying their desires for stylish clothing and desirous of engaging in something ressembling the sporting life. George Haydock was in his late teens when he began to make a living, if not a fortune, in Hudson in the 1820s. He "soon had plenty of money and new clothes." With other young men he formed the "society of genteel drinkers, all well dressed, and having plenty of money to spend." That account probably failed to reflect the whole reality of the conspicuous consumption of clothing. After George Tipple's death in 1834, his employer, Abner Austin, wrote to Tipple's father in England, "during the last year in my employ, he clothed himself very well, & by so doing he ran ahead of his wages." The turn of events showed the risk that came with such spending for purposes of ostentation. And people knew. A friend of John Olmsted's commented in 1833 that "a double-breasted vest [even when worn at a wedding] . . . is a great vanity in the country," one that required a young resident of the Hudson Valley to sacrifice other, quotidian expenses. In the 1840s William Hoffman revealed the importance of clothing to young people when he bought boots and broadcloth, which he had sewn into a coat. It "suits me much and sits like a Pin," he noted, and continued that it was "also the first tight Bodied coat I ever had." Hoffman's personal expenses amounted to $37.72 between April 1847 and March 1848, $30.76 (81.5 percent) of which he spent on clothing.[38] This sum exceeded the value of an entire wardrobe thirty years earlier.

The eminently public role of clothing among male youths concurred with spending on entertainment. Farm laborer Egbert Miller purchased $17.94 worth of clothes and disbursed $15.00 on nights on the town in Kinderhook and after military training, respectively 27.6 percent and 23.1 percent of his wages during an employment stint on Ephraim Best's farm in the mid-1840s. Such outings also favored the consumption of other ephemeral goods. The son of a farmer in Dutchess County, Vincent Morgan Townsend lived it up in December 1833 when he "smoked two cigars at the Inn—Drank nothing," combining stimulants and good fellowship. Family life put a check on such expenditures. Recently married farm laborer Richard Ebo's sartorial expenses for himself and his wife came to $18.12, or 17.5 percent of his yearly wage of $103.50, while entertainment accounted for $6.85 (6.6 percent) when he worked alongside Egbert Miller and paid a yearly house rent of $23.00 (22.2 percent of his yearly wages) to his employer Best. The restriction, however, may have intensified the pleasure that came with such purchases, especially when experienced with members of the family. William Hoffman took note when his mother bought fabric and had it cut and sewn into a dress. Hannah Bushnell, too, delighted in a shopping trip in 1854 during which Calvin "got him[self] a pair of shoes; I got Aurelia a pair. Hers cost 10 shilling, his cost 13s." Then, she emphasized, "I got me a dress."[39] The memorandum reveals Bushnell's awareness of the experience's limits. Her satisfaction was evident—

ILLUS. 8. A farm family's ideal winter evening. (From *Stoddard's Diary: or, the Columbia Almanack* [Hudson, 1830]. Courtesy of the Division of Rare and Manuscript Collections, Carl A. Kroch Library, Cornell University.)

and counted: consumer excitement was an uncommon event whose price raised it beyond the ordinary course of rural existence.

THE AIR OF defensiveness with which the *Rural Repository* described an obviously idealized farming household in 1830 and the palpable satisfaction it took nineteen years later when portraying the pastoral, if fictional, country retreat of a prosperous family in the mercantile business hint at the social distance between entrepreneurs on the one hand and farmers and artisans on the other. Perhaps the evolving tone, and the greater assurance with which the magazine took a stand on the emerging social configuration, even signals how the changes in agriculture, manufacturing, and distribution affected, and effectively reinforced, the unequal distribution of consumer goods in the mid–Hudson Valley. It thus adds to the evidence of social processes that contributed to the constitution of class differences in the antebellum period. According to the *Rural Repository,* simplicity and frugality characterized the agricultural household. "The winter evening at the farmer's fireside is not as intolerable as many would suppose," it asserted euphemistically. "The log burns ruddily in the wide chimney, and the family are gathered around it" (see illus. 8). Material possessions changed altogether in the business class. A visitor entered the household through "the parlor, where one glance was sufficient to betray the hand of elegance and true refinement. Nothing superfluous—nothing wanting, for the union of comfort and beauty. The *fauteuil* and sofa invited repose; the unstudied display of books, prints and paintings promised luxury to the mind, while fresh flowers in antique vases grace every nook and corner." The ornate furnishings of the parlor stood in contrast to the parsimonious furniture in the farm's living room. While the women of the farm were sewing or spinning in the evenings when the family found time to gather, the parlor offered space for intellectual pursuits even in daytime. Without clearly stating it, the literary construct of the two lifestyles opposed the supposedly natural conduct on the farm and the social etiquette in the business household, which was one of the reasons why Andrew Jackson Downing saw little use for parlors in cottages. They would have disturbed the perceived unaffected, maybe even artless, mode of interaction and impede the functionality and efficiency of farm life. The *North American Review* carried condescension for manual labor further when it deemed parlors in the houses of husbandmen and mechanics incongruous and mocked their expression of social ambition outright, declaring that, in the unlikely existence of such a room on a farm, "the parlor is carefully shut up three hundred and sixty days in the year, and the family eat and live in the kitchen."[40] Laboring hands and gentility did not consort.

The distinction drawn by the *Rural Repository* between the plain living room in the farmhouse and the genteel parlor in the villa stylized differences, degrees and tinges of which we can locate in the everyday experiences of people in the mid–Hudson Valley. The presence of farmers, rich and poor, with their distinctive mode of life and the variety of their social and economic experiences complicates any description of patterns of consumption in the countryside. Nevertheless, it is possible to recognize a resemblance to the tripartite social configuration that came to characterize American cities in the antebellum era. The transformation originated with the growth of agricultural productivity and the fall of the price of manufactured goods. The first put more money into people's pockets, and the second augmented the number of goods within the reach of rural inhabitants. Economic development enhanced differences in revenue, which in turn distinctly shaped the social experience in the countryside. Wealth proved less determinant for well-being than disposable income. Farmers' assets were tied to their land. They increased their property while subjecting them to substantial maintenance costs without freeing much of their income for sumptuous expenditures. The mercantile community chose differently. Its members generally earned more than husbandsmen, and the divergence showed. It was not just that merchant Klein's daughter received piano lessons from an Italian maestro in Catskill during the second decade of the nineteenth century. Storekeepers and merchants were more likely to live in brick buildings with more space than farmhouses, a bifurcation that appeared clearly in women's household tasks. Both Ann-Janette Dubois and Sarah Mynderse Campbell described their housecleaning. Whereas two generations of Duboises scrubbed and whitewashed floors and walls in the kitchen, the cellar, the bedrooms, and the garret of their farm, Sarah Campbell hired Black Betty and Caty Miller to scour and polish shop, hall, rooms, and parlor in her mercantile home. Hudson Valley residents in nonmanual occupations consumed beef and veal with wheaten bread rather than pork and mutton with rye or corn loaves. They acquired a series of objects that expressed their aspirations toward urbanity. Finally, they could pay attention to beauty in gardens and paintings in ways that people in manual occupations could not. Even their social activities set them apart: while farm wife Hannah Bushnell went to singing school and practiced her voice as well as her conviviality, merchant widow Harriet Van Orden paid to attend monthly concerts. Hers as well as her relatives' was a style of life that befitted the distinctive social identity of the middle class. The top of the social pyramid regrouped the proprietors of large landed estates, who drew, like the members of the Livingston family, an important part of their income from rents. They lived in "gentlemen's seats, many of them extremely handsome," a fact that did not escape Fanny Trollope when she journeyed up the Hudson in the late 1820s. They engaged in pursuits "like the English gentry, cultivated the mind, and followed certain traditions and manners," as one of them—somewhat nostalgically, it is true—described their lifestyle to Alexis de Tocqueville in the early 1830s.[41]

Economic development benefited a large majority of the Hudson Valley population. Abraham J. Hasbrouck's average customer family spent between $30 and $40 per year on merchandise at the end of the eighteenth century. By 1855, per capita expenditures reached between $25 and $29 at groceries and retail stores alone in the mid–Hudson Valley. Much of this money served to buy commodities that replaced things no longer produced on the farm or wares that rendered life more comfortable without making it a stage for conspicuous consumption among farmers and artisans. Maybe it is this general improvement in living standards that Richard Bushman had in mind when he asserted that the impulse toward refinement tightened America's social fabric, for "the realm of beauty and taste

knew no bounds." After all, young schoolmaster Wilbur Fisk Strong revealed a penchant toward vanity when he "bought 3 yds flannel at 3/ pr
yd. 3 yds satinett at 6/ pr yd. 1 looking glass &c. to the amount of $5.25"
in 1858.[42] It is certain that the people of the mid–Hudson Valley enjoyed
individual gratification in the expanding world of goods, and they apparently liked to turn the occasional consumption thrill into a family or social
event. But, and this is the important point to remember, every kind of
evidence on consumer behavior demonstrates the social determination of
this experience because it occurred within a process of class formation that
sorted individuals and families according to income and occupation.

SEVEN

The Culture of Public Life

A hamlet known as "mill village" in the town of Catskill was the hotbed of peculiarly hostile encounters in the 1820s and early 1830s. "For many months a practice, vulgarly called *Scimmelton,* has prevailed in the village of Madison," the *Catskill Recorder* began an article in March 1821 before it detailed a remarkably scripted ritual:

> When a marriage is to be solemnized, a gang of men and boys meet in the evening, and parade through the village with drums, fifes, bells, tin pans, kettles, horns, &c. to the great annoyance of the citizens generally, and particularly to the company assembled for the above mentioned purpose. "To cap the climax," on Wednesday evening last, a number of the lower class (for such they must be) enlisted under their banner a worthless boy, who went near the door of the house in which was the assembled party, and in the midst of the company, sounded his horn and whistle, when these women sallied forth, and paraded the streets with their instruments of discord and confusion.

This was not a singular and isolated incident. Three wedding assemblies in Delaware County on the western slope of the Catskills were honored with the same jamboree, and a word geography reveals a high concentration of *skimertons* and *skimiltons* in the Hudson Valley. It was, however, less violent than other episodes in the same series of events. In 1832, the *Catskill Recorder* reported on a "Riot" during which "a large collection of men and boys made an attack upon a house in the upper part of the Village [Madison], storming the inmates, &c. The cause of the disturbance was the marriage of a female of more than exceptionable character. A number of shots were fired from the house on the assailants, and several persons wounded."[1]

The confrontations between the rackety crowds and the wedding parties amounted to more than European forms of rough music, *Katzenmusik* and *charivari*, which aimed at extorting a repast to compensate men, at least symbolically, for the removal of a woman from the pool of eligible maidens.[2] The conflict opposed, in the newspaper's taxonomy of indictment, "lower-class" and "respectable" groups of people, both of which included women and men. Their contrasting behaviors revealed a struggle over the definition of the boundary between the private and public spheres. The crowd's action intruded on marriages that had become private, segregated affairs among families that sought to reduce their contact with lesser sorts. Even more, members of these groups began to develop a moralizing posture toward the lower class in which they linked defective private conduct with public disorder. Complaints about other unmannerly comportments accompanied the condemnation of scimmeltons. "The open violation of the sabbath, both by adults and children, in the above village [Madison], is another practice which I feel bound to complain of," the correspondent of the *Catskill Recorder* concluded. The portrait of Madison as a busy industrial village and home to several manufacturing establishments, mills, and stores (it was, among others, the site of blacksmith Samuel Fowks's expanding furnace business) included the cavil that, "besides, we, as all other villages, are contaminated with drunkards, sabbath-breakers, thieves, rioters and debauchees." Belittlement of these putatively licentious habits bespoke the culture of the emerging middle class, whose members' own conduct was governed by an ethic of discretion. While its repudiation of unbecoming manners concentrated on such predominantly male activities as drinking, spitting, swearing, gambling, and fighting, which could be reformed in the sanctity of a home dominated by a wife and mother, the objection to the scimmelton also depicted a disreputable demeanor among women of the lower class. Their participation in the cacophonous and all too public display of hostility toward bride, bridegroom, and their refined companions did not conform to the norms of commendable and polite deportment; it surely betrayed the expectation of women's civilizing influence on men. The stigmatization of scimmeltons revealed them as attempts at subversion in the battle for respectability and other Victorian values, whose dominion the new-fledged middle class still had to impose.[3]

The examination of public actions and their meanings in the eyes of people who performed or observed them in the mid–Hudson Valley aims at understanding the practices that constituted communal life. The question of social order and disorder figures at the center of the following analysis. Public conflicts and their contemporary interpretations are moments in which a society exposes its self-representation. They suspend social routines that assure, but often veil, everday operations of power. If the allocation of material resources in the first half of the nineteenth century illustrated the social determinants behind the unequal gains of economic development, exploding tensions unmasked conventional accommodations of divergent moral assumptions on the workings of society. However, it is worth remembering that a public presence presupposes a system of norms that legitimizes social behavior. The ordinary and extraordinary aspects of public events thus require close attention to institutions that shape the values commonly assumed to endow men and women with the attributes necessary for their public acts. To probe the nature of culture and its transformation in the mid–Hudson Valley after 1800 demands a joint investigation of religion and politics, on the one hand, and churches and parties on the other. These institutional groupings, along with voluntary associations often devoted to causes of moral reform, organized segments of public life without dictating individual religious or political experiences. Indeed, one of the tasks of this inquiry is to establish the reach of formal organizations and the social implications of public engagements.[4] After all, scimmeltons escaped the hold of both an institutional political sphere, in which conflicts found peaceful solutions through reasoned argument, and a moral order whose ascendency forced the internalization of standards prohibiting public displays of discontent, let alone anger. The shifting meaning of violence forms the starting point of this study of the mid–Hudson Valley's public life.

Violence, Honor, and Honesty

Disapproval of the roguish noise and ritualistic violence that characterized scimmeltons occurred in a social environment that saw a rift between honor and respectability. The former concerned the good name of a family as the source of a reputation. The latter pertained to the emerging moral code of "small virtues" (as Alexis de Tocqueville called them) that prized privacy, tranquility, comfort, security, and regularity. Physical violence, whose most highly formalized expression was the duel among gentlemen, functioned as the ultimate vindication of the male value of

honor and of family reputation in societies of rank and face-to-face relations. The emerging middle class cherished refinement and privacy and
abhorred force; it excluded fisticuffs, brawls, and duels from acceptable
behavior among respectable men. Indeed, attributes like strength and a
fondness for hard liquor, which had signaled manliness in Alexander and
William Coventry's society at the turn of the nineteenth century, became
badges of crudeness and vulgarity in the milieu of nonmanual occupations
after the 1820s: although gentlemen still, if rarely, resorted to punches to
resolve "affairs of honor" and while the exertion of physical force to harm
others endures to this day, it lost its legitimacy as a means of redressing
injury and insult caused by men of like status.[5]

Physical violence did not necessarily, and certainly did not always, relate to the defense of a man's honor, although the pattern of trial causes
suggests a change in behavior in the first half of the nineteenth century.
As late as 1829, a fellow named Hill "took hold of Truesdell's hat & nose &
pulled the nose pretty hard" after a disagreement had arisen between them,
but the number of court cases that dealt with bodily injuries (and certainly
those with such overtones of assaults on a man's masculinity and the rather
more tangible threat of losing his face) declined slowly in the first half
of the nineteenth century. It is difficult to untangle the exact causes that
motivated the cases before the Greene County Court of Common Pleas
during this period, and many parties settled out of court. Even so, and
without overstating the precision of our knowledge, we can sketch the
distribution of grievances that pushed people to sue each other: between
1801 and 1810, 41 out of 131 trials (31 percent) revolved around violence; the
1820s registered an increase when 39 out of 102 cases (38 percent) included
assaults; the dockets and minutes of the 1840s recorded 63 hearings, 12 of
which (19 percent) concerned the use of force.[6]

The modification of the perception of force and its role in the honor
code, however, is suggested by the disappearance of public notices an-
nouncing challenges of supposed slanderers and calumnists. "The Public
may take notice," Alexander Thompson entitled a note in the *Northern
Whig* of 1811: "Whereas David Knapp, Esq. Attorney at Law of the village
of Spencertown, having reported scandalous falsehoods respecting my private character, I waited on him and demanded redress. He challenged me
to meet him at a certain time and place, to settle the controversy in an hon-
orable way. I attended at the time and place appointed, armed as agreed;
and waited more than an hour and said Knapp did not make his appear-
ence—I therefore publish him to the world, as a *liar, coward* and *scoundrel*."

The accusation of cowardice was a severe insult to a gentleman's public standing. In a case in Catskill, Moses I. Cantine defended himself against such a charge, which Abraham Van Dyck had leveled against him in 1809. Respected men like Ira Day and Judge Bronk attested to Cantine's honor, but their support did not induce Van Dyck to back down. So it came to a showdown, which Moses Cantine described in the following terms:

> I held a horse-whip in my left hand, without even raising it in an attitude to strike him [Van Dyck]; my right hand was extended towards him, twisting my fingers round his nose, without *absolutely* wringing it, and told him he might now give another certificate of my cowardice; he replied he would certify as he pleased; I repeated the insult a second time, and told him he was a mean cowardly puppy and liar; he raised not a finger to resist. Perceiving that I had to deal with a being as destitute of spirit as of every other qualification for a gentleman, I bid him be gone out of my sight, to take further notice of him was beneath me, and the puppy walked away as quietly as a spaniel sneaks off after having been corrected.[7]

This kind of public notice faded from the mid–Hudson Valley press after the second decade of the nineteenth century. For a while, however, the public arena remained the place where, as the scimmeltons demonstrated, shaming practices castigated dishonorable neighbors. Elam Garret, for example, composed a song about Ann Owen's traffic with a black man named Tom. Garret's performance of the verses on 8 January 1810 led to a lawsuit because Owen's family wanted to fend off the brunt of slander. In 1815, Moika Conine circulated rumors about the dishonorable behavior of John Vosburgh, who responded with legal action. A ballad pitted inhabitants of Greenville against each other. It had grown out of neighborhood rumors about the Rundle family's purchase of a coffin before their ailing mother passed away in the late 1820s.[8] But such dramatic settlements, in which members of the local community acted as incriminators, witnesses, and an engaged audience (somewhat like the chorus in Greek tragedies) that judged the actions and honor of one of their neighbors, became obsolete as the social structure and the system of values changed.

Conscience replaced honor in the makeup of people's reputation. Character—the ethical integrity distinguishing a person—and conscience—a person's moral center of experience and judgment—designated private, individual qualities that were rewarded with public recognition. Traditionally, esteem was ascribed to a social station in a society whose rules demanded that its members defend their honor in public. Now it was achieved through personal enterprise, maintained through judicious management, and lost through personal failings. The development from public honor to private honesty as a core value in the evaluation of a person and his fitness for active involvement in community affairs sapped the foundations of the field of force in which matters of social standing and respect eventuated. The press ceased to function as a vehicle of defense and the arena where wounded gentlemen denounced their adversaries. Kingston merchant Nathaniel Booth revealed just how different things were in 1849 when he commented on a fellow resident's attempt to explicate his position on a domestic quarrel in a public statement. "What do the people care about him or his affairs," Booth asked, hinting at the anachronism of the quest. "I doubt if any beyond his immediate neighborhood has even heard of him."[9] The lack of public explanation indicated not only the consequences of urban growth with its attendant anonymity. It pointed to the sway of new means of self-definition in a society that had left behind the hierarchical but personalized social relations carried over from the prerevolutionary era.

The process of social reconfiguration that began during the second decade of the nineteenth century forged a novel set of attributes to define the worth of a person. This was the epochal cultural change. Prior social attachments were discarded as influences on a man's standing in the community. Members of the aristocratic Livingston family were born with honor and could, indeed did, lose it throughout the 1800s as a result of excessive gambling, conceiving illegitimate children, divorcing, and running into debt. By the 1820s respect came with individual success in economic ventures. The requisite features of individual achievement and consequent public recognition did not fail to appear in published biographies in the 1840s. The pattern informed the portraits of businessmen like tanner Zadock Pratt who were to inspire emulation among contemporaries: "He was a poor boy, without friends, and picked blackberries for a living. But by honest industry, he made a fortune, was elected to Congress, and a large and flourishing town now bears his name."[10] There was no better acknowledgment than a place on the map and in government to emphasize private virtues as the tools for achieving wealth and respectability.

The insistence on a person's character brought about paradoxical consequences. Its primary area of deployment was the expanding private sphere, and so its mere operation limited men's involvement in public affairs, whereas the honor code had made participation in government an obligation among the community's notable members. However, the rising prominence of character and dignity enabled women to enter the public sphere. Their virtues—chastity and purity—had always been private as opposed to men's valor and virility, which came into existence, so to speak, only when displayed in public. Because probity was a question of behavior, not social antecedents, it was possible to teach it. And who better than women to teach the lessons of their experience with private virtue to society at large? Hence the irony of rising cultural standards whose emphasis on privacy and peacefulness for men enhanced and legitimized the public role and militancy of women. Women's increased visibility did not elude a correspondent of the *Hudson Bee,* who in 1816 declared: "We have an age for everything, and this emphatically appears to be an age of Societies. Almost every city, town and village in our country boasts its Bible Societies, and the female sex, ever found in the ranks of benevolence, vie with our own in disseminating the scriptures of truth."[11] But a community in which values and norms needed promotion did not take them for granted. The classification of vice and virtue proved, as the scimmeltons amply illustrated, to be an issue at stake.

The Topography of Vice and Virtue

The Female Society of Hudson announced its foundation in 1811. A year later, the Durham Female Cent Society, so named because the weekly membership contribution amounted to one cent, announced its existence. The two assocations pursued distinct vectors of action. While the women of Durham promised to exert themselves so "that Christ shall have the Heathen for his inheritance & the uttermost part of the Earth for his possession" (where, "it is computed . . . thirty thousand females are burnt alive every year on the funeral pile of their Deceased Husbands"), the Hudson group got involved in local concerns. "We often hear of the ill consequence of indiscriminate charity," one of its public statements read in 1816. "And we all know that it is wrong to encourage idleness and vice. But let it be remembered that the sick and the needy, whether worthy or undeserving, require our care. . . . Fellow beings in distress have claims upon humanity." The Female Benevolent Society (as it had dubbed itself by the middle of the decade) distributed food, clothing, and wood to the poor in Hudson and contributed to the cost of schooling indigent children.[12]

Whether the impulse behind these organizations was proselytism or benevolence, they are most remarkable for their social features. Both were exclusively female, nondenominational, and run by the wives of prominent citizens. Six of the eleven Hudson officers were the spouses of merchants and lawyers, and Hannah Barnard had made herself a name as a headstrong Quakeress. The Durham leadership was in the hands of women from more affluent families at the society's founding. The rank and file seemed quite inclusive then, but their number declined from about a hundred in 1813 to fifty in 1830 while attendance at trimestrial meetings faded, too. All the same, these voluntary associations allowed women to think about and discuss their roles and responsibilities in the community. The Durham Female Cent Society, although ostentatiously pursuing missionary goals, provided a formal space for sociability between women of different social standing who sang, prayed, read evangelical magazines, and engaged in religious conversations. At these gatherings ministers sometimes preached sermons on themes such as "Help those women which laboured with me in Gospel" or "And she was a Widow," which addressed women's concerns as much as they affirmed their crucial contribution in spreading and sustaining Christian teachings.[13]

When men gathered in voluntary associations, they augmented their public purpose and narrowed their social inclusiveness. The Columbia, Greene & Delaware Auxiliary Bible & Common Prayer Book Society and the Columbia Society for the Promotion of Good Morals also distributed Bibles and propagated Christian instruction without denominational discrimination. In addition, they engaged in a fight against Sabbath breaking, intemperance, profane language, horse racing, and other, unspecified "prevailing immoralities." No women served on the governing boards of these organizations, where membership fees were $1 per year. Ministers such as Beriah Hotchkiss of Catskill and Jacob Sickles of Kinderhook provided spiritual guidance to the campaign, but leadership fell to affluent men in mid–Hudson Valley communities. The average wealth of nineteen identifiable members (out of twenty-six) of Greene County committees was $5,572, more than twice the mean property of the county's wealthiest town, Catskill, but not at the top of the area's fortunes in 1813.[14] The movement was thus both a sign and an instrument of self-affirmation among men of middling condition. Membership in the voluntary association proved their social difference and asserted the importance, indeed the necessity, of character as an attribute of respectability. It was, in short, a means of sustaining middle-class values.

Where philanthropy had guided women's organizations and in some ways transcended class lines, order mattered to the men, whose associations regularly published appeals for the enforcement of laws to prevent the profaning of the Sabbath in the 1820s and 1830s. These exhortations attest to the tenacity of moral reformers — and also to their uncertain success. The village of Catskill adopted bylaws prohibiting the sale of liquor, the opening of the public market, bathing, skating, and butchering on Sundays in 1825, but calls for the strict implementation of the law prohibiting Sabbath breaking as "an evil of disquieting magnitude" revealed its practical inefficiency in 1828 and 1836. Friends of "good order" and "good morals" continued to condemn the "vulgar and profane fellows" who visited the circus and disturbed the peace on holy days, frivolous amusements that demonstrated the local decline of morals.[15]

If sanctification of Sundays, and as a consequence respect for the church as a place of rectitude, was a paramount goal of middle-class reformers between 1815 and 1830, then the promoters of moral regeneration had no problem identifying one important vector of dissipation in liquor and the site of its influence in taverns. Inn and church staked out the topography of vice and virtue, and societies that advocated temperance and total abstinence from alcoholic beverages became active in the 1820s. John Beekman of Kinderhook dated the bifurcation of middle- and lower-class behavior from about that time. Before, he recalled, it was still "the custom for white men, both old and young, to collect at the nearest public-houses. In the many townships there were scores of these, and Kinderhook had its share. Here they remained talking and drinking till early dinner-time, returned again by five in the afternoon, and spent the evening, till probably mid-night, in drinking, gambling, cock-fighting, horse-racing, or perhaps fighting among themselves. Idleness led the way to immorality, and to frequent ruin, on the parts of the whites." George Haydock, whose moral progress led him from the tavern to temperance halls and lectures, insisted in his autobiography on the heavy drinking of respectable men before the dawn of the temperance movement. The particulars of Beekman's and Haydock's descriptions may exaggerate the character of a tavern culture in the countryside, but both Alexander Coventry and Basil Hall commented on the numerous and at times noisy inns in Greene County. On the other side of the Hudson River, a tavern on the Columbia Turnpike in Chatham was the regular meeting place of Chester Upham, Jesse Matthias, Joseph Price, James Williams, Abner Bristol, and Joshua Loax between 1816 and 1818. Brawls like the fight between Henry Jones and Matthew Bogardus in a Greenville tavern in 1826 confirmed reformers' views of grog shops as settings of debauchery and depravity from which respectable men had better keep their distance.[16]

The assertion of the middle-class values of sobriety and decorum prompted reactions that led to a consolidation of the front lines. The reform movement was fighting a "war," as the assistant secretary of the Greene County Society for the Promotion of Temperance declared in 1833, in which "no inconsiderable part of the work remains to be done." Temperance stores sprang up and withered away. Their owners were "determined not to sell any Rum or any kind of Spirits" and invited those "who do not wish to find a store filled with *Rum drinkers,* to patronize them." The Greene County Society reported that "much has already been achieved" in 1833, but "some violent opponents" in Athens and "very peculiar circumstances" in Lexington impeded its prospects. Indeed, the Lexington branch committee had visited "a few neighborhoods, and find in some a spirit of inquiry on the subject, and a willingness to give temperance papers a favorable reception if sent gratuitously." Their report concluded that "in other sections of the town they found individuals who manifested, in some cases, indifference to the temperance movement, in others prejudice, bordering on hostility." The opposition originated in tanning neighborhoods like Jewett, where membership contributions in the Total Abstinence Society had plummeted from $27.75 to $3.50 between 1822 and 1825. In Catskill, the social geography of resistance to the movement appeared quite clearly in 1838 when the Catskill Mechanical Society announced a debate about the question of whether temperance had been carried too far with total abstinence from alcoholic beverages (the answer seemed to be positive).[17]

The antagonism between lower- and middle-class behavior with respect to alcohol consumption diminished after the mid-1830s. Significantly, the inclusion of women into the ranks of the Greene County Society for the Promotion of Temperance was a strategic modification that helped restore and sustain its efforts. Women brought a more convivial tone to the movement, which abandoned the pursuit of total abstinence to advocate self-restraint and moderation in drinking, although it hardly lost sight of the rejection of liquor as the ultimate aim of its efforts. In turn, these two changes attracted working-class men into temperance associations. National events influenced local happenings. The Mechanics' and Laboring Men's Temperance Association of Catskill followed the example of the Washingtonian movement and adopted its means of persuasion.[18] The movement now took to lecture halls and streets. In Greenville, the temperance society participated in the Fourth of July parade under its own banner in 1844, and it organized processions with music in October and November of 1845. "Solemn pomp and proud hearts" marked these occasions at which the ladies "signalized themselves as to numbers and decorum, which reflects much honor upon the finer sex." Temperance meetings in the 1820s had usually featured sermons. Now singing made up a large part of such get-togethers. John Bower noted the pleasure of participating in performances of a more secular tone. On 21 January 1844, he "went in the evening to the Juvenile Franklin Temperance Society [where] a number of odes were sung and all went well and were worth hearing." In August 1841, the *Catskill Recorder* recounted, three new organizations had collected 700 temperance pledges, representing one-fourth of the town's adult population. The Gayhead Temperance Society reached the same proportion with its 375 constituents in 1843.[19]

Theatricality pervaded temperance lectures and indeed proved crucial to their success. George Haydock, the one-legged lecturer of Hudson, "was extremely desultory and excentric," the log of an event in 1845 read. He "evidently disregarded any thing like system or arrangement— full of anecdotes severe and sarcastic upon our opponents, and by his shrewdness and witticism kept the audience in a burst of laughter." Some speakers stirred "a thrilling interest" in the audience or kept it "breathless." Less excitement brought dire results. One speech maker got away with "some good remarks" and a frustrated public in Greenville. Worse happened when "the Temperance society was addressed by Doct. Tappan, a Mesmerizer & Phrenologist (a stranger) in the Gayhead School House on Saturday Evening the 3rd February 1844. A good attendance, the lecture a failure, the people disappointed and the members mortified—consequently no names to the pledge."[20] The style of delivery and assembly made all the difference. Companionship and entertainment figured prominently in the arsenal of their movement and attracted mechanics who had remained unfavorable or indifferent to the cause just a few years earlier.

Inclusiveness was the goal of the Gayhead Temperance Society. It aspired to recruit as many people as possible. The road to temperance, one orator declared, "is not a road of tolls, not designed to favor monopolies, but a free road philanthropic in its nature, designed to benefit all—political, religious & social societies. It is an individual as well as a national benefit. It is designed for the youth, middle aged, the old, the female sex, for all." The pursuit of an extensive and participatory membership contained the seeds of difficulties and reversals. Soon after having founded their organization in 1841, the managers of the Gayhead Temperance Society had to castigate delinquent drinkers, and exclusions occurred with some regularity. The degree of inconsistency appeared in William Smith's behavior. An inhabitant of Hudson, Smith enjoyed a big party with his firefighting company on 11 August 1843, after which he suffered from a "bad headache." Maybe he saw the pain as a punishment rather than a consequence of the excess, for five days later he attended a temperance lecture. The problem of temperance organizations was their inability to impose sanctions on people who broke the pledge; where members were a minority in the community, stigmatizing renegades lost the efficacy to bring them back in line. But it is also undeniable that, as temperance lecturer and reformed drinker George Haydock argued, increased respectability formed a significant social reward. It was not for everybody, of course, and so the fire brigade and its sprees remained an important part of William Smith's life.[21]

African Americans in the mid–Hudson Valley, however, recognized the benefits of a value system that emphasized private character rather than public honor. Just like women, who had transcended the limits of public activities imposed on them by male notions of what it took to enter the public arena, black residents formed a distinct Colored Temperance Society in the 1840s to publicize both their independence of white guidance and the moral dignity so regularly denied them. However limited the effect of this organizational taking charge was on their social position, their collective comportment and the solemnity of their gatherings elicited positive remarks in the *Kinderhook Sentinel*. In 1843, in a vocabulary that itself expressed the new standards of social evaluation, it lauded the "propriety and decorum . . . , the talent, respectability and gentility" of black people after a temperance convention.[22] The voluntary association helped African Americans to take advantage of rising cultural forms to mark their moral character and announce their claim to the entitlements of social consideration and respect, if not recognition as political actors in community life.

Religion and Church

Christian teachings inspired and often justified the efforts of moral reform associations. Yet by many accounts church attendance was low. Describing the hamlet of Spencertown in the Taconic Mountains in a letter to her fiancé, John Olmsted, in 1834, Lucinda Davenport wrote that "the Church and Society remain about as usual—I go to meetings seldom. It seems gloomy and lonesome when I do, so few attend." The occasional revival to foster "hope in Christ," as one minister put it, failed to leave a lasting impact on church membership in the Hudson Valley. The region's religious equanimity distinguished it from the waves of millenarianism and perfectionism that rocked western New York's burned-over district.[23] At midcentury, and in spite of what seemed to be an increase over the feeble attendance of the 1780s, only four in ten adults in Columbia and Greene Counties were members of a church, a situation that prompted some clergymen to ponder the use of the temperance movement as a vehicle to extend the church's reach; they likely targeted the seven in ten adults who attended services every once in a while without full church membership. Women found in their domestic solitude a compelling impetus to join a formal organization. "My mother found life very lonely," Maria Edwards Park remembered of the early days of Hunter's tanning community in the 1820s and 1830s. Lucretia Warner Hall of Canaan devoured a large number of books in the 1840s despite her weak eyes, but in December 1841, after having put down yet another volume (was it Combs's *Physiology,* "Washington Ervin," or *The Life of Napoleon?*), she sighed, "loneliness reigns here." Sundays at religious services palliated these feelings of isolation. The possibility of escaping the confining realm of the household certainly figured disproportionately among the reasons why women made up two-thirds of the church membership and participated in other social movements.[24]

Their circumscribed scope did not prevent churches from enforcing discipline among their members. In the late 1830s and the early 1840s the Valatie Presbyterian Church denounced brethren Rivenberg and Hoover for Sabbath breaking, the use of profane language, and the consumption of alcoholic beverages. It charged Louisa VanDeBogart with "quarrelling with neighbors and the use of wicked and opprobrious language." Charles Snyder and Henry D. Longworthy were accused of "unchristian behavior." The number of communicants obviously circumscribed the reach of parish discipline. In 1842, the Valatie Presbyterian Church went so far as to appoint a commission whose task it was to inform shiftless parishioners of "the sinfulness of their wanderings" after the recognition that "several members of our church were very negligent in their attendance at public worship and at the communion table." However, the results of such disciplinary measures were mixed, to say the least. In a lengthy process Anthony J. Pulver was indicted for "vending intoxicating liquors to persons of intemperate habit and that too without a license, allowing gambling and other disorderly practices in his shop or store," an allegation that "he peremptuously denies and challenges proof." The investigation ended with a "guilty" verdict to which Pulver paid no attention. He had already left the Presbyterians to attend the Reformed Dutch Church of Kinderhook.[25]

Pulver's choice demonstrated the importance of religion and the limits of church influence in people's lives. Christianity remained central in the lives of the region's inhabitants who, like most Americans, believed in a day of judgment and the danger of eternal damnation. Doctrinal issues, however, did not cause perturbation among the inhabitants of the mid–Hudson Valley. If institutional discipline failed, the cultivation of neighborhood relations—and religious feeling—fueled churchgoing. William Youngs had no qualms about going to the "Methodist quarterly Meeting at Coeymans Stone church," to listen to black preachers and "to hear quakers preach" in 1811 and 1812. Members of the Dubois family of Catskill "went to universalous church" in the morning on 2 August 1835 and "at 2, Methodist." Two weeks later, they went to a Presbyterian mass. Christmas saw them in the Episcopal church, and in February 1836 they took part in a Baptist celebration. Lucretia Warner Hall went to Baptist and Methodist meetings. Though inclined toward the Universalist creed, William Smith of Hudson listened to a Presbyterian, a Catholic, and to what he perceived to be a Jewish preacher. In Cairo, Episcopalians and Methodists shared a building for their services. John Bower of Poughkeepsie saw no contradiction in attending Presbyterian, Methodist, and Quaker meetings. And, while Benjamin Gue was curious enough to listen to an African American preacher and then promised himself never to do it again, Hannah Bushnell delighted in "the colored man [who] preached again" in Cooksburg, north of Durham, in 1856, and had attracted "a very full house." The Episcopalian pastor of Athens seemed, not altogether surprisingly, unconcerned about dogmatic systems and his flock's understanding of their subtleties. He gleefully informed a colleague in 1844 that "there is one feature in our prospects here which looks more encouraging for the church than at any previous time of my Rectorship. Two of 'the denominations around us,' the Lutheran & Dutch Reformed are incompetent to sustain preaching: and their Dominies are preparing to leave now shortly. We shall have some accessions, doubtless, by this measure. I shall at least be quite a Patriarch in the place, notwithstanding I have been here but little over 3 years."[26]

Indifference to religious doctrines weakened the churches' influence as identity-forming factors in people's lives. Nonperformance of church duties and even expulsion from a specific religious group did not expose a person to sanctions in the community. Since church membership and attendance did not contribute to the positive or negative identification of people, do we have to conclude that religious (non)practices and tolerance actually obliterated or at least attenuated the class-structured social experience in the mid–Hudson Valley? To extend the spectrum of religious inclinations and include overt antagonism to the church as an institution promises to throw more light on the population's religious attitudes. Then, too, the widespread indifference to the social practice of churchgoing did not mean that religion mattered little. Adolescents, for example, detested going to church. Lucinda Davenport recapitulated one excruciating meeting at which she "heard Rev. J. Osborne. He whiled away *four long* tedious hours reading Newspapers." William Hoffman, too, complained about Mr. Brice, the minister of Claverack, who "addressed us in his old fashioned style & which is rather dry having that same monotonous strain & delivery." (Granted, ministers did not necessarily enjoy preaching and the work it involved, either: Thomas Mallaby once wrote to his colleague, the Rev. Robert Shaw, that he "would rather ride 10 miles any time than write a new sermon.") But it was still the religious imagination that supplied people, young and old, with a vocabulary with which to raise existential questions. Ann-Janette Dubois "had a talk with Betsy on religion, [and] felt bad" afterward in 1835. Thirteen years later William Hoffman discussed religious ideas with his mother and then decided to pay "unflagging attention" to biblical teachings. John Burroughs's parents Chauncey and Amy only occasionally attended church in the 1840s, but religious questions animated discussions in the household and with neighbors.[27] Religious thought, especially in the guise of biblical parables, contributed to the foundation of the self, the matrix of the perception of the world.

Alienation from churches took different forms and expressed different attitudes. When prompted by his brother in Massachusetts to adhere to Universalist doctrines in 1823, paper maker Abner Austin replied, "I really have no time to spare from my every day business to reply to such lengthy matters. . . . My days are occupied abroad & the evenings are required to keep up with my current business. Besides, there would never be an end to a religious controversy carried on by written communication." When his brother persevered and went so far as to suggest books and pamphlets to read, Austin did "not find that reading controversial writings upon Religion tends to settle religious principles in my own mind, but rather seems to confirm the correctness of advice I received from a Clergyman more than twenty years ago, which was 'to read the Bible without Comment.' "[28] Here, then, this businessman's religious solace did not depend on ministerial exegesis inculcated in church services. It matured through the quite traditionally Protestant, individual immersion in Scripture—when work allowed! Austin described both the extent and the nature of church and religion in a middle-class existence, and if the former seemed limited and clearly bounded by the time spared from business the latter attested the degree to which the withdrawal from honor and the operation of a Christian conscience conditioned each other.

Uneven attendance at church events reflected insouciance among parts of the population. It was, of course, a disposition that worried those contemporaries who construed religious observances as requisites of an orderly society. Erastus Pratt, a wealthy farmer of Spencertown, noted in 1820 "some Revivals of Religion in Pittsfield & the eastward, some at the Northward." Then he bemoaned that "here we remain much as we were rather in a broken state of Society." Only a narrow space separated the general concern for religious habits as a constituent element of community life from an interpretation of their neglect as an act of hostility. In the eyes of commentators, such adverse behavior predominated in the lower class. The inhabitants of Hunter, a town of farmers and tanners of low average wealth in the 1820s, were said to "have no more sense of the worth of the privileges of Gospel than the savages west of the Mississippi, and will do little or nothing to support it." When the Marshall brothers of Stockport erected a Methodist church for their English hands in 1829, they encountered only lukewarm interest. Their workmen maintained a dispassionate attitude toward public religious exercises and attended services only sporadically.[29] The perception of observable devotional conduct, if not the inner experience of faith, about which little evidence survives and which remained remote even from contemporary view, indicates a divergence between the religious worlds of the lower and middle classes. Whereas a great deal of nonchalance and variety characterized what one might call plebeian religious behavior, middle-class observers appreciated churches as a civilizing influence.

The mid–Hudson Valley thus experienced moral reform movements without the commotions associated with the Second Great Awakening. Indeed, the revivals of the period largely bypassed the area. Although the region had been transformed from the traditional world of the late eighteenth century to one discernibly more modern (and closer to ours), this development was evolutionary rather than revolutionary. Much historical writing linked the anxieties generated by so-called modernization with the escalation of efforts to re-create a community spirit shattered by social and economic dislocations. However consequential, change in the Hudson Valley was less fraught with acute disruptions. This may well explain why its residents did not need recourse to an outpouring of religious fervor in order to cope with changing conditions.

The Reordering of the Political Sphere

Voting regulated the beat of political life in 1800 as in 1850. The persistence of the selfsame rhythm, however, obscures the fact that only with the adoption of the general suffrage in 1821 did white men twenty-one years and older gain access to the full entitlements of citizenship in state affairs. If the abolition of suffrage requirements altogether put an end to formal restrictions on their participation in politics in 1824 (except for African Americans), modes of electoral mobilization determined it among the citizenry. And no man maneuvered so skillfully to transform the means of electioneering in New York State and perhaps the United States, was so keenly aware of the radical change in the first half of the nineteenth century, and analyzed the reordering of politics with such a penetrating mind at the end of his career as did Columbia County native Martin Van Buren. Reflecting on his life in politics, Van Buren intended his autobiography to be "a true and frank account of the rise and progress of one, who, without the aid of powerful family connexions, and with but few of the adventitious facilities for the acquisition of political power had been elevated by his countrymen to a succession of official trusts." Family and patronage determined a citizen's political outlook and chances before the lawyer from Kinderhook and his allies substituted partisan allegiance for "influence." When Van Buren's Bucktails and a handful of disappointed, renegade Federalists opposed Governor De Witt Clinton, a politician of the old school, in the decade after 1816, Van Buren noted that his tactical allies, "Federalists from their birth, and of the oldest and strictest sect, . . . could not make much impression by their efforts upon the democratic ranks. . . , neither were they treated by our party with the consideration which they thought they deserved. . . . Most of these gentlemen had from early manhood enjoyed high and influential positions in what was called good society, and the supposition that they expected to occupy, on that account, greater consideration in the democratic organization was not acceptable in that quarter." Politics, Van Buren contended, had evolved from a gentlemanly exercise in the exchange of personal favors for power to a struggle among disciplined parties. His own formation broke new ground and became the prototype of the reconstructed system's constitutive organization. It largely contributed to the emergence of a partisan political culture.[30]

The transformation had begun with the recruitment of Van Buren supporters in 1812 and 1814. In the 1820s the system had been perfected, and J. A. Van Valkenburgh of Hudson organized a meeting at Van Bramer's tavern in Ghent to collect contributions, which would be used to drum up voters. The presidential election of 1828 united the friends of the Adams administration, who organized themselves with greater efficiency to face their more professional opponents. "This measure may be considered as the first movement of the Administration men in this county [Greene] towards organizing as a party, and will afford some index of the strength, character, and materials of which it is to be composed," the *Greene County Republican* editorialized with great keenness of insight. The observer understood this event as the inception of a new kind of politics and the birth of a party system. He continued, "a new order of things has arisen, and parties must necessarily assume a new form and character, and be designated by new boundaries, springing from the divisions of opinion, upon a new and important question, and the heat of discussion, that is rapidly obliterating their ancient distinctions."[31] The primary issue pertained to the nature of governance raised by Andrew Jackson's candidacy, but the article's principal merit (for us as historians) stems from its discernment of the profound alteration of the political sphere. Personal relations had given way to party programs behind which citizens sorted themselves out. Political agendas, partisan discipline, and governmental spoils rather than influence, deference, and personal favors now informed political behavior.

Sharper partisan competition increased voter participation. By the 1840s, nine of ten eligible men went to the polls (table 23). For a short time in the beginning of the 1820s, the organizational strategy worked for the Van Buren Republicans. They targeted formerly disenfranchised yet still propertied voters and benefited from higher voter turnout. In Columbia County, elections won by Federalists showed participation of 54 percent; those in which Republicans prevailed reached 65 percent participation. Greene County Federalists won with 62 percent and Republicans with 68 percent participation. The gain was short-lived. As parties perfected their methods of bringing citizens to the polls and participation increased to

TABLE 23. Voting Participation of Adult White Men, 1815–40 (percentages)

County	1815	1820–22[a]	1830	1840
Columbia	59.1	55.6	72.5	90.8
Greene	56.1	61.0	63.1	89.4

Sources: Northern Whig, 10 May 1814, 2 May 1820; *Catskill Recorder,* 10 May 1815, 13 Nov. 1822, 11 Nov. 1830, 12 Nov. 1840; Edwin Williams, *New York Annual Register for 1831* (New York, 1831); *The Tribune Almanac for the Years 1838 to 1868* (New York, 1868); New York (State), Assembly, *Journal,* 38th sess. (Albany, 1815), appendix; U.S. Census Office, *Fourth Census, 1820* (Washington, D.C., 1821); United States. Census Office. *Fifth Census, 1830* (Washington, D.C., 1832); United States. Census Office. *Sixth Census, 1840* (Washington, D.C., 1841).
[a] Columbia County elections in 1820, Greene County in 1822.

very high levels, the advantage disappeared. General tendencies, although not infallibly at work, nevertheless appeared throughout the 1840s. River towns leaned toward the Federalist and later the Whig persuasion. "The concentration of wealth has placed Aristocratic Federalism above Democracy" in the river towns of Athens and Catskill, the Democratically inclined *Catskill Recorder* commented several times in the late 1830s and 1840s. Hill towns, however, were chiefly Democratic turf. "There is nothing that puts Federalism in Greene County into such woeful fright as to behold in full force the honest countenances and the determined mien of the hard working Democracy of Lexington, Hunter and Prattsville." The Democrats then carried elections by a four-to-one margin in those towns. The same sectional division characterized the political landscape in Columbia County, where Van Buren Democrats tended to prevail in mountainous districts like Austerlitz and Hillsdale and to lose along the river.[32]

Electoral slogans were not merely rhetorical devices concocted by cynical professional political enterpreneurs to seduce a gullible citizenry. The question of people's best representation superseded doubts about their capacity to govern themselves, an idle issue for white men after 1824. The Democrats saw political confrontation in the 1830s as a contest that opposed "the stern unsofisticated democracy" and former elites. In turn, the Whigs did not hesitate to depict their adversaries, without as much as a hint of caution, as the expression of a "floating population . . . destitute of any fixed principles" and given to drunken bouts after militia training.[33] The opposition was real. Nominations to state offices disadvantaged voters in Greene County hill towns. An inhabitant of Windham, disgruntled at the stranglehold of Catskill and Coxsackie on political nominations until 1824, exclaimed: "Is there no one fit to fill these important stations in the backtowns? Are all the talents, all the honesty, all the ability concentrated in Catskill and Coxsackie? Forbid it truth! forbid it ye hardy and enlightened yeomanry of the backtowns! It is evident that it is owing to the management and intrigue of the political trimmers of the two towns aforesaid, and it is high time for us to arouse from this lethargy and assert our right in the west part of the country." The call to arms resounded a few more times, but the Democratic organization showed its opportunism. Henry Goslee of Lexington was their candidate in 1826. Ten years later, they had made it a rule to nominate inhabitants from the hills to state offices.[34]

The conquest of popular legitimacy in government and the emergence of partisan politics meant the removal of traditional elites from the centers of power. Episodes and effects of the struggle appeared most clearly in Columbia County, where the Livingston and Van Rensselaer families had manorial interests. As late as 1828, Englishman Simeon Bloodgood marveled at the "immense influence" of landlords in New York, among whom he singled out patroon and congressman Stephen Van Rensselaer (1764–1839). Foreign observers and local commentators had wondered at the beginning of the nineteenth century about "the republicanism of the landlords of hundreds of life leases, where tenants vote only on the proprietor's will, and are brought to the polls in posse comitatus to support federalism." Extrapolitical, economic pressure on tenants was the leverage in the hands of the great proprietors. With the decline of manorial ownership, this influence diminished, too, but several Livingstons continued to participate in politics and presume their preeminence. When Alexis de Tocqueville asked about the impact of political equality on elections in the early 1830s, a Livingston of Dutchess County replied, "in general, people have no repugnance to electing the wealthiest and best educated," among whom he counted himself. Tocqueville speculated about the Livingstons' loss of "the paternal influence over their leaseholders that of old they had been accustomed to exercise[.] The loss had probably been due to long-standing dissatisfaction with the rental system, and more particularly to the substitution of the secret ballot for the *viva voce* voting just after the Revolution." The decline in influence of manorial interests proceeded more slowly than the French visitor had reckoned, and the buildup of parties had more to do with the loss of power than voting procedures. "Party mixes with every question," the last "patroon" had written in 1824. Stephen Van Rensselaer retired from politics in 1828 because partisan battles were "too disgusting for my Ear as I have ever kept good company. Vulgarity disgusts me." With him one of the last great representatives of the old regime left the political stage. The hold of the new men who made a living from politics appeared quite clearly in 1859 when former Whig turned Republican Ira Harris of Albany asked Henry Greene of Coxsackie to throw his weight behind his candidacy (he would go on to the U.S. Senate in 1861). Many Democrats, he asserted, would vote for him if they "will not be controlled by party considerations."[35] Yet that was just it: the partisan imperative governed voting behavior. The time when personal influence exclusively commanded voting behavior was a thing of the past.

Activities around the polls could be riotous and confusing. Cooper Sayre of Rensselaerville found "the political character" of the fall season in 1836 reinvigorating. He surmised that "these commotions and jars in community only serve to shake off the dust that accumulated on the body politic, and if wisely managed will present our institutions faultless before the world." Politics and the candidacy of Martin Van Buren for president then dominated public life so much that Ann-Janette Dubois "got the extra Recorder" on November 8, 1836. Eight years later after another presidential campaign, the Gayhead Temperance Society observed: "Having just passed through a political campaign and one too that has excited the publick mind to that extent that we presume to say that scarce any society either moral or religious has escaped injury. Politicks has in a measure triumphed over every other subject." It is true that political events left entries, however brief, in the diaries of William Smith and William Hoffman, too.[36]

But had politics really triumphed over every other activity? Did it really dominate every aspect of public life in the mid–Hudson Valley? The timing of commentaries on political events strongly suggests the periodical nature of political interest. Parties had permanent structures with headquarters and small staffs, but involvement among grassroots voters and concern among bystanders overwhelmingly occurred at election time. Moreover, not everybody shared Cooper Sayre's optimistic view when it came to the mechanics of the political system. Washington Irving decided in 1804 to abstain from public political activity. "My fellow countrymen do not know the blessings they enjoy," he wrote during a visit in Europe. "They are trifling with their felicity and are in fact themselves their worst enemies. I sicken when I think of our political broils, slanders & enemities and I think when I again find myself in New York I shall never meddle any more in Politicks." Fellow artist Thomas Cole, temperamentally inclined toward inner discipline and private virtue, considered partisan politics a vulgar activity in the mid-1830s. "While we were in the Valley we heard shouts of a company of Jacksonians who were rejoicing at the defeat of the Whigs of this county [Greene]. Why were they rejoicing? because of the triumph of good principles or the cause of virtue & morality? No! but because *their party* was victorious." The *Rural Repository,* the Hudson magazine fashioning itself as an agent of refinement, declared in an early editorial statement that "we have zealously avoided all Political and Religious discussions. . . . Ours is the humble province of preparing a 'feast of reason' spreading the table with VIANDS gathered with care from Books of Travels, etc." It succeeded in keeping politics out of its pages over the following twenty years and provided a mental space into which its readers could withdraw from the turbulent political sphere.[37]

When it came to advice for farmers, politics earned critical rather than commendatory remarks. Agricultural reformer Jesse Buel equated "launching about a tavern" and "wrangling in politics." Both pastimes were contrary to the work ethic necessary to thrive in a commercial world. They distracted agriculturalists from their business. Voting was an indispensable act of the responsible citizen-farmer. It signified a man's membership in the political community. However, the election of representatives in government only required a minimum of expenditure in time and effort beyond which political involvement intruded too much on family life and farm activities. Community and the roles he and other inhabitants assumed to maintain it very much mattered to Coxsackie town supervisor Jacob Van Dyck. But his high opinion of public service also drove him to deplore that "in each district the [electoral] meeting is merely an occasion for a row."[38] The periodical peaks of rough-and-tumble political manifestations verged on unbecoming behavior. They jeopardized the republican idea in the eyes of men who considered a certain amount of decorum a cardinal component in both public and private life.

Unlike the public sphere, which in principle at least was open to every resident in the United States, the political sphere remained exclusive. But concerns whose settlement required political identification and recourse to government authority generated social movements whose purpose it was to force the agenda of state institutions. Attempts to stretch the limits of citizenship and enlarge the content of politics took different paths. African Americans protested their claims to the unfulfilled promises of the Declaration of Independence in separate Fifth of July parades in the mid–Hudson Valley. They pursued public and political recognition by living up to the highest expectations of formal, genteel behavior. In 1846, the *Kinderhood Sentinel* applauded "the concluding parts of [Reverend Beman's] address in particular—contrasting the situation, the social, literary, and religious privileges of the white, with those of the black man, [which] were finely conceived and delivered with pathos and eloquence" at the anniversary ceremonials of the black population's freedom day. So far, the endeavor had been successful. But the *Sentinel* paid them an ambiguous compliment when it commended African Americans on their capacity to raise themselves "in the scale of refinement and improvement on a level with those whose veins are not cursed by African blood." William Hoffman revealed similar feelings. On 7 July 1847, he visited Hudson "as today the Negroes celebrated this day in lieu of the 4th. . . . Heard them speak, they seemed to be uncommonly smart for Blacks. Did not remain a great while."[39] Close observation of public etiquette may have raised the esteem for African Americans in the mid–Hudson Valley. It did little to alleviate their political plight or to further their accession to civil rights.

Suffrage did not automatically guarantee hearings with politicians. Lessees on the estates of the Livingston family launched petitions urging state authorities to examine the legality of manorial titles in the early republic. They met with little sympathy from the political establishment. Courts, too, safeguarded manorial property on which tenants had, so they argued in 1811, earned "by the sweat of the brow a princely and endless fortune for their lords and masters."[40] With the failure of these two paths to recognition as owners of the lands they tilled, tenants founded associations. They organized meetings in which antirenters appeared disguised as Indians. In 1844, one such gathering in Copake saw five hundred Indians and at least one hundred bystanders among whom there were women. They protested against the state-sanctioned repossession of farms whose leaseholders had fallen behind in, or defaulted on, rent payments. Occasionally they damaged their adversaries' property before and during the outbreak of the so-called Anti-Rent Wars upon Stephen Van Rensselaer's death in 1839. They committed acts of civil disobedience in resisting the sheriffs and militia who enforced the landlords' property rights. Their county associations met regularly after 1839, held statewide meetings between 1845 and 1851, and continued to send petitions to the New York legislature to call for the abolition of manorial property relations. While these parapolitical activities were futile as long as interests rather than parties organized politics, in the late 1830s tenant movements succeeded in arousing the interest of professional politicians among Whigs as well as Democrats. Democracy worked: no politician could afford to dismiss a concern that shook public order over a protracted period of time, mobilized a sizable part of the population in the Hudson Valley and upstate New York, and attracted nationwide attention and commentary. Votes counted, whether a candidate advocated or opposed antirent claims. Grassroots social activism and statewide political lobbying, including the public support of nominees at elections, transformed a local matter into a momentous item on the state's political agenda, which previously had mostly been stirred by national business.[41]

The antirent movement's success in heaving their concern into politics demonstrated the resilience and flexibility of the reordered political sphere. The alliance of professional politicians and antirent agitators proved uneasy, but the political system as such withstood the challenge posed by the tenants' organization. Political institutions—and shrewd politicians—permitted the outcome to find a constitutional solution. The provisions of the new Constitution, adopted in 1846, stipulated that "all feudal tenures of every description, with all their incidents, are declared to be abolished."[42] The principle did not settle the question of property rights, the passage of tenant farms from manorial proprietors to occupants, and the retrieval of accumulated rent arrears. Given the medley of court opinions to follow, it also fell short of guiding judges in their decisions on those unresolved problems. But it clearly marked the end of an era: personal dependence stopped dominating rental arrangements. From a political point of view, the elimination of the feudal setup of landholdings and of representations of authority based on personal influence and patronage completed the emergence of a politics in which individual white male citizens freely exerted their political rights. Their political empowerment removed, at least in theory, impediments to political participation that had originated in other spheres of life. In doing so, the new New York Constitution effected a slightly ironic feat: it proclaimed the emancipation of the political sphere while placing it next to other activities that competed for men's time and interest. This explains why politics could at certain times be everything in public life and, in turn, why public life rarely was nothing but politics.

The Composition of Social Identities

Public life thus bore the imprint of contending class cultures in the countryside after the first decade of the nineteenth century with the acceleration of economic development and the increasing differentiation of the area's social structure. If the making of social identities certainly included determinants that related positively or negatively to religious sensibility, political conduct did not seem to respond unequivocally to pressures from institutionalized religion. The casualness with which the region's inhabitants chose to attend one church *and* another *as well as* a third makes church adherence a weak predictor of a community's overall political inclination. In other words, the lack of friction between the diverse denominations, formal or evangelical, Puritan or non-Puritan, suggests a tolerance in matters ecclesiastic that seems to preclude a straightforward determination of voting behavior by church membership: the indifference to religious doctrine and the regular, effortless mixing of religious groups in neighborhoods would seem to make difficult the separation of their relative impact on a man's vote. The microhistorical analysis of everyday life, and in this case practices of churchgoing, invalidates generalizations of political behavior predicated on aggregate data. This is not to gainsay at least some influence because reform movements, for example, occasionally benefited individual churches and benefited from them as well. However, only once in the first half of the nineteenth century did a local editor comment on an electoral outcome in terms of religious affiliation. In 1841, the *Catskill Recorder* considered the "Quaker town" of New Baltimore "always good for a Democratic victory." He had a point insofar as the town attracted a great many Friends from the vicinity, where only Athens provided another, much smaller locale in which to gather. In New Baltimore, the Friends' meetinghouse was one of five places of worship, and it regularly welcomed about 40 percent of New Baltimore's churchgoing people in 1855. This was enough to imprint a distinct, visible character on the town. The comment seemed well taken, but what did it prove? No other town in the mid–Hudson Valley with like scores for different denominations in similar competitive circumstances showed such a sweeping and noticeable correspondence between the character of an administrative unit and its inhabitants' political preferences. The other Quaker town in the area, the city of Hudson, regularly voted against the Democrats.[43]

The impact of ethnic identity on politics proves more difficult to assess. In the near absence of numerical figures on Yankees and Yorkers, discursive evidence must bear the weight of the argument. Any documentation on ethnicity in the mid–Hudson Valley is rare, an indication of its relative weakness as a self-consciously experienced organizing principle of everyday life in formal organizations as well as informal social environments like taverns, where a sense of belonging could find expression. Recall that around 1800 ethnic labels surfaced once or twice in comments on conduct at the polls, a fact that should attract our attention to the relational determination of ethnic consciousness in conflicts of interest that encouraged the assignment of undesirable characteristics to adversaries. But an analysis of the surnames in corresponding committees and electoral delegations from 1790 to 1820 reveals no significant difference in their ethnic composition. Later on, and through the 1840s, no private evidence ever referred to ethnic groups. The mention in Spafford's *Gazetteer* of "an old Dutch Burgher" who cursed "Yankee notions" when turnpikes were built at the beginning of the century is so rare that it sounds apocryphal. An almost ethnographic account in the *Catskill Messenger* of 1836 asserted that Dutch funeral rites, "which to us appeared more like some festival or convivial party . . . are in the main abrogated" even in the remoter parts of the Catskills. So while the salience of the Yankee-Yorker distinction seemed to fade in everyday life, where its relevance was limited to begin with at the turn of the century, it gained a life of its own—and one that captured the historiographical imagination—in a literature that indulged in the description of a group's picturesque traits for dramatic effect. African Americans, on the other hand, appeared regularly as employees or clients in the private papers of white people and their press but were denied significance in the very literary genre that invented ethnic qualities. Only the arrival of Irish immigrants after the famine years in the mid-1840s apparently activated ethnic resentment. Kinderhook farmer Ephraim P. Best, at least, occasionally spiced his ledger with the mention of "Yankees" and used derogatory terms like *sow* and *slut* to describe his Irish maid, Joanah Geary, who quit his service rather quickly.[44] Poetic license and literary tropes make for a fallacious historical case. While evidence of discriminatory conduct hints at a larger pattern, its infrequent occurrence prevents it from sustaining an interpretation that derives men's voting behavior from their ethnic backgrounds.

As ECONOMIC development in the first half of the nineteenth century had prompted classes to sort themselves out in terms of patterns of consumption and, as suggested here, by adhering to different codes of behavior in the public sphere, respectability replaced honor as the core value against which comportment began to be measured. New precepts of decency and dignity defined an emerging middle class that cherished the privacy of a refined home. Efforts at both social distinction and self-discipline governed the private as well as public conduct of middle-class people. Paper maker Abner Austin, who was sympathetic to moral reform throughout his life without, however, joining a formal association, illustrated the twin motivation of self-control and public order that quickened his middle-class neighbors to associate in a moral crusade. Looking for a foreman for his paper mill, he informed a candidate in 1833, "I will state fairly in the outset what I wish. It is a man that does not drink ardent spirits, or smoke tobacco. None of my family use tobacco in any shape—but smoking is particularly offensive. As to strong drink, I do not furnish it to any of my workmen." Entrepreneurs had an interest in prohibiting habits that impeded production. While Austin lived by these standards so as to provide a model for his workmen, the owners of the Matteawan Manufacturing village in Fishkill enforced a ban on alcoholic beverages on its grounds.[45]

As mores evolved, politics, too, witnessed a profound shift that in turn reflected a transformation of public sensibility. A stout Columbia County Federalist and ally of manorial interests at the beginning of the nineteenth century and a stalwart adversary of Martin Van Buren's politics throughout the 1830s, attorney Elisha Williams relished a good political fight. Yet the accepted means of engaging political rivals changed over these thirty years. Williams knocked out the editor of the Republican *Hudson Bee* in 1802 after a fierce attack on him had been published in the newspaper. Thirty years later and at an age perhaps less sanguine, Williams endured a polemical assault that the *Catskill Recorder* couched in the idiom of partisanship. Gone were the days when the opposite of honor was cowardice. Now Williams was singled out merely as a representative of the Whigs, who had, so the charge went, an aversion to the "ring-streaked and speckled population of our large towns and cities, comprising people of every kind and tongue." Of course, the polls saw the occasional brawl between members of the contending parties. But the emergence of party bureaucracies contributed to the pacification of political battles and the decline of honor as a man's defining quality in public. Individual reputations now engaged the opposition of virtue and vice to gauge a man's fitness for public office. While partisan rhetoric remained vehement, physical violence was banned as a way of solving problems between the leading men in politics.[46]

The new standards of public behavior ushered in a conflicted situation. Workers like William Smith or George Haydock grew up in an environment where drinking and toasting were part of a lifestyle. At the same time, however, the philanthropic impulse of temperance movements, which emphasized individual responsibility and moral regeneration (and health and well-being), also promised the social reward of respectability to popular classes. In an almost contrapuntal development, then, when members of the lower classes joined the ranks of reform movements they introduced some uncouth elements of the tavern culture into formal organizations and events. Noisy performances, shunned by middle-class people, who probably preferred an evening of moral and intellectual elevation (however much Thomas Cole disparaged "the illustrious and learned Lyceum and gentry of Catskill" after a lecture on Sicilian scenery in 1843), became the hallmark of Washingtonian temperance drives in the mid–Hudson Valley as elsewhere.[47]

Middle-class women found causes to adopt outside their homes in early philantropic organizations. Scimmeltons, antirent pow-wows, and reform movements saw lower-class women occupy a portion of the streets and lecture halls, where at times they assumed vociferous stands. Between private and public, between oversight and acknowledgment, women negotiated their place in the community. Firefighting companies, like inns, remained locales of male sociability, but when William Schunemans's tavern and barn burned down in 1818 the "ladies" of the village of Jefferson helped extinguish the blaze. Thirty-five years later, the Female Benevolent Association of Leeds, which comprised a majority of the hamlet's wives and daughters, staked out its position in terms that both illustrated their assertiveness and betrayed their solicitudes:

> Whereas, in these days of excitement and innovation there is so much dispute with regard to the appropriate sphere of women, we the ladies of the congregation of the Reformed Dutch Church of Leeds take this opportunity to state the ground which we assume on this disputed point. While we distinctly repudiate the doctrine advocated by many that women should sally forth into the field of action side by side with man and push forward with him upon the same terms in his most arduous labors;—neither do we fall into the opposite extreme and hold that woman is required to fold her hands in idleness and spend her days in vain pursuits.

The result of gathering in an association with a public, if not political, purpose consisted in these women's demarcation of their domain. They performed a balancing act in which they reworked the demands of domesticity into claims to consequential, if still limited, public responsibilities and recognition.[48]

The opening of venues into the public sphere must not dissimulate their prohibitive, selective function. While physical violence declined in the encounters between individual respectable white men and lost its status as a legitimate way of righting wrongs inflicted on a man's name or family, symbolic violence continued to curb the access of other groups to an encompassing equality. African Americans were a case in point. They walked the line between conspicuousness and invisibility with more circumspection than women, and their attitudes revealed how adversity was constitutive of identity and self-consciousness. When pressed to testify about the nightly visitors of supposedly doubtful morality to one Judith Snyder in Valatie that he had noticed in 1844, Henry Shoemaker apprehensively declared, "he did not like to make those facts public, from fear the whole would be called a negro lie."[49] Outsiders to politics, where the ideal type of community membership was defined, African Americans and women gained access to public space when character and conscience replaced honor and virility as the necessary qualities of a public persona. However, citizenship and participation in the delegation of authority required the acknowledgment of these groups' full humanity and the removal of assumptions about their innate insufficiencies. In spite of their efforts to live up to the expectations of legitimate culture, this recognition was denied to them. The unequal distribution of power and the means to enforce it through electoral disfranchisement—as well as other mechanisms of the social reproduction of inequality and the perpetuation of feelings of inferiority, such as the small chances of access to substantial education or the numerus clausus in the labor market—maintained them in a subordinate social position. Autonomy remained, like the promise of equality, a thing of the future and, as the antirenters had learned, the object of a struggle to be won.

Conclusion

Labor, the Manor, and the Market

Work was the category through which Alexander Coventry apprehended the society of the Hudson Valley—and his cousin William Coventry—upon his arrival in 1785. He admired the beauty of the area but left no doubt about the toil required to cultivate the soil. Three generations later, a sickly William Hoffman returned to his "native Home" in Claverack after having spent two years as a sales clerk in New York City. The "gorgeous scenery" and the "loveliness of nature" touched Hoffman's "sensibilities of feeling." Whereas Coventry had recorded the efforts necessary to maintain farms, Hoffman indulged in a pastoral description of the countryside. "What pen can delineate the contrast . . . with the bustle like & monotonous every day scenes constantly experienced by the citizen of New York with all its mammon—its business—its would be luxuries—its plethoric 'markets' affording the most exquisite delicacies for the Palate; with Palaces & Paradises for its people [that] cannot compare in point of luxury with the ordinary *Country location & Residence.* The country—the Garden & Paradise of Eden—man's first existence." A literary trope of simplicity and pastoralism had submerged Hoffman's own experience of work on the farm. By the 1850s, indeed, mid–Hudson Valley farmers labored hard to send dairy products, hay, and coarse grains to market while manufacturers produced straw paper, textile and bricks to supply a national market. Between Coventry's journey upriver in 1785 and Hoffman's in 1850, the mid–Hudson Valley had developed from a local, indeed parochial, society into an integral part of a wider world. It was precisely the confrontation with new realities arising from population growth, increasing production, expanding commercial relations, and more intensive communication that pushed the area's inhabitants to forge more abstract concepts in order to make sense of, organize, and cope with the transformation of their everyday experiences.[1]

The roots of the restricted horizon and field of experience at the end of the eighteenth century lay with the struggle of the rural population to assure its subsistence. Nature and its vagaries figured prominently in the worldview of Hudson Valley residents. A shortage of labor exacerbated the incapacity of their agro-technical skills to halt soil exhaustion. Scarcity and scantiness appeared to threaten their supplies. The precariousness of existence, the awareness of which was heightened by the memory of war deprivations and a series of difficult harvests, gave rise to relational strategies that ensured production and the distribution of losses among neighbors. These close relationships defined the scale and meaning of community. Social bonds, not "individual autonomy and self-fulfillment," as Jack P. Greene would have it, characterized the behavior of Marietta Staats, Caleb Lobdell, and their fellow villagers in the 1780s and 1790s.[2] Economic arrangements responded to a social imperative. Local give-and-take, never disinterested and already containing the grain of conflict, helped constitute and maintain the neighborhood. Long-distance trade at the landings conformed to a constellation of features that revolved around the instability of rural life. Personal ties linked farmer and merchant. Clientization regulated their exchanges by providing a guarantee of long-term credit to the producer and of supply to the commercial middleman. This privileged connection kept volatile forces of supply and demand at a distance and afforded a sense of security to both participants. Farmers, artisans, and their spouses and children perceived this small world of face-to-face relations through concepts that expressed its immediacy as well as the paramount importance of subsistence-related activities. Hence work, in its transparent form and with concrete results, shaped their understanding of the social relations that created their universe. It was the standard in the circulation of goods and services among neighbors, who determined value equivalence on the basis of the effort it took to accomplish a productive act.

If mid–Hudson Valley farmers followed long-established practices, they nevertheless adopted implements and methods that enhanced agricultural production. They championed new, permanent grasses and began to spread manure and fertilizers; they introduced cradle scythes and cast iron plows; they acquired resistant Merino sheep to produce wool. Gains in production came with the extension of better-cultivated land. Increases in productivity resulted from specialization and the consequent reallocation of labor according to gender-defined skills. Together these advances eventually stimulated the growth of a year-round, often nonlocal, agricultural wage-labor force next to a local pool of seasonal and temporary help. Better grasses, deeper plowing, regular harrowing, and restorative soil treatment on fenced land improved crops and animal well-being: these were capital improvements in both senses of the word, a fact that found reflection in the appreciation of the region's land values. Innovations, technical as well as organizational, helped farmers increase their control over the environment. Of course, nothing protected them against erratic weather, as in 1816 when the area "from the 7th to the 11th of June had frosts every night & some places had some snow."[3] But comments revealing anxiety about the material standard of living disappeared from the diaries and ledgers of the agricultural population in the nineteenth century, when richer husbandmen first succeeded in exporting more produce. By 1820 a majority of farmers regularly engaged in long-distance trade to satisfy metropolitan and even extraregional demand.

The development of a denser transportation network sustained the region's comparative ability to compete in the expanding market. Turnpikes and steamboats lowered conveyance charges after the turn of the century. Specializing middlemen, often financially involved in the construction of roads and interested in riverboats, reduced transaction costs; butter, for example, was collected at the farm gate by the 1830s, when farmers began to deal with different brokers to market their produce. Mass-produced, generic commodities from the mid–Hudson Valley—shoes as well as cloth, hats as well as steel forks—eventually flowed to New York City and western lands, while complex machines (as well as clocks, it is worth remembering) were assembled in industrial towns like Stockport and Kinderhook from parts produced in the metropolitan factory belt.[4]

Politics influenced economic opportunities and impregnated the growing impact of the market principle. State administrations chartered turnpikes, gave tax breaks to industrialists, and supported textile factories when the Napoleonic Wars in Europe diverted investments toward American manufactures. On a local level, town authorities abolished assizes on bread and enforced the tenets of a free market economy in which supply and demand, not personal relationships, regulated the flow of goods.

Agricultural development supplied work to artisans who catered to the needs of the farming population. Waterpower attracted textile manufactures. Natural resources like hemlock bark and Hudson River clay brought tanners and brick makers to the area. For a short period, a small number of farm families and professional weavers entered into a symbiotic relationship with textile manufactures because looms remained hand operated after mechanization had sped up spinning procedures. But industrial development produced a new population of workers whose recruitment tended to target young men, often women, and certainly immigrants. Factory operatives, tanners, and brick makers clustered around their work sites. They stayed aloof from the farm neighborhood with its rhythms and rituals. They consumed agricultural goods, however, for which, as Alexander Coventry observed in 1828, they paid in cash rather than with reciprocating labor, just as their employers bought local raw materials and foodstuffs. They could expect to earn an adequate living during their gainful employment, although their exclusive dependence on paid labor kept them only one crisis away from the state's or the town's relief rolls, where their contingent eventually outnumbered the traditional poor—the old, the infant, and the invalid.[5]

More pervasive cash transactions suggest how the social morphology generated by the rising regional division of labor, emerging local industrial structure, and growing social differentiation had altered the ways in which people in the countryside related to each other. "Cash sales cannot cause you much loss," Peter Ousterhout imparted to aspiring storekeeper Frederick Kirtland in 1834. "A limited safe business is always to be preferred to that which is overextended and done on a credit system." Metropolitan banks increasingly endorsed and discounted legal tender; they transformed promissory notes and bills of lading into reserves that backed the expansion of the volume of circulating cash. Enhanced monetary liquidity, not unlike the regular schedules of ships on the Hudson, became a way to brace and control, in short, to coordinate, longer and more complex chains of social interdependence that linked different segments of the Hudson Valley population to each other as well as the outside world. The change in the quality of social relations is perhaps best illustrated with an example from the manorial lands in Columbia County. As proprietors, the Livingstons had often exhibited their entrepreneurial drive, if not always their business acumen, with attempts to make their estate more productive. As landlords, their attitude toward tenants bore the mark of a paternalism that suffered rent arrears and displayed largesse. They abandoned their paternalistic posture with the advancing nineteenth century when commerce took on greater importance and their revenues from rents encountered sharper public criticism. They began to pressure tenants for regular and full rent payments until, in 1845, Peter L. Livingston "determined to collect at once, with all the rigor of law, every cent due on his share of the estate." Formalized, monetary accounts rather than ritualized, reciprocal relationships eventually prevailed among neighbors and at times in families, too. Theodore Cole hired his laborer Nick out to plough for G. Thornton in 1857, and this construction of work as a fleeting and paid interaction rather than an act in a succession of events signaled the final step in the shift of the balance from an encompassing moral to a differentiated rational universe. The market principle now permeated the social and economic organization of the neighborhood.[6]

Just as money helped connect people who did not know each other in an ever larger economic space, it allowed the introduction of social distance in the proximity of the neighborhood, where housing served as a clear marker of social status. In the late eighteenth century, society remained articulated around the value of hierarchy. Men in the mid–Hudson Valley knew their station and could mingle without much trouble because their difference in kind appeared so self-evident that fistfights and duels were status-exclusive ways to solve animosities and enmities in the public arena. If labor was the standard of exchange among farmers and artisans, it distinguished them from gentlemen, who considered physical toil an opprobrium unbecoming to their elevated social position. The Society of Mechanics in the City of Hudson contested the superior intelligence of wealth but expressed no doubt about their own location among the middling sorts in 1792 when public wedding announcements did not fail to pay homage to a man's high rank. A generation later, the assumption of superiority still shone through in a letter on the matrimonial strategies of New York's "good society" by the distinguished Kinderhook lawyer Peter Van Schaack, who wrote, "the union between the branches of two ancient families of the highest respectability very much interests me & immediately affecting affords me the sincerest pleasure." But by this time the joy was melancholy, and the attention to patrician lineage and status displayed a note of defensiveness. The era in which families could take for granted their preeminence in society and politics was coming to an end. While access to the levers of power opened up when an egalitarian ideology inspired hitherto excluded Hudson Valley residents to fight for political participation and inclusion, other spheres of social experience underwent processes of refinement and exclusion. Income contributed to successful distinction. Homes and gardens provided not only comfort and shelter and expressed professional achievement; they also kept less fortunate people out of sight. The conditions and measures of public recognition were changing: the value of birth and name declined in the face of work and occupational proficiency. Respectability replaced honor, a shift from which an emerging middle class had much to gain. Merit earned in the economy, not a pedigree, supported its members' struggle for social prestige and high status. Skill and professionalism, not birthright, sustained their claims to power.[7]

The twins of self-discipline and the search for public order accompanied the mutation and elevation of labor to the core value of social taxonomy. Accordingly, behavior that impeded steady work habits became the target of reform efforts. Good morals, manners and taste, whose canons were often derived from aristocratic etiquette, denoted the domination of baser affects and inclinations associated with intemperance, bloody sports, and Sabbath breaking—in short, with wasting time. The adoption of these standards promised public rewards in the form of economic success and respectability, on the one hand, and private gains such as health and well-being as a result of more moderate consumption of alcohol and pacified sociability on the other. William Hoffman clearly perceived the connection (and in some sense revealed the anxiety associated with the internalization of new standards of behavior) in March 1848 when, on the threshold of a clerkship at a general store and thus of a career in a nonmanual occupation, he resolved "to remove all corruption from my morals & moreover instill me with purer, nobler & higher feelings than I ever before expressed." The decision soon after seduced him into objecting to a neighboring farmer's "consummate folly of chewing tobacco." The elimination of putative vices was a means of self-definition and a declaration of adhesion to, if perhaps not always the respect of, the codes by which the middle class lived. It propelled the antebellum moral crusade that not only included people in search of their social bearings but aimed to correct the conduct of less refined groups. The rise of labor as a value thus occurred simultaneously with the lowering of tolerance for crudeness and coarseness. The new protocol of behavior located unpolished and vulgar demeanor among people cursed to toil in manual occupations, among whom farmers labored to obtain more recognition than mere lip service to their national utility. If the work of independent artisans and husbandmen remained an unlikely source of upward mobility even when pursued on par with the emerging principles of business, they, and certainly their wives at first, perceived the benefits of behavioral regeneration and reform associations in terms of vitality and sociability. At least, they did so after some run-ins with the better sorts and with the adaptation of middle-class and elite organizations to the predilections among the popular classes for the combination of spiritual elevation and entertainment.[8]

Zest and frolic also characterized a number of meetings at which antirent activists appeared in Indian disguises ("so outlandish as to beggar description" according to *Niles' National Register* of 1845) to promote the abolition of manorial property relations. Antirent pow-wows with their tin horns and masks expressed the lessees' contempt for their genteel adversaries, who gave formal balls with dignified music and dances in honor of illustrious visitors such as the Marquis de Lafayette in 1824. Their purpose was to voice a profound opposition to the system of land tenure in upstate New York. The "feudal incidences," as antirenters labeled lease conditions, consisted of rent payments in kind, currency, and services, the landlord's right to impose a fine of alienation, or quarter-sales, that ranged from 10 to 25 percent of a farm's value when a tenant sold his lease, and the right of first purchase of the produce the tenant wished to market. As a matter of course, the landlord benefited from any economic transaction in which the tenant engaged. The project of the lessees was to overthrow this feudal order, which combined, in their eyes, economic exploitation, social segregation, and symbolic exclusion. Naturally, the rentiers-landlords were unwilling to give up their "pleasant revenue" without a fight. The conflict engaged different notions of work, and the growing positive resonance that tenant grievances achieved in public opinion and the political sphere provides an illustration of, and a measure with which to gauge, the advance of a market society and culture in the mid–Hudson Valley.[9]

The social vision shared by the rebellious population rejected the legitimacy of the landlords' leisurely way of life. Lifting their words directly from Thomas Jefferson, the roughly four hundred tenants on Livingston property in Columbia County in 1800 considered themselves "tillers of the earth, the chosen people of God." They aspired to join ranks with the "virtuous and independent yeomanry." Theirs was a worldview of people who strove for a competence, a secure way of life based on family labor in agriculture. This position was remarkable for its longevity in a society that was changing fast. In 1845, antirenters continued to argue that it was the tenant who had "increased the value of the premises to $30 [from $1.75] per acre, by his labor and money invested in tillage and fixtures." Work created wealth, the tenant theory went, but "life leases with their slavish appendages" deprived the lessees of the fruits of their toil. The leases resulted in "the superior wealth and influence of their opponents, [circumstances that] compelled them to submit & to accept from them such terms of accommodation as they saw fit to offer." However much the tenants' struggle was antiseigneurial in character and origin, it did not result from opposition to a perceived capitalist intrusion that threatened the renters' subsistence. Tenants saw the market not as an abstract entity but as a concrete place where they, like their freehold neighbors, could sell the produce of their farms. When they formulated their desire to become "members of civilized society," they hoped to gain the independence promised in the American Constitution but denied to them by the "relics of barbarism" and "the feudal polity" inherited from prerevolutionary, colonial New York.[10] Antirenters interpreted their resistance to seigneurial domination as a fight against feudalism. They did not have a minute, legalistic understanding of its social organization but associated it with a complex of negative characteristics: barbarity rather than civilization, oppression rather than liberty, exploitation rather than independence, privilege rather than equality. To claim economic autonomy—and free, untrammeled access to the market fell into that broad objective—was to demand the rights of an independent citizenry made up of free men whose work supported, and whose authority governed, their families. Coercion had no place in their understanding of the political sphere.

Landlords insisted on property's traditional inviolability, which had found confirmation in the courts. In 1812, Judge Van Ness, a friend of the family, had confirmed the Livingston title. Mary Livingston exulted that the tenant leaders "returned home, mortified & disappointed & the tenants will probably return to their duty, pay their rents which they have withheld, & remain quiet for many years to come." Chancellor James Kent, another Livingston confidant, recognized the legality of manorial landholdings on the Circuit Court in 1813. A generation later, Daniel Dewey Barnard pleaded the landlords' cause by attacking the antirent movement's "agrarian spirit" and its plea "for land to every man without paying for it. Property in land, beyond what a man can personally occupy and cultivate, is especially denounced." Another conservative observer, former New York mayor Philip Hone, picked up and expanded on the same reasoning when he expressed his fear of "the vile disorganizing spirit" among the antirenters, whose appeals and actions threatened public order in the state.[11]

The labor theory of value and property proved unsuccessful in challenging the landlords' status as proprietors of manorial lands. But absolute, unimpeded ownership suffered the assault of a new conception of property that emphasized economic development. Its increasing pervasiveness hinged on the growing influence of the middle class, whose entrepreneurial and political segments promoted a free market agenda. The rise of the market principle spawned a worldview and an ideology in which obstacles to the free exchange of land, labor, and commodities needed to be eliminated as impediments to economic growth. Manorial circumstances and the landlord's interference with any tenant's economic transactions restricted the free flow of real estate and agricultural goods. "Vested rights," proclaimed a group of businessmen of Schodack, located north of Columbia County and sourrounded by Van Rensselaer lands, in 1845, formed "impassible barriers to improvements" because manors appeared to stifle commercial relations. A few members of the state assembly had built a case for "the free course of alienating real property" in 1812. By the 1840s the argument had grown more sweeping and gathered more support. The government-nominated committee to recommend legislation to solve the manorial conundrum and restore public order stated in 1846: "In addition to the restraints on alienation imposed in many of the leases, serious impediments have existed to a free exchange of the lands, in the inconvenience and legal embarrassments which surround such transfers, and which tend to restrain labor from seeking, through shifting employments, its most advantageous application, and to repress the disposition, the habit, and the opportunities of enterprise." Hudson Valley manors, John Van Buren still noted in 1850, acted "as clogs on industry . . . they have been and are a curse to this country, especially to agriculture, manufacturing industry and enterprise."[12]

The abolition of manorial property in 1846 was the Hudson Valley's equivalent of the abrogation of Great Britain's Speenhamland legislation in 1834 insofar as it inaugurated the era of the self-regulating market. However, the antimanorial struggle owed its efficacy not to the hatred inspired by the recognition of minimum wage entitlements of the laboring classes but to capitalism's destruction of a specific kind of property and the removal of a set of privileged, indeed quite entrepreneurial, owners who appeared to obstruct the efficient allocation of resources. The assumptions of laissez-faire efficiency debilitated the traditional ideological foundations of property, depicting it as an obstacle to moneymaking propositions and general welfare. The claim to serve a public purpose had, after all, won state charters for bridges, turnpikes, toll roads, and canals. Such charters granted these quasi-public enterprises the right of eminent domain, which allowed the state to appropriate private property if its projected use would realize an increase in public wealth. This legal premise permitted the businessmen of Schodack to urge executive intervention to abolish manorial property relations when the labor theory of property still justified the arguments deployed in the same cause by tenant organizations like the Taghkanic Mutual Association. "The Boston Rail Road passes through this town," the resolution of the Schodack meeting, presided over by ten men worth a substantial $10,417 on average, declared, "and so far as they occupy the lands, the landlord's covenants have been extinguished without their consent, and that under a power granted by our legislature. This would be justified on the ground, not that it was strictly for the public use, but that prosperity and welfare of the country require it. Then if the prosperity and welfare of the country would be promoted by removing the evils we complain of, why should not the same rule be applied and a similar course adopted?" While entrepreneurial, middle-class adversaries of manorial estates saw land as a commodity best subjected to the abstract laws of supply and demand within an economic system in which capital flowed freely (or with a minimum of transaction costs), antirenters conceived of landed property as the foundation of working farmers' independence and dignity.[13]

The rift in the coalition was patent. It was a tension that Tocqueville put at the center of his inquiry into the emergence of modern polities but one he thought had been resolved in the United States. However, a historical examination of the rise of a market society and culture on the farms, in the shops, and at the landings of the mid-Hudson Valley during the first half of the nineteenth shows that liberty and equality, rather than coexisting harmoniously in New York society, wielded the power to move people. The protracted struggle to abolish manorial conditions was certainly the most consummate manifestation of their competition, but in one form or another their uneasy relation inspired women, African Americans, freehold farmers, artisans, factory operatives, and storekeepers as well as merchants. The editor of the *Catskill Messenger*, for one, advocated free public dances in 1836 because dancing "dissipates those arbitrary distinctions in society, so repugnant to enlightened liberality."[14] It was a playful, practical proposition to further a serious cause. Others shared the ideal but chose different means and ways to promote it. Antirent tenants sought economic and social equality and believed it would lead to political liberty. Their middle-class consociates desired economic liberty and held that it would promote social and political equality. These rival aspirations live on in the political repertoire of our own times. While their actualization takes different forms today, the recovery of their history in the mid–Hudson Valley shows them as the legacy of ordinary people whose actions were possible and meaningful precisely because they participated, eagerly or reluctantly, in the construction of a market society.

Notes

List of Acronyms Used

COLCHS Columbia County Historical Society, Kinderhook
GTCHS Greene County Historical Society, Coxsackie
N-YHS New-York Historical Society, New York
NYPL New York Public Library, Rare Books and Manuscripts, New York
NYSArc New York State Archives, Albany
NYSHA New York State Historical Association, Cooperstown
NYSL New York State Library, Albany

Introduction: *Everyday Life and the Making of Rural Development in the Hudson Valley*

1 Anne Grant, *Memoirs of an American Lady, with Sketches of Manners and Scenery in America as They Existed Previous to the Revolution* (London, 1808), 1:64; *Hudson Weekly Gazette,* 30 Sept. 1788, 4; William Coventry Diary, 3 July 1798, NYSHA.

2 *Hudson Northern Whig,* 7 March 1815; 17 Sept. 1816.

3 *Hudson Rural Repository,* 19 March 1836, 167. See also *Catskill Messenger,* 28 March 1833, 2; 1 Jan. 1834, 2.

4 George Holcomb Diary, 22 Dec. 1838, NYSL; see also Ann-Janette Dubois Diary, 28 Dec. 1839, GTCHS.

5 *Report of the Greene County Agricultural Society for 1847* (n.p., 1847), 3. My reference is to a special printing located at GTCHS. The report originally appeared in *Transactions of the New York State Agricultural Society for 1847* (Albany, 1848).

6 Alexander Coventry Diary, 23 June 1786 (typescript edited by the Albany Institute of History and Art and NYSL, 1978); William Hoffman Diary, 16, 19, and 23 Aug. 1847 (also see 26 June 1847), N-YHS.

7 Alexander Coventry Diary, 11 Nov. 1785, 15 May 1787; Theodore A. Cole Diary, 14 Sept. 1857, MV 1207, GTCHS; Wilbur Fisk Strong Diary, 5 and 20 Oct. 1858, MV 231, GTCHS. Eight shillings were the equivalent of one dollar.

8 Alexander Coventry Diary, 23 June 1786, 26 April 1787; William Hoffman Diary, 1 (quote), 4, 5, 7, and 8 Feb. 1850.

9 Account Joseph White, Elijah Hudson Account Book, 16 April 1787, Sept. 1788, NYSHA; Account of Isaac Mills, Unidentified Account Book (Kinderhook), 12 Jan. 1804, NYSL; Hannah Bushnell Diary, 2 July 1855, 1 Sept. 1856, MV 366, GrCHS; Theodore A. Cole Diary, 12 June 1857, 24 June, 21 and 23 Nov. 1857; William Hoffman Diary, 2 March 1847.

10 William Youngs Diary, 4 May and 16 June 1811, NYSHA; To the president and directors of the Albany & Weststockbridge Railroad Company, 7 June 1842, Van Valkenburg Papers, COlCHS; *New York Spectator,* 3 Sept. 1824, 1; Nathaniel Bartlett Sylvester, *History of Ulster County, New York* (Philadelphia, 1880), 203–4; *Coxsackie Standard,* 21 Sept. 1837, 2; "Reminiscences of Matilda Metcalf," in Edward A. Collier, *A History of Kinderhook* (New York, 1914), 496.

11 *Hudson Gazette,* 16 Aug. 1792, 3; Mary Livingston Memorandum, 1 Dec. 1811, COlCHS; *Kinderhook Sentinel,* 8 Oct. 1846, 2.

12 For the classic debate between Maurice Dobb and Paul Sweezy, see Rodney Hilton, ed., *The Transition from Feudalism to Capitalism* (London, 1976). For a more recent installment, see Robert Brenner, "Agrarian Class Structure and Economic Development in Pre-industrial Europe," *Past and Present* 70 (1976): 30–75; Immanuel Wallerstein, *The Modern World System* (New York, [1974] 1980), 1:308, 2:236–41; Franklin F. Mendels, "Proto-industrialization: The First Phase of the Industrial Revolution," *Journal of Economic History* 32 (1972): 241–61; and Peter Kriedte, Hans Medick, and Jürgen Schlumbohm, *Industrialization before Industrialization: Rural Industry in the Genesis of Industrial Capitalism* (Cambridge, Engl., 1981), 30–31, 82–85.

13 Karl Polanyi, *The Great Transformation: The Political and Economic Origins of Our Time* (Boston, 1957), esp. 58–67; Fernand Braudel, *Civilisation matérielle, économie et capitalisme, 15e–18e siècle,* vol. 2: *Les jeux de l'échange* (Paris, 1979). On market rationality, see also Max Weber, *Wirtschaft und Gesellschaft; Grundriss der verstehenden Soziologie* (Tübingen, 1972), 382–85.

14 These labels are Allan Kulikoff's. See his *The Agrarian Origins of American Capitalism* (Charlottesville, 1992), 13–33. On development on the frontier, see Charles E. Brooks, *Frontier Settlement and Market Revolution: The Holland Land Purchase* (Ithaca, 1996); and Alan Taylor, *William Cooper's Town: Power and Persuasion on the Frontier of the Early American Republic* (New York, 1995). For a fine account of frontier exchange, see Daniel H. Usner, *Indians, Settlers, and Slaves in a Frontier Exchange Economy: The Lower Mississippi Valley before 1783* (Chapel Hill, 1992). Older historiographies include David M. Potter, *People of Plenty: Economic Abundance and the American Character* (Chicago, 1954); Richard Hofstadter, *America at 1750: A Social Portrait* (New York, 1971); and Jack P. Greene, *Imperatives, Behaviors, and Identities; Essays in Early American Cultural History* (Charlottesville, 1992). For examples of regional histories, see Richard L. Bushman, *From Puritan to Yankee: Character and the Social Order in Connecticut, 1690–1765* (Cambridge, Mass., 1967); James T. Lemon, *The Best Poor Man's Country: A Geographical Study of Early Southeastern Pennsylvania* (Baltimore, 1972); and John Frederick Martin, *Profits in the Wilderness: Entrepreneurship and the Founding of New England Towns in the Seventeenth Century* (Chapel Hill, 1991).

15 Michael Merrill, "Cash Is Good to Eat: Self-Sufficiency and Exchange in the Rural Economy of the United States," *Radical History Review* 3 (1977): 42–71; Christopher Clark, "Household Economy, Market Exchange, and the Rise of Capitalism in the Connecticut Valley, 1800–1860," *Journal of Social History* 13 (1979): 169–89; James A. Henretta, "Families and Farms: *Mentalité* in Pre-industrial America," *William and Mary Quarterly,* 3d ser., 35 (1978): 3–32; Daniel Vickers, *Farmers and Fishermen: Two Centuries of Work in Essex County, Massachusetts, 1630–1850* (Chapel Hill, 1994).

16 Braudel, *Civilisation,* esp. 2: 49–54. On the land market, see Giovanni Levi, *Inheriting Power: The Story of an Exorcist* (Chicago, 1988), 66–99.

17 Vincent Morgan Townsend Diary, 3 Jan. 1834, 15 Feb. 1834, Cornell University Archives.

18 Winifred Rothenberg's articles are conveniently collected in *From Market-Places to a Market Economy: The Transformation of Rural Massachusetts, 1750–1850* (Chicago, 1992), quote on p. 4. See also her "The Productivity Consequences of Market Integration: Agriculture in Massachusetts, 1771–1801," in *American Economic Growth and the Standard of Living before the Civil War,* edited by Robert E. Gallman and John Joseph Wallis (Chicago, 1992), 312–14.

19 Francis Hall, *Travels in Canada and the United States in 1816 and 1817* (London, 1818), 35; Louis Hartz, *The Liberal Tradition in America: An Interpretation of American Political Thought since the Revolution* (New York, 1955), 3–20, 43, 52; Hofstadter, *America at 1750,* 11, 151–53, 174. On manorial relations, see Martin Bruegel, "Unrest: Manorial Society and the Market in the Hudson Valley, 1780–1850," *Journal of American History* 82 (1996): 1393–1424. For a political history of antirentism, see Reeve Huston, *Land and Freedom: Rural Society, Popular Protest, and Party Politics in Antebellum New York* (New York, 2000).

20 The information for this paragraph comes from Horatio Gates Spafford, *A Gazetteer of the State of New York* (Albany, 1824), 125–27, 208–10; Thomas F. Gordon, *Gazetteer of the State of New York* (Philadelphia, 1836), 64, 402–13, 468–75; J. Disturnell, *A Gazetteer of the State of New York* (Albany, 1842), 127, 189; J. H. French, *Gazetteer of the State of New York* (Syracuse, 1860), 241, 329; Alexander Coventry Diary, 4 Sept. 1791; Heinrich Luden, ed., *Reise Sr. Hoheit des Herzogs Bernhard zu Sachsen-Weimar-Eisenach durch Nordamerika in den Jahren 1825 und 1826* (Weimar, 1828), 1:110, 173; Horatio Gates Spafford, *A Gazetteer of the State of New York* (Albany, 1813), 150; James Macaulay, *The Natural, Statistical, and Civil History of the State of New York* (New York, 1829), 1:378–79; J. H. Mather, L. P. Brockett, *Geography of the State of New York* (Hartford, 1847), 296; *Catskill Messenger,* 11 Aug. 1849, 2; and *Catskill Messenger,* 1 Sept. 1849, 2.

21 Julian Ursyn Niemcewicz, *Under Their Vine and Fig Tree; Travels through America in 1797–1799, 1805,* translated and edited by Metchie J. E. Budka (Elizabeth, 1965), 192; Tyrone Power, *Impressions of America during the Years 1833, 1834, and 1835* (London, 1836), 1:430; Washington Irving to Sarah Storrow, 1 Aug. 1843, in Ralph M. Alderman, Herbert L. Kleinfield, Jenifer S. Banks, eds., *Washington Irving: Letters,* vol. 3: *1839–1845* (Boston, 1982), 149–50; *Catskill Messenger,* 1 July 1848, 2.

22 See Franklin F. Mendels, "Agriculture and Peasant Industry in Eighteenth-Century Flanders," in *European Peasants and Their Markets,* edited by William N. Parker and Eric L. Jones (Princeton, 1975), 179–204; Kenneth A. Lockridge, "Land, Population, and the Evolution of New England Society, 1630–1790," *Past and Present* 39 (1968): 62–

80; and David W. Sabean, *Property, Production, and the Family in Neckarhausen, 1700–1870* (New York, 1990), 21–22, 450–51. Christopher Clark uses a demographic model to explain the rise of capitalist relations in the Connecticut River valley. See his *The Roots of Rural Capitalism: Western Massachusetts, 1780–1860* (Ithaca, 1990). On population, see *Census of the State of New York for 1855* (Albany, 1857).

23 Alfred F. Young, *The Democratic Republicans of New York: The Origins, 1763–1797* (Chapel Hill, 1967), 90–91; Cynthia A. Kierner, *Traders and Gentlefolks: The Livingstons of New York, 1675–1790* (Ithaca, 1992), 93; J. Hector St. John de Crèvecoeur, *Letters from an American Farmer* (New York, 1982), 81.

24 My understanding of class derives from Max Weber's analysis of "class situation" as a group's location with respect to income-producing assets and the congruence of material living conditions. See Hans Gerth and C. Wright Mills, eds., *From Max Weber: Essays in Sociology* (New York, 1946), 181–82.

25 S. Granby Spees, *Memorial Celebration Comprising the Address Delivered on the Occasion* (Saratoga, 1872), 13.

ONE *Exchange and the Creation of the Neighborhood in the Late Eighteenth Century*

1 Alexander Coventry Diary, 29 Sept. 1786 (typescript edited by the Albany Institute of History and Art and the New York State Library); William Coventry recorded some of his activities on his cousin's behalf in William Coventry Diary, 18 and 21 Sept. 1786, NYSHA.

2 Alexander Coventry Diary, 16–30 Sept. 1786; the frolic took place on 28 September 1786.

3 Ibid., 28 April 1788; Robert Livingston to James Duane, 30 April 1788, quoted in Alfred F. Young, *The Democratic Republicans of New York: The Origins, 1763–1797* (Chapel Hill, 1967), 95. On politics, see Alan Taylor, " 'The Art of Hook and Snivey': Political Culture in Upstate New York during the 1790s," *Journal of American History* 79 (1993): 1371–96.

4 Alexander Coventry Diary, 30 April and 26 July 1788.

5 Tench Coxe, *A View of the United States* (London, 1795), 88 (a bushel contains 35.24 liters or about 9.00 American gallons); J. Hector St. John de Crèvecoeur, "Sketches of Eighteenth-Century America," in *Letters from an American Farmer* (New York, 1982), 297; Crèvecoeur, *Letters,* 80–81. For a comparison with other rural populations, see George M. Foster, "Peasant Society and the Image of Limited Good," *American Anthropologist* 67 (1965): 293–315; and Frank Cancian, "Economic Behavior in Peasant Communities," in *Economic Anthropology,* edited by Stuart Plattner (Stanford, 1989), 127–70.

6 John Beebe Diary, 1 May 1780, 6–15 June 1779, quotes from 5 and 7 June 1779, Chatham Public Library; William Smith Jr., *Historical Memoirs,* edited by William H. W. Sabine (New York, 1969), 3:365 (3 May 1778), 323 (15 March 1778), 373 (7 May 1778). For Albany, see also Rutger Bleecker to Leonard Bronk, 16 Sept. 1780, Bronk Ms. 1780, GRCHS. In general, see Edward Countryman, *A People in Revolution: The American Revolution and Political Society in New York, 1760–1790* (New York, 1989), 180–86. Eight shillings were worth a dollar.

7　John Beebe Diary, 8 Oct. 1779, 25 and 29 Jan. 1780; see also 6, 7, 17, and 24 May 1779. Compare this with Staughton Lynd, *Class Conflict, Slavery, and the United States Constitution* (Indianapolis, 1967), 49–50.

8　John Beebe Diary, 9 July and 4 Aug. 1785; William Coventry Diary, 30 July and 1 Aug. 1790; Alexander Coventry Diary, 25 March 1791; *Hudson Bee,* 23 July 1805, 3. See also comments collected from newspapers in Joel Munsell, *The Annals of Albany* (Albany, 1852), 3:155, 174.

9　*Hudson Weekly Gazette,* 25 Jan. 1787, 3; *Hudson Weekly Gazette,* 30 Sept. 1788, 4; William Coventry Diary, 24, 25, 31 July and 13 Aug. 1799, 15 Aug. and 30 Oct. 1800, 27 June 1807; *Hudson Gazette,* 14 July 1801, 3. See also Munsell, *Annals,* 4:309: "An Albany newspaper from June 21, 1799 stated that 'Wheat is 14s cash, and rising. The Hessian fly is making its ravages in our wheat fields, and in some part of Montgomery County the most promising are already cut off'."

10　Alexander Coventry Diary, 13 and 26 Jan. 1791, 6 Feb. 1791; Crèvecoeur, "Sketches," 304; Charles Rockwell, *The Catskills* (New York, 1867), 124–39; *History of Greene County* (New York, 1884), 64, 326.

11　Alexander Coventry Diary, 13 July and 17 Sept. 1787; William Coventry Diary, 9 and 24 Aug., 4 Sept., 10 Oct. 1792.

12　William Coventry Diary, 17 Oct. 1795; 1, 17, and 31 Oct. and 12 and 30 Nov. 1796; 19 Sept. 1800; 4, 12, and 16 July 1801; 3 Aug. 1802. See also *Catskill Packet and Western Mail,* 5 Sept. 1796, 3.

13　Silah Strong Diary, 22 Sept. 1784, quoted in *History of Greene County,* 263; Alexander Coventry Diary, 25 Feb. 1791; William Coventry Diary, 27 Oct. 1798, 25 and 27 Feb. 1799, 2 Jan. and 7 May 1800; 6 April 1798. See also William Coventry Diary, 26 Jan. and 14 Nov. 1799, 23 Feb. and 2 April 1800 (quote from 3 July 1798 and similarly 7 Nov. 1790); and *Hudson Bee,* 6 Aug. 1805, 3.

14　Timothy Dwight, *Travels in New England and New York* (New Haven, 1820–22), 4:3–4; *Transactions of the Society for the Promotion of Agriculture, Arts, and Manufacture,* 2d ed. (Albany, 1801), 1:294–95; and Alexander Coventry Diary, 3 Sept. 1790. For an instructive timetable of agricultural work, see Winifred B. Rothenberg, "Structural Change in the Farm Labor Force: Contract Labor in Massachusetts Agriculture, 1750–1865," in *Strategic Factors in Nineteenth-Century American Economic History,* edited by Claudia Goldin and Hugh Rockoff (Chicago, 1992), 105–34.

15　Alexander Coventry Diary, 31 Aug. 1786, 14 Feb. 1787; William Coventry Diary, Jan. 1800. Economists will have recognized the Coventry cousins' quandary as a problem of moral hazard, a costly incapacity to monitor somebody else's work completely. See Bengt Holmström, "Moral Hazard and Observability," *Bell Journal of Economics* 10 (1979): 74–91.

16　Caleb Dill's Will of 23 Feb. 1786, in Gustave Anjou, ed., *Ulster County, New York: Probate Records* (New York, 1906), 2:10–11. On the relation between labor demand and a family's life cycle, see Laurel Thatcher Ulrich, "Martha Ballard and Her Girls: Women's Work in Eighteenth-Century Maine," in *Work and Labor in Early America,* edited by Stephen Innes (Chapel Hill, 1988), 70–105.

17　The slave population varied between these two extremes, the mean percentage lying somewhere over 10 percent. See *Heads of Families at the First Census of the United States taken in the Year 1790* (Baltimore, 1966).

18 John Beebe Jr. Diary, 23 June 1785. For other collective house raisings, see William Coventry Diary, 2 July 1798, 29 Sept. 1800. Twenty-three out of 81 houses worth more than $100 in Hurley and 62 out of 174 in Marbletown fitted these categories. See Particular List or Description of Each Dwelling-House . . . Owned, Possessed, or Occupied on the First Day of October, 1798, in Hurley, N-YHS; and Particular List or Description of Each Dwelling-House . . . Owned, Possessed, or Occupied on the First Day of October, 1798, in Marbletown, N-YHS. Crèvecoeur, of course, describes a house-raising frolic in "What Is an American?" in *Letters,* 103–4.

19 Alexander Coventry Diary, 22 July 1786, 7 Oct. 1790; William Coventry Diary, 6 and 12 July, 21 Aug. 1792. Anthropologists long ago discovered the essential quality of these cooperative efforts for the constitution of communities. See Sydel Silverman, "The Peasant Concept in Anthropology," *Journal of Peasant Studies* 7 (1979): 49–69.

20 Alexander Coventry Diary, 20 June 1790. See, for example, Christopher Clark, *The Roots of Rural Capitalism: Western Massachusetts, 1780–1860* (Ithaca, 1991), 38; Christopher Clark, "Household Economy, Market Exchange, and the Rise of Capitalism in the Connecticut Valley, 1800–1860," *Journal of Social History* 13 (1979): 173–76; and Max Schumacher, *The Northern Farmer and His Markets during the Late Colonial Period* (New York, [1948] 1969), 88–89.

21 Zephaniah Chase Account Book, 1787 and 1799, NYSL; Alexander Coventry Diary, 18 and 22 Feb. 1790 (shoes), 1 Sept. 1790; George Holcomb Diary, 7 and 19 March 1814 (see also 22 Aug. 1807), NYSL; Selah Strong Account Book, 4 June 1788, 24 June 1790, GTCHS.

22 Cyril S. Belshaw, *Traditional Exchange and Modern Markets* (Englewood Cliffs, 1965), 56; Marcel Mauss, *Manuel d'éthnographie* (Paris, 1967), 128–33; Joseph Jenkins Account Book, 1803–1806, NYSHA; William Coventry Diary, 6 Feb. 1792.

23 George Holcomb Diary, 3 March 1814, 22 August and 9 Dec. 1807, 23 Nov. 1810, 16 Aug. 1811, 20 Aug. 1812; see also William Coventry Diary, 4 June 1799.

24 George Holcomb Diary, 8 Aug. 1811; Alexander Coventry Diary, 18 Jan. 1787.

25 On Europe, see David W. Sabean, *Property, Production, and Family in Neckarhausen, 1700–1870* (New York, 1990); Giovanni Levi, *Inheriting Power: The Story of an Exorcist* (Chicago, 1988), 66–99; Hans Medick, "The Proto-industrial Family Economy," *Social History* 3 (1976): 291–315; and David Levine, "The Demographic Implications of Rural Industrialization: A Family Reconstitution Study of Shepshed, Leicestershire, 1600–1851," *Social History* 2 (1976): 177–96. On colonial America, see Kenneth A. Lockridge, "Land, Population, and the Evolution of New England Society, 1630–1790: And an Afterthought," in *Colonial America: Essays in Politics and Social Development,* edited by Stanley N. Katz (Boston, 1971), 466–91; Christopher Clark, "Household Economy"; and James A. Henretta, "Families and Farms: *Mentalité* in Pre-industrial America," *William & Mary Quarterly,* 3d ser., 35 (1978): 31.

26 The combination of different types of extant documents and the difficulty of dealing with the creation of new towns imposed the choice of Kinderhook. Information extracted from *Heads of Families at the First Census of the United States, 1790;* Manuscript Population Schedules of the Second Census, 1800 (microfilm edition); Manuscript

Population Schedules of the Third Census, 1810 (microfilm edition); Tax Assessment of Kinderhook, 1800, NYSL; and "Assessment Roll of the Real and Personal Estates in the Town of Kinderhook . . . in 1809," reprinted in Edward A. Collier, *A History of Old Kinderhook* (New York, 1914), 112–24. For a methodological comparison, see Richard H. Steckel, "Household Migration and Rural Settlement in the United States, 1850–1860," *Explorations in Economic History* 26 (1989): 190–218. I have calculated the ratio of migration to total population for every decade between 1790 and 1850 with the help of birth and death rates interpolated from census data, and the first decade of the nineteenth century turns out to be the most mobile, so to speak, for Columbia County and its midland section. In spite of this peak, I found only one public reference to westward migration in local newspapers (*Hudson Bee*, 26 Feb. 1805, 3), which I construe as an indication that there were no anomic consequences to emigration for those who stayed behind. In Greene County, mobility increased after 1835 to reach a high point in 1855. On a later period in Vermont, see Hal S. Barron, *Those Who Stayed Behind: Rural Society in Nineteenth Century America* (New York, 1980).

27 According to David Paul Davenport's data ("The Yankee Settlement of New York," *Genealogical Journal* 17 [1988–89]: 73, 79), New Yorkers coming from eastern counties that were settled before the revolutionary war, as was the case of Columbia and Greene, contributed 12.8 percent to the postrevolutionary settlement of western New York whereas New England states supplied 61 percent.

28 Forty-six out of the 75 transfers were analyzed randomly (I excluded the city of Hudson), from Deeds A, 1787–93, Columbia County Court House. See also Patrich McClaghry's Will, 28 Sept. 1774, in Anjou, *Ulster County*, 2:13; Isaac Belknap's Will, 27 Sept. 1787, in Anjou, *Ulster County*, 16; William Coventry Diary, Jan. 1800.

29 Bond of Lawrence Van Deusen, 26 Nov. 1788, Deeds A, 38–39, Columbia County Court House; Abrahm Donaldson's Will, 16 May 1808, in Anjou, *Ulster County*, 1:168; Helmus Weller's Will, 20 March 1777, in Anjou, *Ulster County*, 57; Patrick Barber's Will, 22 Sept. 1791, in Anjou, *Ulster County*, 75. The general statement is based on an analysis of eighty wills dated from 1774 to 1808 published in Anjou, *Ulster County*, vols. 1 and 2.

30 Analysis based on fifty-eight wills in Anjou, *Ulster County*, 2; forty-nine times sons received all real estate. This practice conformed to the legal prescription found by Norma Basch in *In the Eyes of the Law: Women, Marriage, and Property in Nineteenth-Century New York* (Ithaca, 1982), 110, and to the pattern discovered in Connecticut by Toby L. Ditz in *Property and Kinship: Inheritance in Early Connecticut, 1750–1830* (Princeton, 1986), 26–27, 37. On conflicts, see Alexander Coventry Diary, 22 Aug. 1786; William *Van Den Bergh v. John & Richard Van Den Bergh*, Bronk Ms. 1792, and *People v. Martin Van Bergen*, Bronk Ms. 1792, GrCHS; William Coventry Diary, Jan. 1800; and Archibald McCurdy's Will, 12 Nov. 1787, in Anjou, *Ulster County*, 2:23.

31 William W. Hagen, "Capitalism and the Countryside in Early Modern Europe: Interpretations, Models, Debates," *Agricultural History* 62 (1988): 13–47; Eric R. Wolf, *Peasants* (Englewood Cliffs, N.J., 1966).

32 Leonard Gaansevoort to Leonard Bronk, 13 April 1783, Bronk Ms. 1783, GrCHS; *Hudson Weekly Gazette*, 5 Oct. 1786, 1; *Catskill Recorder*, 14 April 1807, 2.

33 Horse thefts: Spaulding, *New York*, 26; Anna Bradbury, *History of the City of Hudson*,

New York (Hudson, 1908), 74; *Hudson Weekly Gazette,* 19 Oct. 1786, 2–3; *Hudson Weekly Gazette,* 13 Dec. 1787, 4; *Hudson Weekly Gazette,* 3 Jan. 1788, 4; *Hudson Gazette,* 11 June 1799, 2. Threats: Alexander Coventry Diary, 12 Oct. 1789; see also John Homer French, *Gazetteer of the State of New York* (Syracuse, 1860), 242. Brigands: Robert Mandrou, *La France aux 17e et 18e siècles* (Paris, 1974), 60, 99–100. Hangings: Alexander Coventry Diary, 18 Dec. 1789.

34 Alexander Coventry Diary, 22 July 1786, 16 Sept. 1786. Alcohol consumption during harvest: John and Tobias Teller Day Book, July and Aug. 1798, NYSHA. Dances and neighborhood sociability: Alexander Coventry Diary, 23 June 1786, 7 Feb. and 2 June 1786; 26 April 1787; see also George Holcomb Diary, 9 Dec. 1808.

35 John Beebe Diary, 22 Jan. 1780; William Coventry Diary, 6 May and 2 June 1801.

36 Alexander Coventry Diary, 10 Sept. 1786; *Catskill Recorder,* 21 Oct. 1805.

37 *Walter Tyler v. Reuben Jeacocks,* 14 May 1798, Bronk Ms. 1798, GTCHS; Alexander Coventry Diary, 24 Nov. 1789, 10 Jan. 1787; William Coventry Diary, 3 Aug. 1799. On tensions in old regime French villages, see Philip T. Hoffman, *Growth in a Traditional Society: The French Countryside* (Princeton, 1996), 24–25.

38 Abraham Wells to Leonard Bronk, 8 March 1787, Bronk Ms. 1787, GTCHS; Alexander Coventry Diary, 7 Feb. 1786, 2 and 27–28 Feb., 7–8 April, and 3 Aug. 1791.

39 *Catskill Messenger,* 1 Dec. 1836, 2; Alexander Coventry Diary, 23–24 Oct. 1790.

40 "Journal of Colonel Von Specht," transcript at the Saratoga National Historic Park (I would like to thank Ms. Ruth Piwonka for sharing her notes with me); Alexander Coventry Diary, 3 Feb. 1786; Stuart M. Blumin, *The Urban Threshold: Growth and Change in a Nineteenth-Century American Community* (Chicago, 1976), 13–14.

41 "Journal of Colonel Von Specht"; François Jean Chastellux, *Travels in North America in the Years 1780, 1781, and 1782* (Chapel Hill, 1963), 196; Strickland, *Journal,* 126. The proportion of houses worth less than one hundred dollars was 49 percent in Hurley and 57 percent in Marbletown. Calculations are based on Manuscript Schedules of the Federal Census for New York State for 1800 (microfilm edition); Particular List or Description of Each Dwelling House . . . in 1798 in Hurley and Marbletown; and Alexander Coventry Diary, 13 Nov. 1785, 28 Nov. 1786.

42 *History of Greene County,* 117, 121; William Coventry Diary, 22 April 1791, 22 Dec. 1798; Alexander Coventry Diary, 25 Nov. 1786, 2 Jan. 1789; George Holcomb Diary, 30 March 1809, 26 Sept. and 25 Oct. 1810. See also *Catskill Packet,* 21 Jan. 1794, 3.

43 This paragraph was inspired by J. G. Peristiani, Introduction to *Honour and Shame: The Values of Mediterranean Society,* edited by J. G. Peristiani (London, 1965), 9–18; Julian Pitt-Rivers, "Honour and Social Status," in Peristiani, *Honour,* 21–77; and Alexander Coventry Diary, 16 Sept. 1786.

44 Alexander Coventry Diary, 16 Aug. 1790, 16 Sept. 1786; Memorandum of Evidence Taken on Inquisition on the Body of Sanders Goes Laying Dead, 7 June 1780, Bronk Ms. 1780, GTCHS. See also William Coventry Diary, 22 Dec. 1798.

45 LaRochefoucauld-Liancourt, *Voyage,* 5:276. See also *Catskill Packet,* 11 Feb. 1793, 1 and 3; 4 March 1793, 3; 18 March 1793, 3; and 29 April 1793, 3.

46 Pitt-Rivers, "Honour," 31. See also *Hudson Weekly Gazette,* 21 Oct. 1788, 3; 21 April 1789, 1; 3 May 1783, 1.

47 *Hudson Gazette,* 15 March 1792, 1–2. See also J. G. A. Pocock, "The Classical Theory of

Deference," *American Historical Review* 81 (1976): 516–23; and R. W. Nicholas, "Segmentary Factional Political Systems," in *Political Anthropology,* edited by M. J. Swartz, V. W. Turner, and A. Tuden (Chicago, 1966), 49–60.

48 See Dixon Ryan Fox, *The Decline of Aristocracy in the Politics of New York* (New York, 1919); "The Autobiography of Martin Van Buren," edited by John C. Fitzpatrick, in *Annual Report of the American Historical Association* (Washington, D.C., 1918), 2:13, 21.

49 Stephen Haight to Leonard Bronk, 30 May 1777, Bronk Ms. 1777, GrCHS; Henry Livingston to Walter Livingston, 24 April 1785, quoted in Young, *Democratic Republicans,* 61; Peter Livingston to Peter Van Schaack, 2 April 1791, Misc. Mss. Livingston, P.R., N-YHS; Laurence Merkel to Leonard Bronk, 8 March 1800, and William Fraser and Henry Wells Jr. to Leonard Bronk, 5 April 1800, both in Bronk Ms. 1800, GrCHS.

50 On influence, see Taylor, "Art of Hook," 1374, 1393; *Catskill Packet,* 29 April 1794, 3; *Catskill Packet,* 6 May 1793, 1; *Catskill Packet,* 13 May 1793, 1; Dorrance Kirtland to Leonard Bronk, 25 March 1799, Bronk Ms. 1799, GrCHS; *Hudson Weekly Gazette,* 5 April 1787, 2; *Hudson Weekly Gazette,* 12 April 1787, 1–2.

51 *Catskill Packet,* 1 April 1793, 2–3; 15 April 1793, 1. See also Thomas Tillotson to Robert R. Livingston, 23 March 1787, and Robert R. Livingston to James Duane, 30 April 1789, both quoted in Young, *Democratic Republicans,* 95–96; Alvin Kass, *Politics in New York State, 1800–1860* (Syracuse, 1965), 59; Lunenburgh Federalist Meeting, 5 April 1800, Bronk Ms. 1800, GrCHS; and John Van Den Berck to Leonard Bronk, 3 April 1787, Bronk Ms. 1787, GrCHS.

52 See Patricia U. Bonomi, *A Factious People: Politics and Society in Colonial New York* (New York, 1971); Carl L. Becker, *The History of Political Parties in the Province of New York, 1760–1776* (Madison, 1909); Irving Mark, *Agrarian Conflicts in Colonial New York, 1711–1775* (New York, 1940); and Countryman, *A People.* On hierarchy, see Gordon S. Wood, *The Radicalism of the American Revolution* (New York, 1992), 11–92; and Stuart M. Blumin, *The Emergence of the Middle Class: Social Experience in the American City, 1760–1900* (New York, 1989), 17–30, 58–65.

53 F. Backer [?] to Robert R. Livingston, 10 Sept. 1801, Robert R. Livingston Papers, microfilm reel 19, series 1. On loans, see Robert R. Livingston Loan Book, Robert R. Livingston Papers, microfilm reel 54, series 1. On arrears, see James Duane Livingston Rent Book, 1806–1810, Wilson Papers, Eckert Collection, Bard College; and Conclusion. See also notes in the hand of Leon. Bronk, 2 Jan. 1797, and every year through 1816, in Bronk Ms. 1797–1816, GrCHS.

54 *Catskill Packet,* 13 Aug. 1792, 3; Mortgages B, 1800–1801, Columbia County Court House; Deeds D, 1798–1802, Greene County Court House; William Coventry Diary, 4 May 1791; F. Backer [?] to Robert R. Livingston, 10 Sept. 1801; Seats in Church of Coxsackie Sold on November 30th, 1798, Bronk Ms. 1798, GrCHS. See also Collier, *History,* 273.

55 Percentages were calculated from "A Census of Electors and Inhabitants of the State of New York . . . 1790," *New York Daily Advertiser,* 15 Jan. 1791. The numbers are consistent with Young's in *Democratic Republicans,* 19, 83–84, 585–88, and somewhat lower than Kass's in *Politics,* 3; Taylor, "Art of Hook," 1392; and John Van Den Berck to Leonard Bronk, 3 April 1787. The reference to ethnic groups here is puzzling, for the Bronk interest was as Dutch and English as the people who opposed it. In 1800–1801,

Federalist and Republican correspondents contained the same proportion of Dutch and English surnames. See (Catskill) *Western Constellation*, 30 March 1801, 6 April 1801; Lounenburgh Federalist Meeting, 5 April 1800; and *Catskill Recorder*, 25 March 1805, 2.

56 Based on election returns in *Hudson Weekly Gazette*, 28 April 1789, 4; and 28 Feb. 1793, 2.

57 *Catskill Packet*, 4 March 1793, 2–3; *Catskill Packet*, 25 March 1793, 3; John Beebe Diary, 21 Feb. 1780; *Hudson Weekly Gazette*, 12 April 1787, 2–3. See also Spaulding, *New York*, 81; Wood, *Radicalism*, 229–325; and Countryman, *People*, 221–51.

58 *Catskill Packet*, 4 March 1793, 2–3; *Catskill Packet*, 15 April 1793, 1; *Catskill Packet*, 13 May 1793, 1; John Van Den Berck to Leonard Bronk, 3 April 1783; *Hudson Bee*, 22 April 1806, 2. Calculations are based on *Census of the State of New York for 1855* (Albany, 1857), ix.

59 On the connection between anxiety and ritual, see the review by George C. Homans, "Anxiety and Ritual: The Theories of Malinowski and Radcliffe-Brown," *American Anthropologist* 43 (1941): 161–72.

60 Isaac Rosa to Leonard Bronk, 22 Jan. 1801, Bronk Ms. 1801, GrCHS.

61 Lawrence Van Alstine and a certain Howe appointed three neighbors to arbitrate their dispute (Alexander Coventry Diary, 10 April 1786). Noah Hatch and Noah Candy chose Dirick Spoor, Leonard Bronk, and Jocham Tryon "to deside certain Disputes & Controversies Subsiding" between them (Bronk Ms. 1786, GrCHS).

TWO *To Market, to Mill, to the Woods*

1 Abraham Wells to Leonard Bronk, 26 June 1798, Bronk Ms. 1798, GrCHS.

2 J. Hector St. John de Crèvecoeur, "Sketches of Eighteenth-Century America," in *Letters from an American Farmer* (New York, 1986), 238 (title), 304, 299, and, on price setting, 316; Abraham J. Hasbrouck Journal, 20 Sept., 12 and 23 Oct. 1798, N-YHS.

3 Daniel Vickers, "Competency and Competition: Economic Culture in Early America," *William and Mary Quarterly*, 3d ser., 47 (1990): 3–29; Winifred B. Rothenberg, "The Emergence of a Capital Market in Rural Massachusetts, 1730–1838," *Journal of Economic History* 44 (1985): 781–808; Winifred B. Rothenberg, *From Market-Places to a Market Economy: The Transformation of Rural Massachusetts, 1750–1850* (Chicago, 1992).

4 Crèvecoeur, "Sketches," 238–39, 316 (on winter), 271; Alexander Coventry Diary, 15 July 1786 (typescript edited by the Albany Institute of History and Art and NYSL, 1978); William Strickland, *Journal of a Tour in the United States of America, 1794–1795*, edited by J. E. Strickland (New York, 1971), 112; *American Husbandry* (London, 1775), 2:266–67; William Coventry Diary, 13–29 Jan. 1791, 3 Jan. 1793, NYSHA; Alexander Coventry Diary, 2 March and 24 Nov. 1786, 2 Jan. 1788.

5 Robert R. Livingston, "American Agriculture," in *Edinburgh Encyclopedia*, 1st American ed. (Philadelphia, 1832), 1:338; William Coventry Diary, 7, 16–18 Oct. 1800, 21 Sept. 1801, 31 Oct. 1801, 2, 3, and 27 Nov. 1801, 24 Jan. 1796, 19–22 Nov. 1798. See also *American Husbandry*, 2:260–61.

6 Zephaniah Chase Account Book, 1786 and 1797, NYSL. For information about Chase, see John Homer French, *Gazetteer of the State of New York* (Syracuse, 1860), 334. The occupational itinerary and diversification of Reuben Rundle very much resembled Chase's. See *History of Greene County, New York* (New York, 1884), 298.

7 Account Mills Garrit, 22 July 1793, David Cullen Account Book, Baker Library, Harvard University.

8 On farm size and soil exhaustion, see *American Husbandry,* 1:127–29. For European data, see Philip Hoffman, *Growth in a Traditional Society: The French Countryside* (Princeton, 1996), 184, 190. See Charles S. Grant, *Democracy in the Connecticut Frontier Town of Kent* (New York, 1961), 36–38. For a different evaluation that puts the necessary acreage much higher, see James T. Lemon, "Household Consumption in Eighteenth-Century America and Its Relationship to Production and Trade: The Situation among Farmers in Southeastern Pennsylvania," *Agricultural History* 41 (1967): 69. Hoffman, *Growth,* 36–37, estimates that twenty-five acres were necessary to support a family in old regime France.

9 For inventories, see table 1. Information about occupations was extracted from the transcription made by Marquis E. Shattuck (comp.) in "Entries in the Account Book of Teunis Van Vechten, 1753–1782," *Detroit Genealogical Research* 16 (1953): 49–54; 240 accounts (60.9 percent) belonged to farmers, 23 (5.5 percent) to women, 13 (3.3 percent) to professionals and gentlemen, and 10 (2.5 percent) to innkeepers and merchants. Van Vechten died "at an advanced age" in Catskill in 1792 (*Catskill Packet,* 13 Sept. 1792).

10 Livingston, "American Agriculture," 333; *Transactions of the Society for the Promotion of Agriculture, Art, and Manufactures,* 2d ed. (Albany, 1801), 1:306–12; Strickland, *Journal,* 112–13, 50; Alexander Coventry Diary, 6 and 13 Oct. 1787, 31 July 1789; Elijah Hudson Farm Account Book, fol. 36 (1789–1790), NYSHA. Data for Ulster County, N.Y., are from Thomas S. Wermuth, " 'To Market, to Market': Yeoman Farmers, Merchant Capitalists, and the Transition to Capitalism in the Hudson Valley, Ulster County, 1760–1840, Ph.D. diss., State University of New York at Binghamton, 1991, 199. Hoffman, *Growth,* 36–37, allows a man to cultivate thirty-five acres of a specialized, wheat-growing farm in old regime France.

11 A year's work: William Coventry Diary, 15 April through 3 May 1786; Alexander Coventry Diary, 25 March 1791. A year's yields: William Coventry Diary, 4 and 13 Oct. 1791, 1 Nov. 1800, 28 Oct. 1801.

12 Crèvecoeur, *Letters,* 80. Hudson Valley yields: William Strickland, *Observations on the Agriculture of the United States of America* (London, 1801), 40; Strickland, *Journal,* 113; François Alexandre Frédéric De LaRochefoucauld-Liancourt, *Voyage dans les Etats-Unis d'Amérique fait en 1795, 1796, et 1797* (Paris, 1799), 5:273; *Transactions* 1 (1801): 309–10; Livingston, "American Agriculture," 335. French data are from Gilles Postel-Vinay, "A la recherche de la révolution économique dans les campagnes (1789–1815)," *Revue économique* 6 (1989): 1015–45.

13 Livingston, "American Agriculture," 334; William Coventry Diary, July–Oct. 1801, July–Oct. 1802. Coventry noted his output under the heading 20 July–31 Sept. [*sic*] 1801. See also John Beebe Jr. Diary, 23 July 1781, 4 Aug. 1785, Chatham Public Library. According to Crèvecoeur, a wagon could transport one ton of hay ("Sketches," 310), although loads carried on carts from the field to the barn probably weighed considerably less.

14 Livingston, "American Agriculture," 336; Alexander Coventry Diary, 21 Aug. 1786. On women and dairying, see Joan M. Jensen, *Loosening the Bonds: Mid-Atlantic Farm*

Women, 1750–1850 (New Haven, 1986); and Sally McMurry, *Transforming Rural Life: Dairying Families and Agricultural Change, 1820–1885* (Baltimore, 1995). See also chapter 4.

15 Abstract of Valuations and Assessments in the County of Columbia in the Year One Thousand Seven Hundred and Ninety-nine, Coll. B 0315, NYS Arc; Manuscript Census for 1800 (microfilm). Tamás Faragó found three draft animals on mixed agriculture farms in Hungary in the eighteenth century. See his "Formen bäuerlicher Haushalts- und Arbeitsorganisation in Ungarn um die Mitte des 18. Jahrhunderts," in *Familien-struktur und Arbeitsorganisation in ländlichen Gesellschaften,* edited by Josef Ehmer and Michael Mitterauer (Vienna, 1986), 152–53.

16 Crèvecoeur, *Letters,* 81; Alexander Coventry Diary, 1 Feb. 1788; William Coventry Diary, 9 April 1794.

17 Will of Abraham Donaldson, 16 May 1805, in Anjou, *Ulster County,* 1:168.

18 This is a caveat with probate records, too. In general, see Winifred Rothenberg, "Farm Account Books: Problems and Possibilities," *Agricultural History* 58 (1984): 106–12. Meat consumption calculated with information from Abstract of the Valuations and Assessments of the County of Columbia in the Year 1800, Collection B 0315, NYS Arc. The weight of a dressed carcass is given as four hundred pounds in Lemon, *Best Poor Man's,* 163. On meat consumption among the French nobility, see "Histoire de la consommation," *Annales E.S.C.* 2–3 (1975): 402–631.

19 Alexander Coventry Diary, 14 Dec. 1787. On European peasants and their diet, see *Histoire de l'alimentation,* edited by Jean-Louis Flandrin and Massimo Montanari (Paris, 1996), 599–627.

20 Strickland, *Journal,* 119; Anna Grant, *Memoirs of an American Lady* (London, 1808), 1:39–41. The Coventry cousins worked in their gardens. See Alexander Coventry Diary, 6, 12–15 May 1786, 23 Oct. 1787 (apples), 12–14 April, 25 May 1789; William Coventry Diary, 8–17 May 1790, 19–23 April 1791, 6–8 May 1792, 22 April 1793; Crèvecoeur, "Sketches," 315; Sarah F. McMahon, "A Comfortable Subsistence: The Changing Composition of Diet in Rural New England, 1620–1840," *William and Mary Quarterly,* 3d ser., 42 (1985): 26–65, esp. 42; and Sarah F. McMahon, "All Things in Their Proper Season: Seasonal Rhythms of Diet in Nineteenth-Century New England," *Agricultural History* 63 (1989): 130–51.

21 Alexander Coventry Diary, 7 May 1789, 13 May 1789; William Coventry Diary, 27 May 1795, 27 Oct. 1798, 25 Feb. 1799, 2 Jan. and 6 May 1800, 27 Feb. and 22 March 1801; "Recollections of Edward McGraw," in Edward M. Ruttenber, *History of the Town of New Windsor, Orange County, New York* (Newburgh, 1911), 49.

22 Court Officer's Ledger, 22 March 1792, MV 144, Durham Center Museum.

23 Inventory of the Goods and Chattels of Catherine Overbagh, Widow of Godfrey Brandow, 18 Jan. 1805, Bronk Ms. 1805, GrCHS; *Stoddard's Diary; or, The Columbia Almanack for the Year of Our Lord 1801* (Hudson, n.d.).

24 Account of John Teller, 26 Sept. 1798 (see also 12 Dec. 1797), John and Tobias Teller Day Book, NYSHA; Alexander Coventry Diary, 16 Feb., 23 April, 17 July, 24 Sept. 1791, 20 Jan. 1792 (see also 12 Feb. and 5 April 1787). For general background, see Mary Beth Norton, *Liberty's Daughters: The Revolutionary Experience of American Women, 1750–1800*

(Boston, 1980), 9–20; and Laurel Thatcher Ulrich, *A Midwife's Tale: The Life of Martha Ballard Based on Her Diary, 1785–1812* (New York, 1991).

25 Zephaniah Chase Account Book, 1785–1787; James Mason Account, 10 Dec. 1789 through 10 May 1791, Unidentified Store Ledger of Claverack, COLCHS; *Heads of Families at the First Census of the United States Taken in 1790 in New York* (Baltimore, 1966); Alexander Coventry Diary, 25 Nov. 1789, 12 Oct. 1790.

26 Account Gideon Brockway, 1789–1790, Selah Strong Diary, MV 135, GICHS. On dairying in the Mid-Atlantic region, see Joan M. Jensen, *Loosening the Bonds.*

27 Account Joseph White, Elijah Hudson Farm Account Book, fol. 6 (1787–1789), NYSHA; Joseph Jenkins Account Book, 1803, NYSHA; Unidentified Account Book, Kinderhook, N.Y., 5 Jan. 1804, NYSL; Reynolds Account Book, June 1809, 1808–1811, MV 434, GICHS; Abraham J. Hasbrouck Journals, 1797–1799, N-YHS; Crèvecoeur, "Sketches," 310.

28 Abraham J. Hasbrouck Journals, 1797–1799; Tax Assessment for Ulster County 1799, Garrett Lansing Papers, NYSL; Marius Schoonmaker, *The History of Kingston, N.Y.* (New York, 1888), 454. I have converted barrels of flour into bushels of wheat to facilitate comparisons; the ratio was four bushels of wheat for every barrel of flour. See William Carter Hughes, *The American Miller and Millwright's Assistant* (Philadelphia, 1851), 85; John and Tobias Teller Ledger, 1798–1802, NYSHA; and Alexander Coventry Diary, 13 Dec. 1787.

29 Alexander Coventry Diary, 5 Oct. 1786, 16 June 1787.

30 *Transactions* 1 (1801): 306–12; Alexander Coventry Diary, 9 Jan. 1786.

31 Hudson: Hudson Proprietors, Articles of Agreement 1785, COLCHS; Wilson C. Watson, ed., *Men and Times of the Revolution; or, Memoirs of Elkanah Watson* (New York, 1856), 266; Strickland, *Journal,* 121; John Lambert, *Travels through Canada and the United States of America in the Years 1806, 1807, and 1808,* 3d ed. (London, 1816), 2:41; Luigi Castiglioni, *Travels in the United States of North America, 1785–1787,* edited by Antonio Pace (Syracuse, 1983), 90–91. Catskill: *Catskill Western Constellation,* 16 Feb. 1801, 3; Reverend Clark Brown, Topographical Description (1803), Catskill Vertical File, GICHS; *New York Magazine or Literary Repository* (Sept. 1797): 449.

32 *Catskill Western Constellation,* 16 Feb. 1801, 3; Rev. Clark Brown, Topographical Description (1803), Catskill Vertical File, GICHS. My own computation is based on the potential number of farm families delivering produce at Catskill landing (1,066 families), which I multiplied by the average amount of grain supplied to Kingston's Hasbrouck by his customers (16.8 bushels). Census data are from *Census for the State of New York for 1855* (Albany, 1857), xxi.

33 Timothy Dwight, *Travels in New England and New York* (New Haven, 1821–1822), 4:6. Anthropologists call such personal relationships *pratik.* See Cyril S. Belshaw, *Traditional Exchange and Modern Markets* (Englewood Cliffs, 1965), 56–58.

34 Account Jesse W. Baker, 16 April 1800, Abraham J. Hasbrouck Journal, 1799–1802, fol. 120; Account Benjamin DeMyer, 12 Jan. 1799, Abraham J. Hasbrouck Journal, 1797–1799, fol. 334. For a case in which a recommendation turned out badly and led to conflict, see *Hudson Balance,* 25 June 1805, 206.

35 Abraham J. Hasbrouck Journals, 1797–1802, 15 Feb., 14 and 17 Nov. 1798, 5 March 1800. See also Sheldon Graham's advertisement in the *Catskill Packet,* 17 Sept. 1792.

36 On assizes, see, for example, *Hudson Weekly Gazette,* 5 April 1787, 1; *Hudson Weekly Gazette,* 17 Jan. 1790, 2; *Hudson Bee,* 7 July 1807, 3; *Catskill Packet,* 15 July 1793, 3; and *Catskill American Eagle,* 3 Aug. 1808, 3. For fair price notions, see *Preston v. Pomroy,* Bronk Ms. 1798, GrCHS; *Hudson Weekly Gazette,* 10 May 1787, 2; and *Hudson Weekly Gazette,* 17 May 1787, 2.

37 *Catskill Packet,* 22 March 1793, 2; William Coventry Diary, 22 March 1801. Prices were observed in *New York Price Current,* 1797–1800; and Columbia and Greene County Account Books.

38 Rothenberg, *From Market-Places;* and "A Price Index for Rural Massachusetts, 1750–1855," *Journal of Economic History* 39 (1979): 975–1001. Price convergence, however, occurred only after the turn of the nineteenth century.

39 William Coventry spent fourteen days in the woods. See his Diary, 13–29 Jan., 1–4 and 14 Feb. 1791, and 3 Jan. 1793; and *Catskill Packet,* 4 Feb. 1793, 4. On wood arriving at the landings, see Benjamin Moore Ledger, Coxsackie, 1793–1795, MV 889, GrCHS; Castiglioni, *Travels,* 90–91; LaRochefoucauld-Liancourt, *Voyage,* 5:271–72; *Catskill Recorder,* 17 Sept. 1804, 3; and *History of Greene County,* 125, 275, 293.

40 Crèvecoeur, "Sketches," 291; Alexander Coventry Diary, 18 April 1790, 2 June 1790, 25 Sept. 1790 (ashes); William Coventry Diary, 22–23 June 1801.

THREE *Natural Resources and Economic Development*

1 Thomas Cole, "Lecture on American Scenery Delivered before the Catskill Lyceum, April 1st, 1841," *Northern Light* 1 (May 1841): 25–26; Thomas Cole, "Essay on American Scenery," *American Monthly* 7 (June 1836): 12, quoted in Nicolai Cikovsky, " 'The Ravages of the Axe': The Meaning of the Tree Stump in Nineteenth-Century American Art," *Art Bulletin* (1979): 611–26. On Cole, see Howard S. Merritt, *Thomas Cole* (Rochester, 1969).

2 Thomas Cole to Asher Durand, 11 Sept. 1836, in Louis Legrand Noble, *The Life and Works of Thomas Cole,* edited by Elliott S. Vesell (Cambridge, Mass. [1856] 1964), 164; Thomas Cole to David Wadworth, 6 July 1826, in J. Bard McNulty, ed., *The Correspondance of Thomas Cole and David Wadworth* (Hartford, 1983), 1; Cole, "Lecture," 25.

3 *Catskill Recorder,* 12 July 1832, 2.

4 Horatio Gates Spafford, *Gazetteer of the State of New York* (Albany, 1824), 101.

5 Cole, "Lecture," 25; *Hudson Bee,* 17 Dec. 1816, 3. Thomas C. Cochran, in "The Business Revolution," *American Historical Review* 79 (1974): 1456, discovered the first signs of accounting specialization around 1800 in seabord cities involved in maritime trade. Hudson Valley merchants thus encountered the opportunity to adopt the innovation with a twenty-year delay.

6 Max Weber, *Wirtschaft und Gesellschaft: Grundriss der verstehenden Soziologie* (Tübingen, 1972), 53–65. On the role of state authorities, I follow Karl Polanyi, *The Great Transformation: The Political and Economic Origins of Our Time* (Boston, 1957), 139–80. George R. Taylor, "American Urban Growth Preceding the Railway Age," *Journal of Economic History* 27 (1967): 328.

7 Alexis de Tocqueville, *De la démocratie en Amérique* (Paris, 1840), vol. 2, chaps. 13 and 17. On government action in New York, see Nathan Miller, *The Enterprise of a Free People:*

Aspects of the Economic Development in New York State during the Canal Period, 1792–1838 (Ithaca, 1962), 10–17; and Harry J. Carman, "The Beginnings of the Industrial Revolution," in *History of the State of New York,* edited by Alexander C. Flick (New York; 1933–1937), 5:344–45. For an overview, see L. Ray Gunn, *The Decline of Authority: Public Economic Policy and Political Development in New York, 1800–1860* (Ithaca, 1988), 99–143; and Morton J. Horwitz, *The Transformation of American Law, 1780–1860* (Boston, 1977), 160–210, 266.

8 Joseph Dorfman, *The Economic Mind in American Civilization* (New York, 1947), 2:516–26, describes two theorists of laissez-faire doctrines who played an active part in the state-sponsored construction of canals. See also *Hudson Balance,* 11 Oct. 1803, 321; *Hudson Bee,* 21 Sept. 1810, 3; and *Hudson Bee,* 9 July 1816, 3.

9 For examples of rural apprehension of, and prejudice against, New York City as a place of seduction and corruption where country merchants risked material and spiritual perdition before the War of Independence, see Charlotte C. Finkel, "The Store Account Books of Hendrick Schenk, Fishkill Landing, Dutchess County, New York," *Yearbook* 50 (1965): 36–49; and *Catskill Messenger,* 24 March 1849, 2. For short-lived market columns, see *Hudson Gazette,* 11 Aug. 1801, 3; *Hudson Balance,* 26 Jan. 1808; and *Catskill Recorder,* 30 April 1829 through Dec. 1830 and April 1837 through Dec. 1837. On commercial interests in local councils, see *Columbia County at the End of the Century* (Hudson, 1900), 407–30; and *History of Greene County, New York* (New York, 1884), 126–27.

10 *Catskill Recorder,* 19 May 1819, 2. On the New York bread assize, see Howard B. Rock, *Artisans of the New Republic: The Tradesmen of New York City in the Age of Jefferson* (New York, 1979), 183–97. The town of Kingston adapted its assize to New York's in 1807. See Nathaniel B. Sylvester, *History of Ulster County, New York* (Philadelphia, 1880), 1202.

11 Petition of Thomas Frothingham and others [1790s] and Petition of Cornelius Muller & Moore & Peter Wiesmer and Other Inhabitants of the District of Claverack, Bronk Ms., Undated Folder 1, GTCHS.

12 *Catskill Recorder,* 16 Sept. 1818, 2.

13 *Coxsackie Standard,* 10 May 1838, 2; *Catskill Messenger,* 24 March 1849, 2. See also *Catskill Democrat,* 7 May 1845, 2; and *Catskill Messenger,* 19 May 1849, 2.

14 On the diminution of government intervention in the economy, see Gunn, *Decline,* 232–45; Roger L. Ransom and Richard Sutch, *One Kind of Freedom: The Economic Consequences of Emancipation* (Cambridge, Engl., 1977), 89–90; Francis Hall, *Travels in Canada and the United States in 1816 and 1817* (London, 1818), 35; and *Constitution of the State of New York Adopted in 1846,* edited by Franklin B. Hough (Albany, 1867), Art. 1, sec. 12. On state officials, see "Annual Message of Governor Washington Hunt [1851]," in *State of New York: Messages from the Governors,* edited by Charles Z. Lincoln (Albany, 1904), 4:559–60; and A. G. Johnson, *A Chapter in History of the Progress of Judicial Usurpation* (Troy, 1863), 4–6. On tenant activism and the social developments that led to this decision, see chapter 7 and the conclusion.

15 Horatio Gates Spafford, *Gazetteer of the State of New York* (Albany, 1813), 78. On different turnpike companies, see Peter H. Stott, "Industrial Archeology in Columbia County, New York" (manuscript located at COLCHS, 1990); *History of Greene County,* 42–47; Oliver W. Holmes, "The Turnpike Era," in Flick, *History,* 5:269; Joseph Austin

Durrenberger, *Turnpikes: A Study of the Toll Road Movement in the Middle Atlantic States and Maryland* (Valdosta, 1931), 58–65; David M. Ellis, *Landlords and Farmers in the Hudson-Mohawk Region, 1790–1850* (Ithaca, 1946), 83–88; George R. Taylor, *The Transportation Revolution* (New York, 1951), 27; and David R. Meyer, "Midwestern Industrialization and the American Manufacturing Belt in the Nineteenth Century," *Journal of Economic History* 49 (1989): esp. 921–25. The latter source defines an economic region as the integration of a metropolis with its hinterland.

16 Benjamin DeWitt, "A Sketch of the Turnpike Roads in the State of New York," *Transactions of the Society for the Promotion of the Useful Arts* 2 (1807): 193, 200; Julian Ursyn Niemcewicz, *Under Their Vine and Fig Tree; Travels through America in 1797–1799, 1805,* edited by Metchic J. E. Budka (Elizabeth, 1965), 237. See also *Memoirs of the New York State Board of Agriculture* 3 (1826): 7.

17 DeWitt, "Sketch," 199. On central place theory, see Martin Beckmann, *Location Theory* (New York, 1968).

18 *Hudson Bee,* 14 Jan. 1806, 12. Stockholders: Chatham Turnpike, Columbia Turnpike Papers, COLCHS; Assessment of Real and Personal Estate in the Town of Kinderhook . . . for 1799, NYS Arc; George Crawford Papers, April 1814, NYSHA; Coxsackie Turnpike Papers, GrCHS; Jehoakim Bergh Ledger, fol. 129, 1811, Rare Book and Manuscript Division, NYPL; *History of Greene County,* 42–47.

19 Columbia Turnpike Papers, COLCHS; Mary Livingston Memorandum, 1 Jan. 1811, COLCHS; Joseph Howland to William Wilson, 13 July 1811 (see also 23 Oct. and 5 Dec. 1809), Highland Turnpike Correspondence, Eckert Collection, Bard College.

20 *Catskill Recorder,* 8 June 1827, 2; 21 Dec. 1827, 2. The complaint about bad roads was common. See Jesse Everett to Nathan Clark, 22 May 1815, Fox-Clark Papers, Box 16, GrCHS; Henry Pudget to Abner Austin, 4 March 1818, Incoming Letters, Austin Collection, GrCHS; Niemcewicz, *Under,* 237; James Stuart, *Three Years in North America* (Edinburgh, 1833), 2:3; *Catskill Messenger,* 7 April 1849, 2; and *Transactions of the New York State Agricultural Society* 9 (1849): 156. On plank roads, see Holmes, "Era," 270–73.

21 *Albany Argus,* 11 Jan. 1833, 2. The article is mentioned in Clarence Danhof, *Change in Agriculture: The Northern United States* (Cambridge, Mass., 1969), 144, from which I traced it through the *Northern Farmer* 1 (1833): 101. See also *Catskill Recorder,* 2 June 1826, 2; and Russell H. Anderson, "New York Agriculture Meets the West, 1830–1850," *Wisconsin Magazine of History* 16 (1932): 163–98, 285–96.

22 Jesse Buel, *The Farmer's Companion* (Boston, 1839), in *Jesse Buel, Agricultural Reformer: Selections from His Writings,* edited by Harry J. Carman (New York, 1947), 424; *Catskill Recorder,* 4 Jan. 1815, 1; *Hudson Bee,* 22 Jan. 1805, 3; Abraham J. Hasbrouck Day Book, Jan.–March 1824, N-YHS; John Fowler, *Journal of a Tour in the State of New York in 1830* (London, 1831), 51; Patrick Shirreff, *A Tour through North America Together with a Comprehensive View of the Canadas and United States as Adapted for Agricultural Emigration* (Edinburgh, 1835), 33. Production figures are from *Census of the State of New York for 1845* (Albany, 1846); *Census of the State of New York for 1855* (Albany, 1857); *Aggregate Value and Produce and Number of Persons Employed in Mines, Agriculture, Commerce, and Manufacture . . . 6th Census 1840* (Washington, D.C., 1840); and John Homer French, *Gazetteer of the State of New York* (Syracuse, 1860), 329, 246, n. 7.

23 *Rural Repository,* 1 Jan. 1842, 116–17; *Transactions* 3 (1843): 69; Spafford, *Gazetteer* (1813), 218; *Northern Whig,* 6 May 1817; Isaac Holmes, *An Account of the United States* (London, 1823), 167; Stuart, *Three Years,* 1:494; Freeman Hunt, *Letters about the Hudson River and Its Vicinity* (New York, 1837), 222; *Transactions* 1 (1841): 271; *Kinderhook Sentinel,* 23 July 1844, 2.

24 *Memoirs of the New York State Board of Agriculture* 2 (Albany, 1823): 137; *Memoirs* 1 (1820): 251; Spafford, *Gazetteer* (1824), 127. See also John W. Barber and Henry Howe, *Historical Collections of the State of New York* (New York, 1841), 114; and Erastus Pratt to "My Dear Cousin," 28 June 1825, Pratt Family Papers, Cornell University Archives. For numbers on sheep and cattle, see *New York State Assembly Journal,* 45th sess. (Albany, 1822), appendix; and *Census of the State of New York for 1835* (Albany, 1836).

25 *Catskill Recorder,* 19 Aug. 1827, 3. On the advantages of Merino sheep, see Robert R. Livingston, *Essay on Sheep* (New York, 1809); *Niles' Weekly Register,* 9 July 1814, 333–34; and *Transactions* 11 (1851): 406–7. On the context, see Chester Whitney Wright, *Wool-Growing and the Tariff* (Boston, 1910), 12–19; and L. G. Connor, "Brief History of the Sheep Industry in the United States," in *Annual Report of the American Historical Association for the Year 1918* (Washington, D.C., 1921), 101–6.

26 William Cobbett, *A Year's Residence in the United States* (Carbondale, Ill. [1819] 1964), 179; "The Battles of Saratoga from an 'Enemy Perspective,'" translated by Helga Döblin, *Tamkang Journal of American Studies* 3 (1987): 31; Niemcewicz, *Under,* 192; *Hudson Balance and Columbian Repository,* 19 Jan. 1802, 2; *Hudson Balance and Columbia Repository,* 5 Jan. 1802, 2; Stuart, *Three Years,* 1:494; Heinrich Luden, ed., *Reise Sr. Hoheit des Herzogs Bernhard zu Sachsen-Weimar-Eisenach durch Nordamerika in den Jahren 1825 und 1826* (Weimar, 1828), 110, 173; *Greene County Republican,* 28 Nov. 1827, 2; Alexander Coventry Diary, 8 Aug. 1822 (transcript edited by the Albany Institute of History and Art and NYSL, 1978); Andrew Jackson Downing, *The Architecture of Country Houses* (New York, [1850] 1968), 83.

27 Henry Dubois Account Book, May 1823 and May 1824, NYSL. Calcium-rich gypsum, known as plaster of Paris, was used to fertilize meadows and fields (Holmes, *Account,* 174–75; Spafford, *Gazetteer* [1824], 18; Fowler, *Journal,* 181). Asa Webster bought it in 1849 (Asa Webster Account, 26 and 29 June 1849, Joseph Ford Papers, COLCHS) and William Hoffman noted in 1847 that "never have seen so much Plaster used as there has been this month" after he unsuccessfully attempted to purchase some (William Hoffman Diary, 31 May 1847, N-YHS).

28 Alexander Coventry Diary, 22 Aug. 1822; *Transactions* 2 (1843): 339–41; *Transactions* 6 (1846): 117–18; John Burroughs, *My Boyhood* (Garden City, 1924), 27–29; John Burroughs, "Phases of Farm Life," in *Signs and Seasons,* vol. 7 of *The Writings of John Burroughs* (Boston, 1895), 243. See also Stuart, *Three Years,* 1:255.

29 *Catskill Messenger,* 6 Dec. 1832, 2; *Transactions* 7 (1847): 648. Dollar values were calculated according to prices given in *New York Shipping and Commercial List,* 1843 and 1847. For additional information, see *Catskill Recorder,* 14 Nov. 1833, 2; Gordon, *Gazetteer,* 472; *Catskill Messenger,* 13 Apr. 1837, 2. The firkin is roughly equal to a quarter of a barrel or about nine gallons. On the necessity of food importation, see *Catskill Messenger,* 20 March 1834, 3; and French, *Gazetteer,* 101, 329–30.

30 Ann-Janette Dubois Diary, 24 May 1838, GrCHS; William Hoffman Diary, 31 July 1847, 13 April 1847; Hannah Bushnell Diary, 14 Aug. 1854, 30 May 1855, 16 Sept. 1856, MV 366, GrCHS; Edward Thurston to Oliver H. Jones, 5 July 1832 (see also 24 Oct. 1832 and 26 June 1833), Oliver H. Jones Correspondence, NYSL; James Reynolds Diary, 24 Jan. 1847, Adriance Memorial Library.

31 *Hudson Bee,* 22 Feb. 1811, 3; Catskill Mountains, Anonymous ms. [ca. 1815], GrCHS; William Darby, *A Tour from the City of New York to Detroit* (Chicago [1819] 1962), 30. See also *Catskill Recorder,* 18 Oct. 1820, 2. On waterpower, see William Youngs Diary, 5 Jan. 1814; Abner Austin Diary, 14 July 1818 and 31 Aug. 1821, Austin Collection MV 1084; and Manuscript Schedules, Census of Manufactures for 1850 (microfilm).

32 *Kinderhook Sentinel,* 1 Jan. 1846, 1; Thomas F. Gordon, *Gazetteer of the State of New York* (Philadelphia, 1836), 411 (quote; see also 403, 405, 471); Sterling Goodenow, *A Brief Topographical and Statistical Manual of the State of New-York* (New York, 1811), 7.

33 Stephen B. Miller, *Historical Sketches of Hudson* (Hudson, 1862), 64; *Catskill Recorder,* 18 Oct. 1820, 2; *Catskill Recorder,* 12 July 1832, 2.

34 *Catskill Recorder,* 19 July 1832, 2; *Catskill Messenger,* 1 July 1848, 2. See *Rural Repository* 25 (1849): 113–16, which stated that Pratt subdued the wilderness by consuming ten square miles of hemlock woods. See also J. S. E. Julia de Fontenelle and Francis Malepeyre, *The Arts of Tanning, Currying, and Leather-Dressing,* edited with numerous emendations and additions by Campbell Morfit (Philadelphia, 1852), 332; and Lucius F. Ellsworth, *Craft to National Industry in the Nineteenth Century: A Case Study of the Transformation of the New York State Tanning Industry* (New York, 1975), 77.

35 *Memoirs of Col. William Edwards . . . Written by Himself in his 76th Year, 1847* (Washington, D.C., 1847), 98–99; *History of Greene County,* 83, 213.

36 Lewis Mumford, *Technics and Civilization* (New York, 1934), 13–14, 23; David S. Landes, *Revolution in Time: Clocks and the Making of the Modern World* (Cambridge, Mass., 1983), 72. See also Michael O'Malley, *Keeping Watch: A History of American Time* (New York, 1990), 55–72.

37 Zephaniah Chase Account Book, Oct. 1785, NYSL; Elijah Hudson Farm Account Book, 1789–1791, NYSHA; [Henry Van Schaack] Account Book, 11 May 1795, ColCHS. On time in the Middle Ages, see Jacques LeGoff, "Le temps dans la 'crise' du 14e siècle: Du temps médiéval au temps moderne," *Le Moyen Age* 69 (1963): 597–613. I learned a great deal from A. J. Gurevich, "Time as a Problem of Cultural History," in *Cultures and Time* (Paris, 1976), 229–45.

38 Reverend H. H. Prout, *Old Time Letters,* quoted in *History of Greene County,* 347. On the Shaker clockmaker, see Jerry V. Grant and Douglas R. Allen, *Shaker Furniture Makers* (Hanover, 1989), 48; Abstract of the Valuations and Assessments in the County of Columbia in the Year 1800 and Valuations and Assessments in the County of Green [*sic*] in the Year 1800, Collection B 0315, NYS Arc; and Manuscript Schedules, Federal Census for 1800 (microfilm).

39 John Beebe Jr. Diary, 4 Aug. 1785, Chatham Public Library; Margaret Washington, ed., *Narrative of Sojourner Truth* (New York, 1993), 6, 9, 16, 27. See also J. Hector St. John de Crèvecoeur, "Sketches of Eighteenth-Century America," in *Letters from an American Farmer* (New York, 1986), 271.

40 Abraham J. Hasbrouck Journals 1824, N-YHS; *Catskill Recorder,* 15 July 1818, 3. See also Marius Schoonmaker, *History of Kingston* (New York, 1883), 412–14.

41 *History of the American Clock Business for the Past Sixty Years and Life of Chauncy Jerome, Written by himself* (New Haven, 1860), 36–44; Harriet Martineau, *Society in America* (New York, 1837), 2:27. See also David Jaffee, "Peddlers of Progress and the Transformation of the Rural North, 1760–1860," *Journal of American History* 78 (1991): 511–35.

42 William Bessac Daybook, fol. 41 (22 March 1826), MV 1329, GTCHS; Accounts of Titus Jansen and James O. Dubois, Aug. 1835, and Account of Peter Cristiana, May 1836, J. D. LaMontanye Account Book, Ulster County Community College; William Hoffman Diary, 17 Feb. 1848, 9 August and 23 Aug. 1847.

43 Cobbett, *Year's Residence,* 180; Jesse Buel, *The Farmer's Instructor* (New York, 1840), 1:143; *Transactions* 12 (1852): 29.

44 Lexington Temperance Society Minutes, fol. 24, NYSL; Abner Austin to Messrs. Dwight, 28 June 1828, Letter Copies, Austin Collection, MV 1095, GTCHS. See also Washington, *Narrative,* 9, 71–72.

45 William Coventry Diary, 1 and 8 May 1786, NYSHA; Hannah Bushnell Diary, 14 May 1855. See also *Stoddard's Diary; or, the Columbia Almanack for the Year of Our Lord 1830* (Hudson, n.d.); James Hopkins to Charles Hopkins, 18 March 1843, Caleb Hopkins Papers, NYSL; *Catskill Messenger,* 17 March 1849, 2. See also William Hoffman Diary, 23 March 1848.

46 William Coventry Diary, 31 July 1801 (see also 31 March, 3 April, and 17 and 21 April 1800); William Youngs Diary, 24 March and 6 Aug. 1811, NYSHA; *Kinderhook Sentinel,* 30 Oct. 1845, 2. Artisans: *Catskill Recorder,* 20 Nov. 1811, 3; *Kinderhook Sentinel,* 29 Feb. 1844, 3; entries for *punctuality* and *strict* in the *Oxford English Dictionary,* 2d ed. (Oxford, 1989), 12:840, 16:898–900. Women's time: Sally McMurry, *Families and Farmhouses in Nineteenth-Century America: Vernacular Design and Social Change* (New York, 1988), 62– 88; Jeanne Boydston, *Home and Work: Housework, Wages, and the Ideology of Labor in the Early Republic* (New York, 1990), 104–5; *Coxsackie Standard,* 21 Sept. 1837, 2.

47 Noble, *Life,* 164. On Hawthorne, see Leo Marx, *The Machine in the Garden: Technology and the Pastoral Ideal in America* (New York: 1964), 11–33. Washington Irving complained about the noise of the locomotives that desecrated his Hudson Valley retreat in the late 1840s. See Ralph M. Alderman et al., *Washington Irving: Letters,* vol. 4: *1846– 1859* (Boston, 1982), 167–70; and Washington Irving, *Life and Letters* (New York, 1864), 4:36–38.

48 On modes of industrialization that contemporaries deemed acceptable, see Marx, *Machine,* 155–69, 249 (on Thoreau); Thomas Bender, *Toward an Urban Vision: Ideas and Institutions in America* (Louisville, 1975), 22–51; John E. Kasson, *Civilizing the Machine: Technology and Republican Values in America, 1776–1900* (New York, 1976), 3–51; and Max Weber, "Capitalism and Rural Society in Germany," in *From Max Weber; Essays in Sociology,* edited by Hans Gerth and C. Wright Mills (New York, 1946), 366.

49 *Hudson Bee,* 30 Nov. 1810, 2–3; Spafford, *Gazetteer* (1824), 311; French, *Gazetteer,* 330; *Catskill Messenger,* 13 March 1834, 2. See also *Memoirs of Col. Wm. Edwards,* 101.

50 Theodore A. Cole Diary, 31 Oct. 1857, MV 1207, GTCHS.

1 Abner Austin to John J. Hill, 31 March 1835, Austin Collection, MV 1096, GrCHS; Louis LeGrand, *The Life and Works of Thomas Cole,* edited by Elliott S. Vesell (Cambridge, Mass., [1853] 1964), 65; *Census of the State of New York for 1845* (Albany, 1846).

2 Ebenezer Emmons, *Agriculture of New York* (Albany, 1846), 1:327–30; Russell H. Anderson, "New York Agriculture Meets the West, 1830–1850," *Wisconsin Magazine of History* 16 (1932): 163–98, 285–96.

3 Reynolds Account Book, 1808–1810, MV 434, GrCHS; Samuel Fowks Account Book, 1817–1822, MV 1146, GrCHS (Fowks' credits were £412 13s 2d from twenty accounts, of which he received £164 18s 4d in cash payments); Butler General Store Daybook, 1851, MV 319, GrCHS (Garruson settled his bill on 7 June 1853); Theodore A. Cole Diary, 28 Sept. 1827, MV 1207, GrCHS. Eight shillings added up to $1.00 and £1 to $2.50.

4 Resolution of the Republican Citizens of Canaan, Columbia County, 15 April 1812, Canaan Ms., NYSL. See also *Catskill Recorder,* 2 June 1812, 2; and 11 May 1814, 3. I analyzed 309 mortgages for the years 1800–1801, 1823–24, and 1847–48 and found only two men, Elias Haight of Austerlitz in 1823 and Edward G. Bugsby of Ghent in 1847, who dealt with banks (Mortgages B, G2, G3, and DD, Columbia County Court House). The deposits at the Bank of Kinderhook, founded in 1838, never formed more than 40 percent of its assets (see *Kinderhook Sentinel,* 15 Nov. 1838, 2; and the bank's quarterly reports in *Kinderhook Sentinel,* 1844–49).

5 *Hudson Bee,* 15 March 1803, 87. For a similar incident, see *Hudson Balance and Columbia Repository,* 28 Feb. 1804, 70; and *Catskill Recorder,* 18 Jan. 1828, 2.

6 The development of a wage-earning farm labor force occurred in New England during the same period. See Christopher Clark, *The Roots of Rural Capitalism: Western Massachusetts, 1780–1860* (Ithaca, 1990); Daniel P. Jones, *The Economic and Social Transformation of Rural Rhode Island, 1780–1850* (Boston, 1992); and Daniel Vickers, *Farmers and Fishermen: Two Centuries of Work in Essex County, Massachusetts, 1630–1850* (Chapel Hill, 1994).

7 This is the argument deployed to explain the decline in the gross fertility rate in Richard Easterlin, "Population Change and Farm Settlement in the Northern United States," *Journal of Economic History* 36 (1976): 45–75; and William A. Sundstrom and Paul A. David, "Old-Age Security Motives, Labor Markets, and Farm Family Fertility in Antebellum America," *Explorations in Economic History* 25 (1988): 164–97. The number of children aged one to five per 1,000 women age sixteen to forty-five declined, between 1800 and 1855, from 1,471 to 988 in Columbia County, and from 2,086 to 1,125 in Greene County (*Return of the Whole Number of Persons within the Several Districts of the United States* [Washington, D.C., 1802]; *Census of the State of New York for 1855* [Albany, 1857]).

8 Abraham J. Hasbrouck Journals, 1801 and 1824, N-YHS; *Greene County Republican,* 11 June 1828, 2.

9 *Transactions of the New York State Agricultural Society* 4 (1844): 35, 38–39.

10 *Catskill Messenger,* 3 March 1836, 1 (I have corrected a calculation error); *Catskill Messenger,* 21 April 1836, 1; Ephraim P. Best Farm Account Book, 1849, ColCHS; Agricultural Schedules, Federal Census for 1850 (microfilm).

11 *Catskill Democrat,* 5 Nov. 1844, 2; *Transactions* 17 (1857): 92, 18 (1858): 155, 19 (1859): 99, 20 (1860): 160, 14 (1854): 120; Ephraim P. Best Farm Account Book, 1844–1854.

12 Manuscript Agricultural Schedules, Federal Census for 1850 (microfilm).

13 Alexander Coventry Diary, 31 Jan. 1828 (typescript edited by the Albany Institute of History and Art and NYSL, 1978); *Kinderhook Sentinel,* 28 Feb. 1839, 2; Russell Cady to Elias W. Cady, 26 March 1835, Elias W. Cady Papers, Cornell University Archives. See also John F. Collins, *History of Hillsdale, New York* (Philmont, 1883), 55; Abstract of the Valuations and Assessments in the County of Columbia in the Year One Thousand Seven Hundred and Ninety-nine, NYS Archives; New York State, Secretary of State, *Census of the State of New York for 1835* (Albany, 1836); and "Corrected Valuations and Taxes for the Year 1847," *Kinderhook Sentinel,* 20 Jan. 1848, 1.

14 Abraham J. Hasbrouck Journals, 1824; Horatio Gates Spafford, *Gazetteer of the State of New York* (Albany, 1813), 78. See also Horatio Gates Spafford, *Gazetteer of the State of New York* (Albany, 1824), 32–33; Diary of an Unidentified Scottsman, 17 June 1824, BV Diary, N-YHS; and Thomas Hamilton, *Men and Manners in America* (Edinburgh, 1833), 1:78.

15 For hay, see Reuben Rundle Daybook, 1834–1835, 257–58, MV 1218, GrCHS; Sherman Ledgers (New Baltimore) 1841–1854, MV 1213–1215, GrCHS; *Lampman vs. Van Loon,* Court of Common Pleas, 1827, GrCHS; and *Edget vs. Botsford,* Court of Common Pleas, 1828, GrCHS. For butter circuits and commission houses, see John Burroughs, *My Boyhood* (Garden City, 1924), 13–20; *Catskill Recorder,* 28 May 1835, 3; *Kinderhook Sentinel,* 21 Oct. 1836, 3; and Sally McMurry, *Transforming Rural Life: Dairying Families and Agricultural Change, 1820–1885* (Baltimore, 1995), 46–51. For drovers and adjacent businesses, see "Catskill Horse Ferry," Thomson Family Papers, Box 3, GrCHS. In general, see the description of mercantile specialization in Kingston as it changed from a rural village into a bustling river town before the Civil War in Stuart M. Blumin, *The Urban Threshold: Growth and Change in an American Community* (Chicago, 1976), 59–63, 104–14.

16 Burroughs, *My Boyhood,* 60; John Burroughs, "Phases of Farm Life," in *Signs and Seasons,* vol. 7 of *The Writings of John Burroughs* (Boston, 1895), 231. See Agricultural Schedules for Roxbury, Delaware County, New York, Federal Census for 1850 (microfilm) for information about John's father Chauncy and the farm. See also George Holcomb Diary, 25 April, 30 Sept., 3, 4, and 6 Oct. 1831, 25 and 26 May, 10 and 11 June, 13 July, 22 Sept., 3 and 4 Oct. 1832, NYSL; Ephraim Best Farm Account Book, fall and winter 1849; and William Hoffman Diary, 20 July 1850.

17 Cooper Sayre to Frederick Kirtland, 13 Oct. 1836, Caroline A. Morss Papers, NYSL; Theodore A. Cole Diary, 3 Dec. 1857; William Hoffman Diary, 9 Aug. 1847, N-YHS.

18 For examples of the social calendar, see Sarah M. Campbell Diary, 5 July, 1825, N-YHS; *Catskill Recorder,* 28 Oct. 1825, 3; Ann-Janette Dubois Diary, 14 and 21 Sept. 1835, GrCHS; Leeds Female Benevolent Association, 24 March 1853, MV 1211, GrCHS; Ephraim P. Best Farm Account Book, 1849–1850; Hannah Bushnell Diary, 17 May 1855, 2 July 1855, 20 and 21 May 1856, 1 Sept. 1856, MV 366, GrCHS; and Nancy Grey Osterud, *Bonds of Community: The Lives of Farm Women in Nineteenth-Century New York* (Ithaca, 1991), 12, 202–27.

19 *Transactions,* 12 (1852): 191; New York State Census for 1855, Kinderhook, ms; *Trans-*

actions 6 (1846): 118 (see also 121); Burroughs, *My Boyhood,* 49. Unlike art historians, who construe Francis Williams Edmonds's *Taking the Census* (1854) as a depiction of the farmer's boorish awkwardness (he uses his fingers to enumerate crops, etc.), I believe the painting, which is set in the Hudson Valley, catches a rationalistic outlook nicely expressed by the clock in the living room (reproduced in Sarah Burns, *Pastoral Inventions: Rural Life in Nineteenth-Century American Art and Culture* [Philadelphia, 1989], 184).

20 Data from "Census of the State of New York for 1821," in New York State Assembly, *Journal,* 45th sess. (Albany, 1822), appendix, and "Census of the State of New York for 1825," 49th sess. (Albany, 1826), appendix; *Census of the State of New York for 1835;* and New York State Secretary, *Census of the State of New York for 1845* (Albany, 1846), and *Census of the State of New York for 1855* (Albany, 1857).

21 Robert R. Livingston, "American Agriculture," in *Edinburgh Encyclopedia,* 1st American ed. (Philadelphia, 1832), 1:334. On crop rotation after 1820, see Isaac Holmes, *An Account of the United States of America* (London, 1823), 172–74; Fowler, *Journal,* 181–82; James Stuart, *Three Years in North America* (Edinburgh, 1833), 1:255, 264–66; Burroughs, *My Boyhood,* 30–50; *Transactions* 6 (1846): 111–18; and Ellis, *Landlords and Tenants,* 118–56, 184–224.

22 Late-eighteenth-century figures were calculated from Abstract of the Valuations; *Transactions* 14 (1854): 205; *Transactions for the Society for the Promotion of Agriculture, Art, Manufacture,* 2d ed. 1 (Albany, 1801), 309–10; Holmes, *Account,* 170; and *Kinderhook Sentinel,* 23 July 1844, 2. Land allocation was calculated from "Census of the State of New York for 1821," and "Census of the State of New York for 1825." All the subsequent information is calculated according to these assumptions of land requirements on the basis of the New York State censuses of 1845 and 1855.

23 McMurry, *Transforming Women's Work,* 175. See also Joan M. Jensen, *Loosening the Bonds: Mid-Atlantic Farm Women, 1750–1850* (New Haven, 1986); *Transactions* 14 (1855): 120; George W. Best Account Book, 1846–1854.

24 Clark, *Roots,* 59–64, 72–74; Susan Geib, "Changing Works: Agriculture and Society in Brookfield, Massachusetts," Ph.D. diss., Boston University, 1981, 40–41, 54; Thomas Dublin, *Transforming Women's Work: New England Lives in the Industrial Revolution* (Ithaca, 1994).

25 On the Dubois family, see Anson Dubois and James G. Dubois, *Documents and Genealogical Chart of the Family of Benjamin Dubois of Catskill, New York* (New York, 1978), esp. 87–90; Clermont data from Rent Roll of Clermont Estate, 1799, Wilson Papers, Eckert Collection, Bard College (Annandale-on-Hudson, N.Y.); Assessment Roll of the Real and Personal Estate of the Town of Clermont for 1826 (microfilm reel 52, series 5), Robert R. Livingston, New-York Historical Society, New York; Clermont Rent Roll 1826, box 9, Livingston Family Papers (Clermont Historical Site, Clermont, N.Y.); Greene County Property Assessment Roll for 1813, MV 109, GrCHS; New York State Census for 1825, Austerlitz, Austerlitz Town Clerk; 1827 Tax Assessment for Austerlitz, CoICHS; and Manuscript Agricultural Schedules, Federal Census for 1850.

26 Thomas F. Gordon, *Gazetteer of the State of New York* (Philadelphia, 1836), 405, 409.

27 For examples of "countercyclical" activities, see Account Joseph Boccus, 17 and 21 Sept. 1808, Reynolds Account Book, MV 434, GrCHS (shoemaking); Account Isaac

Bromyhan, May 1823, Henry Dubois Account Book, NYSL (fence making); Account James Walker, 17 March 1830, Isaac Reed Ledger, Eastfield Village Collections (spinning); Account James Stambridge, 2 Sept. 1837, Henry Groat Account Book, NYSL (ditching); and Account Barney McGuinnis, 8 Feb., 1 March, 24 April 1848, Asa H. Beach Farm Account Book, NYSHA (woodcutting, wall building).

28 On the impact of enclosures on labor intensity, see J. D. Chambers, "Enclosure and Labour Supply in the Industrial Revolution," *Economic History Review,* 2d ser., 5 (1953): 319–43. Agricultural reformer Jesse Buel sketched the development of farming in the Hudson Valley in *The Cultivator* 5 (Feb. 1839) and 1 (April 1834), reproduced in *Jesse Buel, Agricultural Reformer: Selections from His Writings,* edited by Harry J. Carman (New York, 1947), 27, 47–48.

29 *Transactions* 4 (1844): 39; Livingston, "American Agriculture," 336; *Catskill Recorder,* 25 Dec. 1811, 2; *Memoirs of the New York State Board of Agriculture* 3 (1826): preface; Samuel Fowks Account Books, 1817–1823, MV 1144–1146, GtCHS; *New York Spectator,* 3 Sept. 1824, 1. On Samuel Fowks, see *Catskill Recorder,* 21 March 1821, 3.

30 *Memoirs* 1 (1821), 213; *Memoirs* 3 (1826), 77; *Transactions* 4 (1844): 35–39; Carman, *Jesse Buel,* 390. See also Robert L. Ardrey, *American Agricultural Implements* (Chicago, 1894), 9–12; Leo Rogin, *The Introduction of Farm Machinery in Its Relation to Productivity of Labor in the Agriculture of the United States during the Nineteenth Century* (Berkeley, 1931), 25–26, 30; and Clarence Danhof, *Change in Agriculture: The Northern United States* (Cambridge, Mass., 1969), 278–79. For a minute description of innovation in farm implements that emphasizes the revolutionary nature of the second and third decades of American agriculture, see Peter D. McClelland, *Sowing Modernity: America's First Agricultural Revolution* (Ithaca, 1997), esp. 14–63.

31 Account Barney McGuinnis, 8 April 1848, Asa H. Beach Farm Account Book; John Fowler, *Journal of a Tour in the State of New York in 1830* (London, 1831), 51; Burroughs, *My Boyhood,* 11–16; J. B. Bordley, *Essays and Notes on Husbandry and Rural Affairs,* 2d ed. (Philadelphia, 1801), 274. See also the detailed account in Jensen, *Loosening the Bonds,* 79–141. McMurry, *Transforming Women's Work,* 15–24, explains the impossibility of ascertaining the impact of different breeds as well as the resulting crossbreeds on milk production before the Civil War. In the Hudson Valley, Isaac Holmes saw Durham cows in the early 1820s while the Burroughs family kept Devonshire Ayrshire cows. See Holmes, *Account,* 169–70; Burroughs, *My Boyhood,* 12–13; and Clare Barrus, *John Burroughs: Boy and Man* (Garden City, 1920), 83. On sheep, see *Memoirs of the New York State Board of Agriculture* 1 (Albany, 1820), 307; and *Kinderhook Sentinel,* 23 July 1844, 2.

32 For evidence of the preponderance of sickle use at the beginning of the nineteenth century, see "Ninety-five Years Ago: An Interview with Killian Scott of Hillsdale," *Hillsdale Herald,* April 1880, quoted in Peter Stott, "Industrial Archeology in Columbia County, New York" (1990, typescript located at the COlCHS); "Recollections of Edward McGraw," in Edward M. Ruttenber, *History of the Town of New Windsor, Orange County, New York* (Newburgh: 1911), 48; Lucius Moll Account Book, July 1821, COlCHS; and *Transactions* 4 (1844): 35.

33 Livingston, "American Agriculture," 338; William Cobbett, *A Year's Residence in the United States of America* (Carbondale, Ill., [1819] 1964), 178; Henry Fearon, *Sketches of America* (London, 1819), 69; Stuart, *Three Years,* 1:257–58, 261–62, 280; Thomas Hamil-

ton, *Men and Manners in America* (Philadelphia, 1831), 1:51; William Thomson, *A Tradesman's Travels in the United States and Canada* (Edinburgh, 1842), excerpted in Roger Haydon, ed., *Upstate Travels: British Views of Nineteenth-Century New York* (Syracuse, 1982), 47.

34 I found six seasonal contracts for 1800–1810, twenty for 1811–20 (average length 5.6 months), eleven for 1821–30, sixteen for the 1830s (6.7 months on average), and eight for 1841 to 1850. In Lexington, 20.8 percent of farm families hired help; in Kinderhook, Greenville, and Hillsdale, the rates were 28.2, 35.6, and 37.2 percent, respectively (Population Schedules, Federal Census for 1850). On a different set of labor contracts, see Paul E. Clemens and Lucy Simler, "Rural Labor and the Farm Household in Chester County, Pennsylvania, 1750–1820," in *Work and Labor in Early America,* edited by Stephen Innes (Chapel Hill, 1988), 106–43. Robert A. Gross finds strong evidence that the 1820s marked a dividing line in the decline of family labor and the emergence of wage work in Concord, Massachusetts ("Culture and Cultivation: Agriculture and Society in Thoreau's Concord," *Journal of American History* 69 [1982]: 51–52).

35 Isaac Reed Ledger, December 1827, Eastfield Village Collections (East Nassau, New York). Income stood at $389 and labor expenses at $221 at Great Imbaught near Catskill (Farm Account Book, Great Imbaught, 1815–16, N-YHS). Best's labor costs were $269 out of $1,635 in 1846, of which $219 covered permanent employees and $49 seasonal hands (Ephraim P. Best Farm Account Book 1846). Coffin's were $314 out of $1,552 (*Transactions* 14 [1854]: 120), and here I included inventory from the preceding year, 1853. Crispell's labor costs were $454 on a balance of $2,154 (*Transactions* 7 [1847]: 217–19).

36 Day Book of Asa Webster, Hillsdale, Columbia County, 6 and 14 Aug. 1849 (see 3 Aug. 1849 for the liquor supply, Joseph Ford Papers, COLCHS). Age data are from Population Schedules, Federal Census for 1850; William Hoffman Diary, 12 March 1847; and Ephraim P. Best Farm Account Book, 1844–1848. See also George Holcomb Diary, 16 March 1839; and Contract between Andrew A. Houghtaling and John L. Bronk, 31 March 1849, New Baltimore Ms File, GRCHS; and Thomson, *Tradesman,* 46. On deductions from seasonal wages, see Account Joseph Boccus, 21 Sept. 1808 ("To one Day lost make yourself Boots"), Reynolds Account Book; Account William Jones, August 1812 ("sick with collack"); Account Robert, colored man, 4 May 1840 ("Pinkster"), John and Tobias Teller Account Books, 1812–1835, 1834–1851, NYSHA; and Account John Sitser, 25 Dec. 1846 and 1 Jan. 1847, Ephraim P. Best Farm Account Book ("Lost two days Christmas and New Year").

37 Harriet Olmsted to John Olmsted, 14 Jan. 1837, in "Selections from the Correspondence and Diaries of John Olmsted, 1826–1838," edited by Elisabeth W. Olmsted, mimeographed typescript located at the Buffalo and Erie County Historical Society, Buffalo, N.Y.; Lucretia Warner Hall Diary, 28 June 1846, N-YHS; George Holcomb Diary, 8 Jan. 1827.

38 Daniel Hatch Account Book, 1816, NYSHA; Lucius Moll Account Book, July 1819, 1821. Henry Dubois, also of Schodack, paid the same rates to neighbor David Neher in 1824 (Henry Dubois Account Book, 1824, NYSL), and it looks as if the only wage rate to change between 1815 and 1825 was that for mowing, which diminished from

six shillings per day to five shillings six pence. See William Hoffman Diary, fol. 342, 31 Dec. 1846 ($60), 31 Dec. 1847 ($100); Wilbur Fisk Strong Diary, 20 Sept. 1858, MV 231, GrCHS; and Ephraim P. Best Farm Account Book, 1849. See also Peter Crispell's account in *Transactions* 7 (1847): 217.

39 Holmes, *Account*, preface; among the many books detailing the continuity of the family farm, see Osterud, *Bonds of Community*, 46–47, 53–72. On the sexual division of labor, see Elizabeth Fox-Genovese, "Women in Agriculture during the Nineteenth Century," in *Agriculture and National Development: Views on the Nineteenth Century*, edited by Lou Ferleger (Ames, 1990), 267–301; and M. L. Burton and D. White, "Sexual Division of Labor in Agriculture," *American Anthropologist* 86 (1984): 568–83.

40 Hannah Barnard, *Dialogues on Domestic and Rural Economy and the Fashionable Follies of the World* (Hudson, 1820), esp. 44–45. On the ideology of domesticity, see Nancy F. Cott, *The Bonds of Womanhood: 'Women's Sphere' in New England, 1780–1830* (New Haven, 1976). Stuart M. Blumin, *The Emergence of the Middle Class: Social Experience in the American City, 1760–1900* (New York, 1989), esp. 179–91, provides this ideology's social sphere of origin and grounding. This is not to say that domestic ideals did not reach the countryside (see, e.g., *Hudson Balance*, 16 March 1802, 84) but to stress their accessory place in the discourse on, and as they are directed to, the agricultural population. On Hannah Barnard, who was well known in Hudson for her strong mind and her independent stand on issues of religion, see *Hudson Balance*, 30 Oct. 1804, 349–50; *Some Facts Relating to Hannah Barnard* (Hudson, 1802), esp. iv, 3–6, 12; and Gorham A. Worth, *Recollections of Hudson*, in *Random Recollections of Albany, from 1800 to 1808*, 2d ed. (Albany, 1850), 42–43.

41 Barnard, *Dialogues*, 43; see also 8, 11, 17, 33, 41. This conception did not seem to hold among farmers or segments of the agricultural press in New England, where Linda J. Boorish found a depreciating depiction of farm women. See her " 'Another Domestic Beast of Burden': New England Farm Women's Work and Well-Being in the 19th Century," *Journal of American Culture* 18 (1995): 83–100, esp. 86–87.

42 Barnard, *Dialogues*, 16, 28, 50, 29, 66.

43 *Samuel Burns v. Jane Claw*, Court of Common Pleas Collection 1808, GrCHS; Burroughs, *My Boyhood*, 12–16; Ann-Janette Dubois Diary, 14 July 1835. See also Nathalia Wright, ed., *Washington Irving: Journals and Notebooks*, vol. 1: *1803–1806* (Madison, 1969), 4 (diary of a trip on the Hudson in 1803); Silvina Bramhell to Mehetable Bramhell, 27 Dec. 1818, Elias W. Cady Papers; George Holcomb Diary, 25 April 1831, 25–26 May 1832; and Lucretia Warner Hall Diary, 7 Sept. 1841, 15 May 1844. Edward McGraw recalled that "the women milked the cows" ("Recollections of Edward McGraw," 48). Sarah McMahon confirmed the cooperation of women and men in food preservation for domestic consumption in her "Laying Foods by: Gender, Dietary Decisions, and the Technology of Food Preservation in New England Households, 1750–1850," in *Early American Technology: Making and Doing Things from the Colonial Era to 1850*, edited by Judith A. McGaw (Chapel Hill, 1994), 164–96.

44 Harriet Martineau, *Society in America* (New York, 1837), 2:54; Stuart, *Three Years*, 1:280 (see also 264 and 275). On Europe, see Louise A. Tilly and Joan W. Scott, *Women, Work, and Family* (New York, 1978), 46–47; and Martine Segalen, *Mari et femme dans la société paysanne* (Paris, 1980), 105–18.

45 See Jack Larkin, *The Reshaping of Everyday Life, 1790–1840* (New York, 1989), 23–24; Fox-Genovese, "Women," 270; Hal S. Baron, "Listening to the Silent Majority: Change and Continuity in the Nineteenth-Century Rural North," in Ferleger, *Agriculture*, 14–16; and John Mack Farragher, *Sugar Creek: Life on the Illinois Prairie* (New Haven, 1986), 100–101.

46 Livingston, "American Agriculture," 338; "Ninety-five Years Ago: An Interview with Killian Scott."

47 Ann-Janette Dubois Diary, 13 Aug. 1838, 1 and 2 Aug. 1839; Burroughs, "Phases of Farm Life," in *Signs and Seasons*, vol. 7 of *The Writings of John Burroughs* (Boston, 1895), 236; Jeremiah Bogart's haying season began on 28 June and finished on 18 August 1856. See Jeremiah Bogart Account Book, MV 930, GtCHS; *Rural Repository*, 17 Aug. 1839, 33; and Diary of a Trip through Woodstock and Shandaken, 14 Aug. 1844, in *Thomas Cole: The Collected Essays and Prose Sketches*, edited by Marshall Tymn (St. Paul, 1980), 178. See also Lucretia Warner Hall Diary, 24 July 1833; and Rogin, *Introduction*, 128. Jerome Thompson's "The Haymakers, Mount Mansfield, Vermont" (1839) depicts a woman with a pitchfork (reproduction in Burns, *Pastoral Inventions*, 40; for later illustrations, see 49 and 115).

48 *Memoirs* 1 (1820): 307. Spinning and weaving were mostly, but not exclusively women's concern until the arrival of machine-produced cloth in the 1820s. Between 1821 and 1835 household textile production fell from 6.17 yards per capita to 3.52 in Greene County and from 7.17 to 3.64 in Columbia County ("Census of the State of New York for 1821"; New York State Secretary, "Census of the State of New York for 1835" [Albany, 1836]). In the Hudson Valley, young women hired themselves out to spin and weave for a few weeks or months at a time. See Jacques Gérard Milbert, *Itinéraire pittoresque du fleuve Hudson et des parties latérales de l'Amérique du Nord, d'après les dessins originaux pris sur les lieux* (Paris, 1828–29), 1:xxvi; "Recollections of Edward McGraw," 49; Mehetable Bramhell to Silvina Bramhell, 1 Aug. 1821, Elias W. Cady Papers; Ralph Lefevre, *History of New Paltz, New York* (Albany, 1903), 215–16; [Henry Van Schaack] Account Book, 12 Nov. 1810, 12 Dec. 1811, 30 March 1812, COLCHS; Elisha Blackmar Account Book, 14 and 29 March 1814, 12 Dec. 1815, 4 April 1818, MV 538, GtCHS; Elisha Blackmar Account Book, 10 March, 11 May, 25 June, and 31 Aug. 1829, MV 525, GtCHS; and Blacksmith Account Book, 27 May 1833, Pratt Museum, Prattsville. See also Laurel Thatcher Ulrich, "Wheels, Looms, and the Gender Division of Labor in Eighteenth-Century New England," *William and Mary Quarterly*, 3d ser., 55 (1998): 1–38.

49 Michael Mitterauer, "Formen ländlicher Familienwirtschaft," in *Familienstruktur und Arbeitsorganisation in ländlichen Gesellschaften*, edited by Joseph Ehmer and Michael Mitterauer (Vienna, 1986), 200–204, 212–16. On cattle, see Fred Bateman, "Labor Inputs and Productivity in American Dairy Agriculture, 1850–1910," *Journal of Economic History* 29 (1969): 206–29.

50 For yearly wages, see Account Ruth Taylor, 19 Dec. 1811, and Account Phebe Spencer, 3 May 1817, Reynolds Account Book. For weekly wages, see Isaac DeWitt Account Book 1823; Farm and Saw Mill Day Book, 5 February 1829, Dutchess County Historical Society; Willis Gaylord, Luther Tucker, *American Husbandry* (New York, 1844), 2:235; John and Tobias Teller Day Book, 6 Nov. 1832, NYSHA; Ephraim P. Best Farm

Account Book 1850; George Holcomb Diary, 4 Jan., 10, 12 and 16 March 1832; and *Transactions* 6 (1846): 147.

51 "Ninety-five years ago: an interview with Killian Scott"; "Recollections of Edward McGraw," 48. On productivity, see Rogin, *Introduction,* 69–72. On the English experience, see E. J. T. Collins, "Harvest Technology and the Labour Supply in Britain, 1790–1870," *Economic History Review,* 2d ser., 22 (1969): 453–73; Michael Roberts, "Sickles and Scythes: Women's Work and Men's Work at Harvest Time," *History Workshop* 7 (1979): 8, 20; and K. D. M. Snell, "Agricultural Seasonal Unemployment, the Standard of Living, and Women's Work in the South and East, 1690–1860," *Economic History Review,* 2d ser., 34 (1981): 419, 425.

52 Robert R. Livingston, *Essay on Sheep* (New York, 1809), 77–86; Livingston, "Agriculture," 334; *The Cultivator* 1 (March 1834) and 4 (Nov. 1837), in Carman, *Jesse Buel,* 154–55, 183–84. On labor input, see Franklin M. Mendels, "Agriculture and Peasant Industry in Eighteenth-Century Flanders," in *European Peasants and Their Markets,* edited by William N. Parker and Eric L. Jones (Princeton: 1975), 202; Stuart, *Three Years,* 1:266; Ann-Janette Dubois Diary, 28 Aug. 1839, 20 May 1837, 22 June 1839, 15 Aug. 1835, 3 Aug. 1844; Lucretia Warner Hall Diary, 15 Oct. 1840; Hannah Bushnell Diary, 29 Sept. 1855.

53 Patrick Shirreff, *A Tour through North America* (Edinburgh, 1835), 35; Stuart's comments in *Three Years,* 1:264, 275, 280.

54 Silvina Bramhell to Mehetable Bramhell, 12 Nov. 1820, Elias W. Cady Papers; Sara Mynderse Campbell Diary, 4 Aug. 1826, N-YHS; Ann-Janette Dubois Diary, 2 Sept. 1837; Lucinda Davenport to John Olmsted, 13 Feb. 1835, in Olmsted, "Selections," 104.

55 Gaylord, Tucker, *American Husbandry,* 2:222. On the differently paced paths toward factory production of butter and cheese, for which men controlled the process of production in England and the United States, see Sally McMurry, "Women's Work in Agriculture: Divergent Trends in England and America, 1800–1930," *Comparative Studies in Society and History* 34 (1992): 248–70; and the discussion of ideas on the value of male and female dairy labor in Deborah Valenze, "The Art of Women and the Business of Men: Women's Work and the Dairy Industry c. 1740–1840," *Past and Present* 130 (1991): 142–69.

56 George Holcomb Diary, 25 April 1831, 17, 25, 26 May, 3 and 22 Sept. 1832; Hannah Bushnell Diary, 23 Oct. 1855, 11 Sept., 25 Nov. and 2 Dec. 1854, 21 and 25 April 1855; *Transactions* 6 (1846): 115. See also Lucretia Warner Hall Diary, 15 May 1844; and Burroughs, *My Boyhood,* 17–20.

57 Ann-Janette Dubois Diary, 25 July, 1 Oct., 8 Nov., and 7 Dec. 1838, 28 Jan., 11 Feb., and 12 April 1839, 26 July, 3 and 21 Sept. 1842; 20 Jan. 1840. Tensions arose between Ann-Janette's husband Peter Whitaker and her father and grandfather about the control of hay sales, but Whitaker was unable to wrest concessions from his in-laws (Ann-Janette Dubois Diary, 30 June 1840).

58 Norma Basch, *In the Eyes of the Law: Women, Marriage, and Property in Nineteenth-Century New York* (Ithaca, 1982), 42–69. I analyzed seventy-five deeds from Deeds A (1787–1794), sixteen of which included women, and ninety-six deeds from Deeds M (1827–1828), on seventy of which women appeared (Columbia County Court House).

59 Will of Joseph Peckham, 10 March 1828, Wills F (1827–1833), Columbia County Court

House; data from Wills F (1827–1828). In a study of Connecticut inheritance practices, Toby Ditz found the same development. See her *Property and Kinship: Inheritance
in Early Connecticut, 1750–1830* (Princeton, 1986).

60 Anson Dubois and James Dubois, comps., *Documents and Genealogical Chart of the
Family of Benjamin DuBois of Catskill, N.Y.* (New York, 1878), 87–90; Pratt Family
Papers and Elias W. Cady Papers, Cornell University Archives; William Hoffman
Diary, 30 March 1848. For a longer biographical sketch of one Hudson Valley native
who left for Wisconsin in the 1850s, see Merle Curti, *The Making of an American
Community: A Case Study of Democracy in a Frontier County* (Stanford, 1959), 426–38.
See also Allan Stanley Horlick, *Country Boys and Merchant Princes: The Social Control
of Young Men in New York* (Lewisburg, 1975), 106–21; and Hannah Bushnell Diary,
28 March 1856, 2 June 1857. For outmigration in the decades before the Civil War,
Donald H. Parkerson's *The Agricultural Transition in New York: Markets and Migration in
Mid-nineteenth-century America* (Ames, 1995), 112–16, finds a high persistence rate and
relatively low renewal of the population along the Hudson River in the 1850s.

61 *Kinderhook Sentinel,* 8 Oct. 1846, 2. See also Basch, *Eyes of the Law,* 136–61.

62 Allan Kulikoff, *The Agrarian Origins of American Capitalism* (Charlottesville, 1992), 43;
Abner Austin Diary, 11–26 July 1822, MV 1084, GrCHS; Hannah Bushnell Diary, 20 and
21 May 1856.

FIVE *Country Shops and Factory Creeks, 1807–1850s*

1 *Hudson Bee,* 15 May 1810, 2; *Northern Whig,* 11 June 1816.

2 *Hudson Bee,* 14 Sept. 1810, 3; 18 Jan. 1811, 3. See also *Catskill Recorder,* 12 Aug. 1812, 3;
Franklin Ellis, *History of Columbia County, New York* (Philadelphia, 1878); Thomas F.
Gordon, *Gazetteer of the State of New York* (Philadelphia, 1836), 403, 411, 471; and
William Darby, *A Tour from the City of New York to Detroit* (Chicago, [1819] 1962), 30.

3 *Catskill Recorder,* 26 Sept. 1810, 2; *Northern Whig,* 17 Jan. 1815; *Catskill Recorder,* 20 Aug.
1817, 2; *Hudson Bee,* 23 Jan. 1816, 2; *Catskill Recorder,* 3 Sept. 1817, 2.

4 For a traditional account, see Harry J. Carman, "The Beginnings of the Industrial
Revolution," in *History of the State of New York,* edited by Alexander C. Flick (New
York, 1933–37), 5:337–57; and Harry J. Carman and August B. Gold, "The Rise of the
Factory System," in Flick, *History,* 6:191–245. The best analysis of regional industri-
alization is Richard B. Stott, "Hinterland Development and Differences in Work Set-
ting: The New York City Region, 1820–1870," in *New York City and the Rise of American
Capitalism,* edited by William Pencak and Conrad E. Wright (New York, 1989), 45–
71. See also Sean Wilentz, *Chants Democratic: New York City and the Rise of the American
Working Class, 1788–1850* (New York, 1984), 107–34; Thomas Dublin, *Women at Work:
The Transformation of Work and Community in Lowell, Massachusetts, 1826–1860* (New
York, 1979); Thomas Dublin, "Rural Putting-Out Work in Nineteenth-Century New
England: Women and the Transition to Capitalism in the Countryside," *New England
Quarterly* 64 (1991): 531–73; Paul Faler, *Mechanics and Manufacturers in the Early Industrial
Revolution. Lynn, Massachusetts, 1780–1860* (Albany, 1981); Philip Scranton, *Proprietory
Capitalism: The Textile Manufacture at Philadelphia, 1800–1885* (New York, 1983); Mary H.
Blewett, *Men, Women, and Work: Class, Gender, and Protest in the New England Shoe In-*

dustry, 1780–1910 (Urbana, 1990); and David R. Meyer, "Midwestern Industrialization and the American Manufacturing Belt in the Nineteenth Century," *Journal of Economic History* 49 (1989): 921–37.

5 Jonathan Prude, *The Coming of Industrial Order: Town and Factory Life in Rural Massachusetts, 1810–1860* (Cambridge, Engl., 1983), 183–216; Christopher Clark, *The Roots of Rural Capitalism: Western Massachusetts, 1780–1860* (Ithaca, 1990), 228–55; Richard B. Stott, *Workers in the Metropolis: Class, Ethnicity, and Youth in Antebellum New York* (Ithaca, 1990), 12, 38–39, 66 (quote).

6 On Kinderhook, see J. Disturnell, *A Gazetteer of the State of New York* (Albany, 1842), 406; and *Kinderhook Sentinel,* 29 Feb. 1844, 3. On Lebanon Creek, see Horatio Gates Spafford, *A Gazetteer of the State of New York* (Albany, 1824), 101; New York Secretary of State, *Census of the State of New York for 1855* (Albany, 1857), 18–23; John Homer French, *Gazetteer of the State of New York* (Syracuse, 1860), 244; Hamilton Child, *Gazetteer and Business Directory of Columbia County for 1871–72* (Syracuse, 1871), 100–104, 200–212; and *Columbia County at the End of the Century* (Hudson, 1900), 1:538–39.

7 Raphael Samuels, "Workshop of the World," *History Workshop* 3 (1977): 8; Jeremy Atack, "Firm Size and Industrial Structure in the United States during the Nineteenth Century," *Journal of Economic History* 46 (1986): 474. The quotation is, of course, a reference to Adam Smith, *An Inquiry into the Nature and Causes of the Wealth of Nations* (Chicago, 1976), bk. 1, 21.

8 William H. Sewell, "Social Change and the Rise of Working-Class Politics in Nineteenth-Century Marseilles," *Past and Present* 65 (1974): 75–109; Christopher H. Johnson, "Economic Change and Artisan Discontent: The Tailors' History, 1800–1845," in *Revolution and Reaction: 1848 and the Second French Republic,* edited by Roger Price (London, 1977), 87–114; Herbert G. Gutman, *Work, Culture, and Society in Industrializing America: Essays in American Working-Class and Social History* (New York, 1977), 19–32; Wilentz, *Chants,* 107–71. On the "green hands" interpretation of early labor struggles, see John R. Commons et al., *History of Labor in the United States,* 6th ed. (New York, [1918] 1951), vol. 1, esp. 381–423.

9 *Catskill Messenger,* 11 Feb. 1837, 2.

10 *Catskill Recorder,* 25 March 1805, 3. A similar persistence characterized Essex County, Massachusetts. See Daniel Vickers, *Farmers and Fishermen: Two Centuries of Work in Essex County, Massachusetts, 1630–1850* (Chapel Hill, 1994), 315–16.

11 Unlike the regional model of economic development proposed by Diane Lindstrom, Hudson Valley textiles and leather, if not bricks, ended up with customers residing in various parts of the United States (*Economic Development in the Philadelphia Region, 1810–1850* [New York, 1978]). On factory villages, see *Northern Whig,* 8 June 1812; *Catskill Recorder,* 15 Jan. 1823, 2; extract of *Albany Argus* (undated, but undoubtedly 1837), in Zadock Pratt Papers, N-YHS; *Memoirs of Col. Wm. Edwards* (Washington, D.C., 1897), 96; and *Kinderhook Sentinel,* 1 Jan. 1846, 1. See also Raymond Beecher, " 'Also Known as Mill Village' at Leeds," *Greene County Historical Society Journal* 11 (1987): 11–15.

12 Kinderhook Manufacturing Society, Journal 1815, COLCHS; *Documents Relative to Manufactures in the United States (a.k.a. McLane Report)* (Washington, D.C., 1833), 2:30–37, 69–71; Federal Census for 1820; French, *Gazetteer,* 110; Contract between Abraham Vosburg and George Fuller, 10 May 1833, and Contract between Amos Puffer and Storm

Rosa, 27 March 1848, Brick Manufactures Collection, Coxsackie, GrCHS; Charles Lockwood, *Bricks and Brownstones: The New York City Row House, 1783–1929* (New York, 1972), 6–7; Pratt Misc. Mss, N-YHS; *Catskill Messenger,* 13 April 1837, 2, and 7 April 1849, 2; Gordon, *Gazetteer,* 469.

13 *Catskill Recorder,* 27 June 1810, 3; and 6 March 1811, 1. See also Probate Inventory of Henry G. Phillips, Claverack, 1830, Columbia County Surrogates' Court; and Samuel Adams to John A. Thomson, 7 Jan. 1817, Thomson Family Papers, box 1, folder 2, NYSL.

14 Freeman Hunt, *Letters about the Hudson River and Its Vicinity* (New York, 1837), 218. See also *Catskill Messenger,* 27 Feb. 1834, 2; *Catskill Messenger,* 6 March 1834, 2; *Northern Whig,* 15 and 22 June 1819; and Abner Austin to Elisha Williams, 14 Dec. 1830 and 3 Jan. 1831, Letter Copies, Austin Collection, MV 1096, GrCHS.

15 Jeanne Chase, "L'organisation de l'espace économique dans le Nord-Est des Etats-Unis après la Guerre d'Indépendance," *Annales E.S.C.* (1988): 1008, 1014, 1017; *Memoirs of Col. Wm. Edwards,* 76, 81, 117–18; Mortgages H, 1823, 40 and 69, Greene County Court House; Pratt Misc. Mss., N-YHS; Lucius F. Ellsworth, *Craft to National Industry in the Nineteenth Century: A Case Study of the Transformation of the New York State Tanning Industry* (New York, 1975), 65, 103, 128, 145, 242–47.

16 *Documents Relative to Manufactures,* 2:30, 34; New York State Assembly, *Journal,* 36th sess., 1813, 234; Charles M. Haar, "Legislative Regulations of New York Industrial Corporations, 1800–1850," *New York History* 22 (1941): 205; Stott, "Industrial Archeology." On Nathan Wild, see Dun and Company Ledger, vol. 56, Columbia County, April 1843; and Mortgages DD, 1847, Columbia County Court House. On sources of industrial capital in general, see Victor S. Clark, *History of Manufactures in the United States,* vol. 1: *1607–1860* (New York, 1929), 367–68.

17 R. G. Dun and Company Ledgers, vols. 55 and 56, Columbia County, N.Y., and vol. 107, Greene County, N.Y. For the ratio of large- to small-scale operators, see Schedules of Manufactures 1850; *Census for 1855,* 330–44; and *Columbia County at the End of the Century,* 2:23–24. On occupational mobility in a later period, see Clyde Griffen and Sally Griffen, *Natives and Newcomers: The Ordering of Opportunity in Mid-nineteenth-century Poughkeepsie* (Cambridge, Mass., 1978); and Prude, *Coming,* 59–62. My interpretation differs from Harvey A. Wooster, "Manufacturer and Artisan, 1790–1840," *Journal of Political Economy* 34 (1926): 61–77. For vertical integration in the wool industry, see William Dalton, *Travels in the United States of America and Part of Canada [in 1819]* (Appleby, 1821), 106–7; William Thomson, *A Tradesman's Travels in the United States and Canada* (Edinburgh: 1842), excerpted in Roger Haydon, ed., *Upstate Travels: British Views of Nineteenth-Century New York* (Syracuse, 1982), 42–43; Robert R. Livingston, *Essay on Sheep* (New York, 1809), 144; Rolla M. Tryon, *Household Manufactures in the United States, 1640–1860* (Chicago, 1917), 277; and *Northern Whig,* 3 Jan. 1815.

18 John Burroughs, "Phases of Farm Life," in *Signs and Seasons,* vol. 7: *The Writings of John Burroughs* (Boston, 1895), 236; Thomson, *Tradesman,* 45–46; Lucas Moll Account Book 1818–1823, COlCHS. The potters at Nathan Clark's shop in Athens took time off in May 1821 for planting and in August 1821 for harvesting. See Fox-Clark Pottery Manuscripts, Manuscript box 19, GrCHS.

19 Kinderhook Manufacturing Company Journal 1814–1815; Workmen's Ledger 1820–

1827, Austin Collection, MV 1060; Employee time book, unidentified Textile Mill, 1847–1852, Dutchess County Historical Society; New York Tannery, Schedules of Manufactures, no. 1583, Federal Census for 1820, Greene County, N.Y. (microfilm); *Catskill Recorder,* 19 Dec. 1810, 2; *Catskill Recorder,* 8 Aug. 1828, 3.

20 *Documents Relative to Manufactures,* 2:9; Nathan Wild to James Wild, 17 November 1816, Wild Family Files, COLCHS; Abner Austin Diary, 5 Oct. and 17 Nov. 1818, Austin Collection, MV 1084; Abner Austin to Ruth Benjamin, 19 April 1821, Letter Copies, Austin Collection, MV 1095; Thomas Thomson to ?, 22 Oct. 1816, Thomson Family Papers, box 9. See also Entry Nathan Clark, Greene County Schedules of Manufactures, Federal Census for 1820.

21 Stephen B. Miller, *Historical Sketches of Hudson* (Hudson, 1862), 104–5; *Catskill Recorder,* 28 Nov. 1833, 2; Peter Ousterhout to Frederick Kirtland, 11 March 1835, Caroline A. Morss Papers, NYSL. See also Gorham A. Worth, *Recollections of Hudson* in *Random Recollections of Albany from 1800 to 1808,* 2d ed. (Albany, 1850), 3–6; Francis Hopkins to Charles Hopkins, 8 March 1842, and James Hopkins to Charles Hopkins, 18 March 1843, Caleb Hopkins Papers, NYSL; R. G. Dun and Company Ledger, vol. 56: Columbia County, New York, 404–12; and *Census of the State of New York for 1845.*

22 *Catskill Recorder,* 27 June 1810, 3; 5 Aug. 1825, 3; 31 Dec. 1835, 3; 18 Feb. 1836, 3; 3 March 1836, 3.

23 On job ads, see *Hudson Bee,* 1 Aug. 1809, 3; and *Catskill Recorder,* 19 Dec. 1810, 2. For employment figures, see U.S. Census Office, Federal Census for 1820, Columbia and Greene Counties (microfilm); and Population Schedules, Federal Census for 1850, Columbia and Greene Counties. See also descriptions of Kinderhook in Gordon, *Gazetteer,* 409, and of Windham in *Catskill Messenger,* 1 July 1848, 2.

24 Abner Austin to John Jay Lapham, 21 April 1821, Letter Copies, Austin Collection, MV 1095; Alexander Coventry Diary, 11 Feb. 1828 (typescript edited by the Albany Institute of History and Art and NYSL, 1978).

25 James Montgomery, *A Practical Detail of the Cotton Manufacture of the United States of America* (Glasgow, 1840), 41; Prude, *Coming,* 227–37; Clark, *Roots,* 259–61; Allan Kulikoff, *The Agrarian Origins of American Capitalism* (Charlottesville, 1992), 208–9; Dublin, *Women,* 70, 184–85.

26 *Catskill Recorder,* 21 Feb. 1839, 3. Logan's testimony in *People v. Cooper* (1836) is reproduced in John R. Commons et al, eds., *A Documentary History of American Industrial Society* (New York, 1958), 4:286. See also American Manufactory Company Daybook, 29 Aug., 21 Sept., 1 Dec. 1815; Minutes of the Total Abstinence Society of Jewett, 1 Feb. 1834, 20 Feb. 1835, 26 April 1836, NYSL; *Catskill Recorder,* 11 Nov. 1825, 3; New York State Census for 1855, ms., Kinderhook and Stockport; and Population Schedules, Federal Census for 1860, Kinderhook and Stockport.

27 *Documents Relative to Manufactures,* 2:10, 12 (quote), 15; Dublin, *Women,* 24–25, 35–57.

28 Chandler Holbrook to E. Lord, 3 Oct. 1828, Chandler Holbrook Diary and Correspondence, Adriance Memorial Library; Alexander Coventry Diary, 11 Feb. 1828. See also James Stuart, *Three Years in North America* (Edinburgh, 1833), 2:5. Wage data were calculated on the basis of information on twelve factories enumerated in *Documents Relative to Manufactures,* vol. 2; and Schedule of Manufactures, Federal Census for 1850.

29 Kenneth L. Sokoloff and Georgia C. Villaflor, "The Market for Manufacturing

Workers during Early Industrialization: The American Northeast, 1820–1860," in *Strategic Factors in Nineteenth-Century American Economic History,* edited by Claudia Goldin and Hugh Rockoff (Chicago, 1992), 45–47. Calculations were based on seventeen tanneries and eleven brickyards listed in Schedules of Manufactures, Federal Census for 1820, and twenty-five tanneries and twenty-five brickyards listed in Schedules of Manufactures, Federal Census for 1850. I counted boys' wages as one-half a man's wage.

30 The average yearly income of artisans is based on data from forty-eight shops that employed only male workers in Columbia, Dutchess, Greene, and Ulster Counties in 1820. Boys have been assigned one-half of an adult male's wage (Schedules of Manufactures, Federal Census of 1820). See also Stott, *Workers,* 36, 53; and Sokoloff and Villaflor, "Market," 54.

31 Agricultural Schedules, Federal Census for 1850, Greenville, Greene County, New York. In both Durham and Coxsackie, one hundred families fit in the same uncertain category. See Agricultural Schedules, Federal Census for 1850; New York State Census for 1825, Austerlitz, Austerlitz Town Clerk; and Thomson, *Tradesman,* 44.

32 On immigrants, see Stott, *Workers,* 72–73; *Census of the State of New York for 1855.* On contemporary perceptions, see *Hudson Bee,* 30 Nov. 1810, 2–3; Charles H. Cochrane, *The History of the Town of Marlborough, Ulster County, New York* (Poughkeepsie, 1887), 63–64; and Alexander Coventry Diary, 11 Feb. 1828. See also W. E. Lingelbach, "Historical Investigation and Commercial History of the Napoleonic Era," *American Historical Review* 19 (1914): 277–79. The various origins of this labor force distinguished it from New England's rather more uniform but young farmers, fishermen, and factory operatives. See Vickers, *Farmers,* 314–15.

33 Carl Ludwig Fleischmann, *Der Nordamerikanische Landwirth: Ein Handbuch für den Ansiedler in den Vereinigten Staaten* (Frankfurt am Main, 1852), 307. On immigrants, see Stott, *Workers,* 76–80.

34 Anonymous Journal of a Trip to the Catskill Mountains [ca. 1815], GrCHS; Edward S. Abdy, *Journal of a Residence and Tour of North America, from April 1833 to October 1834* (London, 1835), 1:263; *Census of the State of New York for 1855.* Occupations were listed for 262 black men in Population Schedules, Federal Census for 1850, Columbia County. See also *Catskill Recorder,* 5 Aug. 1830, 2; and R. G. Dun and Company, vol. 107, Greene County, 1 April 1851, 1 March 1852, 5 Oct. 1852.

35 Carl Bridenbaugh, *The Colonial Craftsman* (New York, 1950), 127, 147, 153–54; Jackson Turner Main, *The Social Structure of Revolutionary America* (Princeton, 1965), 134–35, 199, 274–75; Stuart M. Blumin, *The Emergence of the Middle Class: Social Experience in the American City, 1760–1900* (New York, 1989), 17–65, 133–37. On itinerants, see *History of Greene County,* 114, 334; Tryon, *Household,* 244; and Moses Mead Account Book, April and Sept. 1823, MV 520, GrCHS.

36 Account Martin Lane, Reynolds Account Book, July 1808, MV 434, GrCHS; *Catskill Messenger,* 1 July 1848, 2; Schedules of Manufactures, Federal Census for 1850, Columbia and Greene Counties.

37 On blacksmiths, see Samuel Fowks Daybook 1826, MV 1144, GrCHS; and Bristol Glass Factory Ledger 1816–1817, Ulster County Genealogical Society. See also Account of Leonard Bronk with Dedymus Shephard, 1823–1824, Bronk Ms. 1823–1824, GrCHS;

Fleischmann, *Erwerbszweige,* 170–71; and D. E. Rugg Daybook 1846, MV 171, Durham Center Museum. On shoemakers, see Lucas Moll Account Book 1818; and Daniel Ives Ledger 1821–1824, Durham Center Museum. See also Workmen's Ledger 1820–1827, fol. 224 (April 1826), Austin Collection, MV 1060; and Schedules of Manufactures, Federal Census for 1850, Hudson, Columbia County. On the evolution of shoemaking, see Paul Faler, *Mechanics,* 8–27; and Mary H. Blewett, *Men, Women,* 3–19, 44–67. On tailors, see Samuel Fowks Daybook, 1 Jan. 1822; and J. D. LaMontanye Account Book 1828–1838.

38 On mill capital, see Gristmills identified on Greene County Property Assessment Roll for 1813, MV 109, GrCHS; Manuscript Schedules of Manufactures, Federal Census for 1850, Columbia and Greene Counties, N.Y. (microfilm); and Rev. Clark Brown Topographical Description 1803, Catskill Unbound Ms, GrCHS. See also Timothy Dwight, *Travels in New England and New York* (New Haven, 1822), 4:7–8; William Youngs Diary, 1811–1814, 26 Oct. 1814 (quote), NYSHA; and William Carter Hughes, *The American Miller and Millwright's Assistant* (Philadelphia, 1851), 83, 85 (conversion of wheat into flour). An article in the *Hudson Bee* (15 May 1810, 2) mentioned a technical improvement without explanation and implied a mill's daily production of 20 to 24 barrels of superfine flour.

39 For a short period before the introduction of gins in the mid–Hudson Valley, mills had families in the neighborhood pick—that is, clean—cotton. See *Hudson Bee,* 21 Nov. 1809, 4, 15 June 1810, 3, and 10 Aug. 1810, 1; and Kinderhook Manufacturing Society Journal 1814–1815. On the ideology of domestic production, see *Hudson Bee,* 10 Jan. 1815, 4; *Northern Whig,* 2 Dec. 1817; and *Catskill Recorder,* 6 Aug. 1823, 28 May 1824 (quote). See also J. § R. Bronson, *The Domestic Manufacturer's Assistant and Family Directory in the Arts of Weaving and Dyeing* (Utica, 1817), 9–10. On weaving women, see Account of Ezeriah Winegar, Daniel Hatch Account Book, Oct. 1822, Feb. and Dec. 1824, June 1828, NYSHA; Elisha Blackburn Account Book, 12 Nov. 1829, MV 525, GrCHS; Martin Van Gerritsen Day Book, April 1827, GrCHS; especially Account Catherine Van Ness 1832, Ledger D, fols. 68, 69, and 182, Van Ness–Philip Papers, N-YHS; Robert R. Livingston, *Essay,* 140–44, 151–52; and, on the tradition of weaving women, Laurel Thatcher Ulrich, "Wheels, Looms, and the Gender Division of Labor in in Eighteenth-Century New England," *William and Mary Quarterly,* 3d ser., 55 (1998): 1–38.

40 Abner Austin to Henry P. Franklin, 15 Sept. 1809, Letter Copies, Austin Collection, MV 1095; *Hudson Bee,* 7 Feb. 1815; *Kinderhook Sentinel,* 21 Dec. 1837, 3. See also Alfred Hand to John A. Thomson, 1 July 1835, Thomson Family Papers, box 1, folder 3. On looms, see Horatio Gates Spafford, *Gazetteer of the State of New York* (Albany, 1813), 149, 153, 156, 163, 195; and probate inventories at Columbia County Court House. On production, see Elizabeth Hitz, *A Technical and Business Revolution: American Woolens to 1832* (New York, 1986), 160–62; Clark, *History of Manufactures,* 1:246–47, 368; Arthur H. Cole, *The American Wool Manufacture* (Cambridge, 1926), 1:110–12, 134; and Chester Whitney Wright, *Wool-Growing and the Tariff* (Boston, 1910), 57–60.

41 Spafford, *Gazetteer* (1813), 198. On weavers' shops, see *Northern Whig,* 29 March 1810 and 27 Aug. 1816; *Hudson Bee,* 27 Aug. 1816, 3; *Hudson Bee,* 9 May 1820, 3. On Matteawan, see Spafford, *Gazetteer* (1824), 311; and *Niles' Weekly Register,*

29 March 1828, 76. For parallel developments in New England, see Clark, *Roots,* 177–79. It is impossible to do justice to the literature on rural industries and proto-industrialization in Europe, but for good starting points, see Franklin F. Mendels, "Proto-industrialization: The First Phase of the Industrializing Process," *Journal of Economic History* 32 (1972): 241–61; and Gay Gullickson, "Agriculture and Cottage Industry: Redefining the Causes of Proto-industrialization," *Journal of Economic History* 43 (1983): 831–50.

42 Kinderhook Manufacturing Society Journal, 1814–1816; Ronald Vern Jackson and Gary Ronald Teeples, *New York 1820 Census Index* (Bountiful, 1977); Federal Census for 1820, Population Schedules (microfilm). For the production of full-time weavers, I chose the months of October to April for reasons of compatibility because Nelson and Nichols began to deliver in October 1815. But note that these are winter months.

43 For instances of negligent weaving by farmers, see Kinderhook Manufacturing Society Journal, 1 and 7 Feb., 24 and 29 April 1815. At the level of twenty-six dollars over two years, farmers' income from weaving was slightly lower than the receipts of a typical straw-hat-braiding family in Fitzwilliam, New Hampshire, in the 1820s. See Thomas Dublin, "Women and Outwork in a Nineteenth-Century New England Town: Fitzwilliam, New Hampshire, 1830–1850," in *The Countryside in the Age of Capitalist Transformation,* edited by Steven Hahn and Jonathan Prude (Chapel Hill, 1985), 51–69; and his "Rural Putting-out Work in Early Nineteenth-Century New England: Women and the Transition to Capitalism in the Countryside," *New England Quarterly* 64 (1991): 531–73, esp. 552. Rhode Island weavers involved in putting-out systems during the 1820s delivered roughly two hundred yards per year, probably just about as many as the nine outweavers of the American Manufactory Company in Amenia, Dutchess County, would have if they had worked steadily in 1815 (this is impossible to verify due to lack of continuous data). See American Manufactory Company Daybook, 1815, Amenia, Dutchess County, NYSHA; and Gail Fowler Mohanty, "Putting up with Putting-out: Power-Loom Diffusion and Outwork for Rhode Island Mills, 1821–1829," *Journal of the Early Republic* 9 (1989): 191–216.

44 On quality, see "Duties on Imports: Testimony in Relation to Wool [in 1828]," U.S. Congress, American State Papers, *Finance* (Washington, D.C., 1859), 5:818, 824; Mohanty, "Putting up," 203, 207; and Sterling Goodenow, *A Brief Topographical and Statistical Manual of the State of New York,* 2d ed. (New York, 1822), 14. On prices, see *Documents Relative to Manufactures,* 2:41, 44, 46; *Census of the State of New York for 1855,* lv; and Fleischmann, *Erwerbszweige,* 36–37.

45 Tryon, *Household,* 11, 184, 268, 306–7; *Documents Relative to Manufactures,* 2:61; Schedules of Manufactures, Federal Census for 1820.

46 *Documents Relative to Manufactures,* 2:61, 44; Ann-Janette Dubois Diary, 13 Jan. 1838, 23 Feb. 1838, 2 Oct. 1834, GrCHS; Ephraim P. Best Account Book, 17 Sept. and 21 Oct. 1845, ColCHS; Hannah Bushnell Diary, 1 and 26 Nov. 1853, 24 June 1854, MV 366, GrCHS. See also Wilbur Fisk Strong Diary, 4 Nov. 1858, MV 231, GrCHS. One shilling was worth 12.5 cents; 8 pence were worth just about 8.0 cents.

47 At the beginning of the nineteenth century, Hudson mechanics seemed to have organized separate Fourth of July parades occasionally (Miller, *Sketches,* 46). For sporadic evidence on artisans' associations, see *Hudson Balance,* 6 May 1806, 144; *Catskill Re-*

corder, 19 Dec. 1810, 2; *Catskill Recorder*, 26 Jan. 1827, 4; *Catskill Recorder*, 20 Nov. 1834, 3; *Catskill Recorder*, 18 Dec. 1834, 2; *Catskill Recorder*, 15 Feb. 1838, 1; *Catskill Recorder*, 30 Jan. 1840, 2; and *History of Greene County*, 138.

48 On New England, see Prude, *Coming*, 116–32; Dublin, *Women*, 75–79; and Spafford, *Gazetteer* (1824), 311. See also Edwin Williams, *The New York Annual Register . . . for 1830* (New York, n.d.), 156–57; Edwin Williams, *The New York Annual Register . . . for 1831* (New York, n.d.), 108–9; Blumin, *Emergence*, 199; and Abner Austin to Messrs. Dwight, 28 June 1826, Letter Copies, Austin Collection, MV 1095, GICHS.

49 Workmen's Ledger 1816, Austin Collection, MV 1052 (for Shortman, fol. 53 [8 Oct. 1816]); Kinderhook Manufacturing Society Journal 1814–1816, COLCHS. See also American Manufactory Company Ledger 1815–1817, NYSHA; and Employee Time Book of Unidentified Textile Mill, fol. 2, Dutchess County Historical Society. Low remuneration made women desirable workers in general. See George S. Mackenzie, *A Treatise on the Diseases and Management of Sheep* (New York, 1810), 241–42; and Population Schedules, Federal Census for 1860, Kinderhook and Stockport. Although 164 operatives had no immediately recognizable relatives in the factories, a substantial minority boarded with other workers.

50 *Memoirs of Col. William Edwards*, 88–89; Thomson, *Tradesman*, 43–44; Kinderhook Manufacturing Company Journal, 1 April 1816; *Documents Relative to Manufactures*, 2: 66, 31 (see also 33, 35).

51 Workmen's Ledger, fol. 96 (30 April 1823), fol. 139 (10 May 1824) (see also fols. 106, 232, and 241 [31 July 1821 and 1 April 1828]), Austin Collection, MV 1060; Bristol Glass Factory Ledger, 14 Nov. 1816. On apprentices, see *Catskill Recorder* 26 Sept. 1810, 2; *Hudson Balance-Advertiser*, 19 Jan. 1808; and John Olmsted to Mary Olmsted, 30 Aug. 1828, in Elizabeth Olmsted, ed., "Selections from the Correspondence and Diaries of John Olmsted, 1826–1838," 9–10 (transcript located at the Buffalo and Erie County Historical Society, 1968). On brickmakers, see *Zachariah Sickles v. Eli Botsford*, Court of Common Pleas 1827, and *Root v. Ambrose Gaw*, Court of Common Pleas, 1848, GICHS.

52 *Catskill Recorder*, 19 Aug. 1825, 3; *Catskill Recorder*, 3 March 1836, 3; "People v. Cooper," in Commons, *Documentary History*, 279–312, 281–82 (quote); *Catskill Recorder*, 21 Feb. 1839, 3.

53 *People v. Cooper*, 279; *Catskill Recorder*, 2 Jan. 1834, 2; *Catskill Recorder*, 7 Feb. 1839, 3. The argument, of course, was a staple. See Commons et al., *History of Labour*, 1:404–12.

54 *Catskill Recorder*, 7 Feb. 1839, 3; *Catskill Recorder*, 21 Feb. 1839, 3; *Catskill Messenger*, 4 April 1839, 4; *People v. Cooper*, 308–9, 277, 285. Family connections and responsibilities diminished a worker's propensity to strike in France between 1871 and 1890. See Michelle Perrot, *Les ouvriers en grève: France, 1871–1890* (Paris, 1974), 2:504–7. In Amoskeag after World War I, however, strikes did break up family connections. See Tamara K. Hareven, *Family Time and Industrial Time: The Relationship between the Family and Work in a New England Industrial Community* (New York, 1982), 114, 152.

55 *Catskill Messenger*, 6 Feb. 1834, 2; *Catskill Recorder*, 21 Feb. 1839, 3; *Catskill Recorder*, 10 Dec. 1835, 2. For examples of recent historiography, see Wilentz, *Chants*, 61–103; and Robert J. Steinfeld, "The Philadelphia Cordwainers' Case of 1806: The Struggle over Alternative Legal Constructions of a Free Market in Labor," in *Labor Law in America*, edited by Christopher L. Tomlins and Andrew J. King (Baltimore, 1992), 20–

43. For a judicious critique, see Richard Stott, "Artisans and Capitalist Development," *Journal of the Early Republic* 16 (1996): 257–71.

56 Stephen Hedges, of Hillsdale (Population Schedules, Federal Census of 1850 [microfilm]) was the only one of Columbia County's 274 shoemakers listed with a double occupation. See K. K. Mallaby to Thomas Mallaby, 28 Sept. 1843, Rev. Thomas Mallaby Correspondence, Pers. box 19, Rare Books and Manuscripts, NYPL. Commons et al., *History of Labour*, 1:404–11, esp. 411, describes the three New York State cases in which artisans had to stand trial between 1833 and 1837. See Bristol Glass Factory Ledger, 3 and 11 Nov. 1816; and Alexander Coventry Diary, 11 Feb. 1828 (typescript edited by the Albany Institute of Art and the NYSL, 1978). In New York City, Blue Mondays seemed to have occurred rarely. See Stott, *Workers*, 131, 247.

57 *Catskill Messenger*, 30 Aug. 1832, 2; see also 18 Oct. 1832, 3.

SIX *"Things, Not Thought"*: *Wealth, Income, and Patterns of Consumption, 1800–1850s*

1 *Catskill Recorder*, 28 March 1828, 3. For relative prices, see U. S. Bureau of the Census, *Historical Statistics: Colonial Times to 1957* (Washington, D.C., 1960), ser. E1–12, E68.

2 Richard L. Bushman, *The Refinement of America: Persons, Houses, Cities* (New York, 1992), 402, xv, 231–37, 423–31; Gordon S. Wood, *The Radicalism of the American Revolution* (New York, 1992), 347–54. See also Adam Smith's well-known statement on luxuries, decencies, and necessities in *An Inquiry into the Nature and Causes of the Wealth of Nations*, edited by Edwin Cannan (Chicago, 1976), 2:399–400.

3 Stuart M. Blumin, *The Emergence of the Middle Class: Social Experience in the American City, 1760–1900* (New York, 1989), 109–21, 146–63; David Jaffee, "One of the Primitive Sort: Portrait Makers of the Rural North, 1760–1860," in *The Countryside in the Age of Capitalist Transformation*, edited by Steven Hahn and Jonathan Prude (Chapel Hill, 1985), 104; Sally McMurry, *Families and Farm Houses in Nineteenth-Century America: Vernacular Design and Social Change* (New York, 1988), 141–48.

4 For a good introduction to research on consumption that is attentive to its indigenous construction and objective limitations, see Claude Grignon and Jean-Claude Passeron, *Le savant et le populaire* (Paris, 1989), 115–51.

5 John Burroughs, "Phases of Farm Life," in *Signs and Seasons*, vol. 7 of *The Writings of John Burroughs* (Boston, 1895), 231; Daniel Bell, *The Cultural Contradictions of Capitalism* (New York, 1976), 22.

6 The ratio of property owners (beyond $250) to renters declined from 2.4 to 0.9 in Columbia County and from 2.8 to 1.4 in Greene County between 1801 and 1821. See *Census of the State of New York for 1855* (Albany, 1857), ix. This approach to patterns of consumption owes a great deal to the concept of structuration that Blumin culled from Anthony Giddens, *The Class Structure of the Advanced Societies* (New York, 1975). See Stuart M. Blumin, "The Hypothesis of Middle-Class Formation in Nineteenth-Century America: A Critique and Some Proposals," *American Historical Review* 90 (1985): 299–338.

7 Harvey A. Wooster, "A Forgotten Factor in American Industrial History," *American Economic Review* 16 (1926): 14–18; Christopher Clark, *The Roots of Rural Capitalism: Western Massachusetts, 1780–1860* (Ithaca, 1990), 156–91; Gregory Nobles, "The Rise of

Merchants in Rural Market Towns: A Case Study of Eighteenth-Century Northampton, Massachusetts," *Journal of Social History* 24 (1990): 5–23.

8 Reuben Swift Receipt Book, 1802–1809, Rare Book and Manuscript Division, NYPL; *Catskill Recorder,* 23 May 1810, 3; *Catskill Recorder,* 8 June 1843, 2; *Longworth's American Almanach, New-York Register and City Register* (New York, 1802); *Longworth's American Almanac* (New York, 1809); Thomas Thomson to Alexander Thomson, 4 Nov. 1815, Thomson Family Papers, box 1, folder 2, NYSL; Elizabeth W. Olmsted, ed., "Selections from the Correspondence and Diaries of John Olmsted, 1826–1838," 1 (typescript located at the Buffalo and Erie County Historical Society, 1968); *Kinderhook Sentinel,* 5 Dec. 1844, 2; William Hoffman Diary, 22 June, 7 July, 26 and 30 Aug., 23 Sept. 1850, N-YHS.

9 William Dalton, *Travels in the United States of America and Part of Upper Canada* (Appleby, 1821), 100; John and Tobias Teller Account Books 1797 and 1815, NYSHA; Warren H. Wilson, *Quaker Hill: A Sociological Study* (New York, 1907), 72–74; Carl Ludwig Fleischmann, *Erwerbszweige, Fabrikwesen und Handel der Vereinigten Staaten von Nordamerika* (Stuttgart, 1852), 540–41.

10 R. G. Dun and Co. Ledgers, vols. 55, 56, and 107, Baker Library, Harvard University; Stuart M. Blumin, *The Urban Threshold: Growth and Change in a Nineteenth-Century American Community* (Chicago, 1976), 59–62; Thomas F. Gordon, *Gazetteer of the State of New York* (Philadelphia, 1836), 409.

11 George Crawford Inventory 1815–1826, NYSHA; Probate Inventory of Simon Sayre (Cairo), 1829, Greene County Surrogates' Court.

12 Dun and Co. Ledger, vol. 107, Jan. 1843, Aug. 1841, May 1844 (quotes), and vols. 55 and 56; Solomon Crandall to his parents, 8 March 1829, Crandall Papers, COLCHS.

13 *Catskill Recorder,* 27 Dec. 1815, 2; *Catskill Democrat,* 7 May 1845, 2.

14 Dun and Co. Ledgers, vols. 55, 56, and 107. Numbers are based on George Crawford's inventories from 1815 to 1830 and were confirmed by Lewis A. Atherton, *The Southern Country Store, 1800–1860* (Baton Rouge, 1949), 207–12. According to Fred Mitchell Jones, *Middlemen in the Domestic Trade of the United States* (Urbana, 1937), 71, the average capital per retail store in the state of New York was $3,452 in 1839.

15 Blumin, *Emergence,* 113–16. Gross profits were calculated for 259 shops with $500 or less of capital and twelve shops with $1,500 of capital (Manuscript Manufacturing Schedules, Federal Census for 1850, Columbia and Greene Counties, New York).

16 Manuscript Population Schedules, Federal Census for 1850, Columbia and Greene Counties; Dun and Co. Ledger, vol. 107, 5 April 1850, Aug. 1848, April 1848.

17 See chapter 4.

18 *Catskill Recorder,* 19 June 1811, 3; *Catskill Recorder,* 6 Dec. 1809, 3; Greene County Tax Assessment for 1813, MV 109, GrCHS; R. G. Dun and Company Ledger, vol. 107, Greene County, New York, Oct. 1844 and March 1847.

19 Poor of Coxsackie and Athens, Bronk Ms. 1814–1815, GrCHS; Town of Austerlitz Minutes, April 1818–April 1828, COLCHS; Harriet Olmsted to John Olmsted, 5 Oct. 1834, in Olmsted, "Selections," 93; *Catskill Recorder,* 14 Oct. 1825, 2 (quote); *Catskill Recorder,* 13 Oct. 1826, 2; Town of Austerlitz Minutes, 3 April 1832 and 2 April 1833; New York State Census for 1825, Town of Austerlitz, Austerlitz Town Clerk.

20 *Hudson Bee,* 25 Feb. 1817, 3; *Catskill Messenger,* 11 Feb. 1837, 2. On the growth of poor

relief, especially outdoor aid (as opposed to almshouses), in New York State from 1823 through 1859, see Joan Underhill Hannon, "Poverty in the Antebellum Northeast: The View from New York State's Poor Relief Rolls," *Journal of Economic History* 44 (1984): 1007–32, esp. 1025.

21 Thomas Cole to Francis Alexander, 23 Sept. 1834, in Louis LeGrand Noble, *The Life and Works of Thomas Cole,* edited by Elliott Vesell (Cambridge, Mass., [1853] 1964), 137.

22 Manuscript Population Schedules, Federal Census for 1850. Information on housing was collected from Gordon, *Gazetteer;* and J. Disturnell, *A Gazetteer of the State of New York* (Albany, 1842). On surfaces, see Mary Olmsted to John Olmsted, 3 Oct. 1826, in Olmsted, "Selections," 4; *Catskill Recorder,* 15 April 1818, 2; and *Transactions of the New York State Agricultural Society* 7 (1847): 216–17.

23 *Narrative of Sojourner Truth,* edited by Margaret Washington (New York, 1993), 4, 10, 13; Census of the State of New York for 1855, ms. (microfilm); "Reminiscences of Matilda Metcalf," in Edward R. Collier, *A History of Kinderhook* (New York, 1914), 497.

24 Andrew Jackson Downing, *The Architecture of Country Houses* (New York, [1850] 1968), 40, 143, 73–92; *Census of the State of New York for 1855* (Albany, 1857), 231–32, 234. I have excluded the city of Hudson from the computation; houses there were assessed at $1,201 on average. See James Stuart, *Three Years in North America* (Edinburgh, 1833), 1:260; and John Fowler, *Journal of a Tour in the State of New York in 1830* (London, 1830), 181–82. Both Bushman, *Refinement,* and Wood, *Radicalism,* apply this type of trickle-down model to the diffusion of refinement and gentility and so replicate the value judgments of members of the era's upper class, who elevated their own tastes to the legitimate measure of decorum and etiquette.

25 Alexander Coventry Diary, 7 and 10 Aug. 1822; Rev. Thomas Mallaby to Rev. A. S. Murray, 27 Oct. 1843, Rev. Thomas Mallaby Papers, Rare Book and Manuscript Division, NYPL. On changes in construction after fires in Hudson, see *Hudson Balance,* 28 March 1801, 1; *Hudson Balance,* 1 March 1803, 68; and *Census of the State of New York for 1855.* Overrepresentation of nonmanual occupations in ownership is based on a sample of 176 brick buildings (again exclusive of the city of Hudson) in Census of the State of New York for 1855, ms. (microfilm).

26 Thorstein Veblen, *The Theory of the Leisure Class* (New York, [1899] 1994), 115–66; *Albany Argus,* 19 Jan. 1833, 2; Stuart, *Three Years,* 1:260; Fowler, *Journal,* 181–82; George Holcomb Diary, 29 March 1832, NYSL; John Bower Diary, 1844–45, Adriance Memorial Library; Ann-Janette Dubois Diary, 8 June 1836, GrCHS; Hannah Bushnell Diary, 17 May 1854, MV 366, GrCHS; Caroline A. Morss to Frederick Kirtland, 26 April 1830, Caroline A. Morss Papers, NYSL.

27 Horatio Gates Spafford, *Gazetteer of the State of New York* (Albany, 1813), 163–64; Sarah Mynderse Campbell Diary, 22 and 26 April 1825 (see also 8 May 1824, 4 May 1826, 5 May 1827, and 16 and 18 April 1829), N-YHS; *Rural Repository* 10 (24 May 1834): 205–6. For an insightful brief on gardening and its multiple significances in people's lives, see Karl Polanyi, *The Great Transformation: The Political and Economic Origins of Our Time* (Boston, [1944] 1957), 270–71.

28 Henry B. Fearon, *Sketches of America* (London, 1819), 75–85; Thomas Thomson to Alexander Thomson, 4 Nov. 1815, Thomson Family Papers, box 1, folder 2; Richard

Weston, *A Visit to the United States and Canada in 1833* (Edinburgh, 1836), 137–38; William Thomson, *A Tradesman's Travels in the United States and Canada* (Edinburgh, 1842), excerpted in Roger Haydon, ed., *Upstate Travels: British View of Nineteenth-Century New York* (Syracuse, 1982), 46; William Hoffman Diary, 21 March 1848.

29 Smith, *Inquiry*, 2:399. On cooking stoves, see *Catskill Messenger*, 15 Oct. 1835, 3; *Catskill Messenger*, 22 Oct. 1835, 3; Ann-Janette Dubois Diary, 21 Nov. 1840; and *Coxsackie Standard*, 10 May 1838, 2. See also *Catskill Democrat*, 7 May 1845, 2; *Rural Repository*, 12 June 1824, 7; and *Rural Repository*, 9 June 1827, 7. On portraits, see Jaffee, "One of the Primitive Sort," 103–38; and Noble, *Life and Works*, 196.

30 All probate inventories at Greene County Surrogates' Court, 1841–1850. See Ann-Janette Dubois Diary, 13 May 1839, 29 April and 14 May 1840.

31 All probate inventories at Greene County Surrogates' Court, 1821–1830.

32 Abraham J. Hasbrouck Journal 1797–1799, N-YHS; Asa H. Beach Farm Account Book 1848, NYSHA.

33 Harriet Van Orden Account Book 1834, NYSL. Van Orden's total household expenditures amounted to $266.31 in 1834, of which $156.73 (58.9 percent) went for foodstuffs. Van Orden, who came from a prominent Albany family, had married Catskill merchant Jacob Van Orden in 1815 (Genealogical Files, GRCHS) and upon his death received $25 monthly from Abraham Van Vechten to foot her bills. She finished the year with a $21.31 deficit. See Ephraim Best Account Book, 6 Dec. 1845; *Transactions* 14 (1854): 120; *Niles' Weekly Register* 29 March 1834, 76; Lucinda Davenport to John Olmsted, 30 Dec. 1834, in Olmsted, "Selections," 39; and Vincent Morgan Townsend Diary, 12 Jan. 1834, Cornell University Archives. See also Frederike Bremer, *Die Heimath in der neuen Welt* (Stuttgart, 1854), 1:39–40; and Ann-Janette Dubois Diary, 9 and 11 Dec. 1835.

34 Fleischmann, *Erwerbszweige*, 259; "Narrative of Marks Barker," Aug. 1828 (typescript at COLCHS); William Youngs Diary, 27 Oct. 1811; Vincent Morgan Townsend Diary, 15 Jan. 1834; Ann-Janette Dubois Diary, 25 Dec. 1839, 1 Jan. 1840; Sarah Mynderse Campbell Diary, 24 Feb. 1827, 24 Feb. 1827 (and see 16 Jan. and 16 March 1827 and 23 Feb. 1829); Stuart, *Three Years*, 1:279; Patrick Shirreff, *A Tour through North America* (Edinburgh, 1835), 455; Bristol Glass Factory Ledger, Nov. 1816–Jan. 1817, Ulster County Genealogical Society; *Transactions* 9 (1849): 60–61.

35 Noble, *Life and Work*, 42; Washington, *Narrative*, 9–10; John Burroughs, *My Boyhood* (Garden City, 1924), 55; Harriet Van Orden Account Book 1834. On Europe, see Massimo Montanari, *La faim et l'abondance: Histoire de l'alimentation en Europe* (Paris, 1995), 205–30.

36 Horatio Gates Spafford, *Gazetteer* (1813), 37 (his emphasis); Robert Sutcliff, *Travels in Some Parts of North America in the Years 1804, 1805, and 1806* (York, 1811), 127; Martha Hoag to James Van der Poel, 17 April 1814, 5 Oct. 1815, Misc. Mss Hoag, N-YHS; *Catskill Recorder*, 3 July 1811, 2.

37 Probate inventories located at the Columbia County Surrogates' Court. Information is from sixteen probates codified between 1789 and 1799 and fifty-six between 1820 and 1823.

38 *Incidents in the Life of George Haydock, Ex-Professional Woodsawyer, of Hudson* (Hudson, 1846), 11; Abner Austin to William Tipple, 1 May 1834 (see also Abner Austin to Gard-

ner Burbank, 28 May 1827 and 4 Oct. 1827), Letter Copies, Austin Collection, MV 1096; C. W. Mayhew to John Olmsted, 1 Jan. 1833, in Olmsted, "Selections," 42–43; William Hoffman Diary, 16, 19, 23 Aug. 1847 (accounts are on pp. 337–41).

39 Miller and Ebo in Ephraim Best Account Book, 1845–46; Vincent Morgan Townsend Diary, 28 Dec. 1833; William Hoffman Diary, 7 and 9 March 1847; Hannah Bushnell Diary, 24 June 1854 (see also 14 Aug. 1856). Ten shillings equaled $1.25, and 13 shillings equaled $1.63.

40 *Rural Repository,* 21 Dec. 1830, 119; *Rural Repository,* 28 April 1849, 122; Downing, *Architecture,* 97; *North American Review,* October 1849, 334.

41 Catskill Mountain Manuscript, ca. 1815, GrCHS; Ann-Janette Dubois Diary, 4 May 1837, 26–27 April 1838, 20–22 May 1839, 19 April, 4 and 15 May 1840, 6 May 1841, 2 and 4 May 1842, 27 April 1843, 2–4 May 1844, 24–26 April 1845; Sarah Mynderse Campbell Diary, 11 Nov. 1824, 18 and 27 May 1825, 9 June 1826, 23 Oct. 1827; Hannah Bushnell Diary, 19 Sept. and 22 Oct. 1855, 2 Jan. and 17 Sept. 1856; Harriet Van Orden Account Book, 1 Dec. 1834; Fanny Trollope, *Domestic Manners of the Americans* (London, [1832] 1997), 286; Jacques-Gérard Milbert, *Itinéraire pittoresque du fleuve Hudson* (Paris, 1828–29), 1:59–60; George Wilson Pierson, *Tocqueville and Beaumont in America* (New York, 1938), 117. On the social experience in cities, see Blumin, *Emergence,* esp. 138–91, 298–305.

42 Abraham J. Hasbrouck Journal 1798. For 1855, calculations are based on the number of retail stores and groceries in Columbia and Greene Counties and on cash flow of $4,000 per store, adjusted slightly upward from figures found in the R. G. Dun & Co. ledgers (*Census for the State of New York for 1855,* 479); Bushman, *Refinement,* 273; and Wilbur Fisk Strong Diary, 4 Nov. 1858, MV 231, GrCHS.

SEVEN *The Culture of Public Life*

1 *Catskill Recorder,* 14 March 1821, 3; *Catskill Recorder,* 2 Aug. 1832, 2 (I have been unsuccessful in identifying the wedding parties); Julia Hull Winner, "A Skimeton," *New York Folklore Quarterly* 20 (1964): 134–36; Hans Kurath, *A Word Geography of the Eastern United States* (Ann Arbor, 1949), 79, fig. 184. On the industrial nature of Madison, see *Catskill Recorder,* 28 Oct. 1825, 3; and Raymond Beecher, " 'Also Known as Mill Village' at Leeds," *Greene County Historical Society Journal* 11 (1987): 11–15.

2 See Edward P. Thompson, "Rough Music," in *Customs in Common: Studies in Traditional Popular Culture* (New York, 1993), 467–533; and Natalie Zemon Davis, *Society and Culture in Early Modern France* (Stanford, 1975), 97–123. For a review, see Bryan D. Palmer, "Discordant Music," *Labour - Le Travail* 3 (1978): 5–62. A hiatus of more than one century separates sporadic mentions of similar practices in colonial New York from those documented in the Hudson Valley. See Alice Earle Morse, *Colonial Days in Old New York* (New York, 1896), 62–63.

3 *Catskill Recorder,* 14 March 1821, 3; 28 Oct. 1825, 3. On issues of public behavior, see Daniel Walker Howe, "The Evangelical Movement and Political Culture in the North during the Second Party System," *Journal of American History* 77 (1991): 1216–39. On the private character of middle-class marriages, see the short mentions in Edward S. Abdy, *Journal of a Residence and Tour of North America from April 1833 to October 1834*

(London, 1835), 1:253; and Isaac Fidler, *Observations on Professions, Literature, Manners, and Emigration in the United States and Canada* (New York, 1833), 26–27.

4 This choice lies closer to an encompassing, quite Durkheimian understanding of institutions that both reflect and express social taxonomies with their enabling (as well as sanctioning) force than to the traditional institutional history of churches, parties, trade unions, and so on. See Emile Durkheim, *Les règles de la méthode sociologique* (Paris, [1895] 1993), esp. xi–xxiv, 3–14. On the difficulty of understanding an individual's spiritual experience, we are well advised to remember Tocqueville, who reckoned, "I do not know whether Americans have faith in their religion, for who can read hearts?" See Alexis de Tocqueville, *De la démocratie en Amérique* (Paris, [1835] 1981), 1:399.

5 Julian A. Pitt-Rivers, "Honour and Social Status," in *Honour and Shame: The Values of Mediterranean Society,* edited by J. G. Peristiani (London, 1965), 21–31; *The Fate of Shechem or the Politics of Sex* (Cambridge, 1977), 1–17. Tocqueville's approach to honor in its various guises is very helpful, although it misses the persistence of its archaic forms in the early republic and among the great landowners. See Tocqueville, *De la démocratie en Amérique,* 2:285–98.

6 *Truesdell v. Hill,* Court of Common Pleas 1829, GrCHS. All data come from these files. On the varying case load of the Court of Common Pleas, see *Catskill Recorder,* 9 Feb. 1827, 2; *Catskill Recorder,* 3 June 1830, 2; and *Catskill Messenger,* 31 May 1832, 2. In general, see *History of Greene County, New York* (New York, 1884), 32–33.

7 *Northern Whig,* 26 July 1811; *Catskill Recorder,* 6 Sept. 1809, 3; *Catskill Recorder,* 11 Oct. 1809, 2.

8 The last examples of reporting on "affairs of honor" appear in *Catskill Recorder,* 25 May 1814, 3; 29 June 1814, 3. See also *Ann Owen and Edward Austin v. Elam Garret,* Court of Common Pleas 1810; *John Vosburgh v. Leonard C. Conine and Moika, his wife,* Court of Common Pleas 1815; and Raymond Beecher, *Out of Greenville and Beyond: Historical Sketches of Greene County* (Cornwallville, 1977), 27–33. On gossip, see Karen W. Hansen, "The Power of Talk in Antebellum New England," *Agricultural History* 67 (1993): 43–64.

9 Booth is quoted in Stuart M. Blumin, *The Urban Threshold: Growth and Change in a Nineteenth-Century American Community* (Chicago, 1976), 118.

10 For examples of dishonorable behavior and the shame associated with it among the Livingstons, see Clare McCurdy, "Domestic Politics and Inheritance Patterns: The Family Papers of William Livingston," in *The Livingston Legacy: Three Centuries of American History,* edited by Richard D. Wiles (Annandale-on-Hudson, 1987), 162–86; and *Kinderhook Sentinel,* 25 June 1846, 2.

11 *Hudson Bee,* 1 Oct. 1816, 3.

12 *Northern Whig,* 12 April 1811; Durham Female Cent Society Minutes, 6 Aug. 1812, NYSL; *Hudson Bee,* 19 March 1816, 3; *Northern Whig,* 19 March 1816, 25 Feb. and 22 July 1817, 23 June 1818.

13 Durham Female Cent Society Minutes, 7 Jan. 1817, 3 Jan., 3 April and 9 July 1820; *Hudson Bee,* 19 March 1816, 3; Town of Durham, Greene County Assessment List for 1813, MV 109, GrCHS.

14 *Catskill Recorder,* 26 July 1815, 2; *Catskill Recorder,* 27 Sept. 1815, 1; *Catskill Recorder,*

11 Oct. 1815, 1; *Northern Whig,* 21 Jan. 1815, 22 Oct. 1816. See also *History of Greene County,* 62; and Greene County Assessment Roll for 1813. For similar social patterns, see Clifford S. Griffin, *Their Brothers' Keepers: Moral Stewardship in the United States, 1800–1860* (New Brunswick, 1960); and Christopher Clark, *The Roots of Rural Capitalism: Western Massachusetts, 1780–1860* (Ithaca, 1990), 116–17, 209–14.

15 *Catskill Recorder,* 3 June 1825, 2; *Catskill Recorder,* 12 Jan. 1827, 3; *Greene County Republican,* 16 April 1828, 3; *Catskill Messenger,* 25 Aug. 1836, 2; *Catskill Messenger,* 2 June 1831, 3; *Catskill Messenger,* 10 Jan. 1833, 3; *Catskill Messenger,* 20 June 1833, 2; *Rural Repository,* 3 Jan. 1835, 127.

16 James F. W. Johnston, *Notes on North America: Agricultural, Economical, and Social* (Boston, 1851), 2:270; *Incidents in the Life of George Haydock, Ex-Professional Woodsawyer, of Hudson* (Hudson, 1846), 18–20; Basil Hall, *Travels in North America in the Years 1827 and 1828* (Philadelphia, 1829), 1:55; Alexander Coventry Diary, 10 Aug. 1822 (typescript edited by the Albany Institute of History and Art and the NYSL, 1978); Tavern Day Book, Columbia Turnpike, Chatham, 1816–1818, Eastfield Village Collection; *Henry Jones v. Matthew Bogardus,* Greene County Court of Common Pleas 1826.

17 *Catskill Messenger,* 28 March 1833, 2–3; *Greene County Republican,* 14 May 1828, 3; Temperance Society of Lexington, Minutes, 21 Jan. and 1 Feb. 1834 and 20 Feb. 1835; Total Abstinence Society of Jewett Minutes 1822–1825, NYSL; Catskill Mechanical Society, 15 Feb. 1838, GrCHS.

18 On women, see Temperance Society of Lexington Minutes, 30 Sept. 1829, in Total Abstinence Society of Jewett Minutes; and Report of the Temperance Society of School District No. 1 and 2 in the town of Coxsackie, Bronk Mss 1833, GrCHS. The society was founded in 1827. See *Greene County Republican,* 21 Nov. 1827, 3. For Columbia County, see John F. Collins, *History of Hillsdale, New York* (Philmont, 1885), 9. For an account of national temperance, see Ian R. Tyrrell, *Sobering up: From Temperance to Prohibition in Antebellum America, 1800–1860* (Westport, 1979).

19 Gayhead (Greenville) Temperance Society Minutes, MV 1224, GrCHS, 1843, 25 June 1844, 4 Oct. and 1st Nov. 1845 (see also 3 Feb. 1844 and 29 Nov. 1845); John Bower Diary, 21 Jan. and 17 Nov. 1844; *Catskill Recorder,* 29 July 1841, 2; *Catskill Recorder,* 5 Aug. 1841, 2. On Hudson, see *Incidents in the Life of George Haydock,* 23.

20 Gayhead (Greenville) Temperance Society Minutes, 6 Sept. and 29 Nov. 1845, 3 Feb. and 25 Dec. 1844, 23 Jan. 1845.

21 Gayhead (Greenville) Temperance Society, 29 Nov. 1845, 12 Oct. 1841; exclusions: Aug. and Sept. 1843, Sept. and Nov. 1845; William Smith Journal, 11 and 16 Aug. 1843, N-YHS. The absence of efficient sanctions motivated the historiographical critique of interpretations of reform movements as engines of discipline in the hands of the middle and upper classes. See Lois W. Banner, "Religious Benevolence as Social Control: A Critique of an Interpretation," *Journal of American History* 60 (1973): 23–41. For a local study of great subtlety, see James L. McElroy, "Social Control and Romantic Reform in Antebellum America: The Case of Rochester, New York," *New York History* 58 (1977): 17–46.

22 *Kinderhook Sentinel,* 13 July 1843, 2. See also Ann-Janette Dubois Diary, 5 July 1844, GrCHS.

23 Evidence for revivals was gleaned from David Porter, *A Sermon Delivered November 1st,*

1815, at Chatham (New Concord), N.Y. (Catskill, 1816), 18; Dutch Reformed Church 1821, Bronk Mss. 1821, GTCHS; David Harrower, *A Farewell Sermon Delivered to the Church and Congregation at Lexington, New York, 1826* (Utica, n.d.), 22–23 (quote); Caroline A. Morss to Frederick Kirtland, 5 July 1831 and 17 July 1832, Caroline A. Morss Papers, NYSL; Edward A. Collier, *The Hallowed House: A Historical Discourse on the Reformed Dutch Protestant Church* (Albany, 1866), 13; *History of Greene County,* 131, 279, 327; and *Catskill Recorder,* 11 Feb. 1841, 2.

24 Lucinda Davenport to John Olmsted, 30 Dec. 1834, in Olmsted, "Selections," 100. In Columbia County, 37.5 percent of the adult population were church members in 1855; in Greene, the proportion was 36.2 percent (*Census of the State of New York for 1855* [Albany, 1857], 477). On the rise in church attendance during the antebellum era, see Jon Butler, *Awash in a Sea of Faith: Christianizing the American People* (Cambridge, Mass., 1990), 283–84. On the clergy, see L. King to Thomas Mallaby, 20 Jan. 1843, Rev. Thomas Mallaby Papers, Pers. Misc. Papers, box 19, Rare Book and Manuscript Division, NYPL; Gayhead (Greenville) Temperance Society, 29 June 1844; *Memoirs of Col. William Edwards. . . . , Written by Himself, in His 76th Year, 1847* (Washington, D.C., 1897), 94; and Lucretia Warner Hall Diary, 12 Dec. 1841 ("Spent much of the day reading Washington Ervin.") (see also entries for 18 Jan. 1838, 16 March 1841, 17 June 1844, and 30 Aug. 1845). The proportion of women in churches is based on the membership lists of the Congregational Church in Austerlitz, 1825, Town Hall of Austerlitz; and the First Presbyterian Church of Kinderhook in 1839, Kinderhook box, COLCHS.

25 Valatie Presbyterian Church Records, Kinderhook Box, COLCHS, 6, 9, and 23 Feb. 1839, 3 and 8 April 1840, 14 June and 4 Sept. 1841, 16 May and 15 Aug. 1842, 23 Jan. 1844. See also First Presbyterian Church of Kinderhook in 1839. Curtis D. Johnson, in *Islands of Holiness: Rural Religion in Upstate New York, 1790–1860* (Ithaca, 1989), 24–27, 55–56, 89–93, 173–75, 189–91, delineates the process of enforcing church discipline in Cortland County, New York. Next to the Protestant majority, Catholics remained a distinct minority in Columbia and Greene Counties; they appear only exceptionally in people's diaries. The first Catholic church in Coxsackie opened in 1845 (*History of Greene County,* 250). Catholics made up 5.4 percent of the population in Columbia County and 1.2 percent in Greene in 1855 (*Census of the State of New York for 1855,* 471–72).

26 William Youngs Diary, 22 June, 31 Dec. 1811, 7 March 1812, 10 Feb. 1814; Daniel Merwin Account Book, 1828, Pratt Museum, Prattsville; Ann-Janette Dubois Diary, 2 and 16 Aug., 24 Dec. 1835, 7 Feb. 1836; Lucretia Warner Hall Diary, 29 April 1839; William Smith Journal, 24 April, 5 and 11 May, 4 and 15 June, 27 Aug. 1843; Gordon, *Gazetteer,* 470; John Bower Diary, 4 and 25 Jan., 16 June 1844, 16 Feb. 1845; Benjamin F. Gue Journal, 25 July, 8 and 22 Aug. 1847, NYSL; Hannah Bushnell Diary, 8 June 1856 (see also 1 and 22 June 1856), MV 366, GTCHS; Thomas Mallaby to Robert Shaw, Rev. Thomas Mallaby Papers, 12 March 1844; the two churches still existed in 1855. The level of church attendance in mid–Hudson Valley villages varied with the number of churches in a town because people could walk or ride from, say, one-church Stuyvesant, where 25 percent of the adult population attended, to six-church Kinderhook, where supposedly 90 percent of the adult population went to services (*Census of the State of New York for 1855,* 445–76).

27 Lucinda Davenport to John Olmsted, 8 June 1834, in Olmsted, "Selections," 100, 83; Thomas Mallaby to Robert Shaw, Rev. Thomas Mallaby Papers, 13 March 1844; William Hoffman Diary, 12 and 13 March 1848; Ann-Janette Dubois Diary, 22 Jan. 1835; John Burroughs' recollections, as told to Clara Barrus, in *John Burroughs: Boy and Man* (Garden City, 1920), 78–79.

28 Abner Austin to his brother, 16 July 1823, Letter Copies, MV 1095; Abner Austin to his brother, 15 Jan. 1832, Letter Copies, MV 1096.

29 Erastus Pratt to Joel Pratt, 20 Aug. 1820, Pratt Family Papers, Cornell University Archives; *Catskill Recorder*, 23 and 30 Nov. 1827, 4 Jan. 1828, 3 (quote); Janet A. Lathrop, *The Township of Stockport* (n.p., 1919), 12.

30 *The Autobiography of Martin Van Buren*, edited by John C. Fitzpatrick, vol. 2 of *Annual Report of the American Historical Association* (Washington, D.C., 1918), 7, 67, 105. See the classic narrative by Dixon Ryan Fox, *The Decline of Aristocracy in the Politics of New York* (New York, 1919). For a succinct account of suffrage extension, see Lee Benson, *The Concept of Jacksonian Democracy: New York as a Test Case* (Princeton, 1961), 7–10.

31 *Catskill Recorder*, 27 April 1812, 2; *Catskill Recorder*, 12 April 1815, 2–3; J. A. Van Valkenburgh to Jesse Merwin, 25 Oct. 1824, Merwin Folder, COLCHS; *Greene County Republican*, 21 May 1828, 2.

32 Results of elections to the state assembly 1820 and 1822. Germantown, Columbia County, was the only exception to the regularity between participation and results in elections: 80 percent of eligible citizens overwhelmingly, almost unanimously, supported Federalists and opponents of Van Buren's Bucktails. See *Catskill Recorder*, 23 Aug. 1838, 2; 22 Oct. 1840, 2; 16 Sept. 1841, 2. For other sources, see table 23.

33 Lee Benson (*Concept*, 10–11) is in good company when formulating the hypothesis of a certain regression in New York politics with the rise of professional parties. See Max Weber, *Wirtschaft und Gesellschaft: Grundriss der verstehenden Soziologie* (Tübingen, 1972), 845–48; *Catskill Recorder*, 17 Nov. 1826, 3 (quote); *Catskill Recorder*, 19 Oct., 2 and 9 Nov. 1827, 26 April 1832, 3; *Catskill Recorder*, 13 Sept. 1832, 3; *Catskill Recorder*, 25 Oct. 1832, 2; *Greene County Republican*, 31 Oct. 1831; *Catskill Messenger*, 18 Oct. 1832, 3; *Catskill Messenger*, 22 Nov. 1832, 2.

34 *Catskill Recorder*, 29 Oct. 1824, 2; *Catskill Recorder*, 3 Nov. 1826, 3; *Greene County Republican*, 24 Oct. 1827, 2; *Greene County Republican*, 19 Nov. 1827, 2; *Coxsackie Standard*, 12 Oct. 1837, 2.

35 Simeon DeWitt Bloodgood, *An Englishman's Sketch-Book; or, Letters from New York* (New York, 1828), 119; *Hudson Bee*, 31 March 1807, 3; Julian Ursyn Niemczewicz, *Under Their Vine and Fig Tree: Travels through America in 1797–1799, 1805* (Elizabeth, N.J., 1965), 185; George Wilson Pierson, *Tocqueville and Beaumont in America* (New York, 1938), 118 (Livingston), 127–28 (Tocqueville). Van Rensselaer is quoted in William B. Fink, "Stephen Van Rensselaer: The Last Patroon," Ph.D. diss., Columbia University, 1950, 128. See also Ira Harris to Henry Greene, 19 Oct. 1859, Coxsackie File, GRCHS.

36 For riotous scenes at the polls, see *Catskill Recorder*, 14 April 1831, 2; *Catskill Messenger*, 22 Nov. 1832, 2; Cooper Sayre to Frederick Kirtland, 13 Oct. 1836, Caroline A. Morss Papers; Gayhead (Greenville) Temperance Society Minutes, 11 Dec. 1844; Ann-Janette Dubois Diary, 8 Nov. 1837 (see also 4 and 10 March 1841 on President

William H. Harrison); William Smith Diary, 29 March 1843; and William Hoffman Diary, 29 March 1848.

37 This paragraph owes much to Glenn C. Altschuler and Stuart M. Blumin, "Limits of Political Engagement in Antebellum America: A New Look at the Golden Age of Participatory Democracy," *Journal of American History* 84 (1997): 855–85. See also Washington Irving to William Irving, 27 Oct. 1804, in *Washington Irving: Letters,* vol. 1: *1802–1823,* edited by Ralph M. Aderman, Herbert L. Kleinfield, and Jenifer S. Banks (Boston, 1978), 106; Thomas Cole Diary, 6 Nov. 1834 (Catskill), in Thomas Cole, *The Collected Essays and Prose Sketches,* edited by Marshall Tymn (St. Paul, 1980); and *Rural Repository,* 9 June 1827, 7. In general, see Michael Wallace, "Changing Concepts of Party in the United States: New York, 1815–1828," *American Historical Review* 74 (1968): 453–91.

38 Jesse Buel, *The Farmer's Instructor* (New York, 1840), 1:145; Jacob C. Van Dyck to ?, 8 Jan. 1850, Coxsackie Mss., Education, GTCHS.

39 *Kinderhook Sentinel,* 13 July 1843, 2; *Kinderhook Sentinel,* 16 July 1846, 2; William Hoffman Diary, 7 July 1847. See also Sarah Mynderse Campbell Diary, 5 July 1827, N-YHS; and William Smith Journal, 5 July 1843.

40 "Petition of Petrus Pulver & Others Demanding an Investigation into the Livingstons' Title" [1795], in *The Documentary History of the State of New York,* edited by E. B. O'Callaghan, 4 vols. (Albany, 1850), 3:499–502. Tenant quote: Petition of a few Damn'd Rascals of the Manor of Livingston to the Legislature of New York [1811], item 14, box 2, Livingston Family Papers, Rare Book and Manuscript Library, Columbia University. Court decision: *Jackson v. Schultz,* 18 Johns. 179 (1816); *Livingston v. Stickles,* 8 Paige Ch. 403–4 (1840).

41 For tenant resistance, see *Northern Whig,* 23 Aug. 1811; George Baker Anderson, *Landmarks of Rensselaer County, New York* (Syracuse, 1897), 93–94; *Kinderhook Sentinel,* 26 Dec. 1844, 2; and *Albany Argus,* 13 Jan. 1845, 2. John Burroughs mentioned women in the antirent crowds. See Barrus, *John Burroughs,* 128–29. See also Henry Christman, *Tin Horns and Calico: A Decisive Episode in the Emergence of Democracy* (New York, 1945), 102–4. On antirenters in politics, see David Maldwyn Ellis, *Landlords and Farmers in the Hudson-Mohawk Region, 1790–1850* (Ithaca, 1946), 268–313.

42 Franklin B. Hough, ed., *Constitution of the State of New York Adopted in 1846* (Albany, 1867), Art. 1, sec. 12.

43 See Benson, *Concept,* 191–207, esp. 192. For the distinction between formal and evangelical denominations, see Johnson, *Islands,* 67–76. On the methodological improvement brought about by, and the goals and limits of, the "new political history," see Ronald P. Formisano, "The Invention of the Ethnocultural Interpretation," *American Historical Review* 99 (1994): 453–77; *Catskill Recorder,* 11 Feb. 1841, 2; and *Census of the State of New York for 1855,* 28–29, 34–35, 445–77. Quakers from adjacent towns may have come to New Baltimore, of course; the county's other meetinghouse in Athens enjoyed a customary attendance of 25 to New Baltimore's 210 worshippers out of a total of 750 (or roughly 40 percent) of the town's churchgoing adults ("Census of the State of New York for 1855," 454).

44 On the evidence of electoral committees, see *Catskill Packet,* 22 April 1794, 3; *Cats-*

kill Packet, 29 April 1794, 3; *Western Constellation* (Catskill), March 30 and April 6, 1801; *Hudson Balance,* May 28, 1807; *Northern Whig,* 27 April 1812; *Catskill Recorder,* March 25, 1805, 2; *Catskill Recorder,* 27 April 1812 and 12 April 1815. See also Loonenburgh Federalist Meeting, 5 April 1800, Bronk Ms. 1800, GrCHS; Spafford, *Gazetteer* (1824), 197; and *Catskill Messenger,* 1 Dec. 1836, 2. On African Americans, see Alexander W. Mechan to Leonard Bronk, 10 Dec. 1801, Bronk Ms. 1801; Account Jacob Teal, Ledger 1815–36, Van Ness–Philip Papers, N-YHS; Account Francis Peters, black man, John and Tobias Teller Account Book 1812–1835, fols. 7–8, NYSHA; Peter Van Schaack to Frederick De Peyster, 30 Nov. 1819, De Peyster Papers, vol. 12, N-YHS; Sarah Mynderse Campbell Diary, 24 Aug. 1828; Ann-Janette Dubois Diary, 27 Jan. 1839; Valatie Presbyterian Church Records, 4 Feb. 1840; and Account Robert, colored man, John and Tobias Teller Account Book 1834–1857, fol. 36, NYSHA. Is it worth noting that no named black person with fully developed individual traits appears in Washington Irving's "Rip Van Winkle" and "The Legend of Sleepy Hollow"? Let me reassure the reader that one can appreciate Irving's irony and use of language, that is, his mastery of the art of writing fiction, and be deeply moved by his portrayal of the fate of Native Americans without surreptitiously importing his categories into the historical analysis (Ephraim P. Best Farm Account Book, 15 Oct. and 14 Dec. 1858). Max Weber, in *Wirtschaft und Gesellschaft,* 237, indicated the ideological nature of ethnic consciousness that manipulates other common, but not necessarily shared, characteristics like language, religion, and origin to construct an identity that remains inescapably rooted in historical development.

45 Abner Austin to William Emory, 28 Feb. 1833, Letter Copies, Austin Collection, MV 1096. Austin, however, adhered to the federal Republican adversaries of the Van Buren Bucktails in 1819. See *Catskill Recorder,* April 14, 1819, 2; Spafford, *Gazetteer* (1824), 311; and Edwin Williams, *The New York Annual Register . . . for 1830* (New York, n.d.), 156–57.

46 Stephen B. Miller, *Historical Sketches of Hudson* (Hudson, 1862), 66; *Catskill Recorder,* 25 Oct. 1832, 2. Williams had fervently opposed the extension of the suffrage franchise in 1821. Tocqueville in *De la démocratie en Amérique,* 2:292, spotted the importance of immaculate private behavior for successful political careers.

47 Thomas Cole to C. L. Ver Bryck, 21 Feb. 1843, in Noble, *Life,* 255.

48 *Catskill Recorder,* 4 Nov. 1818, 2; Female Benevolent Association of Leeds, 1853, MV 1211, GrCHS.

49 Valatie Presbyterian Church Records, 12 Aug. 1844.

Conclusion: *Labor, the Manor, and the Market*

1 Alexander Coventry Diary, June 1785 (typescript edited by the Albany Institute of History and Art and NYSL); William Hoffman Diary, 29 June 1850, N-YHS; John Homer French, *Gazetteer of the State of New York* (Syracuse, 1860), 241, 246, 329–30.

2 Jack P. Greene, *Imperatives, Behaviors, and Identities: Essays in Early American Cultural History* (Charlottesville, 1992), 174–75.

3 Ledger 1815–1836, Van Ness–Philip Papers, N-YHS. See also Abner Austin Diary, 23 April 1816, Austin Collection, MV 1084, GrCHS; Abijah Stone to John Thomson,

21 Aug. 1817, Thomson Family Papers, box 1, folder 1, NYSL; and *Catskill Recorder,* 16 Sept. 1818, 2.

4 For an analysis of commodity flows and their determinants, see David R. Meyer, "Midwestern Industrialization and the American Manufacturing Belt in the Nineteenth Century," *Journal of Economic History* 49 (1989): 921–37.

5 Alexander Coventry Diary, 11 Feb. 1828; Thomas F. Gordon, *Gazetteer of the State of New York* (Philadelphia, 1836), 411; *Catskill Messenger,* 1 Sept. 1849, 2.

6 Peter Ousterhout to Frederick Kirtland, 12 Aug. 1834 (see also 11 March 1835), Caroline A. Morss Papers, NYSL; Peter L. Livingston, quoted in *Niles' Weekly Register,* 15 March 1845, 32; Theodore A. Cole Diary, 25 June 1857, GTCHS. On the growing importance of legal tender issued or discounted in New York City, see *Catskill Messenger,* 27 Feb. 1834, 2; 6 March 1834, 2; 10 Sept. 1835, 2.

7 *Hudson Gazette,* 15 March 1792, 2; *Catskill Packet,* 15 Aug. 1792, 3; Peter Van Schaack to Frederick De Peyster, 5 Feb. 1821, De Peyster Papers, vol. 12, item 84, N-YHS. Alexis de Tocqueville emphasized the centrality of work in the creation of identity in the northern United States. See his *De la démocratie en Amérique* (Paris, [1840] 1981), 2:291–93.

8 William Hoffman Diary, 5 and 12 March 1848. Stuart Blumin found a close correlation between industrious virtue and economic success among businessmen in Kingston. See his *The Urban Threshold: Growth and Change in a Nineteenth-Century American Community* (Chicago, 1976), 205–11. On occupation and upward mobility, see Steven Herscovici, "Migration and Economic Mobility: Wealth Accumulation and Occupational Change among Antebellum Migrants and Persisters," *Journal of Economic History* 58 (1998): 927–56, esp. 937–40.

9 *Niles' National Register,* 11 Jan. 1845, 292. On Lafayette, see *New York Spectator,* 20 Sept. 1824, 2–3; and Auguste Levasseur, *Lafayette en Amérique en 1824 et 1825* (Paris, 1829), 1:229–30. On "feudal incidences," see *Hudson Bee,* 16 Aug. 1811, 2; *Catskill Democrat,* 18 Dec. 1844, 2; Clare Barrus, *John Burroughs: Boy and Man* (Garden City, 1920), 128–29; and William Strickland, *Journal of a Tour in the United States of America, 1794-1795* (New York, 1971), 115. For "pleasant revenue," see François A. F. de la Rochefoucauld-Liancourt, *Voyage dans les Etats-Unis d'Amérique fait en 1795, 1796 et 1797* (Paris, 1799), 2:325.

10 *Hudson Bee,* 16 Aug. 1811, 2; *Catskill Democrat,* 25 Jan. 1845, 2; Petition of a few Damn'd Rascals of the Manor of Livingston to the Legislature of New York [1811], item 14, box 2, Livingston Family Papers, Rare Books and Manuscript Library, Columbia University.

11 Mary Livingston Memorandum, 20 March 1812 (Judge Van Ness), Feb. 1813, and March 1816 (Chancellor Kent), COLCHS; *Northern Whig,* 12 Oct. 1813; Daniel Dewey Barnard, "The 'Anti-Rent' Movement and Outbreak in New York," *American Review* 2 (Dec. 1845): 13 (my reference is to a special printing located in the Rare Book and Manuscript Library, Columbia University); *The Diary of Philip Hone, 1828-1851,* edited by Bayard Tuckerman (New York, 1889), 1:392.

12 *Catskill Democrat,* 25 Jan. 1845, 2; *New York State Assembly Journal,* 17 Feb. 1812, quoted in A. G. Johnson, *A Chapter of History; or, The Progress of Judicial Usurpation* (Troy, 1863), 4; "Report of the Select Committee on So Much of the Governor's Message as Relates

to the Difficulties Existing between the Proprietors of Certain Leasehold Estates and Their Tenants," in New York State, *Documents of the Assembly,* 69th sess., 1846 (Albany, 1846), 8; *Mr. John Van Buren's Argument in the Livingston Manor Case* (Hudson, 1850), 7.

13 Karl Polanyi, *The Great Transformation: The Political and Economic Origins of Our Times* (Boston, [1944] 1957), 77–85; *Catskill Democrat,* 25 Jan. 1845, 2. Wealth figures are from Manuscript Population Schedules for Columbia and Rensselaer Counties, New York, Federal Census for 1850 (microfilm); and *History of Columbia County, New York* (Philadelphia, 1878), 54–55. See also *Kinderhook Sentinel,* 27 Jan. 1848, 2.

14 *Catskill Messenger,* 22 Dec. 1836, 2.

Bibliography

Primary Sources

UNPUBLISHED

Adriance Memorial Library, Poughkeepsie
    Henry Booth Account Book, 1806–1825
    John Bower Diary, 1844–1845
    Chandler Holbrook Diary, 1827–1838
    James Reynolds Diary, 1839–1854
Austerlitz Town Clerk
    New York State Census for 1825, Austerlitz
Baker Library, Harvard University
    David Collin Ledger, 1770–1813
    R. G. Dun and Co. Credit Ledgers, vols. 55, 56, and 107
Bard College Library
    Highland Turnpike Correspondence, Eckert Collection
    Wilson Papers, Eckert Collection
Chatham Public Library
    John Beebe Jr. Diary, 1779–1785
Columbia County Court House, Hudson
    Deeds A (1787–1789), M (1827–1828)
    Mortgages A (1786–1788), B (1800–1801), GI and G2 (1823–1824), DD (1847–1848)
    Probate Inventories, 1787–1823
    Wills, 1787–1830
Columbia County Historical Society, Kinderhook (cited as COLCHS)
    Account Book Collection
    William Chase Papers, 1792–1832
    Columbia Turnpike Papers
    Crandell Family Papers
    Joseph P. Ford Papers

Genealogical Files
Mary Livingston Memorandum, 1811–1820
Narrative of Marks Barker [ca. 1828]
Town Files and Boxes
Van Valkenburg Family Papers
Columbia University Library, Rare Books and Manuscripts
Livingston Papers
Cornell University Archives
Elias W. Cady Papers
Pratt Family Papers
Vincent Morgan Townsend Diary, 1833–1834
Durham Center Museum
Account Book Collection
Dutchess County Historical Society, Poughkeepsie
Employee Time Book, Unidentified Textile Mill, 1847–1852
Farm and Saw Mill Account Book, 1821–1828
Carpenters' Account for Housebuilding, 1840, Huntting Papers DC 0109
Eastfield Village, Inc., Collection, East Nassau
Smith Reed Ledger, 1827–1829
Refine Landing Tavern Day Book, Columbia Turnpike, 1816–1818
Greene County Court House, Catskill
Mortgage Books A (1800–1802), H (1823–1824), and V (1847–1848)
Probate Inventories, 1800–1850
Greene County Historical Society, Coxsackie (cited as GrCHS)
Account Book Collection
Anon., Journal of a Journey to the Catskill Mountains [ca. 1815], Catskill Mountains
vertical folder
Austin Collection MV 1158–1189
Bronck Manuscripts, folders 1–39, 1770–1840
Hannah Bushnell Diary, 1854–1856, MV 366
Theodore A. Cole Diary, 1856–1857, MV 1207
Court of Common Pleas Collection, 1800–1850
Ann-Janette Dubois Diary, 1834–1847
Female Benevolent Association Minutes, Leeds, 1853, MV 1211
Fox-Clark Pottery Manuscripts, manuscript box 19
Gayhead (Greenville) Abstinence Society Minutes, 1841–1852, MV 1224
Sherman Collection
Thomson Family Papers
Wilbur Fisk Strong Diary, 1857–1859, MV 231
Town Boxes and Files
New-York Historical Society (cited as N-YHS)
Sarah Mynderse Campbell Diary, 1823–1829
Diary of unidentified Scotsman visiting the eastern United States, 1824
Abraham J. Hasbrouck Journals, 1798, 1801, and 1824
Eunice Hill Papers

William Hoffman Diary, 1847–1850
Great Imbaught Farm Account Book, 1815–1816
Misc. Mss., Hoag
Hudson River Sloop *Jane* Account Book, 1795–1801
Robert R. Livingston Papers, microfilm reels 6–8, 19–20, 52–54
James Masten Account Book, 1781–1828
Van Ness Philip Papers
Zadock Pratt Papers
William Smith Diary, 1842–1851
Benjamin Snyder Day and Sloop Book, 1774–1777
Francis Sylvester Letters
Unidentified Store Account Book, Claverack, 1801–1805
James Vanderpoel Letters, 1808–1826
Henry Van Schaack Correspondence
Lucretia Warner Hall Diary, 1832–1846
New York Public Library, Rare Books and Manuscripts (cited as NYPL)
   Jehoiakim Bergh Ledger, 1801–1818, and Daybook, 1810–1833
   Rev. Thomas Mallaby Correspondence, pers. misc. box 19
   Sloop *Victory* Account Book, 1841–1860
   Reuben Swift Receipt Book, 1802–1813
New York State Archives, Albany (cited as NYS Arc)
   Abstract of State Taxes, 1799–1800
   Garrett Lansing Papers (Tax Assessments)
New York State Historical Association, Cooperstown (cited as NYSHA)
   Account Book Collection
   Bunker Family Papers
   William Coventry Diary, 1786–1817
   George Crawford Papers
   William Youngs Diary, 1811–1814
New York State Library, Albany (cited as NYSL)
   Titus Bedell Papers
   Catskill Residents Account Book, 1813–1814
   Zephaniah Chase Account Book, 1784–1805
   Alexander Coventry Diary, 1785–1831, edited as a typescript by the New York State
      Library in collaboration with the Albany Institute of History and Art
   Durham Female Cent Society Minutes
   Greene County Papers, 1792–1831
   William and Benjamin Guildersleve Account Book, 1830
   George Holcomb Diary, 1806–1840
   Caleb Hopkins Papers
   Oliver H. Jones Correspondence, 1832–1833
   Livingston Manor Residents, Petition, 1786
   Caroline Amelia Morss Letters, 1829–1841
   Thomson Family Papers
   Total Abstinence Society, Jewett, Minutes

Vanderpool Family Papers
Pratt Museum, Prattsville
   Account Book Collection
Ulster County Community College, Stone Ridge
   J. D. LaMontanye Account Book, 1828–1841
Ulster County Genealogical Society, Hurley
   Bristol Glass Factory Ledger, 1816–1817
United States Census Office
   Federal Census of Columbia and Greene Counties, 1800, 1810, 1820, 1830, 1840, 1850
   (microfilm)

NEWSPAPERS AND MAGAZINES

Columbia County

Hudson Balance and Columbia Repository, 1804
Hudson Bee, 1805–1818
Hudson Gazette, 1792–1793, 1801–1803
Hudson Wasp, 1802–1803
Hudson Weekly Gazette, 1786–1790
Hudson Whig, 1809–1820
Kinderhook Sentinel, 1836–1851
Northern Whig, 1809–1820
Rural Repository, 1824–1851

Greene County

Catskill American Eagle, 1808–1811
Catskill Democrat, 1843–1848
Catskill Messenger, 1831–1849
Catskill Packet, 1792–1796
Catskill Packet and Western Mail, 1796–1797
Catskill Recorder, 1804–1845
Coxsackie Standard, 1837–1838
Greene County Republican, 1826–1828
The Packet, 1799
Western Constellation, 1800–1801

New York State

Albany Argus, 1833, 1845
Albany Evening Journal, 1845
Memoirs of the New York State Board of Agriculture, vols. 1–3, Albany, 1821–1826
New York Annual Register, edited by Edwin Williams, 10 vols., New York, 1830–1845
New-York Price Current, 1797–1800
New York Shipping and Commercial List, 1843 and 1847
New York Spectator, 1824
New York Weekly Tribune, 1845

Transactions of the New York State Agricultural Society, vols. 1–20, Albany, 1842–1861
Transactions of the Society for the Promotion of Useful Arts, vols. 1–4, Albany, 1801–1819

OTHER

Niles' Monthly Register, 1814
Niles' Weekly Register, 1828, 1834, 1845
North American Review, 1849

GOVERNMENT PUBLICATIONS

Constitution of the State of New York Adopted in 1846, edited by Franklin B. Hough. Albany, 1867.

Documents Relative to Manufactures in the United States (a.k.a. *McLane Report on Manufactures*). 22d Cong., 1st sess. 1833. H. Exec. Doc. 308.

"Duties on Imports: Testimony in Relation to Wool [1828]." In U.S. Congress, *American State Papers: Finance*. Vol. 5. Washington, D.C., 1859.

Journal of the New York State Assembly. 45th sess., Albany, 1822, appendix; 49th sess., Albany, 1826, appendix.

New York State Secretary. *Census of the State of New York for 1835*. Albany, 1836.

New York State Secretary. *Census of the State of New York for 1845*. Albany, 1846.

New York State Secretary. *Census of the State of New York for 1855*. Albany, 1857.

State of New York. *Messages from the Governors*. Vol. 4: *1843–1856*. Edited by Charles Z. Lincoln. Albany, 1904.

United States Bureau of Census. *Historical Statistics: Colonial Times to 1957*. Washington, D.C., 1960.

United States Census Office. *Aggregate Value and Produce and Number of Persons Employed in Mines, Agriculture, Commerce, Manufacture . . . 6th Census 1840*. Washington, D.C., 1840.

United States Census Office. *Fourth Census, 1820* (Washington, D.C., 1821).

United States Census Office. *Fifth Census, 1830* (Washington, D.C., 1832).

United States Census Office. *Sixth Census, 1840* (Washington, D.C., 1841).

BOOKS AND ARTICLES

Abdy, Edward S. *Journal of a Residence and Tour of North America from April 1833 to October 1834*. 3 vols. London, 1835.

Allardice, Robert Barkley. *Agricultural Tour in the United States and Upper Canada*. London, 1842.

American Husbandry. 2 vols.. London, 1775.

The America of 1750: Peter Kalm's Travels in North America, edited by Benson, Adolph B. 2 vols. New York, 1937.

Anjou, Gustave, comp. *Ulster County, New York: Probate Records*. 2 vols. New York, 1906.

The Autobiography of Martin Van Buren, edited by John E. Fitzpatrick. Vol. 2 of *Annual Report of the American Historical Association*. Washington, D.C., 1918.

Barber, John W., and Henry Howe. *Historical Collections of the State of New York*. New York, 1841.

Barnard, Daniel Dewey. "The 'Anti-Rent' Movement and Outbreak in New York." *American Review* 2 (December 1845): 577–98.

Barnard, Hannah. *Dialogues on Domestic and Rural Economy and the Fashionable Follies of the World.* Hudson, 1820.

Bloodgood, Simeon DeWitt. *An Englishman's Sketch-Book; or, Letters from New York.* New York, 1828.

Bordley, J. B. *Essays and Notes on Husbandry and Rural Affairs.* 2d ed. Philadelphia, 1801.

Bremer, Friederike. *Die Heimath in der neuen Welt.* Stuttgart, 1854.

Bronson, J. and R. *The Domestic Manufacturer's Assistant and Family Directory in the Arts of Weaving and Dyeing.* Utica, 1817.

Buel, Jesse. *Jesse Buel, Agricultural Reformer: Selections from His Writings,* edited by Harry J. Carman. New York, 1947.

———. *The Farmer's Instructor.* Vol. 2. New York, 1840.

Burroughs, John. *My Boyhood,* Garden City, 1924.

———. "Phases of Farm Life." In *Signs and Seasons.* Vol. 7 of *The Writings of John Burroughs.* Boston, 1895. 219–45.

Castiglioni, Luigi. *Travels in the United States of North America, 1785–1787.* Translated and edited by Antonio Pace. Syracuse, 1983.

Chastellux, François Jean. *Travels in North America in the Years 1780, 1781, and 1782.* Translated by Howard C. Ries Jr. Chapel Hill, 1963.

Child, Hamilton. *Gazetteer and Business Directory of Columbia County for 1871–72.* Syracuse, 1871.

Cobbett, William. *A Year's Residence in the United States of America.* Carbondale, Ill. [1819] 1964.

Cole, Thomas. *The Collected Essays and Prose Sketches.* Edited by Marshall Tymn. St. Paul, 1980.

———. "Lecture on American Scenery Delivered before the Catskill Lyceum, April 1st, 1841." *Northern Light* 1 (May 1841): 25–26.

Coppinger, Joseph. *The American Practical Brewer and Tanner.* New York, 1815.

The Correspondance of Thomas Cole and David Wadworth. Edited by Bard McNulty. Hartford, 1983.

Coxe, Tench. *A Statement of the Arts and Manufactures of the United States of America for the Year 1810.* Philadelphia, 1814.

———. *A View of the United States of America.* London, 1795.

Crèvecoeur, J. Hector St. John de. *Letters from an American Farmer.* New York, 1982.

Dalton, William. *Travels in the United States of America and Part of Upper Canada.* Appleby, Engl. 1821.

Darby, William. *A Tour from the City of New York to Detroit.* Chicago, [1819] 1962.

DeWitt, Benjamin. "A Sketch of the Turnpike Roads in the State of New York." *Transactions of the Society for the Promotion of Useful Arts* 2 (1807): 190–204.

The Diary of Philip Hone, 1828–1851. Edited by Bayard Tuckerman. Vol. 1. New York, 1889.

Disturnell, J. *A Gazetteer of the State of New York.* Albany, 1842.

A Documentary History of American Industrial Society. Edited by John R. Commons et al. Vol. 4. New York, 1958.

Downing, Andrew Jackson. *The Architecture of Country Houses.* New York, [1850] 1968.

Dwight, Timothy. *Travels in New England and New-York.* 4 vols. New Haven, 1821–22.

Edmonds, John E. *Reports of Select Cases Decided in the Courts of New York.* New York, 1868.

Emmons, Ebenezer. *Agriculture of New York.* Vol. 1. Albany, 1846.

"Entries in the Account Book of Teunis Van Vechten, 1753–1782." Copied by Marquis E. Shattuck. *Detroit Genealogical Research* 16 (1953): 49–54.

Fearon, Henry B. *Sketches of America.* London, 1819.

Fiat Justitia. *Anti-rent Controversy.* Albany, 1865.

Fidler, Isaac. *Observations on Professions, Literature, Manners, and Emigration in the United States and Canada.* New York, 1833.

Fleischmann, Carl Ludwig. *Agricultural Development in the Old and the New World: The Progress of European and Retrograding Condition of American Agriculture, the Causes and Remedies.* N.p., 1859.

———. *Der nordamerikanische Landwirth: Ein Handbuch für Ansiedler in den Vereinigten Staaten.* Frankfurt am Main, 1852.

———. *Erwerbszweige, Fabrikwesen, und Handel der Vereinigten Staaten von Nordamerika.* Stuttgart, 1852.

Fowler, John. *Journal of a Tour in the State of New York in 1830.* London, 1831.

French, John Homer. *Gazetteer of the State of New York.* Syracuse, 1860.

Gaylord, Willis, and Luther Tucker. *American Husbandry.* Vol. 2. New York, 1844.

[Goodenow, Sterling.] *A Brief Topographical and Statistical Manual of the State of New-York.* Albany, 1811.

Goodenow, Sterling. *A Brief Topographical and Statistical Manual of the State of New-York.* 2d ed. New York, 1822.

Gordon, Thomas F. *Gazetteer of the State of New York.* Philadelphia, 1836.

Grant, Anna. *Memoirs of an American Lady, with Sketches of Manners and Scenery in America as They Existed Previous to the Revolution.* 2 vols. London, 1808.

Grund, Francis J. *Handbuch und Wegweiser für den Auswanderer nach den Vereinigten Staaten von Nordamerika.* Stuttgart, 1843.

Hall, Basil. *Travels in North America in the Years 1827 and 1828.* 2 vols. Philadelphia, 1829.

Hall, Francis. *Travels in Canada and the United States in 1816 and 1817.* London, 1818.

Hamilton, Thomas. *Men and Manners in America.* 2 vols. Philadelphia, 1833.

Harrower, David. *A Farewell Sermon Delivered to the Church and Congregation at Lexington, New York, 1826.* Utica, n.d.

Heads of Families at the First Census of the United States taken in the Year 1790. Baltimore, 1966.

Hill, Henry. *Recollection of an Octogenarian.* Boston, 1884.

History of the American Clock Business For the Past Sixty Years and Life of Chauncy Jerome, Written by Himself. New Haven, 1860.

Holley, O. L. *The New-York State Register.* 2 vols. Albany and New York, 1843, 1846.

Holmes, Isaac. *An Account of the United States of America.* London, 1823.

Hughes, William Carter. *The American Miller and Millwright's Assistant.* Philadelphia, 1851.

Hunt, Freeman. *Letters about the Hudson River and Its Vicinity.* New York, 1837.

Incidents in the Life of George Haydock, Ex–Professional Woodsawyer, of Hudson. Hudson, 1846.

Johnson, A. G. *A Chapter of History; or, the Progress of Judicial Usurpation.* Troy, 1863.

Johnston, James F. W. *Notes on North America: Agricultural, Economical, and Social.* 2 vols. Boston, 1851.

Julia de Fontenelle, J. S. E., and Francis Malepeyre. *The Arts of Tanning, Currying, and Leather-Dressing.* Edited, with numerous emendations and additions, by Campbell Morfit. Philadelphia, 1852.

Lambert, John. *Travels through Canada and the United States of America in the Years 1806, 1807, and 1808.* 2d ed. 2 vols. London, 1814.

LaRochefoucauld-Liancourt, François Alexandre Frédéric de. *Voyage dans les Etats-Unis d'Amérique fait en 1795, 1796 et 1797.* 8 vols. Paris, 1799.

Levasseur, Auguste. *Lafayette en Amérique en 1824 et 1825.* 2 vols. Paris, 1829.

Livingston, Robert R. "American Agriculture." In *Edinburgh Encyclopedia.* 1st American ed. Philadelphia, 1832. 332–42.

———. *Essay on Sheep.* New York, 1809.

Livingston Manor Case: Opinion of Mr. Justice Wright in the Case of the People agt. Herman Livingston, Supreme Court, Columbia County. Hudson, 1851.

Longworth's American Almanac. New York, 1809.

Longworth's American Almanach, New-York Register, and City Register. New York, 1802.

Macauley, James. *The Natural, Statistical, and Civil History of the State of New York.* 3 vols. New York, 1829.

Mackenzie, George Steuart. *A Treatise on the Diseases and Management of Sheep.* New York, 1810.

Martineau, Harriet. *Society in America.* 2 vols. New York, 1837.

Mather, J. H., and L. P. Brockett. *Geography of the State of New York.* Hartford, 1847.

Memoirs of Col. William Edwards, . . . Written by Himself, in His 76th Year, 1847. Washington, D.C., 1897.

Men and Times of the Revolution; or, Memoirs of Elkanah Watson. Edited by Wilson C. Watson. New York, 1856.

Milbert, Jacques Gilbert. *Itinéraire pittoresque du fleuve Hudson et les parties latérales de l'Amérique du Nord d'après les dessins originaux pris sur les lieux.* Paris, 1828–29.

Miller, Stephen B. *Historical Sketches of Hudson.* Hudson, 1862.

Montgomery, James. *A Practical Detail of the Cotton Manufacture of the United States of America.* Glasgow, 1840.

Mr. John Van Buren's Argument in the Livingston Manor Case. Hudson, 1850.

Munsell, Joel. *The Annals of Albany.* Vols. 1–9. Albany, 1850–58.

Narrative of Sojourner Truth. Edited by Margaret Washington. New York, 1993.

Niemcewicz, Julian Ursyn. *Under Their Vine and Fig Tree: Travels through America in 1797–1799, 1805.* Translated by Metchie J. E. Budka. Elizabeth, N.J., 1965.

Pickering, Joseph. *Inquiries of an Emigrant.* London, 1832.

Porter, David. *A Sermon Delivered November 1st, 1815, at Chatham (New Concord), N.Y.* Catskill, 1816.

Power, Tyrone. *Impressions of America during the Years 1833, 1834, and 1835.* 2 vols. London, 1836.

Reise Sr. Hoheit des Herzogs zu Sachsen-Weimar-Eisenach durch Nordamerika in den Jahren 1825 und 1826. Edited by Heinrich Luden. Weimar, 1828.

Review of the Decision of the Court of Appeals upon the Manor Question. Albany, 1859.

Rockwell, Charles. *The Catskills.* New York, 1867.

"Selections from the Correspondance and Diaries of John Olmsted, 1826–1838." Edited by Elizabeth W. Olmsted, 1968. Mimeographed typescript located at the Buffalo and Erie County Historical Society.

Shirreff, Patrick. *A Tour through North America Together with a Comprehensive View of the Canadas and United States as Adapted for Agricultural Emigration.* Edinburgh, 1835.

Smith, Adam. *An Inquiry into the Nature and Causes of the Wealth of Nations.* Chicago, [1776] 1976.

Smith, William, Jr. *Historical Memoirs.* Edited by William H. W. Sabine. 3 vols. New York, 1969.

Some Facts Relating to Hannah Barnard. Hudson, 1802.

Spafford, Horatio Gates. *A Gazetteer of the State of New York.* Albany, 1824.

――――. *A Gazetteer of the State of New York.* Albany, 1813.

Spees, S. Granby. *Memorial Celebration Comprising the Address Delivered on the Occasion.* Saratoga, 1872.

Stoddard's Diary; or, the Columbia Almanack for the Year of Our Lord 1830. Hudson, n.d.

Strickland, William. *Journal of a Tour in the United States of America, 1794–1795.* Edited by J. E. Strickland. New York, 1971.

――――. *Observations on the Agriculture of the United States of America.* London, 1801.

Stuart, James. *Three Years in North America.* 2 vols. Edinburgh, 1833.

Sutcliff, Robert. *Travels in Some Parts of North America in the Years 1804, 1805, and 1806.* York, Engl., 1811.

Thomson, William. *A Tradesman's Travels in the United States and Canada.* Edinburgh, 1842. Excerpted in *Upstate Travels: British Views of Nineteenth-Century New York.* Edited by Roger Haydon. Syracuse, 1982.

Tocqueville, Alexis de. *De la démocratie en Amérique.* 2 vols. Paris, [1839–40] 1981.

Transactions of the Society for the Promotion of Agriculture, Arts, and Manufacture. 2d ed. Albany, 1801.

Trollope, Fanny. *Domestic Manners of the Americans.* London, [1832] 1997.

Von Raumer, Friedrich. *Die Vereinigten Staaten von Nordamerika.* Leipzig, 1845.

Washington Irving: Letters. Edited by Ralph M. Alderman, Herbert L. Kleinfield, and Jenifer S. Banks. 4 vols. Boston, 1978–82.

Weston, Richard. *A Visit to the United States and Canada in 1833.* Edinburgh, 1836.

Worth, Gorham A., "Recollections of Hudson." In *Random Recollections of Albany from 1800 to 1808.* 2d ed. Albany, 1850.

Secondary Sources

Altschuler, Glenn C., and Stuart M. Blumin. "Limits of Political Engagement in Antebellum America: A New Look at the Golden Age of Participatory Democracy." *Journal of American History* 84 (1997): 855–85.

Anderson, Russell H. "New York Agriculture Meets the West, 1830–1850." *Wisconsin Magazine of History* 16 (1932): 163–98, 285–96.

Ardrey, Robert L. *American Agricultural Implements.* Chicago, 1894.

Atack, Jeremy. "The Agricultural Ladder Revisited: A New Look at an Old Question With Some Data for 1860." *Agricultural History* 63 (1989): 1–25.

————. "Firm Size and Industrial Structure in the United States during the 19th Century." *Journal of Economic History* 46 (1986): 463–75.

Atack, Jeremy, and Fred Bateman. *To Their Own Soil: Agriculture in the Antebellum North.* Ames, 1987.

Atherton, Lewis A. *The Southern Country Store, 1800–1860.* Baton Rouge, 1949.

Baker, Andrew H., and Holly V. Izard. "New England Farmers and the Market Place, 1780–1865: A Case Study," *Agricultural History* 65 (1991): 29–52.

Banner, Lois W. "Religious Benevolence as Social Control: A Critique of an Interpretation," *Journal of American History* 60 (1973): 23–41.

Barron, Hal S. "Listening to the Silent Majority: Change and Continuity in the Nineteenth-Century Rural North." In *Agriculture and National Development: Views on the Nineteenth Century,* edited by Lou Ferleger. Ames, 1990. 3–23.

————. "Rediscovering the Majority: The New Rural History of the Nineteenth-Century North." *Historical Methods* 19 (1986): 141–52.

————. *Those Who Stayed Behind: Rural Society in Nineteenth-Century New England.* New York, 1984.

————. "The Impact of Rural Depopulation on the Local Economy: Chelsea, Vermont, 1840–1900." *Agricultural History* 54 (1980): 318–35.

Barrus, Clare. *John Burroughs: Boy and Man.* Garden City, 1920.

Basch, Norma. *In the Eyes of the Law: Women, Marriage, and Property in Nineteenth-Century New York.* Ithaca, 1982.

Bateman, Fred. "Labor Inputs and Productivity American Dairy Agriculture, 1850–1910." *Journal of Economic History* 29 (1969): 206–29.

Becker, Carl L. *The History of Political Parties in the Province of New York, 1760–1776.* Madison, 1909.

Beckmann, Martin. *Location Theory.* New York, 1968.

Beecher, Raymond. "'Also Known as Mill Village' at Leeds." *Greene County Historical Society Journal* 11 (1987): 11–15.

————. *Out of Greenville and Beyond: Historical Sketches of Greene County.* Cornwallville, 1977.

Bell, Daniel. *The Cultural Contradictions of Capitalism.* New York, 1976.

Belshaw, Cyril S. *Traditional Exchange and Modern Markets.* Englewood Cliffs, 1965.

Bender, Thomas. *Toward an Urban Vision: Ideas and Institutions in Nineteenth-Century America.* Lexington, 1975.

Benson, Lee. *The Concept of Jacksonian Democracy: New York as a Test Case.* Princeton, 1961.

Bidwell, Percy W. "Rural Economy in New England at the Beginning of the 19th Century." *Transactions of the Connecticut Academy of Arts and Sciences* 20 (1916): 241–399.

Bidwell, Percy W., and John I. Falconer. *History of Agriculture in the Northern United States, 1620–1860.* New York, 1941.

Blackburn, Roderick, and Ruth Piwonka. *Remembrance of Patria: Dutch Arts and Culture in Colonial America, 1609–1776.* Albany, 1988.

Blewett, Mary H. *Men, Women, and Work: Class, Gender, and Protest in the New England Shoe Industry, 1780–1910.* Urbana, 1990.

Blumin, Stuart M. *The Emergence of the Middle Class: Social Experience in the American City, 1760–1900.* New York, 1990.

―――. "The Hypothesis of Middle-Class Formation in Nineteenth-Century America: A Critique and Some Proposals." *American Historical Review* 90 (1985): 299–338.

―――. *The Urban Threshold: Growth and Change in a Nineteenth-Century American Community.* Chicago, 1976.

―――. "Rip Van Winkle's Grandchildren: Family and Household in the Hudson Valley, 1800–1860." *Journal of Urban History* 1 (1975): 293–315.

Bonomi, Patricia U. *A Factious People: Politics and Society in Colonial New York.* New York, 1971.

Borish, Linda J. " 'Another Domestic Beast of Burden': New England Farm Women's Work and Well-Being in the 19th Century." *Journal of American Culture* 18 (1995): 83–100.

―――. "Farm Females, Fitness, and the Ideology of Physical Health in Antebellum New England." *Agricultural History* 64 (1990): 17–30.

Boyd, Julian P. "Horatio Gates Spafford: Inventor, Author, Promoter of Democracy." *Proceedings of the American Antiquarian Society* 51 (1942): 279–350.

Boydston, Jeanne. *Home and Work: Housework, Wages, and the Ideology of Labor in the Early Republic.* New York, 1990.

Bradbury, Anna R. *History of the City of Hudson, New York.* Hudson, 1908.

Braudel, Fernand. *Civilisation matérielle, économie, et capitalisme, 15e–18e siècle.* Vol. 2: *Les jeux de l'échange.* Paris, 1979.

Braun, Rudolf. *Industrialisierung und Volksleben: Die Veränderungen der Lebensformen in einem ländlichen Industriegebiet (Zürcher Oberland) vor 1800.* Erlenbach and Zurich, 1960.

Brenner, Robert. "Agrarian Class Structure and Economic Development in Pre-industrial Europe." *Past and Present* 70 (1976): 30–75.

Bridenbaugh, Carl. *The Colonial Craftsman.* New York, 1950.

Brooks, Charles E. *Frontier Settlement and Market Revolution: The Holland Land Purchase.* Ithaca, 1996.

Brown, Ralph Adams. "The Lumber Industry in the State of New York, 1790–1830." Ph.D. diss., Columbia University, 1933.

Bruegel, Martin. "Unrest: Manorial Society and the Market in the Hudson Valley, 1780–1850." *Journal of American History* 82 (1996): 1393–1424.

Burns, Sarah. *Pastoral Inventions: Rural Life in Nineteenth-Century American Art and Culture.* Philadelphia, 1989.

Burton, M. L., and D. White. "Sexual Division of Labor in Agriculture." *American Anthropologist* 86 (1984): 568–83.

Bushman, Richard L. *The Refinement of America: Persons, Houses, Cities.* New York, 1992.

―――. "Opening the Countryside." In *The Transformation of Early American History,* edited by James A. Henretta, Michael Kammen, and Stanley N. Katz. New York, 1991. 239–56.

―――. "Family Security in the Transition from Farm to City, 1750–1850." *Journal of Family History* 6 (1981): 238–56.

―――. *From Puritan to Yankee: Character and the Social Order in Connecticut, 1690–1765.* Cambridge, Mass., 1967.

Butler, Jon. *Awash in a Sea of Faith: Christianizing the American People.* Cambridge, Mass., 1990.

Buttel, Frederick H., and Philip McMichael. "Sociology and Rural History: Summary and Critique," *Social Science History* 12 (1988): 93–120.

Cancian, Frank. "Economic Behavior in Peasant Communities." In *Economic Anthropology,* edited by Stuart Plattner. Stanford, 1989. 127–70.

Carman, Harry J. "The Beginnings of the Industrial Revolution." In *History of the State of New York,* edited by Alexander C. Flick. 10 vols. New York, 1933–37. 5:337–57.

Carman, Harry J., and August B. Gold. "The Rise of the Factory System." In *History of the State of New York,* edited by Alexander C. Flick. 10 vols. New York, 1933–37. 6:191–245.

Chambers, J. D. "Enclosure and Labour Supply in the Industrial Revolution." *Economic History Review,* 2d ser., 5 (1953): 319–43.

Chase, Jeanne. "L'organisation de l'espace économique dans le Nord-est des Etats-Unis après la Guerre d'Indépendance." *Annales E.S.C.* (1988): 997–1020.

Cheyney, Edward P. *The Anti-rent Agitation in the State of New York, 1839–1846.* Philadelphia, 1887.

Christman, Henry. *Tin Horns and Calico: A Decisive Episode in the Emergence of Democracy.* New York, 1945.

Cikovsky, Nicolai. "'The Ravages of the Axe': The Meaning of the Tree Stump in Nineteenth-Century American Art." *Art Bulletin* (1979): 611–26.

Clark, Christopher. "Economics and Culture: Opening up the Rural History of the Early American Northeast." *American Quarterly* 43 (1991): 279–301.

———. *The Roots of Rural Capitalism: Western Massachusetts, 1780–1860.* Ithaca, 1990.

———. "Household Economy, Market Exchange, and the Rise of Capitalism in the Connecticut Valley, 1800–1860." *Journal of Social History* 13 (1979): 169–89.

———. "The Household Mode of Production: A Comment." *Radical History Review* 18 (1978): 166–71.

Clark, Victor S. *History of Manufactures in the United States.* Vol. 1: *1607–1860.* New York, 1929.

Clemens, Paul E., and Lucy Simler. "Rural Labor and the Farm Household in Chester County, Pennsylvania, 1750–1820." In *Work and Labor in Early America,* edited by Stephen Innes. Chapel Hill, 1988. 106–43.

Cochran, Thomas C. "The Business Revolution." *American Historical Review* 79 (1974): 1449–66.

Cochrane, Charles H. *The History of the Town of Marlborough, Ulster County, New York.* Poughkeepsie, 1887.

Cohen, David Steven. *The Dutch-American Farm.* New York, 1992.

———. "How Dutch Were the Dutch of New Netherland?" *New York History* 62 (1981): 43–60.

Cole, Arthur H. *The American Wool Manufacture.* 2 vols., Cambridge, Mass., 1926.

Collier, Edward A. *A History of Old Kinderhook.* New York, 1914.

———. *The Hallowed House: A Historical Discourse on the Reformed Dutch Protestant Church.* Albany, 1866.

Collins, E. J. T. "Harvest Technology and the Labour Supply in Britain, 1790–1870." *Economic History Review,* 2d ser., 22 (1969): 453–73.

Collins, John F. *History of Hillsdale, New York.* Philmont, N.Y., 1883.

Columbia County at the End of the Century. 2 vols. Hudson, 1900.

Commons, John R., et al. *History of Labour in the United States*. 4 vols. New York, 1918–35.

Connor, L. C. "Brief History of the Sheep Industry in the United States." In *Annual Report of the American Historical Association for the Year 1918*. Washington, D.C., 1921. 89–197.

Cooke, Edward Strong, Jr. "Rural Artisanal Culture: The Preindustrial Joiners of Newtown and Woodbury, Connecticut, 1760–1820." Ph.D. diss., Boston University, 1984.

Cott, Nancy F. *The Bonds of Womanhood: "Women's Sphere" in New England, 1780–1830*. New Haven, 1976.

Countryman, Edward. *A People in Revolution: The American Revolution and Political Society in New York, 1760–1790*. New York, 1989.

Curti, Merle. *The Making of an American Community: A Case Study of Democracy in a Frontier County*. Stanford, 1959.

Curtiss, John S. "The Sloops of the Hudson, 1800–1850." *New York History* 14 (1933): 61–73.

Dangerfield, George. *Chancellor Robert R. Livingston of New York, 1746–1813*. New York, 1960.

Danhof, Clarence. *Change in Agriculture: The Northern United States, 1820–1860*. Cambridge, Mass., 1969.

Davenport, David Paul. "The Yankee Settlement of New York." *Genealogical Journal* 17 (1988/89): 63–87.

Davis, Natalie Zemon. *Society and Culture in Early Modern France*. Stanford, 1975.

De Peyster, Frederic. *A Biographical Sketch of Robert R. Livingston*. New York, 1876.

Ditz, Toby L. *Property and Kinship: Inheritance in Early Connecticut, 1750–1820*. Princeton, 1986.

Donovan, John L. "Textile Manufactures in New York before 1840." M.A. thesis, Columbia University, 1932.

Dorfman, Joseph. *The Economic Mind in American Civilization*. Vol. 2. New York, 1947.

Dublin, Thomas. *Transforming Women's Work: New England Lives in the Industrial Revolution*. Ithaca, 1994.

———. "Rural Putting-out Work in Early Nineteenth-Century New England: Women and the Transition to Capitalism in the Countryside." *New England Quarterly* 64 (1991): 531–73.

———. *Women at Work: The Transformation of Work and Community in Lowell, Massachusetts, 1826–1860*. New York, 1979.

Dubois, Anson, and James G. Dubois. *Documents and Genealogical Chart of the Family of Benjamin Dubois of Catskill, New York*. New York, 1978.

Durkheim, Emile. *Les règles de la méthode sociologique*. Paris, [1895] 1993.

Durrenberger, Joseph Austin. *Turnpikes: A Study of the Toll Road Movement in the Middle Atlantic States and Maryland*. Valdosta, 1931.

Earle, Alice Morse. *Home Life in Colonial Days*. New York, 1945.

———. *Colonial Days in Old New York*. New York, 1896.

Easterlin, Richard. "Population Change and Farm Settlement in the Northern United States." *Journal of Economic History* 36 (1976): 45–75.

Easterlin, Richard A., George Alter, and Gretchen A. Condran. "Farms and Farm Families in Old and New Areas: The North Eastern States in 1860." In *Family and Population in Nineteenth-Century America*, edited by Tamara K. Hareven and Maris A. Vinovskis. Princeton, 1978. 22–84.

Ellis, David Maldwyn. *Landlords and Farmers in the Hudson-Mohawk Region, 1790–1850.* Ithaca, 1946.

Ellis, Franklin. *History of Columbia County, New York.* Philadelphia, 1878.

Ellsworth, Lucius F. *Craft to National Industry in the Nineteenth Century: A Case Study of the Transformation of the New York State Tanning Industry.* New York, 1975.

Faler, Paul. *Mechanics and Manufacturers in the Early Industrial Revolution: Lynn, Massachusetts, 1780–1860.* Albany, 1981.

Familienstruktur und Arbeitsorganisation in ländlichen Gesellschaften. Edited by Josef Ehmer and Michael Mitterauer. Vienna, 1986.

Farragher, John Mack. *Sugar Creek: Life on the Illinois Prairie.* New Haven, 1986.

———. "History from the Inside-Out: Writing the History of Women in Rural America." *American Quarterly* 33 (1981): 537–57.

———. *Women and Men on the Overland Trail.* New Haven, 1979.

Fink, William B. "Stephen Van Rensselaer: The Last Patroon." Ph.D. diss., Columbia University, 1950.

Finkel, Charlotte C. "The Store Account Books of Hendrick Schenk, Fishkill Landing, Dutchess County, New York." *Yearbook* 50 (1965): 36–49.

Folbre, Nancy. "The Wealth of Patriarchs: Deerfield, Massachusetts, 1760–1840." *Journal of Interdisciplinary History* 16 (1985): 199–220.

———. "Patriarchy in Colonial New England." *Review of Radical Political Economics* 12 (1980): 4–13.

Formisano, Ronald P. "The Invention of the Ethnocultural Interpretation." *American Historical Review* 99 (1994): 453–77.

Foster, George M. "Peasant Society and the Image of Limited Good." *American Anthropologist* 67 (1965): 293–315.

Fox, Dixon Ryan. *Yankees and Yorkers.* New York, 1940.

———. *The Decline of Aristocracy in the Politics of New York.* New York, 1919.

Fox-Genovese, Elizabeth. "Women in Agriculture during the Nineteenth Century." In *Agriculture and National Development: Views on the Nineteenth Century,* edited by Lou Ferleger. Ames, 1990. 267–301.

From Max Weber: Essays in Sociology. Edited by Hans Gerth and C. Wright Mills. New York, 1946.

Gates, Paul Wallace. "Problems in Agricultural History, 1790–1840." *Agricultural History* 46 (1972): 33–58.

Geib, Susan. " 'Changing Works': Agriculture and Society in Brookfield, Massachusetts, 1785–1820." Ph.D. diss., Boston University, 1981.

Goldin, Claudia, and Kenneth Sokoloff. "Women, Children, and Industrialization in the Early Republic: Evidence from the Manufacturing Censuses." *Journal of Economic History* 42 (1982): 741–74.

Grant, Charles S. *Democracy in the Connecticut Frontier Town of Kent.* New York, 1961.

Grant, Jerry V., and Douglas R. Allen. *Shaker Furniture Makers.* Hanover, 1989.

Greene, Jack P. *Imperatives, Behaviors, and Identities; Essays in Early American Cultural History.* Charlottesville, 1992.

Griffen, Clyde, and Sally Griffen. *Natives and Newcomers: The Ordering of Opportunity in Mid-nineteenth-century Poughkeepsie.* Cambridge, Mass., 1978.

Griffin, Clifford S. *Their Brothers' Keepers: Moral Stewardship in the United States, 1800–1860*. New Brunswick, 1960.

Grignon, Claude, and Jean-Claude Passeron. *Le savant et le populaire*. Paris, 1989.

Grimsted, David, "Ante-bellum Labor: Violence, Strike, and Communal Arbitration." *Journal of Social History* 19 (1985): 5–28.

Gross, Robert A. "Culture and Cultivation: Agriculture and Society in Thoreau's Concord." *Journal of American History* 69 (1982): 42–61.

Gullickson, Gay. "Agriculture and Cottage Industry: Redefining the Causes of Proto-Industrialization." *Journal of Economic History* 43 (1983): 831–50.

Gunn, L. Ray. *The Decline of Authority: Public Economic Policy and Political Development in New York, 1800–1860*. Ithaca, 1988.

Gurevich, A. J. "Time as a Problem of Cultural History." In *Cultures and Time*. Edited by L. Gardet et al. Paris, 1976. 229–45.

Gutman, Herbert G. *Work, Culture, and Society in Industrializing America; Essays in American Working-Class and Social History*. New York, 1977.

Haar, Charles M. "Legislative Regulations of New York Industrial Corporations, 1800–1850." *New York History* 22 (1941): 191–207.

Hagen, William W. "Capitalism and the Countryside in Early Modern Europe: Interpretations, Models, Debates." *Agricultural History* 62 (1988): 13–47.

Hammel, E. A., Sheila R. Johansson, and Caren A. Ginsberg. "The Value of Children during Industrialization: Sex Ratios in Childhood in Nineteenth-Century America." *Journal of Family History* 8 (1983): 346–66.

Hannon, Joan Underhill. "Poverty in the Antebellum Northeast: The View from New York State's Poor Relief Rolls." *Journal of Economic History* 44 (1984): 1007–32.

Hansen, Karen W. "The Power of Talk in Antebellum New England." *Agricultural History* 67 (1993): 43–64.

Hareven, Tamara K. *Family Time and Industrial Time: The Relationship between the Family and Work in a New England Industrial Community*. New York, 1982.

Hareven, Tamara K., and Maris A. Vinovskis. Introduction to *Family and Population in Nineteenth-Century America,* edited by Tamara K. Hareven and Maris A. Vinovskis. Princeton, 1978. 3–21.

Hartz, Louis. *The Liberal Tradition in America: An Interpretation of American Political Thought since the Revolution*. New York, 1955.

Haskell, Thomas L. "Capitalism and the Origins of Humanitarian Sensibility." *American Historical Review* 90 (1985): 339–61, 547–66.

Hedrick, Ulysses Prentiss. *A History of Agriculture in the State of New York*. Albany, 1933.

Henretta, James A. "The Transition to Capitalism in America." In *The Transformation of Early American History,* edited by James A. Henretta, Michael Kammen, and Stanley N. Katz. New York, 1991. 218–38.

———. "The War of Independence and American Economic Development." In *The Economy of Early America: The Revolutionary Period, 1763–1790,* edited by Ronald Hoffman, John J. McCusker, Russell R. Menard, and Peter J. Albert. Charlottesville, 1988. 45–87.

———. "Families and Farms: *Mentalité* in Pre-industrial America." *William and Mary Quarterly,* 3d ser., 35 (1978): 3–32.

Herscovici, Steven. "Migration and Economic Mobility: Wealth Accumulation and

Occupational Change among Antebellum Migrants and Persisters." *Journal of Economic History* 58 (1998): 927–56.

Hilton, Rodney, ed. *The Transition from Feudalism to Capitalism.* London, 1976.

Histoire de l'alimentation. Edited by Jean-Louis Flandrin and Massimo Montanari. Paris, 1996.

"Histoire de la consommation." *Annales E.S.C.* 2–3 (1975): 402–631.

History of Greene County, New York. New York, 1884.

Hitz, Elizabeth. *A Technical and Business Revolution: American Woolens to 1832.* New York, 1986.

Hobsbawm, E. J. *Labouring Men.* London, 1964.

Hoffman, Philip T. *Growth in a Traditional Society: The French Countryside.* Princeton, 1996.

Hofstadter, Richard. *America at 1750: A Social Portrait.* New York, 1971.

Holmes, Oliver W. "The Turnpike Era." In *History of the State of New York,* edited by Alexander C. Flick. 10 vols. New York, 1934. 5:255–94.

Holmström, Bengt. "Moral Hazard and Observability." *Bell Journal of Economics* 10 (1979): 74–91.

Homans, George C. "Anxiety and Ritual: The Theories of Malinowski and Radcliffe-Brown." *American Anthropologist* 43 (1941): 161–72.

Horlick, Allan Stanley. *Country Boys and Merchant Princes: The Social Control of Young Men in New York.* Lewisburg, Pa. 1975.

Horwitz, Morton J. *The Transformation of American Law, 1780–1860.* Cambridge, Mass., 1977.

Howe, Daniel Walker. "The Evangelical Movement and Political Culture in the North during the Second Party System." *Journal of American History* 77 (1991): 1216–39.

Huston, Reeve. *Land and Freedom: Rural Society, Popular Protest, and Party Politics in Antebellum New York.* New York, 2000.

Jaffee, David. "Peddlers of Progress and the Transformation of the Rural North, 1760–1860." *Journal of American History* 78 (1991): 511–35.

———. "One of the Primitive Sort: Portrait Makers of the Rural North, 1760–1860." In *The Countryside in the Age of Capitalist Transformation,* edited by Steven Hahn and Jonathan Prude. Chapel Hill, 1985. 103–38.

Jensen, Joan M. *Loosening the Bonds: Mid-Atlantic Farm Women, 1750–1850.* New Haven, 1986.

———. "Cloth, Butter, and Boarders: Women's Household Production for the Market." *Review of Radical Political Economy* 12 (1980): 14–24.

Johnson, Christopher H. "Economic Change and Artisan Discontent: The Tailors' History, 1800–1845." In *Revolution and Reaction: 1848 and the Second French Republic,* edited by Roger Price. London, 1977. 87–114.

Johnson, Curtis D. *Islands of Holiness: Rural Religion in Upstate New York, 1790–1860.* Ithaca, 1989.

Jones, Daniel P. *The Economic and Social Transformation of Rural Rhode Island, 1780–1850.* Boston, 1992.

Jones, Eric L. "Agricultural Origins of Industry." *Past and Present* 40 (1968): 58–71.

Jones, Fred Mitchell. *Middlemen in the Domestic Trade of the United States, 1800–1860.* Urbana, 1937.

Kass, Alvin. *Politics in New York State, 1800–1830*. Syracuse, 1965.

Kasson, John E. *Civilizing the Machine: Technology and Republican Values in America, 1776–1900*. New York, 1976.

Kierner, Cynthia A. *Traders and Gentlefolks: The Livingstons of New York, 1675–1790*. Ithaca, 1992.

Kim, Sung Bok. *Landlord and Tenant in Colonial New York: Manorial Society, 1664–1775*. Chapel Hill, 1978.

Kriedte, Peter, Hans Medick, and Jürgen Schlumbohm. *Industrialization before Industrialization: Rural Industry in the Genesis of Capitalism*. Cambridge, Engl., 1981.

Kulik, Gary. "Pawtucket Village and the Strike of 1824: The Origins of Class Conflict in Rhode Island." *Radical History Review* 17 (1978): 5–37.

Kulikoff, Allan. *The Agrarian Origins of American Capitalism*. Charlottesville, 1992.

Kurath, Hans. *A Word Geography of the Eastern United States*. Ann Arbor, 1949.

Landes, David S. *Revolution in Time: Clocks and the Making of the Modern World*. Cambridge, Mass., 1983.

Larkin, Jack. *The Reshaping of Everyday Life, 1790–1840*. New York, 1988.

Lathrop, Janet. *The Township of Stockport*. N.p., 1919.

Lefevre, Ralph. *History of New Paltz, New York*. Albany, 1903.

LeGoff, Jacques. "Le temps dans la 'crise' du 14e siècle: Du temps médiéval au temps moderne." *Le Moyen Age* 69 (1963): 597–613.

———. "Au Moyen Age: Temps de l'Eglise et temps du marchand." *Annales E.S.C.* (1960): 417–33.

Lemon, James T. *The Best Poor Man's Country: A Geographical Study of Early Southeastern Pennsylvania*. Baltimore, 1972.

———. "Household Consumption in Eighteenth-Century America and Its Relationship to Production and Trade: The Situation among Farmers in Southeastern Pennsylvania." *Agricultural History* 41 (1967): 59–70.

Levi, Giovanni. *Inheriting Power: The Story of an Exorcist*. Chicago, 1988.

Levine, David. "The Demographic Implications of Rural Industrialization: A Family Reconstitution Study of Shepshed, Leicestershire, 1600–1851." *Social History* 2 (1976): 177–96.

Lindstrom, Diane, *Economic Development in the Philadelphia Region, 1810–1850*. New York, 1978.

The Livingston Legacy. Edited by Richard Wiles. Annandale, 1987.

Lockridge, Kenneth A. "Land, Population, and the Evolution of New England Society, 1630–1790: And an Afterthought." In *Colonial America: Essays in Politics and Social Development*, edited by Stanley N. Katz. Boston, 1971. 466–91.

Lockwood, Charles. *Bricks and Brownstone: The New York Row House, 1783–1929: An Architectural and Social History*. New York, 1972.

Loehr, Rodney C. "Self-Sufficiency on the Farm." *Agricultural History* 26 (1952): 37–41.

Lynd, Staughton. *Class Conflict, Slavery, and the United States Constitution*. Indianapolis, 1967.

Main, Gloria L. "Gender, Work, and Wages in Colonial New England." *William and Mary Quarterly*, 3d ser., 51 (1994): 39–66.

Main, Jackson Turner. *The Social Structure of Revolutionary America*. Princeton, 1965.

Mandrou, Robert. *La France aux 17e et 18e siècles.* Paris, 1974.

Manufacture in Town and Country before the Factory. Edited by Maxine Berg, Pat Hudson, and Michael Sonenscher. Cambridge, Engl. 1983.

Mark, Irving. *Agrarian Conflicts in Colonial America, 1711–1775.* New York, 1940.

Marti, Donald B. "Early Agricultural Societies in New York: The Foundations of Improvement." *New York History* 48 (1967): 313–31.

Martin, John Frederick. *Profits in the Wilderness: Entrepreneurship and the Founding of New England Towns in the Seventeenth Century.* Chapel Hill, 1991.

Marx, Leo. *The Machine in the Garden: Technology and the Pastoral Ideal in America.* New York, 1964.

Mauss, Marcel. *Manuel d'éthnographie.* Paris, 1967.

McClelland, Peter D. *Sowing Modernity: America's First Agricultural Revolution.* Ithaca, 1997.

McElroy, James L. "Social Control and Romantic Reform in Antebellum America: The Case of Rochester, New York." *New York History* 58 (1977): 17–46.

McMahon, Sarah F. "Laying Foods by: Gender, Dietary Decisions, and the Technology of Food Preservation in New England Households, 1750–1850." In *Early American Technology: Making and Doing Things from the Colonial Era to 1850,* edited by Judith A. McGaw. Chapel Hill, 1994. 164–96.

———. " 'All Things in Their Proper Season': Seasonal Rhythms of Diet in Nineteenth-Century New England." *Agricultural History* 63 (1989): 130–51.

———. "A Comfortable Subsistence: The Changing Composition of Diet in Rural New England, 1620–1840." *William and Mary Quarterly,* 3d ser., 42 (1985): 26–65.

McMurry, Sally. *Transforming Rural Life: Dairying Families and Agricultural Change, 1820–1885.* Baltimore, 1995.

———. "Women's Work in Agriculture: Divergent Trends in England and America, 1800–1930." *Comparative Studies in Society and History* 34 (1992): 248–70.

———. "Who Read the Agricultural Journals? Evidence from Chenango County, New York, 1839–1865." *Agricultural History* 63 (1989): 1–18.

———. *Families and Farmhouses in Nineteenth-Century America; Vernacular Design and Social Change.* New York, 1988.

Medick, Hans. "The Proto-industrial Family Economy." *Social History* 3 (1976): 291–315.

Mendels, Franklin F. "Seasons and Regions in Agriculture and Industry during the Process of Industrialization." In *Region und Industrialisierung,* edited by Sidney Pollard. Göttingen, 1980. 177–95.

———. "La composition du ménage paysan en France au 19e siècle: Une analyse économique du mode de production domestique." *Annales E.S.C.* (1978): 790–802.

———. "Agriculture and Peasant Industry in Eighteenth-Century Flanders." In *European Peasants and Their Markets,* edited by William N. Parker and Eric L. Jones. Princeton, 1975. 179–204.

———. "Proto-industrialization: The First Phase of the Industrializing Process." *Journal of Economic History* 32 (1972): 241–61.

Merrill, Michael. "Self-Sufficiency and Exchange in Early America: Theory, Structure, Ideology." Ph.D. diss., Columbia University, 1985.

———. "Cash Is Good to Eat: Self-Sufficiency and Exchange in the Rural Economy of the United States." *Radical History Review* 3 (1977): 42–71.

Merritt, Howard S. *Thomas Cole*. Rochester, 1969.

Meyer, David R. "Midwestern Industrialization and the American Manufacturing Belt in the Nineteenth Century." *Journal of Economic History* 49 (1989): 921–37.

Miller, Nathan. *The Enterprise of a Free People: Aspects of the Economic Development in New York State during the Canal Period, 1792–1838*. Ithaca, 1962.

Mintz, Sidney. "Peasant Markets." *Scientific American* 203 (August 1960): 112–22.

Mohanty, Gail Fowler. "Putting up with Putting-Out: Power-Loom Diffusion and Outwork for Rhode Island Mills, 1821–1829." *Journal of the Early Republic* 9 (1989): 191–216.

Montanari, Massimo. *La faim et l'abondance: Histoire de l'alimentation en Europe*. Paris, 1995.

Mumford, Lewis. *Technics and Civilization*. New York, 1934.

Murray, David. "The Anti-rent Episode in the State of New York." In *Annual Report of the American Historical Association*. Washington, D.C., 1896. 1:139–73.

Neale, Walter C. "Monetization, Commercialization, Market Orientation, and Market Dependence." In *Studies in Economic Anthropology*, edited by George Dalton. Washington, D.C., 1971. 25–29.

Newby, Howard. "European Social Theory and the Agrarian Question." In *Technology and Social Change in Rural Areas*, edited by Gene F. Summers. Boulder, 1983. 109–23.

Nicholas, R. W. "Segmentary Factional Political Systems." In *Political Anthropology*, edited by M. J. Swartz, V. W. Turner, and A. Tuden. Chicago, 1966. 49–60.

Niven, A. C. "A Chapter in Anti-Rent History." *Albany Law Journal* 24 (1881): 125–27.

Noble, Louis Legrand. *The Life and Works of Thomas Cole*. Edited by Elliott S. Vesell. Cambridge, Mass., [1853] 1964.

Nobles, Gregory H. "The Rise of Merchants in Rural Market Towns: A Case Study of Eighteenth-Century Northampton, Massachusetts." *Journal of Social History* 24 (1990): 5–23.

———. "Commerce and Community: A Case Study of the Rural Broommaking Business in Antebellum Massachusetts." *Journal of the Early Republic* 4 (1984): 287–302.

Norton, Mary Beth. "The Evolution of White Women's Experience in Early America." *American Historical Review* 89 (1984): 593–619.

———. *Liberty's Daughters: The Revolutionary Experience of American Women, 1750–1800*. Boston, 1980.

O'Connor, Richard P. "The History of Brickmaking in the Hudson Valley." Ph.D. diss., University of Pennsylvania, 1987.

O'Malley, Michael. *Keeping Watch: A History of American Time*. New York, 1990.

Osterud, Nancy Grey. "Gender and the Transition to Capitalism in Rural America." *Agricultural History* 67 (1993): 14–29.

———. *Bonds of Community: The Lives of Farm Women in Nineteenth-Century New York*. Ithaca, 1991.

Palmer, Bryan D. "Discordant Music: Charivaris and White-Capping in Nineteenth-Century North America." *Labour–Le travail* 3 (1978): 5–62.

Parkerson, Donald H. *The Agricultural Transition in New York: Markets and Migration in Mid-nineteenth-century America*. Ames, 1995.

Pendleton, Eric Honaker. "The New York Anti-rent Controversy, 1830–1860." Ph.D. diss., University of Virginia, 1974.

Peristiani, J. G. Introduction to *Honour and Shame: The Values of Mediterranean Society,* edited by J. G. Peristiani. London, 1965. 9–18.

Perrot, Michelle. *Les ouvriers en grève: France, 1871–1890.* 2 vols. Paris, 1974.

Pierson, George Wilson. *Tocqueville and Beaumont in America.* New York, 1938.

Pitt-Rivers, Julian. *The Fate of Shechem or the Politics of Sex.* Cambridge, 1977.

———. "Honour and Social Status." In *Honour and Shame: The Values of Mediterranean Society,* edited by J. G. Peristiani. London, 1965. 21–77.

Pocock, J. G. A. "The Classical Theory of Deference." *American Historical Review* 81 (1976): 516–23.

Polanyi, Karl. "The Economy as an Instituted Process." In *Trade and Market in the Early Empires,* edited by Karl Polanyi, Conrad M. Arensberg, and Harry W. Pearson. Glencoe, 1957. 243–70.

———. *The Great Transformation: The Political and Economic Origins of Our Time.* Boston, 1944.

Postel-Vinay, Gilles. "A la recherche de la révolution économique dans les campagnes (1789–1815)." *Revue économique* 6 (1989): 1015–45.

Potter, David M. *People of Plenty; Economic Abundance and the American Character.* Chicago, 1954.

Prude, Jonathan. *The Coming of Industrial Order: Town and Factory Life in Rural Massachusetts.* Cambridge, Mass., 1983.

Pruitt, Bettye Hobbs. "Self-Sufficiency and the Agricultural Economy of Eighteenth-Century Massachusetts," *William and Mary Quarterly,* 3d ser., 41 (1984): 333–64.

Ransom, Roger L., and Richard Sutch. *One Kind of Freedom: The Economic Consequences of Emancipation.* Cambridge, Engl., 1977.

Roberts, Michael. "Sickles and Scythes: Women's Work and Men's Work at Harvest Time." *History Workshop* 7 (1979): 3–28.

Rock, Howard B. *Artisans of the New Republic: The Tradesmen of New York City in the Age of Jefferson.* New York, 1979.

Rogin, Leo, *The Introduction of Farm Machinery in Its Relation to the Productivity of Labor in the Agriculture of the United States during the Nineteenth Century.* Berkeley, 1931.

Rothenberg, Winifred B. *From Market-Places to a Market Economy: The Transformation of Rural Massachusetts, 1750–1850.* Chicago, 1992.

———. "Structural Change in the Farm Labor Force: Contract Labor in Massachusetts Agriculture, 1750–1865." In *Strategic Factors in Nineteenth-Century American Economic History,* edited by Claudia Goldin and Hugh Rockoff, Chicago, 1992. 105–34.

———. "The Bound Prometheus." *Reviews in American History* 15 (1987): 628–37.

———. "Farm Account Books: Problems and Possibilities." *Agricultural History* 58 (1984): 106–12.

Ruttenber, Edward M. *History of the Town of New Windsor, Orange County, N. Y.* Newburgh, N.Y., 1911.

Sabean, David W. *Property, Production, and the Family in Neckarhausen, 1700–1870.* New York, 1990.

Sahlins, Marshall. *Stone Age Economics.* Chicago, 1972.

Samuels, Raphael. "Workshop of the World: Steam Power and Hand Technology in Mid-Victorian Britain." *History Workshop* 3 (1977): 5–72.

Schlesinger, Arthur M., Jr. *The Age of Jackson.* Boston, 1946.

Schoonmaker, Marius. *The History of Kingston, N. Y.* New York, 1888.

Schulze, Winfried. "Europäische und deutsche Bauernrevolten der frühen Neuzeit: Probleme der vergleichenden Betrachtung." In *Europäische Bauernrevolten der frühen Neuzeit,* edited by Winfried Schulze. Frankfurt am Main, 1982. 10–60.

Schumacher, Max. *The Northern Farmer and His Markets during the late Colonial Period.* New York, [1948] 1969.

Scranton, Philip. *Proprietory Capitalism: The Textile Manufacture at Philadelphia, 1800–1885.* New York, 1983.

Segalen, Martine. *Mari et femme dans la société paysanne.* Paris, 1980.

Sellers, Charles. *The Market Revolution: Jacksonian America, 1815–1846.* New York, 1991.

Sewell, William H. "Social Change and the Rise of Working-Class Politics in Nineteenth-Century Marseilles." *Past and Present* 65 (1974): 75–109.

Shammas, Carole. "How Self-Sufficient Was Early America?" *Journal of Interdisciplinary History* 13 (1982): 247–72.

Shanin, Teodor. "The Nature and Logic of the Peasant Economy." *Journal of Peasant Studies* 1 (1973): 63–80.

Sherman, Constance D. "A French Explorer in the Hudson River Valley." *New York Historical Society Quarterly* 45 (1961): 254–80.

Silverman, Sydel. "The Peasant Concept in Anthropology." *Journal of Peasant Studies* 7 (1979): 49–69.

Smith, Carol A. "Regional Economic Systems: Linking Geographical Models and Socioeconomic Problems." In *Regional Analysis.* Vol. 1: *Economic Systems,* edited by Carol A. Smith. New York, 1976. 3–63.

Snell, K. D. M. "Agricultural Seasonal Unemployment, the Standard of Living, and Women's Work in the South and East, 1690–1860." *Economic History Review,* 2d ser., 34 (1981): 407–37.

Sokoloff, Kenneth L., and Georgia C. Villaflor. "The Market for Manufacturing Workers during the Early Industrialization: The American Northeast, 1820–1860." In *Strategic Factors in Nineteenth-Century American Economic History,* edited by Claudia Goldin and Hugh Rockoff. Chicago, 1992. 29–65.

Spaulding, E. Wilder. *New York in the Critical Period, 1783–1789.* New York, 1932.

Steckel, Richard H. "Household Migration and Rural Settlement in the United States, 1850–1860." *Explorations in Economic History* 26 (1989): 190–218.

Steinfeld, Robert J. "The Philadelphia Cordwainers' Case of 1806: The Struggle over Alternative Legal Constructions of a Free Market in Labor." In *Labor Law in America,* edited by Christopher L. Tomlins and Andrew J. King. Baltimore, 1992. 20–43.

Stott, Peter H. "Industrial Archeology in Columbia County, New York: A History of the Economic and Industrial Development of Hudson and the Several Towns as Portrayed in Their Surviving Structures." 1990. Typescript located at COLCHS.

Stott, Richard B. "Artisans and Capitalist Development." *Journal of the Early Republic* 16 (1996): 257–71.

———. *Workers in the Metropolis: Class, Ethnicity, and Youth in Antebellum New York.* Ithaca, 1990.

———. "Hinterland Development and Differences in Work-Setting: The New York Region, 1820–1870." In *New York City and the Rise of American Capitalism: Economic Development and the Social and Political History of an American State, 1780–1870,* edited by William Pencak and Conrad Edick. New York, 1989. 45–71.

Sundstrom, William A., and Paul A. David. "Old-Age Security Motives, Labor Markets, and Farm Family Fertility in Antebellum America." *Explorations in Economic History* 25 (1988): 164–97.

Sylvester, Nathaniel Bartlett. *History of Ulster County, New York.* Philadelphia, 1880.

Taylor, Alan. *William Cooper's Town: Power and Persuasion on the Frontier of the Early American Republic.* New York, 1995.

———. " 'The Art of Hook and Snivey': Political Culture in Upstate New York during the 1790s." *Journal of American History* 79 (1993): 1371–96.

Taylor, George R. "American Urban Growth Preceding the Railway Age." *Journal of Economic History* 27 (1967): 309–39.

———. *The Transportation Revolution.* New York, 1951.

Thompson, E. P. *Customs in Common: Studies in Traditional Popular Culture.* New York, 1993.

Tilly, Louise A., and Joan W. Scott. *Women, Work, and Family.* New York, 1978.

Todd, C. Lafayette. "Some Nineteenth-Century European Travelers in New York State." *New York History* 43 (1962): 336–70.

Tryon, Rolla Milton. *Household Manufactures in the United States, 1640–1860.* Chicago, 1917.

Tyrrell, Ian R. *Sobering up: From Temperance to Prohibition in Antebellum America, 1800–1860.* Westport, Conn., 1979.

Ulrich, Laurel Thatcher. "Wheels, Looms, and the Gender Division of Labor in Eighteenth-Century New England." *William and Mary Quarterly,* 3d ser., 55 (1998): 1–38.

———. *A Midwife's Tale: The Life of Martha Ballard Based on Her Diary, 1785–1812.* New York, 1991.

———. "Martha Ballard and Her Girls; Women's Work in Eighteenth-Century Maine." In *Work and Labor in Early America,* edited by Stephen Innes. Chapel Hill, 1988. 70–105.

———. "A Friendly Neighbor: Social Dimensions of Daily Work in Northern Colonial New England." *Feminist Studies* 6 (1980): 392–405.

Usner, Daniel H. *Indians, Settlers, and Slaves in a Frontier Exchange Economy: The Lower Mississippi Valley before 1783.* Chapel Hill, 1992.

Valenze, Deborah. "The Art of Women and the Business of Men: Women's Work and the Dairy Industry, c. 1740–1840." *Past and Present* 130 (1991): 142–69.

Van Wagenen, Jared. *Golden Age of Homespun.* Ithaca, 1953.

Veblen, Thorstein. *The Theory of the Leisure Class.* New York, [1899] 1994.

Vickers, Daniel. *Farmers and Fishermen: Two Centuries of Work in Essex County, Massachusetts, 1630–1850.* Chapel Hill, 1994.

———. "Competency and Competition: Economic Culture in Early America." *William and Mary Quarterly,* 3d ser., 47 (1990): 3–29.

Wallace, Michael. "Changing Concepts of Party in the United States: New York, 1815–1828." *American Historical Review* 74 (1968): 453–91.

Wallerstein, Immanuel. *The Modern World System.* Vols. 1–2. New York, 1974, 1980.

Weber, Max. *Wirtschaft und Gesellschaft: Grundriss der verstehenden Soziologie.* Tübingen, [1921–22] 1972.

Weiman, David F. "Families, Farms, and Rural Society in Preindustrial America." *Research in Economic History,* supplement, 5 (1989): 255–77.

Welsh, Peter C. *Tanning in the United States to 1850: A Brief History.* Washington, D.C., 1964.

Wermuth, Thomas S. "New York Farmers and the Market Revolution: Economic Behavior in the Mid-Hudson Valley." *Journal of Social History* 32 (1998): 179–96.

———. "To Market! To Market! Yeomen Farmers, Merchant Capitalists, and the Development of Capitalism in the Hudson River Valley, Ulster County, 1760–1840." Ph.D. diss., State University of New York, Binghamton, 1991.

Wilentz, Sean. *Chants Democratic: New York City and the Rise of the American Working Class, 1788–1850.* New York, 1984.

Wilson, Warren H. *Quaker Hill: A Sociological Study.* New York, 1907.

Winner, Julia Hall. "A Skimeton." *New York Folklore Quarterly* 20 (1964): 134–36.

Wolf, Eric R. *Peasants.* Englewood Cliffs, 1966.

Wood, Gordon S. *The Radicalism of the American Revolution.* New York, 1992.

Wooster, Harvey A. "A Forgotten Factor in American Industrial History." *American Economic Review* 16 (1926): 14–27.

———. "Manufacturer and Artisans, 1790–1840." *Journal of Political Economy* 34 (1926): 61–77.

Wright, Chester Whitney. *Wool-Growing and the Tariff.* Boston, 1910.

Young, Alfred F. *The Democratic Republicans of New York: The Origins, 1763-1797.* Chapel Hill, 1967.

Index

Burroughs, John (*continued*)
trade, 96; on farm work, 79, 109, 117–18; on his parents' religious experience, 201

Bushnell, Hannah (farmer's wife), 2, 14, 86, 125; and church going, 200; and consumption, 122, 151; and dairy, 2, 97, 122; and singing, 185; and wardrobe, 182–83

By-employment, 104; artisanal, 43–46, 49; protoindustrial, 10

Canals, 150. *See also* Erie Canal

Capital, 1–2, 131; requirement in crafts, 131, 165; requirement in manufacturing, 126–27, 129–33; requirement in milling, 146–47; requirement in retailing, 164–66; requirement in road building, 73–74; requirement in sources, 73–74, 131–33, 151, 164–66

Capitalism, 77, 88, 125

Capitalists, 1–2

Carpenters, 13, 44, 53, 83, 137, 144

Cash: social implications of, 14, 40, 220; spread of, 1–2, 6, 14, 20, 57, 91–92, 219

Catskill Lyceum, 64–65, 214

Cattle, 10, 48, 98–105, 118–19, 249 n.31

Changing work, 2, 22–23, 220. *See also* Neighborhood exchange

Character: individual, 191–93

Charivari. *See* Scimmelton

Church affiliation and electoral behavior, 211–12

Church discipline, 199–201

Churches, 198–203, 211, 269 nn.25, 26. *See also* Women

Climate, 8–10, 18, 32, 81. *See also* Seasonality

Clocks, 3, 83–86, 158, 176–77, 248 n.19. *See also* Time-consciousness

Cloth: homemade, 13, 77, 156, 252 n.48

Clothing: and conspicuous consumption, 181–82; farmers, 2, 181; female factory operatives, 141; manufacturing, 77,

146; value (in probate inventories), 181; youth, 181–82

Clover, 76–77, 105, 108

Coachmaking, 139

Cole, Theodore (farmer), 2, 89, 92

Cole, Thomas (artist), 64–66, 78, 87–89, 90, 118, 170, 177, 214; and food, 180; on politics, 207–8

Commensality, 14–15, 28–29, 30–31, 39, 44, 113; in shops and manufactures, 153

Competency, 10–11, 23, 25, 30, 42, 49, 159, 218

Conscience, 191–92

Consumption, 11, 122, 159–86; meaning, 160–62, 166, 181–82, 186; patterns, 183–86; per capita expenses, 185–86

Coventry, Alexander (physician): and agriculture, 17–19, 47, 56, 62–63; on brickmaking, 173; and cash, 219; and competency, 23, 49; and cousin William Coventry (farmer), 2, 13–14, 57, 63, 216; on environmental change, 78; on factory operatives, 139, 141, 143, 157, 219; and food consumption, 50–51; and inheritance, 26; and inns, 195; and neighborhood exchange, 13–16, 21; and neighborhood imagination, 28; and neighbors, 21, 30; and politics, 15–16

Coventry, William (farmer), 2, 47, 63, 86; and artisanal activities, 44, 61; and competency, 25; and food consumption, 51; and frolicking, 32; and harvests, 14, 17–19, 87; and hay sales, 19, 47–48; and hiring laborers, 20, 25; and inheritance, 26–27; and neighbors, 23, 29

Credit, 6, 58–59, 217, 219; and political influence, 36, 42

Crèvecoeur, St. John de: on agriculture, 16, 62; and competency, 10–11, 17; and exchange geography, 42, 59; and wagon loads, 54

Crop rotation, 45, 75–76, 99–100, 111–12

Hand looms, 22, 147–50. *See also* Outwork

Hasbrouck, Abraham J. (Kingston merchant), 42, 54–57, 59, 84, 93, 95–96, 178, 185

Hay, 2, 19, 47–48, 76, 79–80, 89, 96

Haydock, George (temperance lecturer, one-legged), 195, 197, 213; and clothes, 181–82

Hemlock bark, 81–83, 137, 218–19

Hiring. *See* Labor market

Hoffman, William (farmer, then store clerk), 2, 96, 114, 123, 176; and moral reform, 221; and nature, 216; and politics, 207; and time-consciousness, 85–86; and wardrobe, 2, 182

Holbrock, Chandler (fire inspector): on women factory operatives, 141

Holcomb, George (farmer): and banking, 1; and changing work, 22–23; and dairy, 119; and peddling farm produce, 96

Honor, 32–34, 189–92, 213, 221. *See also* Masculinity

Hours. *See* Time-consciousness

Households: consumption, 50–52

Housing, 31–32; and social distinction, 172–74

Housework, 44, 117, 121–22, 141, 176, 184–85

Immigrants, 142–44, 133, 157; and prejudice, 212

Income, 11; commercial middlemen, 167; craftsmen, 45, 138–39; farmers, 56–57, 94–96; multiple sources, 44–45, 61, 236 n.6. *See also* Wages

Industrialization: accounts of, 127; effects on artisans, 145–46, 156

Inequality. *See* Social rank

Influence: political, 35–37, 203–4

Information, 2–3, 41, 60–61, 68, 179

Inheritance, 25–27, 123–24

Inns, 28–29, 31–34, 182, 195–96, 214

Irving, Washington, 199, 272 n.44; on politics, 207

"Just price," 60, 70

Kinship. *See* Family

Labor. *See* Work

Labor market: agricultural, 20–21, 45, 91, 110–13; control, 128, 154–55, 157; entry, 142–44, 152–53; industrial, 93, 128, 138–39. *See also* African Americans; Artisans; Immigrants; Women

Labor scarcity, 20–21, 110–11, 117, 217

Laissez-faire. *See* Market principle

Land, 23–24, 26, 123; meaning, 25, 167–68

Landings, 2, 42, 54–55, 57–58, 95; housing occupancy, 171–72; image, 27–28

Land market, 25–27, 95

Land use, 10, 45, 47, 98–101, 103

Lawyers, 35, 66, 190–91

Livestock, 48, 76–77, 91, 101–3, 109. *See also* Cattle; Sheep

Living standards, 141–42, 157, 168–71, 175–78, 219

Livingston family: and business enterprise, 219–20; and housing, 185; and politics, 35–36, 38, 192, 206

Livingston, Mary (widow): and family, 3; and investments in roads, 74; and tenants, 12, 223

Livingston, Robert R. (chancellor): on agriculture, 44, 47–48, 57, 109–10, 117–18, 120; and social rank, 37, 175

Lobdell, Caleb (tavern keeper), 13–14; and masculinity, 13, 33, 217

Manorial society, 7–8, 222–26; and market principle, 71–72, 222–25; and politics, 15–16, 35–37, 206–7, 209–10

Manure, 76–77

Market economy, 4, 7, 62, 66

Marketplace, 2, 6, 57–62, 66

Market principle, 155, 220; institution of, 66–72

Market, regulation of, 60, 67

Marriage, 3–4, 31, 123–24, 188–89, 220

Martineau, Harriet (author): on agriculture, 117; on Yankee clock peddlers, 85

Masculinity, 13–14, 32–34, 190–91. *See also* Honor

Massachusetts, 7, 61, 152. *See also* New England

McGaw, Edward (memorialist): on farm work, 109, 120; on food monotony, 51

Meadows and pastures, 47–48, 77–79, 91, 99, 105

Merchants, 41–42, 54–57, 65, 69–70, 162–63; image of, 27–28

Middle class, 160, 173–75, 185, 194–95, 202, 212–13, 224–26

Millers, 3, 146–47

Mobility, geographical, 23–25, 104, 139–40, 232 n.26, 233 n.27

Moral hazard, 110–11, 149–50, 231 n.15

Native Americans, 144, 156

Nature (as aesthetic category), 64–65, 217

Neighborhood exchange, 2, 6, 13–16, 19–23, 97, 220. *See also* Bees: as collective work

New England, 10, 24, 43, 51. *See also* Massachusetts

Newspapers. *See* Information

New York City: growing commercial awareness of, 2–3, 60–62, 68–69, 79; investment from, 132–33; marketing in, 55–57, 75–76, 79–80, 84, 89, 93, 95–96, 130, 163, 218

Outwork, 127–28, 147–51, 219; and capital accumulation, 151. *See also* By-employment

Panic of 1817, 130, 137, 169

Panic of 1837, 137–38, 169–70, 176

Parades, 196–98, 208–9, 267 n.47

Parlors, 160, 176, 183–84

Pastures. *See* Meadows and pastures

Plow, 2, 107–9

Polanyi, Karl (economist), 4

Political parties, 204–8, 213

Politics, 15–16, 35–39, 189, 203–10. *See also* Elections; Influence (political)

Population, mid–Hudson Valley: growth, 10; turnover. *See also* Migration

Portraits, 160, 177–78

Potato famine, 80

Poverty, 52, 128–29, 154, 157, 169, 219

Power. *See* Waterpower

Pratt, Zadock (tanner and congressman), 82; as model of self-made man, 192

Price convergence, 69

Price setting, 42

Production: artisanal, 145–46; mass, 145, 156, 181, 218

Profit and loss: calculated, 134–35. *See also* Income

Protestantism, 200, 202

Public good, 68–69

Public space, 11, 188–89; African Americans and, 198; women and, 192–93, 198

Railroad, 3, 225

Real estate: meaning of, 168; value of, 95, 167–68

Religion, 17, 189, 200–201, 267 n.4

Rents (on manorial property), 222

Residential patterns, 80, 82, 127, 130, 171–72, 188, 196, 219

Roads, 65, 72–75, 150, 218

Rumors, 30, 191–92

Scarcity consciousness, 10, 16–19, 27, 29–30, 39–40, 41–42, 45, 51, 58, 125, 159, 217

Scimmelton, 187–88, 214

Scott, Killian (farm hand): on farm women, 118, 120

Seasonality, 43–46, 61, 87, 107, 113–14, 133–36, 139, 141; long-distance trade, 163

Sheep, 48, 76–77, 101–3, 109, 217

Shirreff, Patrick (author): on women in agriculture, 121

Shoemakers, 44, 87, 128, 134–35, 140, 144–46, 156, 168; and strikes, 154–56

Shoes, 21, 22

Shopkeepers, 162–66

Slaves, 14, 21; and food, 180; and housing, 172

Smith, Adam (economist), 68, 128, 160; on decencies, 176

Social class: associations and, 194–96; awareness, 34–38, 160, 188, 225; and consumption, 11, 160, 186; definition, 11, 230 n.24; and housing, 172–74

Social rank, 33–39, 191–92, 220

Stores, 54; differentiation, 164; inventories, 163–65

Stoves, 177

Strikes, 140, 154–56

Strong, Wilbur Fisk (farmer, school teacher), 2, 114; and consumption, 186

Stuart, James (author): on gender in agriculture, 117

Suffrage requirements, 37–39, 203. See also Elections; Politics

Sun dial, 83. See also Time-consciousness

Tailors, 2, 85, 145–46

Tanning, 44, 81–83, 88–89, 92, 127, 141; conflict in industry, 154

Taverns. See Inns

Taxes, 40, 57, 179

Temperance, 188, 194–98; African Americans and, 198; violent opponents to, 196

Tenancy, 7

Textile manufacturing, 80–82, 88, 132–33

Thompson, William (artisan, farm hand, author): on boarding, 153; on labor market, 111, 142; on meals during harvest, 113

Time-consciousness, 3, 65, 83–87, 154, 159, 221

Tocqueville, Alexis de (author), 66, 225–26; and manorial conditions, 185, 206; on religious experience, 267 n.4; and "small virtues," 189

Town clocks, 3, 87. See also Time-consciousness

Townsend, Vincent Morgan (farmer), 6; and festive meals, 180; and smoking, 182

Trade: long-distance, 2, 6, 41, 57–58, 64, 76, 93, 96–97; organization, 42–43, 54–61, 69–70, 84, 95–96; transatlantic, 4, 80, 163, 175–76. See also Landings; Seasonality

Transportation. See Roads

Truth, Sojourner (author): on food, 180; on housing, 172; and time-consciousness, 84

Turnpikes. See Roads

Van Buren, Martin (politician), 203–4, 207, 213; and housing, 174

Van Rensselaer, Stephen ("patroon"), 206–7, 209

Violence, 6, 14, 30, 39, 187–91, 213; on animals, 30, 32. See also Brawling; Duels

Wages: agricultural, 112–14; artisans', 138–39; factory, 138–39, 141; and strikes, 156; women's, 113, 138–39, 141

Wage workers: in agriculture, 20–25

War of Independence, 16–17, 19

Watches, 83–85, 159. See also Time-consciousness

Waterpower, 65, 80–82, 87–88, 128, 146, 218

Wealth, 167–68; artisans, 168

Weaving, 52–53, 252 n.48. See also Outwork

Weber, Max (sociologist), 4, 66, 88; on ethnic categories, 272 n.44

West, the, 5, 75, 93, 117, 124

Widows, 21, 26, 49–50, 52

Women: in associations, 192–96, 214; in churches, 198–99; and exchange, 13, 53–54, 93, 97; in factories, 138, 140–41; on farm, 44, 52–54, 93, 114–24, 218; middle-class, 214; and outwork, 147–48; and property rights, 3, 26, 123–24; and work, 52–54, 83, 93

Woods, 9–10, 64, 76, 78

Work: conditions, 151; as exchange equivalence, 21–23, 39, 216–17; meaning, 170, 216–17, 221, 222–23; seasonal, 44–46, 107
Workers: and religion, 202–3

Workplace: discipline, 153–55; number of employees, 129–30

Youngs, William (miller), 87, 146–47; and festive meals, 180; and news, 3

Martin Bruegel is Chargé de recherche at the Institut
National de la Recherche Agronomique, Laboratoire de
Recherche sur la Consommation, in France.

Library of Congress Cataloging-in-Publication Data
Bruegel, Martin.
Farm, shop, landing : the rise of a market society in the
Hudson Valley, 1780–1860 / Martin Bruegel.
p. cm.
Includes bibliographical references and index.
ISBN 0-8223-2835-6 (cloth : alk. paper)
ISBN 0-8223-2849-6 (pbk. : alk. paper)
1. Columbia County (N.Y.)—Economic conditions—
18th century.   2. Columbia County (N.Y.)—Economic
conditions—19th century.   3. Greene County (N.Y.)—
Economic conditions—18th century.   4. Greene
County (N.Y.)—Economic conditions—19th century.
5. Industrialization—New York (State)—Columbia
County.   6. Industrialization—New York (State)—
Greene County.   I. Title.
HC107.N72 C693   2002
330.9747'3703—dc21   2001050107